THE BUILDINGS OF ENGLAND

BE 14

SOUTH AND WEST SOMERSET

NIKOLAUS PEVSNER

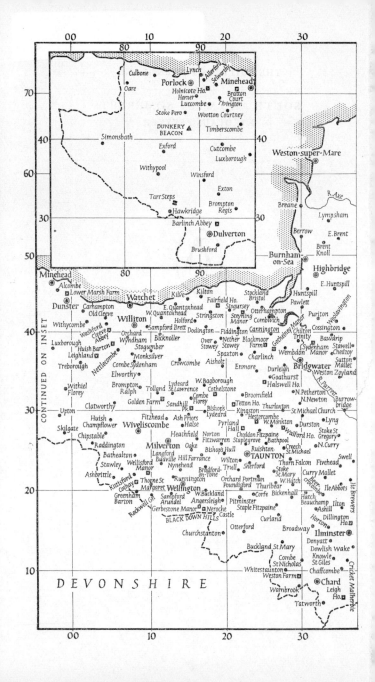

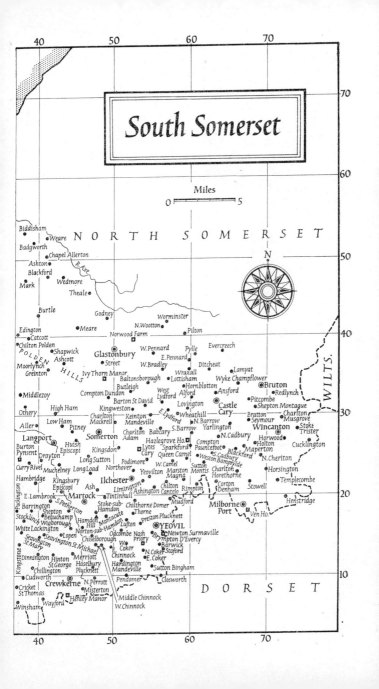

South and West Somerset

BY

NIKOLAUS PEVSNER

★

PENGUIN BOOKS

Penguin Books Ltd, Harmondsworth, Middlesex
U.S.A.: Penguin Books Inc., 3300 Clipper Mill Road, Baltimore 11, Md.
AUSTRALIA: Penguin Books Pty Ltd, 762 Whitehorse Road,
Mitcham, Victoria

—

First published 1958

—

00012740X

TO THE
LEVERHULME TRUST

*

Made and printed in Great Britain
by William Clowes and Sons Ltd, London and Beccles
Collogravure plates by Harrison & Sons Ltd

CONTENTS

*

*

Map References

The numbers printed in italic type in the margin against the place names in the gazetteer of the book indicate the position of the place in question on the index map (pages 2–3), which is divided into sections by the 10–kilometre reference lines of the National Grid. The map contains all those places, whether towns, villages, or isolated buildings, which are the subject of separate entries in the text.

The first two figures of the reference number indicate the grid position of the place in question *East* of the Grid datum point near Land's End : the last two figures its grid position *North* of that point. Thus, for example, Rimpton (reference 6020) will be found in the map square bounded by grid lines 60 and 70 *east* and 20 and 30 *north* of the south-west (bottom left hand) corner of the map ; Enmore (reference 2030) in the square bounded by grid lines 20 and 30 *east* and 30 and 40 *north*.

FOREWORD

Somerset in The Buildings of England *appears in two volumes. There was far too much worth recording even to try and put it into one volume. The natural dividing line runs S of the Mendips. On the other hand, accepting this line, it would have been difficult to keep a balance in bulk between the two volumes, and so, anticipating exactly the same surfeit of material in the case of the treatment of Gloucestershire some time later, I decided to publish Bristol together with North Somerset. Bristol is a county as well as a city. But in spite of all its wealth of monuments it would not have justified a whole volume of its own. So North Somerset became North Somerset and Bristol, and the dividing line runs now as follows.*

North Somerset and Bristol contains everything N of the river Axe from its mouth to Wookey. It then contains Wookey and Wells, and then everything N of the A371 and B3081 roads. That includes – as it seemed reasonable to go by the position of the parish church – Shepton Mallet, but excludes Bruton. The B3081 joins the A303 close to the Wiltshire border and the North Somerset volume in its SE corner follows that road.

The Introduction is the same for both volumes, but all places listed in the North Somerset volume are given an N to distinguish them. References to plates in the margin to this Introduction are marked N where they appear in the North Somerset volume and S where they appear in the South and West Somerset volume. Bristol has of course its own introduction. It could not possibly have been made part of an introduction to Somerset, though points of special Somerset interest are repeated in this.

Users of these two volumes will soon notice that coverage is uneven. It is easier to achieve an adequate approach to completeness in churches than in houses. For secular architecture adequacy or inadequacy depended almost entirely on the lists of buildings of architectural or historic interest which it is the statutory duty of the Ministry of Housing and Local Government to compile. As in the case of previous volumes I have again had access to these unpublished lists and to much other information collected by the Chief Investigator and his staff. The Ministry had at the time of writing completed its lists for urban districts but not for rural districts. Wherever lists for rural districts were available they helped my text enormously, although on the scale of my work only something like one in every twenty buildings included in the lists could be examined and mentioned. I have of course again tried to see everything myself before I described it. Houses for which I had to rely on the Ministry without being able to pay a visit are put in brackets and distinguished by the sign MHLG. The sign GR means, as in previous volumes, that information comes from Mr Goodhart-Rendel's lists of Victorian churches, the sign TK refers to Sir Thomas Kendrick's lists of Victorian stained glass. I am most grateful to both Mr Goodhart-Rendel and Sir Thomas Kendrick for allowing me the use of their lists. My thanks also go to the National Buildings Record (Mr Cecil Farthing, Mrs Parry and others) and to the Somerset Archaeological and Natural History Society at Taunton for much help received. The most valuable material I had to consult at Taunton was the volumes of the Buckler drawings made of churches and houses in Somerset in the 1820s to 1840s for Hugh Smyth Pigott, and the volumes of miscellaneous information and reproductions of the Braikenridge and Tite collections. In addition Mrs Asquith of Mells Manor House owns a collection of drawings made c. 1845–50 by W. W. Wheatley. She kindly allowed me their use. These four collections helped in many cases to clear up doubtful points.

Mr Jon Manchip White, as in several volumes before, has contributed the passages on prehistory and Ancient Rome in the introduction and the gazetteer. The geological remarks are the work of Mr D. T. Donovan of Bristol University. The compiling of nearly all the other information which has gone into these volumes was first done by Mrs Schilling some five years ago and then extensively revised by Miss Mary Littlemore. I am very greatly indebted to Mr Bryan Little and Mr Walter Ison for their excellent publications on Bristol and Bath as well as for the way they have helped me on individual questions, and also to Mr Vivian-Neal, whose specialized knowledge has been of the greatest value. I wish to thank him moreover for having read the proofs of certain parts of my text. The same nuisance I have inflicted on Mr L. S. Colchester for Wells Cathedral, on Miss E. Ralph, City Archivist of Bristol for Bristol, on Miss E. A. Russ of the Bath Municipal Library for Bath, and on Mr Arthur Sabin for Bristol Cathedral. They have all responded undauntedly and most generously. I also sent galleys to all rectors and vicars whose churches were of any architectural significance and there also the response was most gratifying.

Moreover I have to thank many for answers to individual questions or whole batches of questions, notably at Bristol Mr W. S. Haugh and Miss Grinham of the Central Library, Miss Elizabeth Ralph the City Archivist, Mr J. Nelson Meredith the City Architect, Canon Millbourn at the Cathedral, and Mr D. W. Lloyd, who is making a study of the nineteenth-century architecture of Bristol. Miss Elsie A. Russ at the Library at Bath has dealt patiently with my many enquiries about that city and Mr John Hatton has given me much help with regard to Bath Abbey. At Downside I had the benefit of Father Ralph Russell's co-operation. At Wells I wish to thank Mr L. S. Colchester and Dr R. D. Reid for their valuable assistance and likewise I owe a debt of gratitude to Mr A. D. Hallam at Taunton Castle and Mr D. L. Smith the reference assistant at Taunton Public Library. Finally Mr J. D. U. Ward provided me with a list of packhorse bridges – a most welcome contribution. My gratitude to all these helpers for their generosity and the tedious and extensive work to which they were put is greater than I can say.

I have had to write to many rectors and vicars and have received much kindness from them. Some have gone to a great deal of trouble to satisfy my requests for specified information. The same is true of owners of houses. Here also everybody, with the exception of one owner of a really important house who proved intractable, has been most obliging both in showing me their houses and in answering questions. In return I wish to make it quite clear to users of these volumes that houses must not be supposed to be open to the public because they are mentioned or even described in this book.

Now a word on what is and what is not to be found in this volume. I have not included more than a selection of Victorian and post-Victorian churches, the selection being based on what seemed to me aesthetically best or historically most significant. Church bells are not mentioned, church chests and chairs in churches only occasionally, doors and timber roofs, I am afraid, not consistently, fonts not if undecorated. In houses no paintings other than wall-paintings are referred to, and no furniture other than what can be regarded as fixtures.

Finally, as in all previous volumes it is necessary to end the Foreword to this with an appeal to all users to draw my attention to errors and omissions.

*The publication of this volume has been made possible
by a generous contribution from the Leverhulme Trust and
Messrs Arthur Guinness, Son & Company Ltd*

SOUTH AND WEST SOMERSET

*

INTRODUCTION

SOMERSET is a serene county, varied in mood more than most, yet always mild. It has neither the rocks nor the subtropical displays of aloe and palm-tree, as you find them in Devon and Cornwall. Even Exmoor is greener and warmer than Dartmoor and S3a Bodmin Moor. Somerset has stretches almost East Anglian in its flat watery meadows and brick cottages, yet one never feels the endlessness of East Anglian expanses. The plain of Somerset cuts across the county in a SE direction. Much of the land here lies below sea-level. The hills rise to 1700 ft with Dunkery Beacon in Exmoor towards the W end of the county, and to just over 1000 ft in the Mendips to the E of the plain. The coastline W of Porlock where the hills rise to over 900 ft straight out of the sea is the grandest piece of scenery that Somerset has to offer. Again E of Brendon are the Quantocks, a separate line of hills touching the sea by the two Quantoxheads and running SE to separate the Parrett valley with Bridgwater as its centre from the lovely Vale of Taunton, where in fine weather the Quantocks form as clear a horizon on the N as the Blackdown Hills beyond Wellington on the S and Brendon in the distance in the W. Along the S and E boundary, from the Blackdowns by Chard, Crewkerne, Yeovil, to Frome and indeed to Bath, hills and valleys cross in a variety of directions, all green and all lovable. Between Bath and Bristol is perhaps the least attractive part of the county, through no fault of nature. But here towns have spread and industries too. And here there is also some coal-mining. Radstock (N) is the centre of a coalfield which is small, but has done much damage to the amenities of the neighbourhood. Collieries appear right to the walls of Downside (N). Otherwise Somerset is not an industrial and not an urban county. One finds few factories and fewer large factories, little council housing, and no town anywhere of 100,000 inhabitants or more. Bristol is a county of its own, Bath (N) has 80,000 (1951), Taunton, the county town, 34,000, Weston-super-Mare (N), a seaside resort primarily, 40,000, Bridgwater and Yeovil just over 20,000, no other more than 15,000. Yet there are many towns, that is places with an urban character and an urban tradition, and that is also a visual pleasure. They are scattered throughout the county.

From Bath and Bristol to the s the land rises steeply at once, a first step in the direction of the Mendips. The other side of the Mendips, the low lands between them and the Quantocks, a distance of twenty miles, are interrupted by another range of hills: the Polden Hills, no higher anywhere than 300 ft. They are the boundary between the Parrett and the Brue and Axe valleys, between the King's Sedgemoor and the Burnham Level and East Sedgemoor.

N1 &
S3a
The extremes in landscape are the long majestic lines of Exmoor, the crags and caves of Cheddar Gorge in the Mendips, the sudden bumps and mumps and knolls rising in unexpected places, such as Burrow Mump, Brent Knoll, and Glastonbury Tor, and the watery stretches of Sedgemoor, drained by that stately straight canal, the King's Sedgemoor Drain, and by innumerable ditches called rhines. Along the roads and rhines stand lined up the willow trees closely pollarded for osiers. This is the country of brick, though brick never won over stone to the extent it did in East Anglia. There are no brick churches in Somerset, and no major brick houses before the end of the c17.

There are, however, excellent building stones, and to understand them a little GEOLOGY may be useful. The majority of the outcrops are elongated E–W. The Mendips are of hard, cold, grey, Carboniferous Limestone. This was mainly used for rough building, but occasionally, intractable as it is, for carved work. Churches apparently took to it only when there was no other material at hand (e.g. Berrow). At Wells colonnettes, shafts and some carving of Carboniferous Limestone may be explained by the fact that Purbeck marble had become popular and that the Carboniferous Limestone was a cheaper substitute. Carboniferous Limestone also forms the headlands of Brean Down, Worlebury Hill and Sand Point on the coast, and several ridges near Bristol and Clevedon. Along the N and s edges of the Mendips lie narrow strips of Dolomitic Conglomerate, a dull pink rock with grey pebbles of Carboniferous Limestone, easier to work than the limestone and much used where it occurs. It was occasionally polished and used for columns, e.g. in the Victorian work at Ashwick (N). Between the limestone uplands of the N are the basins of Coal Measures already referred to, blanketed by soft Triassic Marls which produce deep red soils. The Pennant Sandstone, in the Coal Measures, has been quarried along the Avon valley; otherwise the rocks are mainly shales. The red marls reappear s of Mendip; alabaster has been got from them near Somerton. Further w, near Taunton and around the Quantocks, their place is taken by red sandstones, used locally as freestone. The Quantocks, the Brendon Hills, and Exmoor are of Devonian slates and hard sandstones.

N of Mendip and in the central lowland are extensive areas of White Lias and Blue Lias, thin, hard bands of limestone interbedded with shale. In the centre of the county they form the Polden Hills. Both white and blue have been much used for building. Associated are clays, dug for brickmaking. Near Somerton, the Blue Lias has been worked as Keinton Stone, and used for paving; at Marston Magna, near Yeovil, a variety full of ammonites forms an ornamental stone, the now forgotten Marston Marble. The Lias stretches w as far as Watchet. Between Clevedon and Weston-super-Mare (N), and s of Mendip from the coast inland to Glastonbury and Langport, are extensive tracts of low-lying, recently-formed alluvium.

The oolitic limestones of the Middle Jurassic form a hilly margin to the county on the E and SE, with an outlier at Dundry Hill (N), s of Bristol. They yield some of the finest building stones in the country: the pale cream Bath Stone (now mined in Wiltshire); Doulting Stone, a crystalline limestone, grey when weathered, quarried near Shepton Mallet (N) (and from which Wells Cathedral is built); Dundry Stone, no longer worked; and, from the neighbouring Upper Lias, the matchless golden brown Ham Hill Stone, quarried near Montacute since Roman times. All these achieved fame far beyond the county boundary and were much used within it. In this belt, whole towns and villages are built of freestone, which in other parts of the country is reserved for the finest work. Those of Ham Hill Stone, in the SE, are unique.

A specially attractive original peculiarity is the mixing of Ham Hill, Doulting, or a similar oolitic limestone with Blue Lias. Famous examples are Ile Abbots and North Petherton.

Tombstones were made of Bath Stone, Ham Hill Stone, Dundry Stone, Pennant Sandstone, and Blue Lias. The latter in particular took very fine carving, but most examples have weathered very badly.

The history of art, or at least of artefacts, in Somerset begins at the dawn of human history. To understand the PREHISTORY of Somerset it must be remembered that the physical appearance of the county at that time was very different from its appearance today. The Bristol Channel had taken a great bite out of the heart of the county, so that the entire central area was covered by the sea or by thick uninhabitable swamp. This wet and barren stretch of land extended from the Mendips to the Quantocks and as far inland as a line between Shepton Mallet (N), Ilchester, and Crewkerne. That is to say, it extended from the River Axe to the edge of the high land s of the River Parrett. Until the onset of Roman times, when the marshy condition of this segment of the county began to improve a little, and when agriculturalists were better equipped to deal with heavy, saturated soils, no settlement was possible in this southern overspill of the Channel. A few hardy souls established themselves on the spine of the Polden Hills, which emerged in lonely isolation from the surrounding bog, and there were also travellers who were expert at finding their way across this difficult terrain, and who left behind them a variety of portable objects to testify to their journeyings. But in general the prehistoric settlement was confined to the rolling downs around modern Bath and Bristol, to the fine dry ridges of the Mendips, and to the rich country round Yeovil and Ilminster. There was also a secondary area consisting of the blocks of hills to the W and SW. But in the main these hills were too remote, bare, and windswept to be looked upon with favour by our earlier ancestors, though they were heavily settled during the long high-summer of the Bronze Age and were a welcome refuge during the military upheavals of the Iron Age.

At the beginning of the Old Stone Age the occupation of Somerset appears to have been chiefly confined to the Yarty and the Otter, roughly inside the shallow triangle Taunton–Otterford–Chard. From here and from the Broome gravels came the crude hand-axes of the earliest periods of the Old Stone Age. There was also an interesting contemporary community that made its home on the Lyonesse-surface or buried strands s of Bridgwater Bay.

Later in the Old Stone Age, Somerset slowly developed into one of the classic British areas of this remote epoch. The Mendips were the main centre of this activity, which was manifested on their N slopes in the vicinity of Burrington Combe (N), on their W slopes in the vicinity of Bleadon Hill and Weston-super-Mare (N), and principally on its s slopes in the vicinity of Cheddar, Priddy, and Wookey (all N). These sites are fully dealt with in the gazetteer. It suffices to say here that there was a splendid cultural efflorescence in Mendip in the later stages of the Old Stone Age, where the remains of the Magdalenian hunters have come to light in significant quantities in the caves that were their homes.

Traces of the Mesolithic Age, intermediate between the Old and New Stone Ages, are meagre in Somerset, but during the Neolithic or New Stone Age the N part of the county was inhabited by members of the so-called Severn culture. Their presence is attested by a number of characteristic long cairns, of which the most highly-evolved is at Stoney Littleton (N). These large pear-shaped tumuli are sometimes unchambered, but in most cases they contain, or once contained, a concave forecourt leading into a passage lined with stone slabs. Off the passage were constructed a series of small lateral chambers with corbelled roofs. The centre of the culture was situated in Gloucestershire and along the coast of Glamorgan, but its extension into Somerset was by no means negligible.

At the close of the New Stone Age a small, warlike, and adventurous band of itinerant metal-smiths of Continental origin reached Britain. They buried their dead either in the megalithic cairns of the preceding epoch or in newly-constructed round barrows of their own. The drinking-cups known as Beakers from which they take their name, and which they inserted in their burials, are found sporadically on Mendip. They are generally of the type known to archaeologists as AC.

The incursion of these bringers of metallurgy into Somerset was not of the first importance, but the county was intensively colonized during the Bronze Age, which the Beaker people ushered in. The Bronze Age was in the main a calm and settled period, during which there was a remarkable advance in the crafts of husbandry and a parallel increase in the growth of population. The compact groups of Bronze Age farmers sought out the high, dry uplands, and their round barrows proliferate on Mendip (N), on the Quantock and Brendon Hills, and on distant Exmoor. In the remote backwaters of the far west of Somerset they found an ideal place to carry on their rural pursuits and erect the stone circles and sanctuaries in which they worshipped their gods. That their principal deity was the sun-god we can infer from the elaborate gold sun-disc found at Lansdown (N), and other gold ornaments from Yeovil and Clevedon (N) indicate their general prosperity. From their barrows and graves have been unearthed a wide variety of funerary urns – globular, barrel-shaped, and cordoned – that point to a long, continuous, and undisturbed period of cultural development. The principal stone circle is Stanton Drew (N) in the Mendips.

The Iron Age that followed, on the other hand, was a stormy, troubled era, an era of battle and pursuit. The population of Somerset withdrew, as it did elsewhere in Britain, to strongly fortified hill-camps. Some of these hill-camps may have dated originally from Bronze Age times, but the tribes of the Iron Age – an epoch when every man's hand was raised against his brother – took them over and added one, two, or even three great banks and ditches to the original fortifications. They also built fortresses of their own, and there still exist ninety camps of this type in Somerset alone. The camps are scattered uniformly over the county, and the largest of them are of an immense size. Their commanding positions and powerful construction still fill the be-S3b holder with a sense of awe (*see* Dolbury, Hamdon Hill, South Cadbury). The descendants of the Bronze Age villagers took these strongholds as their focus and welded themselves into recognizable tribes and tribal alliances. The folk of Somerset – always, as we have remarked, a marginal area – no doubt adhered partly to the Dobuni to the N, whose capital was Corinium (Cirencester), and partly to the Durotriges to the S, who had twin capitals at Lendiniae (Ilchester) and Durnovaria (Dorchester). Probably life continued to be relatively peaceful until the moment when a tribe to the E, the aggressive and greatly-feared Belgae, marched westwards, impelled either by their innately warlike spirit or by the pressure of the newly-landed Roman legions. The Belgae invaded the territories of their neighbours and put their forts and homesteads to fire and sword. There is evidence of a massacre having taken place at Worlebury Camp (N), and at Glastonbury lake village.

The end of Glastonbury was especially tragic, for during the heyday of the Glastonbury and Meare lake villages, at the end of the Iron Age, Somerset had possessed an outstanding cultural influence in the life of Britain. The Glastonbury lake village was a great Celtic emporium rather than a definite tribal centre. The range of goods which it manufactured and exported was so wide and of such high quality that they spread into Gloucestershire, Devon and Cornwall, and across the Channel into South Wales. It is possible that the lake villagers were joined by refugees from Western France who fled to Britain after Caesar's campaign of 56 B.C. and established themselves in what had originally been a kind of overseas branch-office for their commercial enterprises.

Under ROMAN RULE, Somerset reverted to its former quiet condition. It was not densely settled during the early period of

Roman government, and the rival community lived in small villas built in modest imitation of the Roman pattern. Except for incursions by pirates from the sea, Somerset under the *Pax Romana* must indeed have been a pacific corner of these islands. During the later centuries of the occupation, the s w portion of the county became the fashionable preserve of gentlemen farmers, as the great villas with their ostentatious bathing-suites demonstrate. There does not appear to have been any Roman settlement of the country beyond Taunton, and the main agglomerations of villas were either on the Mendips, in the vicinity of the important lead mines of Charterhouse (N), or in the environs of Bristol (Abone) and Bath (Aquae Sulis). Abone and Aquae Sulis were the only Roman townships of any consequence. Although Lendiniae (Ilchester) was certainly a tribal capital, it does not seem to have become romanized to any significant degree. It did, however, stand at the focal point of the s w villa-system.

The Roman roads of Somerset were also confined to the E half of the county. The road from Corinium (Cirencester) led into Bath, from which it led to the E to Ilchester. This road was bisected by a road that carried the products of the Mendip lead-mines to the s through Sorbiodunum (Old Sarum) to Venta Belgarum (Winchester), and thence across the English Channel to Gaul and Italy. From Ilchester there forked two roads, one to Durnovaria (Dorchester) and the other to Isca Dumnoniorum (Exeter).

The only major monument of antiquity which remains for us to mention is the gigantic linear earthwork known as the Wansdyke (N). This, though British, belongs to the years of Anglo-Saxon advance. It is fully described in the gazetteer.

The scarcity of visible ANGLO-SAXON remains is surprising so near Wiltshire and Gloucestershire. Hardly anything is of national importance, all the less so since the excavations of Glastonbury have unfortunately not been left exposed. They show only on paper now: the small church of Ine with its side porticus, the C8 or 9 extensions to the w and E, and St Dunstan's square chancel yet further E, with its transept-like N and s porticus – a composite design which can never have possessed much monumentality. The whole cannot have been larger than 140 ft. Otherwise there is some long-and-short work at Wilton, and there are fragments of carved crosses, mostly, it is suggested, of the C9, at Porlock, Kelston (N), Nunney (N), and Rowberrow (N). There is, however, one interesting problem connected with the Saxon style in architecture: those parts of Milborne Port, the chancel s

side and formerly also the W front, which show unmistakably
Saxon lesenes and triangular arches, just like Bradford-on-Avon
across the Wiltshire border. However, they occur indivisibly
connected with equally typically Norman motifs, such as shafted
windows, and so Milborne seems to be a case of the 'Saxo-
Norman overlap' rather than of Saxon architecture – new motifs
used by men familiar with the old.

For NORMAN architecture also Somerset is not a hunting
ground. It would no doubt be, if Wells and Bath had not so
drastically removed all traces (or at Bath nearly all traces) of their
Norman cathedrals. So the best that remains is at Bristol, and for
Bristol the reader must go to another Introduction. On the other
hand, quantitatively, not qualitatively, there is certainly no short-
age. Of doorways especially there are plenty – more than three
dozen in North Somerset alone – and chancel arches also have
remained in quite a number of places. Nor are they usually bare
and utilitarian – or else they would not have been preserved by
the later Middle Ages. There are all the usual Norman motifs of
abstract ornamentation, from the simple zigzag to bands of zigzags, lozenges formed by the meeting of zigzags, crenellation,
beading, and so on. Norman foliage is rare, decorative figurework
too, and beak-heads, the motif of a monster-head biting into a
roll-moulding, occur only twice, at Lullington (N) and Pawlett.
The colonnettes of doorways and chancel arches also carry their
share of decoration, spiral-fluting, diapering, etc. – to the splen-
N7 didly bold twisted piers of Compton Martin (N) which must in
some remote way depend on Durham (cf. especially Pittington,
County Durham).

Chancel arches range from the comparative simplicity of one
order of colonnettes and one zigzag in the arch to three orders
(Hemington, Montacute, Sutton Bingham) and barbarically pro-
fuse decoration in the arches. Altogether the archaeological
interest should not blind the student to the barbarity of much
Norman work in minor churches. Take the sculpture of tympana
as an instance. The way in which geometrical motifs are sometimes
spread over them without any feeling for the demands of the semi-
circle is aesthetically inexcusable. When it comes to figurework,
S7 again one must distinguish between a case like Langport – actually
a lintel, not a tympanum – where there is the civilizing, if distant,
S6 influence from France, and Stoke-sub-Hamdon with its raw assembly of the Tree of Life, the Lamb, small in one corner, and
Sagittarius and Leo much bigger below. Did in such a case the
carver know what he was doing? Another Tree of Life is at

Wellington, where above the doorway under an oddly convex-sided steep gable Christ is enthroned as he is in French tympana and the tympanum of Malmesbury. Affronted animals without the Tree of Life occur at Milborne Port. Why are they in a tympanum then? Did the carver in this case know? Another sculptural oddity at Milborne Port is the capitals of the crossing S4 arches, which are applied as a strip of plaster and then modelled with foliage.

Yet in its plan Milborne Port is amongst the ambitious churches; for it has transepts and a tower over the crossing. That, S5a one can say, was the standard plan of the major Norman parish church (cf. e.g. Dunster), and often in Perp churches this original plan can still be traced from more or less easily noticeable parts or indications. Where there was no transept, a tower may yet be between nave and chancel (Lullington, Uphill, Englishcombe, Christon, etc.; all N). Norman W towers are not absent but relatively rare (Beckington, N). Other positions also existed, and it seems again that where a tower is in a N or S position we can, even if no actual motifs are visible any longer, conclude early origin. The late F. Bligh Bond has counted eighteen Somerset towers in a SE position, eight in a SW position, and four on the N side.

Three more points of detail must find mention in passing. The first is the survival of a large and extremely oddly detailed rose window at Bristol (St James, founded 1128), the second is the occasional segmental arches found in doorways (Chewton Mendip, Loxton, Periton; all N). The third is that occasionally a chancel arch on the nave side is flanked by shallow arched recesses. They were probably for side altars (Chewton Mendip, Compton Martin, both N; also Ashill) and can be met with in other counties as well.

VAULTING was rare in English parish churches and has remained so all through the centuries. So the few examples ought to be noted specially where C12 rib-vaulting exists in the county. They are the spaces under the towers at Christon (N) and Stoke-sub-Hamdon, and the chancels at Compton Martin (N) and N7 Stogursey.

Both Compton Martin and Stogursey (the chancel) also have aisles, though aisles were not something frequent in Norman churches. Thurlbear and Pilton are other cases of surviving aisles.

Finally two cases of more elaborate plans, Stogursey and Muchelney. Stogursey represents a type more usual in C11 Ger- S5b many than France, but not entirely absent in England either (Old

Shoreham), the plan with nave, crossing and transepts, a chancel, an apse, and an apsidal chapel on the E side of either transept. Muchelney on the other hand had the standard French Romanesque plan which the Normans brought over at once and used often, the plan with transepts, chancel, apse, ambulatory, and radiating chapels. At Muchelney these parts do not stand any longer, but the foundations are exposed.

Now both Stogursey and Muchelney were monastic churches, both Benedictine priories. A survey may here follow of the other MONASTIC HOUSES of Somerset. Benedictines were also at Glastonbury, perhaps the most famous monastery in England, and at Bath (N), at Athelney and Dunster, and Benedictine Nuns at Barrow Gurney (N) and Cannington, and perhaps at Chew Stoke (N), Augustinian Canons were at Barlinch, Bruton, Buckland, Burtle near Moorlynch, Keynsham (N), Stavordale (N), Taunton, and Woodspring (N), Augustinian Canonesses at Ilchester (White Hall). The Cluniacs had only one house in Somerset: Montacute, the Cistercians also only one: Cleeve. Charterhouses were at Witham (N; the oldest in England) and Hinton (N). As for the friars, the Franciscans had a settlement at Bridgwater and the Dominicans at Ilchester. The preceptory of the Knights Templar at Templecombe passed to the Hospitallers after the dissolution of the Templars. Hospitallers also had a preceptory at Buckland which had (*see* above) originally been Augustinian and then became a collecting place for the sisters of the order of the Hospitallers.

With some of these foundations we are right in the C13. And for that we are not ready yet, as a few lines must first be devoted to the TRANSITIONAL style between Norman and E.E. Amongst motifs specially typical of the Transitional of the late C12 are the waterleaf capital and the trumpet capital and the three-dimensional zigzag. The pointed arch also occurs quite frequently in contexts which still look entirely Norman, and the idea should be given up that pointed and Gothic are the same. Of major buildings Malmesbury used it in the 60s, Worcester in the 70s. In Somerset it is, no doubt for sound structural reasons, specially frequent where arches have to carry towers. In doorways it exists in a depressed form (which Wells favoured) at Chesterblade (N) and Buckland Dinham (N), both with vertical pieces between abacus and arch. These vertical pieces are also used below a segmental arch, at Doulting (N). Waterleaf capitals never became a fashion in the county (Doulting, N), but trumpet capitals did. The trumpet capital is a scalloped capital in which the scallop, instead of rising and widening with straight outlines, curves forward as it widens – like a cornucopia or indeed a trumpet. A good example (amongst many) is Pilton. Its more generously three-dimensional character corresponds to the equally Transitional zigzags which stand at an angle of 45 degrees to the wall or even turn straight towards us. Such three-dimensional zigzags exist at Stogursey and go on, in a spirit of playfulness it may be suggested, to Glastonbury and even to Wells (N), where they can be found in a welter of stiff-leaf foliage in the N porch as late as *c.* 1230.

Stiff-leaf foliage is the hallmark of the EARLY ENGLISH style, an English speciality of which we can be proud. The richness and yet the architectural discipline of these forms is the happiest symbol of the C13. French crocket capitals are less natural, French foliage capitals of the late C13 more natural. Neither quite achieves the classic balance of style and nature of the stiff-leaf capital. Stiff-leaf foliage was created as early as *c.* 1185, as can be seen in St Mary's Chapel at Glastonbury, but its development can nowhere be followed better in its course from timid beginnings to summery lushness than at Wells (N), begun at the chancel end also ^N10 &11 about 1180, and gradually carried on to the W parts of the nave. In one capital on the S side of the nave the Transitional trumpet form appears, again perhaps in a playful mood, amongst the stiff-leaves. But there may be more in that appearance, and it is worth considering whether the carver who was going to do a stiff-leaf capital was not supplied by the hewer with a trumpet capital to work into. This suggestion is backed by the capitals in St Cuthbert at Wells, where we can see trumpet and stiff-leaf side by side. If it is accepted, it would explain the same proximity at Shepton Mallet (N) and East Lambrook.

Wells, to say it again, was begun *c.* 1180, Glastonbury after the disastrous fire of 1184, and with these two buildings Somerset suddenly leaps into the forefront of architectural events in England. Of Wells it can be said without hesitation that it was the first English building in which the pointed arch – as a Gothic motif – was accepted throughout and without exceptions. Wells still stands, except for its E end, in all its C13 glory, less interfered with by later alterations than most cathedrals in England. Glastonbury is in ruins, and its beauty is that of cliff-like fragments on the green turf and arches and windows with the light blue sky behind them.

To understand Glastonbury and Wells, one must remember their antecedents, the creation of the Gothic style in the Île de France about 1140, its consistent growth from decade to decade, and its early acceptance by the Cistercian Order. The Cistercians appreciated its structural innovations without believing in that negation of the solid wall which became more and more the credo of the French cathedral architects. About 1150–70 the Cistercians gradually imported the style into England.

The cathedral style was imported by a Frenchman who began the rebuilding of the chancel at Canterbury in 1175. The inspiration of the two men who at the same moment, about ten years later, designed Glastonbury and Wells was, however, not Canterbury, but West-Country work done under the influence of Cistercian buildings, especially Malmesbury, c. 1160–70, and Worcester, c. 1175–85, both already mentioned. Neither of these two can be called Gothic without reservation. Both used Gothic and Norman elements indiscriminately. Even so, however, so many of the motifs at Glastonbury and Wells come straight from Worcester that some must be recorded here: three-dimensional zigzag, trumpet capitals, keeled shafts, paterae in spandrels, a triforium instead of a gallery, continuous mouldings in the triforium. On the significance of these motifs more will be said presently.

S9a   At Glastonbury the Lady Chapel was built first, from 1184–6, and this seems still a Late Norman building, with plenty of intersecting blank arcades inside and out and with round-arched windows. Inside, however, it has rib-vaults which show a clear understanding of Gothic principles and the Gothic spirit. The chancel of Glastonbury was also begun in 1184, but perhaps at first work was done only on the foundations, and masonry above ground was not designed until the Lady Chapel was complete. It is tempting to assume that; for in the chancel Gothic elements dominate, and they are so similar to Wells that they may well be a reflection of the beginnings there.

The distinguishing elements at Wells, elements which distinguish it singly or *in toto* from both Canterbury begun five years earlier and Lincoln begun ten years later, are the following:
N9a a consistent use of the pointed arch throughout, a more and more consistent emphasis on horizontals, oblong quadripartite vaults, piers of great breadth and excessive sub-division (twenty-four shafts), a triforium instead of a gallery, and this triforium detailed with continuous mouldings instead of shafts with capitals and separate arches. An analysis of these motifs shows that they come from very varied sources. It is all the more remarkable how perfectly they are fused into an aesthetic whole. The continuous moulding is an English and more specifically a West-Country speciality. Bristol has it in a purely Norman context (Chapter
N6

House), Malmesbury has it too, and it has been mentioned at Worcester. In Somerset parish churches of the C12 it can also be found (e.g. Frome, N). It is so un-French that it deserves some comment to itself. The idea of the arch on columns or pilasters is of Roman origin: two uprights carrying an arch. The logic of the procedure demands a capital as an expression of the change of function. That logic was not accepted in England. Here the whole was seen rather as two lines bowing to each other and finally meeting. That is the English sense of line – the sense which made Queen Mary's Psalter possible, and flowing tracery, and later William Blake. It does not exhaust English characteristics, but it is one of them. National characteristics can only be described in polarities. Nothing could make that clearer than the next typical element of Wells, the triforium. A triforium instead of a gallery is a feature which the designer of Chartres Cathedral in 1194-5 established as indispensable to the High Gothic style which he created thereby (and by other innovations). But the triforium existed also occasionally in Norman architecture especially in the Trinité at Caen (and, as we have seen, at Worcester), and the character at Wells is emphatically more like Caen than like Chartres. It is different with the oblong quadripartite vault of Wells. This also was an innovation of Chartres (though Durham had had it in England), and one that became *de rigueur* for High Gothic architecture. The vault at Wells looks indeed French and not English. Canterbury was sexpartite, at Worcester the vaults of *c.* 1175 do not survive, Lincoln had curious, novel, and wholly English configurations.

But in spite of its vault, Wells is wholly English too. To feel that fully one has to experience it in the nave – which admittedly N9a is a little later than the end of the C12. The dates between the beginning and the consecration in 1239 are not determinable in detail. There is reason to assume that by 1239 the cathedral, except for the W front, was complete. Of the chancel only the arcade storey survives. What the upper parts were like we know only fragmentarily. If we assume – in a rough and ready way – that work was spaced evenly over the available fifty-odd years, we can say that the chancel was ready before 1200, transepts and crossing and the beginnings of the tower and as much of the nave as was necessary to help to abut it by about 1210, and that the nave then grew from E to W between *c.* 1210 and 1239. Glastonbury, where work went on at the same time though much more slowly, does not help, because too little survives. It is certain, however, that the system of elevation at Glastonbury, as it

S10 can still be seen in one part of one transept, was Anglo-Norman,
a system by which nave and triforium (a triforium here also and
not a gallery) were bound together by one tall wall-arch underneath the clerestory. This had been done at Jedburgh and Oxford
before. At Wells any such stress on vertical ties was avoided, and
so much was the problem of being Gothic without being too
vertical the dominant problem in the mind of the designer that,
as the transept went up, he decided to correct one detail in a
most telling way. In the chancel and transept E and W walls the
triforium is in twins with the vaulting shafts for the high vault
going up between pair and pair. The end walls of the triforium
are an uninterrupted band, and when it came to the nave, this
is what was established as its principle. It is now the essential
characteristic of Wells, an eminently English one. The architect
has succeeded in designing a building which is undeniably Gothic
and yet does not abandon the down-to-earth security of horizontals. Nor does it give up a firm sense of enclosure. The piers
are so broad, the triforium openings so small, that wall remains
wall and never becomes that skeleton of thin verticals which it is
in C13 France. This being so, there could also be enough leisure
to carve the Wells foliage capitals in all their generous richness.
They again, as has already been said, are English – without
parallel on the Continent.

So, before leaving Wells for the moment, it should be made
clear that Wells and Lincoln are, Europeanly speaking, the earliest
cases of a national Gothic. No-one could be Gothic without having first absorbed what France had done in the second half of the
C12. But in Spain, in Italy, in Germany the mid C13 had to come
before Gothic was assimilated and a national idiom found. In
England that moment is c. 1180 for Wells, c. 1190 for Lincoln.

N8   The dating of the W front of Wells has fluctuated a great deal
in writings of the past. In my opinion none of the sculpture can
have been made before 1235. The architectural framework may
have been begun earlier. However that may be, two things are
certain: that the designer was a new man, a man not even in
sympathy with the spirit of the nave, and that the sources of the
sculpture were the France of c. 1225–35, that is of the S porch of
Chartres and the W portals of Reims. Nowhere else in England
N12b does so much C13 sculpture survive as at Wells. It is unfortunately
not of the best. Exposure to weather and wilful damage must of
course be taken into consideration, but the quality can hardly
have been as high as that of the angels at Westminster or that
superb headless figure of an Ecclesia or a Synagogue at Win-

chester. Much is outright bad, especially in the upper tiers. The best has that peculiarly English quality of long, close, rather hard, parallel folds in the draperies – not the fullness of France or indeed of the small figurework amid the stiff-leaf of Wells about 1220–35, although some of the latter can still be seen in the figures of angels in quatrefoils at the lower level of the façade.

The design of the front, architecturally speaking, is of interest too – a screen front in the English sense, with the towers pushed outside the line of the aisles so as to obtain greater breadth, but with on the other hand the buttresses developed so strongly as to call for mighty towers, far mightier than they were executed in the late C14 and early C15. Here there is another attempt at marrying horizontal and vertical, again very English, though not aesthetically as successful as in the nave. The nave is ample, the front is spare, the nave allows the integrity of the wall to have a say in the desired stress on the horizontals; in the façade all is long gaunt shafts of Purbeck marble, and gabled blank arcades for statues to stand under. The verticals and the straight diagonals of the gables dominate.

A few more individual motifs ought to be recorded before we can leave Wells Cathedral: keeled shafts and shafts with fillets, spandrels and paterae of stiff-leaf, shaft-rings, vertical lines of crockets behind Purbeck shafts (this in the W front only), intersected or partly intersected arch-mouldings (N porch, W front), N9b Y-tracery (N porch – a remarkably early occurrence), and buttress set-offs divided into many small steps.

The latter motif also appears in the Bishop's Palace which Bishop Jocelyn built about 1230–40. So far no DOMESTIC ARCHITECTURE has been mentioned in this survey, though Somerset possesses at Saltford near Keynsham (N) the remains of a Norman house as good as the best in the country, and though Bristol possesses an equally valuable fragment of a late C12 house (pieces of an arcade between nave and aisles). Bishop Jocelyn's palace must have been a noble building in its original form. The mid C19 unfortunately has done much to reduce that nobility. It had a great hall on the upper floor with two-light windows with plate tracery, and a vaulted undercroft below. See p. 73

Contemporary are the vaulted remains of the Carthusian Witham Friary (N), no doubt the Lay-Brothers' Chapel, and at Hinton Charterhouse (N). Here also the workmanship is very good, and the two Carthusian houses must have been amongst the best work of the C13 in the county.

What else has to be mentioned is small fry. As for Bristol once again, the Elder Lady Chapel of the abbey church (the present cathedral) is of *c.* 1220–30, and the inner N portal of St Mary Redcliffe is a proud display of the beginning of the C13. But they are referred to in the Bristol Introduction. What remains then? Some work by Wells Cathedral masons at St Cuthbert Wells (N) and at Wedmore, the arcades at Queen Charlton (N), East Coker, and Tickenham (N), and the S porches at Compton Bishop (N) and Tickenham (N). Arches on vertical springers have to be noted at Hemington (N) and Great Elm (N), towers in various places, e.g. Sutton Montis, Dulverton, and Brompton Regis, an octagonal tower at Doulting (N), bellcotes at Brympton d'Evercy, Chillington, Chilthorne Domer, Cricket St Thomas, Cudworth, Dinnington, Knowle St Giles, and Lopen, some of them no doubt later than the C13.

A few words on PIER SHAPES of the C13 are still needed, a few on vaulting, and a few on tracery. C13 and early C14 piers are nowhere of course as elaborate as at Wells and Glastonbury. Scale forbade that, though at St Cuthbert in Wells a successful reduction is carried out. Circular piers, as they had been used by the Normans, continue (Ilchester, East Coker, Kingston, Chedzoy, Hemington, N), octagonal piers are at Queen Charlton (N). The other designs are variations on the theme of the quatrefoil and the quatrefoil with diagonal shafts: plain quatrefoil (South Cadbury, Chewton Mendip, N), quatrefoil but with semi-octagonal foils (Frome, N, Cucklington), square with four demi-shafts (Norton St Philip, N), circular with four demi-shafts (Taunton Magdalene, Wilton, Chedzoy), quatrefoil with four diagonal shafts (Chewton Mendip, Newton St Loe, both N), quatrefoil with four semi-octagonal diagonal shafts (Congresbury, N), and so on. A different principle appears at Congresbury (N), where a circular pier has four detached Purbeck shafts in the diagonals, and at Hemington (N) where to a circular pier four detached Purbeck shafts are added in the main directions.

The type comes from France (cf. e.g. Laon), and appears in England at Canterbury in 1175. But it was the Lincoln Cathedral lodge and also the masons working in the Lincoln parish churches who proved most inventive in the treatment of such piers. And Lincoln Cathedral was also the place where vaulting received its most original and most English impetus in the first half of the C13. From here the ridge-rib comes, and from here the tierceron. Both appear at Wells and in Somerset with some delay. At Wells the passage to the undercroft of the chapter house *c.* N14 1260–70 is the first instance. This is followed later by the chapter

stair and the chapter-house lobby.* The chapel in the Bishop's N15a
Palace adds tiercerons, but that takes us to *c.* 1275–80 and a
different style altogether.

TRACERY did not interest the Wells lodge much. At a time
when bar tracery had already been introduced to Westminster
from Reims, Wells still kept to the lancet. That again is characteristic. For the lancet accepts the wall into which the window is
set, and even plate tracery still accepts it by cutting in separately
two lancet lights and a circle or a quatrefoil above. But bar tracery
makes a two-light window one whole. The bars are only a sub-
division. So bar tracery belongs to the French principle of the
negation of the wall. Hence at Wells and in Somerset generally it
was accepted only tardily. The first example is the doorway into
the passage to the chapter-house undercroft.‡ But the chapter
stair above it has still – like Jocelyn's Palace of *c.* 1230–40 – plate
tracery exclusively, fine displays of foiled circles in groups of
three. All that seems to belong to *c.* 1260–75. It is, with the typical
sunk triangles in the spandrels, a hint at the existence of bar
tracery. Examples of plate tracery outside Wells are Watchet and
St Cuthbert Wells (N), of bar tracery Ile Abbots and Orchardleigh (N).

No sooner, however, had this stage been reached in Somerset,
and especially at Wells, than designers turned away from its
harmoniousness and regularity in pursuit of a new ideal of
complexity, intricacy, perhaps even perversity. It was an attitude
familiar to those who have experienced the revulsion from Im-
pressionism to Post-Impressionism, an attitude comparable also
to that of the Mannerists about 1520 towards the High Renaissance. No more calm perfection; let us have imperfection provided it is not calm. So both in matters of decoration and of space
new ways were explored. Sometimes in the end negation pre-
vailed, but sometimes a new valid expression was found. In this
England was ahead of all other countries.

It is characteristic that the new style is known by the name
DECORATED. Decoration may indeed well be taken first, because
the change is more patent here. In window tracery the classic
French scheme of the lancet lights with foiled circles is abandoned
at once. The first signs of a change are such motifs as pointed
cusping, pointed trefoils in spandrel spaces, also spheric triangles

* The E end of the Elder Lady Chapel at Bristol Cathedral is contemporary
with these.
‡ The corresponding example in Bristol is the E window of the Elder Lady
Chapel.

instead of circles. They were introduced in France and England
as early as the mid C13. But then new combinations appear, no
longer of quite such simplicity and logicality. For instance where
the early C13 had made a group of three or five isolated lancet
windows, the late C13 preferred the three or five as lancet lights
under one arch (Bishop's Chapel, Wells (N), W window). Where
the mid C13 had given each light its own unmistakable arch, the
late C13 liked intersection, that is confusion as to how the arches
should be viewed. The foremost examples of freer late C13 variations are the Bishop's Chapel and the Lady Chapel at Wells,
the first of c. 1285–90, the other of a little after 1300. The
Bishop's Chapel belongs to a magnificent scheme of enlarging
the Bishop's Palace which was done for Bishop Burnell. A hall
also formed part of it, which survives only in ruins, but must have
been one of the proudest secular halls up to that time in England,
115 ft long and nearly 60 ft wide, with tall windows with tracery
still Geometrical, two cusped lancet lights and a foiled circle.
The date may be 1280. But in the Bishop's Chapel, say about
1285–90, there is more variety and less regularity of tracery:
intersection, spheric triangles, pointed trefoils. The Lady Chapel,
of c. 1300–15, goes much further in novelty and wilfulness.
But from about 1300 onwards such an outburst of inventiveness takes place everywhere in the county that only a chart
could do justice to all the new forms. One usual irritant is
to make the outer lights of a three-light window taller than the
middle light and thus gain space for a somewhat squeezed-in
circle (White Lackington, Wrington, N) or spheric triangle (Barrington, Ditcheat) or spheric quadrangle (Whitchurch, N). Alter-
natively the middle lancet can push up higher than the others and
three circles can be arranged above the three lights (Ile Abbots).
Or intersection or Y-tracery can be combined with foiled circles
inserted in a few unexpected places (Yatton, N, St Mary Redcliffe
Bristol W windows, Chapel Bishop's Palace Wells E window).
About 1300–10, the ogee arch comes in (Wells Chapter House;
Wells E transept and chancel aisles; Bristol Cathedral), and reticulation at once too. The oddest use of reticulation is as a grille
in the large oblong window of the chapel at Clevedon Court (N)
and as the pattern to fit a circle at Charlton Mackrell. But flowing tracery of the fantastic kind so favoured in East Anglia is rare
in Somerset. The strangest examples are in the (much restored)
transepts at Bridgwater.

But tracery and decoration in general are only a sign of a change
which went deeper. Architecture is the art of shaping space for

utilitarian as well as emotional purposes. No style has ever existed
in architecture that was not primarily concerned with space. And
in space also 1300 was the moment of a great change in England,
a change of international importance. C13 space had possessed
the same clarity as C13 decoration. Now space began to flow, unexpected interpenetrations were sought, and thus effects obtained
which must have been as disquieting to some and as thrilling to
others as were the spatial innovations of C20 architecture when
first they were seen. Wells and Bristol are again leading for
England and for Europe. At Bristol the rebuilding of the E parts of
the abbey took place from 1298 to about 1330. At Wells, where
the Chapter House was complete by 1319 or perhaps earlier, the N17b
chancel must have been rebuilt between the Lady Chapel and N16
the crossing from c. 1325 to c. 1340. No details can be given in & 20
this Introduction. But the composition of Lady Chapel and N17a
retrochoir at Wells and of chancel, chancel aisles, and Lady N21
Chapel at Bristol and also the sensational strainer arches at Wells, N19
all this is conceived in terms of open spaces merging with each
other and of surprising and not easily understood vistas, diagonally through space. The arrangement of the piers in the Wells
retrochoir seems at first as arbitrary as the arrangement of the
bridges and transverse little vaults of the chancel aisles at Bristol.
The very fact that both Wells and Bristol here worked in terms
of the 'hall', the room with nave and aisles of equal height, is
telling enough. For this became the *leitmotif* of the most creative
Late Gothic style on the Continent, the German *Sondergotik*.
English *Sondergotik*, already with all the characteristics of an
anti-classic style, is 150 years older.

The vaulting at Wells and Bristol is as enterprising as the
management of space. Liernes appear in both places in the first
decades of the C14 (Wells Lady Chapel, Bristol high vault), and
the lierne had only been invented in England just before 1300, it
seems at St Stephen's Chapel, Westminster (in the undercroft).
Wells and Bristol are amongst the earliest to follow. The lierne
even more than the tierceron converts the surfaces of the vault
into a linear pattern. The visible structural logic of the rib-vault
in the French sense was here finally defeated. The cusping of
ribs is first seen at Bristol Cathedral, second in the S aisle at the
parish church of St Mary Redcliffe, third in the chancel of Wells. N20
It also appears in the Tewkesbury chancel. Three-dimensionally
curved ribs were introduced in the S aisle at St Mary Redcliffe and
passed on from there to Ottery St Mary (South Devon).

St Mary Redcliffe has altogether its ample share in all these

N24 innovations: spatial enterprise (in the N porch), the ogee and the nodding ogee arch (which had been used a little earlier in the Sedilia of the Wells Lady Chapel), and the lierne-vault. In addition at St Mary Redcliffe the transition from the Dec style of the early C14 to the Perp style of the second half can be followed most instructively. The first signs – mullions running straight up into an arch – appear inside the S porch.

At Wells the same observations can be made in the upper parts of the chancel and the E window, work which must belong to *c.* 1330–40. That impetus of reckless spatial and decorative inventiveness was maintained, but the spirit of the coming PERPENDICULAR STYLE can already be sensed, verticals standing hard on arches or pushing up against arches. When the renewal of the chancel was complete about 1340, the cathedral recedes. The inadequate completion of the W towers and the vaulting of the crossing were minor tasks. At Glastonbury the chancel was lengthened and remodelled in the Perp style some time about 1350–60, with the typical motif of an even flat panelling of walls.* At Bristol Cathedral the Perp style only carried on with the transepts and did not get very far. In Bristol initiative now passed
N26a on entirely to St Mary Redcliffe, and this change in significance from the cathedral and the abbey church to the parish church is a general characteristic of the later Middle Ages in the whole of England and in most of Europe. In Somerset, Bath Priory (N), rebuilt completely from 1499 onwards, is the one exception to this rule. Kenneth Wickham in the preface to his beautiful book *Churches of Somerset* devotes nearly half his space to the Perp style or what he calls The Great Epoch. It will be seen that that is wholly true of parish churches, though not of churches altogether. The greatness of the Wells nave and the greatness of the Wells retrochoir need not fear comparison with even the proudest of C15 and C16 Somerset church towers.

Somerset is one of the richest counties in large and worthwhile PERPENDICULAR PARISH CHURCHES. The epoch was one of great prosperity in the county. At the end of the C14, it has been calculated, Somerset produced about a quarter of the total of woollens made in England. Wells, Bath, and Frome (all N) were the centres. But small places like Pensford, Beckington (N), Bruton, Croscombe (N), Mells (N) appear also among the chief producers. Again about 1475 according to the alnage ac-

---

* This and some tracery on the Queristers' House along the Wells cloister, built shortly before 1363, are the earliest occurrences of the Perp style in Somerset.

counts the output of cloth in Somerset was as high as in Suffolk or in Yorkshire. This prosperity is reflected in the rebuilding of churches, and it seems that the great epoch started about 1375–80. Datable examples are Yeovil and perhaps Wellow (N), both masculine and sturdy in the Perp forms used. Wraxall (N) seems to belong the same phase.

If we now try to regard the whole of the Perp period, the 150 years of its reign, as one, what can be said in the way of a summary? Nothing new was done in the planning of the church. Rectangularity ruled. Bath and St Cuthbert at Wells are two N25 major examples.* The tower stands at the W end. Where crossing towers were kept from older plans or built afresh (as at Bath, N), the problem of a W front proper arises, and Bath (with its delightful ladders up the buttresses for angels to climb up and down), Crewkerne, and Yatton (N) are examples of such Perp W façades. S13a The preference, however, was for the W tower. The case of St Cuthbert at Wells (N) is characteristic, where the C13 crossing N25a tower stood until 1561, and yet in the C15 a splendid W tower was built as well. A similar case is Bruton, where the C14 had built a modest N tower, but the C15 added, in keeping with an enlarged and heightened church, a much more ambitious W tower. The ideal of the completely new church, where no compromise was necessary with earlier work, is W tower, nave and aisles, chancel and chancel chapels – and every member of this simple assembly decked out as lavishly as could be done.

The chancel is often the part which seems to have been cut short in size and display. This is due to the rule that the parishioners were responsible for the W parts but those in whose gift the church was for the chancel. Now the great pride and prosperity, and also no doubt the desire to make a show, were on the whole with the parishioners rather than with the lord of the manor or the monastery. So cases of a stunted chancel like, say, Bishop's Lydeard, Leigh-on-Mendip (N), or Stoke St Gregory are only too frequent. Nor are the cases rare in which the W tower dwarfs the whole rest of the church. For that there is a purely aesthetic reason. The tower, it seems, in the form of the single tower, no longer the group of towers as in the C12 and C13, was the greatest thrill for the Late Middle Ages, not only in Somerset but in England, and not only in England but in most of Europe. Take Strassburg, take Ulm, take Antwerp. Even so, amongst all

---

* A minor speciality is E vestries behind and below the chancel (North Petherton, Ilminster, Kingsbury, Langport, Porlock, and formerly Crewkerne).

English counties, Somerset remains the tower county *par excellence*, and much will here have to be said about them.

See
p. 73
SOMERSET TOWERS as a rule are square in plan, although the county also possesses a number of towers, all earlier, which turn octagonal higher up. They may be over crossings or to the W, N, or S. One even starts octagonal from the foot (Barton St David).* The oblong instead of the square tower is a freak. Yet so uniform and so costly a church as Bishop King's Bath Priory has one over the crossing, almost twice as broad as it is deep.

The Somerset towers are as a rule towers, in the sense that they have no spires. There are of course quite a number of medieval spires in the county, just under two dozen (eighteen of stone, four of timber), but with the exception of a few they don't count. The finest by far is only just in Somerset, that of St Mary Redcliffe which must have been complete by about 1330 or 1340 and was rebuilt in the C19. Bridgwater may also be mentioned, and perhaps Congresbury (N) and Yatton (N; incomplete).

But the big events were in square-topped towers. Quite a number of them are strikingly tall. The first dozen in height are:

Wells crossing tower (N)	182 ft
(Downside, built in the C20 (N)	166)
Taunton, St Mary Magdalene	163½
Bath Abbey (N)	162
Wells west towers (N)	150
Glastonbury, St John	134½
Chewton Mendip (N)	126
Wells, St Cuthbert (N)	122
Taunton, St James	120
(Probus, a Somerset tower in Cornwall	118½)
Blagdon (N)	116½
(Chittlehampton, a Somerset tower in Devon	115)
Bristol, Temple Church	114
Wrington (N)	113½

But quite apart from height, an immense amount of thought was expended on the details of the towers in Somerset. Masons must have been asked by parishioners, on the strength of one N27a tower, to design another (e.g. Batcombe and Chewton Mendip, both N). In other cases masons must have travelled – the distances

---

* At Stoke St Gregory *c.* 1300 and at Podimore and Pitminster the transition from square to octagon is done by squinches, not a usual thing in England.

were not great – to see what one village was doing, while they were working for another. But whatever inspiration or imitation did to make us recognize groups or schools, there is hardly one amongst the fifty or so best towers which has not also its individual touches. They will be described in the pages of this book in what to some users may seem exaggerated detail. Yet it is just the individuality of the mason, as it comes out in the proportions he chooses, or the detailing of buttresses and pinnacles, that is so fascinating to watch from place to place.

A Classification of Somerset Towers is not a new thing to attempt. Yet for the purpose of this book it must be attempted afresh. The chief areas are (1) the North from Bristol and Bath to the Mendips and Wells; (2) to the sw of the Mendips not quite as far as Burnham and Highbridge with important outliers at Shepton Mallet and Bruton; and (3) the Vale of Taunton. The chief concern of the designers was everywhere with those parts of the tower which rise above the roof line of the nave. Below these may be more or less big w doorways and more or less big w windows. There may also be diagonal or set-back buttresses, and some decoration by canopied image niches or ornamental bands, but even these enrichments must always be seen in conjunction with, and as a preparation for, the upper part. Now for this upper part the chief aesthetic division is in my opinion this. Class One: towers in which it is regarded as one, and Class Two: towers in which it is clearly subdivided horizontally. As for the second class, we need not look for any special source. Towers built up in stages had been usual ever since the first Anglo-Saxon towers went up. The source for the first class is Wells Cathedral (N), and here the two chief sub-species of Class One can be studied at leisure and with much enjoyment. The crossing tower of *c.* 1440, a wonderful achievement of calm power, has three long transomed two-light bell-openings, broader blank transom band in blank two-light windows of almost the same height. So, thanks to the descending mullions and shafts, the whole upper structure is one. But it is lightly divided into two by the transom band. In the late c14 NW tower that band is so much narrower that the whole available height becomes one, even if more than half of these exceedingly long windows is blank. The principle is, however, the same in both towers – the descending mullion used in such a way that the part of the tower above the roof-line is essentially ruled by verticals. The fact that the crossing tower has three two-light openings, the NW tower two, is less significant.

The progeny of these Wells towers is limited. Its distinguishing feature, once again, is the unification of the whole height above the roof-ridge by the verticals of the mullions. Batcombe (N) is the closest follower of the crossing tower, Evercreech the closest follower of the W towers. Wrington (N) is a variation of Evercreech and not an improvement. Two-thirds of the total height are left blank. St Cuthbert at Wells on the other hand is a decided improvement over the W towers of the cathedral. The bell-openings here have three instead of two lights, and the mullions descend so precipitously that verticalism in the design of a tower could hardly go further. Here is an extreme statement, but one that is wholly convincing.

There were others who would not go so far, who were ready to accept the principle of panelling of the tower walls, as it was done at Wells, but did not want to give up the normal staging of a tower either. So the lower stage, instead of a continuation of

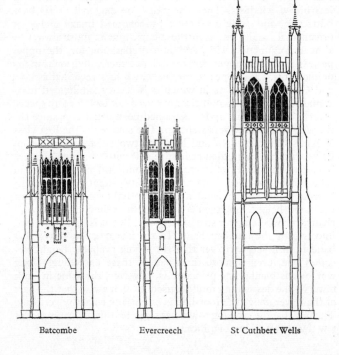

Batcombe   Evercreech   St Cuthbert Wells

the upper, reverted to being one of separate windows, blank or open, with their proper arched heads. Thus the crossing tower, with a proper string-course between lower and upper storey. The crossing tower of Bath Abbey (N) goes with Ilminster, except that it has instead of Ilminster's three-two-lights rhythm a rhythm of one two-light to the N and S and two four-light to the E and W, and that its big octagonal buttresses are Oxfordshire rather than Somerset. Close to Ilminster also are the sister-towers of Mells and Leigh-on-Mendip (both N), though with more emphasis on slenderness. To counterbalance that, there is some wall left above the blank lower windows and above the bell-openings. The result is particularly happy, classic and reposeful. In terms of the two three-light openings of St Cuthbert the same correction – properly arched lower windows, wall above them and a clearly marked string-course – is made at Chewton Mendip (N). A more personal variation finally is St John at Glastonbury, not only because the pairs of long and large upper bell-openings are of four lights, but also because below the vigorous string-course the wall is again panelled as at Wells.

In the sub-group just described the horizontal division was an afterthought, as it were. We now turn to our Class Two, the far more numerous towers in which design starts from the old

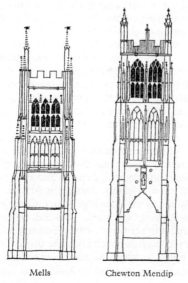

Mells   Chewton Mendip

convention of horizontal stages, and less is done to pull stages together vertically. In Somerset this class consists of two sub-species, the first of minor interest on the whole, the second comprising the most spectacular of all English parish church towers. The principle of the first was laid down at Shepton Mallet (N), a tower which may well belong to the late C14 and thus not be later than the NW tower at Wells. Now Shepton Mallet foreshadows the crossing tower of Wells, as also did the NW tower of Wells itself, but the treatment of the Shepton Mallet designer is the opposite. The NW tower stresses all the vertical elements; the master of Shepton Mallet stresses the horizontals, has no descending mullions at all, establishes a solidly closed wall below, and even makes two of his three two-light bell-openings blank. So his is in fact a very closed tower, though the bell-stage looks opener than it is, by means of the blank repetition of the bell-openings l. and r. This was repeated in plenty of churches, never with aesthetically very thrilling results: at Banwell (N), Cheddar (N), Mark, Weston Zoyland, Winscombe (N), and a little more simply* at Axbridge, Bleadon (both N), South Brent, and Weare. There is incidentally one difference between Shepton Mallet and these followers. They all are of three stages, that is have one two-light window below the tripartite display at the bell-stage, while Shepton Mallet is in four stages, that is has two two-light windows above each other below the bell-stage. But that should not be made a criterion of classification.

Whether a tower received three or four stages depended, it seems, entirely on money available, not on aesthetic considerations. It is true that in a two-stage tower, with only the bell-stage above roof-ridge level, even the best designer could not do much, but whether he had two or three stages above does not seem to have influenced composition. The three-stage arrangement of Shepton Mallet is to be found also at Banwell, Cheddar, Winscombe (all N), and Weston Zoyland. If one plots all these towers on a map, it will be seen that they are nearly all a good distance away from Shepton Mallet and close together within an area of c. 9 by 12 miles round Axbridge and Winscombe (all N). The one exception is Weston Zoyland. Another is Bruton. Here the very fine tower belongs to the Axbridge scheme, except that all three two-light bell-openings are open. This and the richer treatment of the top parts in other ways as well is clearly a sign of inspiration from the second sub-species (i.e. the third of our three main geographical areas) to which we have now to turn.

* No shafts between the blank windows and the bell-openings.

The masterpieces of tower design in the Vale of Taunton are located at and around Taunton in a circle of hardly more than ten miles' radius: Bishop's Lydeard, Huish Episcopi, Ile Abbots, S16b Kingsbury Episcopi, Kingston, North Petherton, Staple Fitz-paine, and of course Taunton itself.   S17

To group them and refer to what must in addition be mentioned, I propose a morphological system. This recommends itself because the rhythm of window openings on the various stages of a tower, their number and width, obviously influence the total effect decisively. We start with one two-light window below, and one two-light bell-opening above. That is the simplest form. It occurs in innumerable towers in England. A big early Somerset tower which belongs to this class is Yeovil. If money was available for a further stage in height, then we get one two-light window, one two-light window, one two-light bell-opening, i.e. $\frac{2}{2}$ (e.g. Batheaston, Chew Magna, and Winsford; all N and all outside the Vale of Taunton). There is no special subtlety about such towers.

Next in our morphology comes one lower two-light window and two two-light bell-openings: $\frac{2\ 2}{2}$. Here at once there is more variety. The lower part can be treated more or less openly to harmonize with the greater openness above. The designer can keep to the two-light window, or give it three, or four, lights. All these variations have been tried with much swagger in the Vale of

| Bleadon | Chew Magna | Ile Abbots | Huish Episcopi |

S16b Taunton. Ile Abbots $2\ 2_2$, Huish Episcopi $2\ 2_3$, Kingsbury Episcopi $2\ 2_4$. As before, the same can of course be done in a four-stage tower, and the Temple Church at Bristol has the arrangement $2\ 2_{2}{}_{2}$.

Now we come to two three-light bell-openings. The ensemble becomes more and more sumptuous. It exists with one three-light window below: $3\ 3_3$ (North Petherton, Probus in Cornwall, but a Somerset tower), with two stages each with one two-light window $3\ 3_{2}{}_{2}$ (Bishop's Lydeard) or with two stages each with a three-light window $3\ 3_{3}{}_{3}$ (St James Taunton). This system culminates in the grandest of all English parish church towers, St

S17 Mary Magdalene Taunton, where there are three stages, each with two large three-light windows: $3\ 3_{3\ 3}{}_{3\ 3}$.

The major examples of the Vale of Taunton group have more in common than the criteria so far mentioned. To the eye it matters indeed much more that they are all enriched to excess by ornament. In the windows is Somerset tracery, an all-over patterning with pierced quatrefoils or similar motifs, which was usual all over the county. The divisions between the stages are emphasized

Kingsbury Episcopi

North Petherton

Bishop's Lydeard

by bands of quatrefoils; and buttresses, battlements, and pinnacles all are given a maximum of interest.

On the strength of the criteria of fenestration so far used exclusively, two classes and their sub-species have been defined and
correlated to three geographical areas. What other criteria might
have been used or might be used in addition? Of Freeman's
attempt at developing a system from the position of the stair-
turret no more need nowadays be said. The only facts about stair-
turrets that might be mentioned are two. At Bristol and in its
surroundings the stair-turret is given a little spire thus making it
the chief, if asymmetrical, accent of the tower. At and around
Wellington in the W (West Buckland, Hill Farrance, Bradford)
the stair-turret is placed not in one corner of the tower but in the
middle of one, usually the S, side. That is a Devon custom
(Totnes, Ashburton) and, as in so many other ways, the W of
Somerset follows Devon.

No more helpful is a distinction between diagonal and set-

St Mary Magdalene   Dundry
Taunton

back buttresses. It is true that some areas prefer the one, some the other, but little is made of it aesthetically. The majority in Somerset, and certainly the majority of the valuable ones, have set-back buttresses, probably because they allowed such a delightful play of shafts and pinnacles in the upper parts. What ingeniousness is displayed in this, especially in the Vale of Taunton, can only be appreciated in going from one to the other. No two of these towers are quite the same in the way in which buttresses turn into diagonal shafts, the angle of the tower is hidden or partially hidden by a diagonal plane laid from buttress to buttress, shafts are attached in relief to buttresses, shafts detach themselves from the wall, pinnacles appear behind pinnacles, and so on, until in the end the top is reached.

This may have four or eight or twelve pinnacles, and the main angle pinnacles may be the final achievement of the buttresses and shafts below or quite independent of them. However it was done, it made a splendid final flourish, and the danger was less that it might be underplayed than overplayed. It can on the whole S16b be said that such towers as Huish, Kingston, Ile Abbots are rich without being top-heavy, but that one group, by trying to emulate the much broader crossing tower of Gloucester Cathedral, overdid what a parish church can do. Such a transparent crown with battlements and big square pinnacles all in openwork could be afforded at Gloucester, and it could be afforded at St Mary S17 Magdalene Taunton, where incidentally the fragile angle shafts and pinnacles standing detached from the main pinnacles against the sky are a typical Taunton addition. But at St Stephen Bristol, at St John Glastonbury, and especially at Dundry (N) they overload the top. There is no longer a harmony of composition between the tower and its crown.

Battlements and pinnacles altogether, not only on towers, but also on any other part of a church which was to be distinguished specially, aisles, clerestories, and in particular chapels given by the wealthy, are of considerable interest. In Somerset they are not used as much as in other counties. The preference is for the yet more elaborate and certainly daintier motif of the decorated parapet. The three main types are blank or pierced arcading, a blank or pierced frieze of quatrefoils set either upright or diagonally, i.e. as cusped lozenges, or cusped triangles. There is no development here. The Lady Chapel at Wells (N) has already the pierced triangles, Shepton Mallet (N) has the pierced lozenges, but St Cuthbert (N) has still the so much more elementary blind arcading.

Inside towers the arches towards the nave are often given the full height of nave and clerestory and thus tend to become the loftiest internal element of the church. The mouldings of the arches correspond to those of arcade piers. In quite a number of cases they are panelled rather than elaborately moulded (St Cuthbert Wells, Wrington, Beckington, Compton Martin, all N, etc.). To enhance the fine effect of the tall arch and also to strengthen the tower it is sometimes vaulted inside. There again no development can be traced. When the parish churches received their towers the tierceron-vault and the lierne-vault were both familiar. So both are found (tiercerons: Yatton (N), Churchill (N), West Pennard, etc.; liernes: Long Sutton, Cheddar (N), Banwell (N), Winscombe (N) – the latter three in the same area). Fan-vaults of course exist only in late towers. On the scale of a tower vault they were hardly attempted before the last quarter of the C15, and most of them belong to the C16. They are a sign of a desire for costliness and splendour. So they appear at Taunton Magdalene, Taunton St James, Bruton, North Petherton, Mells (N), Beckington (N), Chewton Mendip (N), Wrington (N), and in about a dozen other places. Under crossing towers they were built at Wells, at Axbridge (N), Crewkerne, Ditcheat, Ilminster, and also at Woodspring Priory (N).

VAULTING is unusual in English parish churches. Norman vaults have already been enumerated. There are more in the E.E. style. St Mary Redcliffe at Bristol is the only example in the county of the complete vaulting of a parish church. It was begun before 1350. In Somerset apart from Wells Cathedral there is only Bath (N) with its magnificent fan-vaults of the early C16; but Bath was monastic.* In parish churches the porch was the only part other than the tower which was vaulted frequently. Altogether churches with plenty of money liked to make something spectacular of porches. One need only think of those of about 1330–40 at St Mary Redcliffe. Yatton (N) is perhaps the most ornate of all Perp porches. Mells, Doulting, Wellow (all N) have the charming feature of a concave-sided gable. Vaulted porches can again have tierceron-vaults (Montacute, Muchelney, Keynsham (N), Chew Stoke (N), etc.) or lierne-vaults (St John Glastonbury, Yatton, N) or later fan-vaults (Crewkerne, Kingston, Ile Abbots, North Curry, Curry Rivel, Doulting (N), Mells (N), Buckland Dinham (N)). They can also have a pointed tunnel-vault with transverse ribs (Norton-sub-Hamdon, Odcombe,

* The fan-vaulted side-chapel at Stavordale (N) also belonged to a monastic house, as did the fan-vaulted cloister at Muchelney.

Tintinhull, Woolverton (N), etc., and also Yeovil and Hinton St George, both panelled).

This form was occasionally used in other parts of a church too; the Vestry at Croscombe (N), the N transept at Limington, and the N chancel chapel at Portbury (N). At Backwell (N) a chantry chapel built in 1537 has a similar stone ceiling. The transverse ribs here are cusped.

For naves and aisles the TIMBER ROOF remained the standard, and Somerset has produced some of the most beautiful of English timber roofs. The county did not accept the hammerbeam and double-hammerbeam roof (there is not a single example, though the roof of the refectory at Cleeve Abbey makes a curious attempt at looking like one without being one). The two main types are the wagon roof, a general SW English type of which, however, N29a Somerset possesses the grandest of all: Shepton Mallet (N), and the type which is so much a special achievement of Somerset that it is in this volume called the Somerset roof. This is a roof of usually low pitch with tie-beams and kingposts and often tracery above the tie-beam, figures of angels against it and against the wall-plate, and ornamental panelling between the rafters and the N29b purlins. The best of them, Martock, Somerton, Leigh (N), St Cuthbert Wells (N), and so on, are gorgeous to look at. At Mar-S18a tock the tie-beams stand on wall-shafts and these on canopied niches for carved images. But that is an exception, and another feature at Martock not at all at home in Somerset is the blank tracery of the arcade spandrels below the niches. One is used to that in East Anglia, not in the south-west.

A-type

B-type

There are only two more elements now of the Perp style in Somerset which ought to be considered: piers and tracery. PIERS were widely standardized. There are two types in particular which in this book will be called Somerset standard. Both have four shafts in the main directions, the one has four hollows in the diagonals, the other four wave mouldings. Both are just as frequent in the other counties of the SW, and neither is missing in other parts of England. The four-hollows standard has its sources far back. It can even be pointed out that the middle post of the N doorway at Wells Cathedral, c. 1230, has this moulding. Amongst parish churches it occurs specially early at Mark, with unmistakable mid-c14 detail. The W of the county goes on with octagonal piers. Special enrichments are double waves (Bath, N, Dunster, St Cuthbert Wells, N), or shafts placed into the diagonal

hollows as well (St Stephen Bristol, Wrington, N, Yatton, N).
Capitals are usually moulded, and as a rule the hollows of the
piers continue into the arches without a capital or abacus between. If capitals are decorated, there is scarcely more than very
little foliage applied to them. Capitals with bands of foliage all
along belong to the W and to Devon. One group has demi-figures
of angels on all sides of the capitals instead, a very handsome
enrichment (Taunton Magdalene, Lydeard St Lawrence, Combe
Florey, Bishop's Hull, also Shepton Mallet (N), Axbridge (N),
North Petherton, Cheddon Fitzpaine, Chipstable, Pilton).

PERP TRACERY is not of special interest. Perhaps it is nowhere
of special interest. It is a reaction against the licence of the Dec
style, and it remained a comparatively unimaginative way of sub-
dividing large windows. The size of windows is universally large.
Ambitious parish churches may go to five lights all the way
round (St Cuthbert Wells, N). Bath Priory (N) has five lights in
aisles and clerestory, and seven lights at the E end. The E window
and the end windows of the transepts are so tall that they have
three transoms. The feeling of airiness and spaciousness which
these windows create for the interior is an essential part of
English Perp altogether. But if one takes the trouble to analyse
what of ornamental inventiveness has gone into the tracery of
these windows, their barrenness is indeed surprising. The basic
classes are as follows:

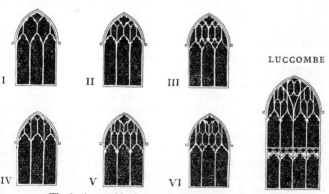

LUCCOMBE

I Woodspring II Merriott III East Pennard IV Evercreech
V Kingston Seymour VI Monksilver

These six classes occur cusped or uncusped (mostly cusped), and
with pointed or ogee-headed lights, and these divisions are in the

following not taken into consideration. Nor is that between two, three, or more lights of a window. Class I has large tracery panels. In Class II they are subdivided. In Class III the dividing mullion inside the panel is split at the foot. In Class IV the main mullions between the lights run straight up against the main arch. In Classes V and VI the main panels are subdivided into three, not two, sub-panels, the third standing on top of the other two, thereby repeating on a small scale the tracery arrangement of Class I. We★ have tried to make a statistical survey of about 350 windows. Of these 34 per cent were of Class II and 14 per cent of Class V, which is an enrichment of it. Another 14 per cent were of Class I. Classes III and VI belong together in the same way as Classes II and V. Class III amounted to 20 per cent, Class V to 10 per cent. Class IV is the rarest. It accounts for only 8 per cent, although in a similar survey made for the Stour Valley by Miss Cora J. Ough‡ it appears as the most popular pattern there, that is on the Suffolk–Essex border.

Only a few more entertaining varieties exist in addition. One is to cusp windows of Classes III and VI at the foot as well (Class III: Ile Abbots, Minehead, Monksilver, Stogumber, Taunton, Deanery Wells, Wrington (N), etc.; Class VI: Curry Rivel, Langport, Luccombe, Minehead, etc.) which adds grace and liveliness. Even more graceful and playful is the tracery in a group, where some of the individual lights have little shouldered arches (Bridgwater, St John Glastonbury, Old Cleeve, Porlock, Selworthy, Watchet), and another where the same part is played by small quatrefoiled circles to fill spandrels. This group seems to be centred round Dunster. Other examples are at Bicknoller, Crowcombe, Curry Rivel, Luccombe, Minehead (1529), Selworthy (1538), the Parsonage Walton, etc., and at Cleeve Abbey and Muchelney Abbey.

The MONASTIC REMAINS in these two places are impressive See p. 73 and instructive as an indication of the comforts of the monastery in the decades before the Reformation. But they are not a sufficient substitute for all that is lost at Glastonbury, at Bristol and Bath. At Bath (N) nothing at all survives. At Bristol, after the Norman remains (three gateways), only a gate tower so much restored as to be almost new, and a confusing much altered group which must once have comprised the refectory and perhaps the abbot's lodgings. That part became the Bishop's Palace when Bristol was made a Cathedral in 1542 and was half destroyed in

---

★ That is Miss Littlemore and I.
‡ Unpublished thesis, University of London, 1939.

the riots of 1831. At Glastonbury the only building which survives is the C14 Abbot's Kitchen, an impressive building indeed, S44 octagonal with a tall central louvre on a substantial rib-vault. So we are left with the C15 to C16 remains at Cleeve and Muchelney. The Refectory is the most interesting part of Cleeve, the Abbot's Lodgings at Muchelney. In the latter we have a comfortable house with large and regularly placed windows, with stonework reduced to a minimum and glazing given the maximum space. There is something curiously modern in this rational system.

It must have applied to the late medieval house as well. We had left DOMESTIC ARCHITECTURE at the end of the C13 with the Bishop's Palace at Wells. For the time from the C14 to the end of the Middle Ages a surprising amount survives in Somerset, more certainly than can be mentioned in this Introduction, and more alas also no doubt than will be found in this volume altogether. An attempt has been made to list every building with at least a pre-Reformation window left. It has certainly not been successful. Even so nearly 100 houses are included.

This does not count CASTLES. Somerset is poor in castles. The only ones which should appear in a general history of English castles are Nunney (N) and Farleigh Hungerford (N). They were N49a both built in the last quarter of the C14 and both belong to the type designed to a regular geometrical plan. They are in fact variants of the most important C14 type of plan, that with four circular towers at the corners. But at Farleigh, where not much more than the plan survives, the area is large, the towers were separated by stretches of wall, and there was a gatehouse with its own rounded towers in the middle of one side. In the middle was a courtyard with buildings in various positions. Nunney is much more impressive. It is just one tall solid block with the four towers attached to it. On the short sides they almost touch. Farleigh is of the type of Harlech, Nunney of a type more usual in the North of England (Langley).

The other castles need not detain us here, although at Taunton the Norman keep has been excavated, and there is the large Hall as well as a tower and walls. Dunster is the most picturesque of the Somerset castles, but archaeologically it has not much to offer – two gatehouses and some masonry. The aesthetic value of the work at Dunster is of the late C17. At Sutton Court (N) an early C14 tower survives and some embattled walls, at Newton St Loe (N) a complete keep greatly altered later, at Stogursey walls without much of a message, at Bridgwater only the Norman watergate, at Bristol some excavated masonry of the Norman Keep.

Of PRIVATE HOUSES the earliest Gothic remains are a door-way of about 1230 at Court Farm Wookey (N), a doorway and traceried windows of the mid C13 in the Treasurer's House at Martock. The most interesting remains of the first half of the C14 S38a are at Clevedon Court (N) and Lytes Cary. At Clevedon Court the typical English plan is already complete. Evidence of that is the position of porch and doorways, the three doorways to kitchen, buttery and pantry from the former screens passage, the N48b bay-window and the chapel above it. The windows of the chapel have reticulated tracery which helps to date the buildings. Reticulated tracery exists also in the E window of the chapel at Lytes Cary. The hall there is of the C15 and has an open timber-roof S38b with collar-beams, arched braces and cusped wind-braces. Other open hall roofs in halls not subdivided horizontally survive at Orchard Wyndham, Coker Court, Cothay, the Chantry House Brympton d'Evercy (first floor hall), Tickenham Court (N), Martock, Hutton Court (N), the former Archdeaconry Wells (N), etc.

PORCHES are the most frequent survival. They go in height from two to four storeys. The tallest is the porch tower at Birdcombe Court, Wraxall (N), with a vault inside. Vaulted also is the porch at Preston Plucknett. Here incidentally a contemporary polygonal chimney-stack and chimney-pot remained until the Second World War and was then renewed. Others are in the Vicars' Close at Wells (N), and at Lyons Farm Whitchurch (N). Sometimes the chapel is placed above the porch entrance, e.g. at Cothay and Lower Marsh Farm. Here and at Lodge House Durston the room has a wagon-roof. More frequent in larger houses seems to have been a chapel wing or a detached chapel. Examples of the former arrangement are, apart from Lytes Cary, Bratton Court and Blackmoor Farm, of the latter Long Ashton (N), Croscombe (N), and Lynch.

STAIRCASES are as a rule of the spiral type. They are placed either by the side of the porch (Gothelney, Nailsea Court (N), Lodge House Dunster) or by the side of the back exit (Poundisford Park, Greenham Barton, Blackmoor Farm, Court House Long Sutton). More than one staircase occurs occasionally, e.g. at Greenham Barton and at Barrington Court. At Barrington Court they are square newel staircases, but Barrington Court is as late as c. 1515. Halls as a rule had a bay-window, as can be seen e.g. at Brympton d'Evercy, Coker Court, West Coker Manor House. In many cases this has disappeared, but the panelled arch survives to indicate its position (Tower House Wells (N), Parsonage Milverton, Slough Farm Stoke St Gregory, Old Manor

House Croscombe (N)). A pair of similar arches from the hall to the porch and the back exit survives at Sutton Court (N).

Much decoration was applied to oriel windows at Wells (Bishop's Palace, Deanery, Vicars' Hall) and in other places N50a (Nash Priory, King Ine's Palace South Petherton, Mellifont S41 Abbey Wookey, N). Highly decorated also is the staircase turret of the delightful early C16 façade of Brympton d'Evercy.

WINDOWS range in size from two lights to as many as six. As a rule the hall windows are the largest, but parlour and solar may have windows of equal size. Six lights are in the parlour wing at Swell Court, five at Ivy Thorn. Large, regular fenestration almost as in a house of the C20 characterizes the Abbot's House at Muchelney and the house at Bristol now inside the Assize Court. N50b The many remaining C15 windows of the W front at Ashton Court (N) are specially ornately traceried. Inside the halls decoration in stone was concentrated on the fireplace, and there are still several ornate fireplaces preserved, such as those in the Bishop's Palace and the Deanery at Wells, and inside the Assize Court at Bristol.

Wooden screens on the other hand seem to have been curiously utilitarian – see the examples in the Deanery at Wells (N) and at Cothay. There is little in Somerset houses of fine carving of Perp roof beams or wall panelling. The spectacular pieces which can be admired at Barrington Court do not belong to the house.

Barrington Court, begun c. 1514–15, stands at the end of Perp S46b domestic architecture and at the beginning of a new style in that it has the E-plan popularly connected with Queen Elizabeth I and a façade almost completely symmetrical. We shall revert to it later.

For the moment we must still deal with some special types of houses. First, often as part of the manor house, the separate GATEHOUSE. Wells has of course the best set, though none of them amongst the best English cathedral gatehouses. They date all four from the C15. Another gatehouse also to a manor of the bishops of Wells has survived at Wiveliscombe; Cothay has one, there is another at Whaley, and Chew Manor House, Chew Magna (N) has one too.

STONE BARNS are fine things in Somerset, much standardized in appearance, with their buttresses, their cross archways, slit windows, and open timber-roofs. It is hard to choose which to record here. Preston Plucknett must of course be among them, S43 and Glastonbury and Pilton and Doulting (N) and perhaps the Bishop's Barn at Wells. But far more interesting is what little remains of the Canons' Barn at Wells; for this seems a building of the late C12 which had nave and aisles divided by tall plain stone pillars rounded at the corners. No other such building seems to survive anywhere.

Other rarities in the county if not the country are the early C16 CHURCH HOUSE at Chew Magna (N), along the Churchyard, with a long open timber-roof, and the GRAMMAR SCHOOL at Taunton, built about 1480 and improved about 1520–30. This is an imposingly large room, also with an open timber-roof. Another fortunate survival is the INN at Norton St Philip (N) with its two stone oriels and its upper timber-framed work.

Half-timber is not a Somerset tradition. There is an odd pre-Reformation house in the Market Place at Axbridge (N) and there were more at Bristol. But what has survived at Bristol, though it looks picturesquely medieval, is of the C17; and at Taunton in Fore Street of the late C16. The Market Cross at Dunster also is S40 of c. 1589 with C17 alterations. The Inn at Glastonbury is often illustrated as another medieval inn, but that was built as a *hospitium* of the abbey, that is not as a private enterprise. The other medieval secular building at Glastonbury also came under the abbey, the Tribunal or Court House.

Urban building otherwise is confined to the interesting NOVA OPERA of Bishop Bekynton at Wells (N), a terrace of houses along one side of the Market Place. At Mells (N) a whole little street of cottages in terrace formation leads from the main road to the church, but curiously without any special axial relation.

The most interesting piece of secular medieval architecture in N48a Somerset is also primarily a piece of planning, the Vicars' Close at Wells (N), a street built by Bishop Ralph of Shrewsbury in 1348 to provide separate houses for the vicars choral of the cathedral and with the houses a hall and a chapel. The whole is a perfect piece of planning, all the houses as identical as in a modern estate or as identical as the cells of a Charterhouse, which is perhaps the most appropriate comparison. The houses have one large and one small room on the ground floor and the same on the upper floor, the two being connected by a spiral staircase. The accommodation is similar in the C15 Priest's House opposite Muchelney church. In the C15 the houses in the Vicars' Close were given front-gardens and little walls and gateways. The hall was enlarged too and several pretty oriel windows were built. In the muniment room attached to the hall the deed cabinet still stands, very much like a modern cupboard for card-index boxes.

FURNISHINGS have so far been neglected, even in churches. We must now try to trace the development of furnishings and the fine arts – what little there is of them. Painting and sculpture need indeed hardly be mentioned.

As for PAINTING there is a fragment of *c.* 1200 at Saltford Manor House (N) and some C13 work at Sutton Bingham S24a church. A fresco of Christ and the Apostles has been found at Watton (N). Two of the familiar St Christophers are at Wedmore and Ditcheat.

Of SCULPTURE the earliest piece not in a strictly architectural context is the seated figure to the l. of the surviving gateway of the former St Bartholomew's Hospital at Bristol, clearly work connected with the Wells W front. The most interesting piece of sculptural church furnishing is in the Taunton Museum, the S23 reredos for Wellington church of *c.* 1380. For here we can see what a complete English reredos was like with figures not spoiled by Victorian sentimentality. In this way the two chipped-off reredoses at St Cuthbert Wells (N) must also be reconstructed in one's mind. It is not too difficult; for of one some good original bodies and heads are still in the church. Otherwise there is the row of apostles in the gable of Wells Cathedral, of the late C14 or the early C15, and no more.

CHURCH MONUMENTS are of course more plentiful, but most of the effigies, principally of knights and ladies of the C13 and C14 which one finds in churches, are in too bad a condition to judge their aesthetic value, though quite often one can still recognize that once they must have been of good quality. An exception is the series of effigies of unknown bishops in Wells Cathedral. There are seven of them, five of *c.* 1220, two of *c.* 1240. N40 They are all well preserved and excellent, the earlier with vigorously characterized features and bold rounded draperies, the later far more realistic and also in higher relief – an object lesson in the change towards a greater consideration of nature which took place everywhere in the course of the first half of the C13. For the later Middle Ages it is advisable to look at monuments rather as architecture than as sculpture. There are, it is true, fine details in a number of monuments, the caryatids of the tomb at Pendomer, S33a the effigy of Bishop Marchia at Wells (N) – both early C14, the two alabaster panels of Annunciation and Trinity on the tomb of John Boleyn at Wells, of the early C15, the brass of *c.* 1430 at South Petherton, the brass of Philip Mede † 1475 at Bristol (which is iconographically interesting because it consists no longer of cut-out figures but is a plate with kneeling figures engraved), the statuettes of mourners at St Stephen Bristol (*c.* 1370), Stogursey, and Farleigh Hungerford (N), and the alabaster effigy

N42b of William Canynge at St Mary Redcliffe of the late c15, and so on – but if one thinks for a moment of the power to carve and the power to characterize in German and French late medieval monuments, one will realize how unrewarding *qua* sculpture are the later bishops' tombs at Wells, and the tombs at Bristol Cathedral and St Mark's Bristol.*

The design of the tomb recesses on the other hand offers an interesting illustration of the development of architectural decoration, starting again from Bishop Marchia, the tomb at Pendomer, and the first of the two odd recesses at Nettlecombe which are so deep that they project beyond the outer wall of the church, and ending with such elaborately Perp pieces as the Newton N42a Monument at Yatton (N), the Choke Monument at Long Ashton (N), the monument to Prior Bird at Bath (N), and the extremely odd surround of the Rodney Monument at Backwell (N). It is only one step from these semi-architectural pieces to chantry chapels. We can see it taken in the Bekynton Tomb of before 1452 at Wells, an effigy on a stone table and a cadaver below, and to the E a wall with a coved top for an altar to be placed against it. There are two real chantry chapels at Wells, Bishop Bubwith's and Treasurer Sugar's of *c.* 1420 and *c.* 1480, and there is finally the fan-vaulted Poyntz Chantry at St Mark's Bristol of *c.* 1520, the size of a normal chapel added to a church.

Now for medieval CHURCH FURNISHING. We take FONTS first. It is a phenomenon noticeable in most counties that Norman fonts were preserved piously in churches where everything else was replaced and rebuilt. Whatever the reason, Somerset also possesses a large number of Norman fonts, many entirely plain, others enriched by just a band of cable-moulding or of saltire crosses, others with some bold scalloping of the underside of the bowl, one, two, three scallops (one: Hinton Blewett, N; two: Edington, Leigh, N; three: Cameley, N, Weston-super-Mare), yet others of the well-known Purbeck type, square with small blank arcading (Templecombe, Odcombe, Milborne Port, Crewkerne, West Buckland, Brushford – all in the s and w), also some with intersected arches (West Camel, Corfe, Halse) and so on to Lullington (N), the most ornate of all, and to Churchstanton which is of the Cornish type of Bodmin with four faces in the corners, and to Ile Abbots with a savage animal. As to the c13 Saltford (N) has eight small carved heads; but more interesting

* The Incised Slab for Bishop Bitton II † 1274 at Wells and that to a Kempe at Chelvey (N), of *c.* 1260–70, ought to be noted in passing. They are among the earliest incised slabs in the country.

are the few purely architectural fonts, that at Winscombe (N) like a moulded capital and that at Wellow (N) of an eight-lobed shape. The most noteworthy C14 font is at Orchardleigh (N) with small seated figures in sexfoils. There are innumerable Perp fonts, and they are nearly all of no interest, though in a few of them demi-figures of angels carry the bowl, just such angels as carry roof-beams or sometimes appear on capitals (Watchet, Axbridge, N, Mark, Doulting, N, Wrington, N, etc.). Other figured Perp fonts are at Minehead, Crowcombe, Taunton St James and at Nemp- S28a nett Thrubwell (N), and so to the far more ambitious font with the Seven Sacraments at Nettlecombe, quite alien to Somerset.

Somerset is not a county of SCREENS like Devon and Cornwall or Suffolk and Norfolk. The best rood screens of wood are in the W, and they belong to the Devon series, with both the varieties of tracery represented which are usual there, that where in each division a middle mullion runs up into the apex of the arch and that where two sub-arches divide the main arch. The best ex-amples are at and round Dunster (Dunster 1498, Minehead, Watchet, Bicknoller, Carhampton, etc.). What is in other parts S29 of the county cannot compare with them. If a few must be men-tioned, they ought to be Banwell (N; 1522), Keynsham (N), and Long Ashton (N). Stone screens on the other hand are plentiful at Wells, but except for the screens of c. 1340–50 from the tran-septs to the chancel aisles they are plain, uninteresting work. Those to the chancel aisles have to the l. and r. of the doorway a vertical frieze of pierced cusped lozenge-shapes, the same idea as in the S transept windows of St Mary Redcliffe and another proof of the close artistic relations in the C14 between Bristol and Wells.

In the case of PULPITS, those of wood can again not compare with Devon (except perhaps for Trull), but there is a fine series S28b of stone pulpits in and around the Mendips, about fifteen of them, the best being perhaps those at Badgworth, and at Wick St N36b Lawrence, Banwell, Bleadon, and Hutton (all N), probably all made by the same workshop.

BENCHES on the other hand are preserved in large numbers and have quite a county character. None of them seems earlier than the C15. It appears indeed that the introduction of benches into churches belongs to that century, an expression of the general late-medieval desire for comfort in the church as well as at home, and an expression also of the growing importance of the sermon in services. The best group is in the W of the county, straight-topped with close tracery or plant motifs, initials, the Instru-

ments of the Passion (but these are never given as much prominence as in Cornwall), and also figure motifs. If one tries to
make a collection of the iconography of these benches one will
S26a find represented a ship (Milverton), a windmill (Bishop's
S27 Lydeard), a fuller and his tools (Spaxton), a rosary (Kingston), a
cock-fight (Hatch Beauchamp), a carpenter (Lyng), a night-
watchman (Bishop's Hull), the Pelican (Stogursey), a whole little
S26b church procession (Trull), the story of a wicked abbot as a fox
(Brent Knoll), and so on. Poppy-heads belong rather to the N
and E of the county. Where dates exist on benches, they are without exception of the C16 and mostly of about 1530–40, a sign
perhaps that benching as a rule took place only in the very years
of the Reformation.

N35b   The MISERICORDS of the choir stalls of Wells (N) of course
are on quite a different plane. They date from c. 1330 and are not
work of the village carpenter but of craftsmen of no doubt far
more than local repute. The series is one of the most enjoyable in
the country. Minor misericords are at Worle (N; early C16) and
Weston-in-Gordano (N).

One DOOR must not be overlooked, that of the late C13 into
the Chapter House undercroft at Wells, with its wild ironwork.
That brings us to metalwork, and there LECTERNS must be mentioned first (especially the brass eagle at Yeovil), then IRON RAIL-
INGS such as that of the Bekynton tomb at Wells (N) of c. 1452,
and SILVER PLATE. The only pre-Reformation pieces in Somerset are a chalice and paten of 1479 at Nettlecombe (the oldest
piece with a date-letter in England), paten of c. 1500 at Pilton, a
paten probably of 1511 at Chewton Mendip (N), and secular
cup also at Chewton Mendip which is dated 1511.* A word in
passing on TILES, because at Cleeve Abbey quite a number are
preserved, especially from the pavement of the original C13 refectory, and a word on VESTMENTS. Somerset has a number of fragments of copes, etc., mostly converted into frontals but still enjoyable in their figure and floral decoration. They are to be found
at Bruton, Chapel Allerton, Chedzoy, St John Glastonbury,
Othery, Pilton, Priddy, and Yatton (N), and are all late C15 or
early C16.

Finally STAINED GLASS.‡ Here Wells Cathedral (N) contains
in the E parts built c. 1310–40 some of the best English glass of the
time, from the exquisite small pieces of c. 1310–20 in the tracery

---

* A C13 chalice of pewter is at Orchardleigh (N).

‡ The earliest stained glass in Somerset is foreign, the beautiful small
panels from Strassburg at Walton-in-Gordano (N).

heads, entirely in the style of contemporary illumination and still in deep colours,* to the Tree of Jesse in the great E window of *c.* 1340, with its rather less numinous colouring in which yellow and green predominate. The yellow may represent the earliest case of the use of silver-stain in England. Village churches have plenty of bits, carefully listed by Canon Woodforde who could thus prove the existence of a Somerset school, but there is little worth mentioning here; perhaps the tracery heads of *c.* 1375 at Compton Bishop (N), the window given by Prior Cantlow of Bath to St Catherine's (N), the two windows at East Brent, the one at Langport, and the three at Winscombe (N). Of these one is of about 1525, and this contains some Italian Renaissance detail.

So the RENAISSANCE makes its appearance, not very early. Nor is there any other piece, in stone or wood or metal, that could be dated earlier.‡ The best stone-work in which the new Renaissance fashion is taken notice of is the porch from Clifton Maybank S47 in Dorset which was re-erected at Montacute. This must date from *c.* 1535, and it is eminently typical of the situation at that moment that an essentially Gothic design is here brightened up just by some putti and some acanthus scrolls. Similarly medallions with heads in profile appear on bench-ends (North Cadbury 1538, Milverton, etc.).

MONUMENTS in Somerset seem to be specially late in accepting pilasters and columns, acanthus and arabesques. The earliest date is 1558, the date of death of Bishop Bush (Bristol Cathedral), and here Renaissance columns still appear together with the *gisant* or cadaver. The monuments at White Lackington of *c.* 1550 S34 or later, at Wookey (N) of *c.* 1555, at Hinton St George of the 1560s, and even at Watchet of *c.* 1575, have no Italian details. Where they appear, they are at once in a Netherlandish–Elizabethan translation (East Harptree † 1568, N, Keynsham † 1587, N, etc.). Far more important, because a document of national interest, is the stone pulpit at Wells given by Bishop Knight, N37 that is *c.* 1545 (he died in 1547); for this is not a piece of pretty Quattrocento decoration (as which it would still be quite up-to-date at that moment) but a heavy, serious piece with plain broad pilasters and a big cornice, a piece in which the Renaissance is taken up in earnest. It is amazingly early for such an attitude and must be explained from Bishop Knight's wide Continental experience.

* Two small pieces of the same date are at Tickenham (N).
‡ The Wells glass of 1507 is not English.

But the Renaissance was a secular movement and so in the c16 secular architecture begins to take precedence over religious. In any case little could be done in CHURCH DECORATION during the decades of religious struggle and uncertainty. Thus no major work was undertaken before Laud, nor even much of minor work. A Marian bench-end with an M and a crown is at Chedzoy, some woodwork dated 1560 at Trull, and 1561 at Spaxton. Pulpits are often called Elizabethan, but that refers to style rather than date. Among two dozen dated examples not one is before 1600. With church monuments of course it is different. They commemorate those who built the houses, and their style in its demonstrative robustness goes with that of the houses.

The transition in DOMESTIC ARCHITECTURE from Late Perp to Elizabethan, that is from Early to Later Tudor, is impercept-
S46b ible. Barrington Court of 1514, etc., already has the E-plan, that is an external symmetry of the façade, although of course no Renaissance detail whatever; the additions at Lytes Cary done about 1533 are also symmetrical, and in addition there is here some of that thin-ribbed 'spider's web' decoration which one connects so firmly with Elizabethan architecture. This was first evolved, it seems, in the 1520s and 1530s, at the Court (Wolsey's cabinets and Great Watching Chamber, Hampton Court, King's College screen, Cambridge). The date at Lytes Cary may be c. 1560; about the same as at Poundisford Park, built shortly after 1546.

Poundisford Park still has mullioned windows in which the individual lights have depressed arches, an early c16 tradition. The full-blown Elizabethan style discards this Gothic relic and builds its mullioned and mullioned and transomed windows without any arches. Of Elizabethan houses the only one in the front
S49 rank, nationally speaking, is Montacute, a perfect example of what Elizabethan designers did not often succeed in: to be large without being showy. Montacute was built from c. 1590 to c. 1599. No major Elizabethan house in Somerset can be dated earlier than 1575. North Cadbury is 1581, Bishop's Hull (rather smaller) 1586, Fairfield 1589, Nailsea Court (N) 1593, St Catherine's Court (N) c. 1594, Nettlecombe 1599. Amongst the undated buildings even the briefest survey will have to include the charming
S48a and very personal work at Cothelstone. There is no break between the Elizabethan and Jacobean styles, and Newton Surmaville (1602–12) and East Quantoxhead do not contribute innovations of external design. Inside the houses, however, the plasterwork changes its style. The thin ribs still carry on, e.g. as late as 1639

at Chelwood, but side by side with it broad bands appear. That is the same all over the country. Somerset examples of the new C17 style are the sumptuous ceiling at Nettlecombe and the tunnel-vaulted ceiling at The Abbey Beckington (N). Fireplaces also get grander with the C17. There are more now with cartouches of three-dimensional strapwork and with caryatids and stories told in relief. Such fireplaces with dates from 1614 to 1630 are, e.g., in the two Luttrell houses at East Quantoxhead and Dunster. Bristol also seems to have gone in for sumptuous fireplaces. They are mentioned in the Introduction to Bristol.*

Before leaving Jacobean architecture attention must be drawn to an interesting freak, Walton Castle near Clevedon (N). This was built c. 1610–20, hardly as a castle, rather as a romantic or chivalric conceit – an octagonal tower surrounded by an octagonal wall with angle turrets. Elizabethan and Jacobean medievalism deserves special notice wherever one finds it, and it is possible that that most curious of church effigies, the so-called Hauteville at Chew Magna (N), is also an Elizabethan attempt at appearing ancient. _{N43b}

To other CHURCH MONUMENTS of c. 1550 to 1650 not much space need be given. The types are the established ones, kneeling figures facing each other across a prayer-desk (Bath (N) 1605, Watchet 1613 and 1624), or recumbent figures (the alabaster effigy at Wiveliscombe, 1622, is specially good), or else now semi-reclining figures (Bishop's Hull 1609, Bridgwater 1620). The effigies were set nearly always, as soon as some money was available, between columns, sometimes with a coffered arch, mostly with an achievement at the top. The most sumptuous are the Sydenham tomb at Stogumber († 1597) and the Popham tomb at Wellington († 1607). Bishop Montague's tomb († 1617) at Bath is no longer in its original state. For Bristol the Bristol Introduction must be compared. One late C16 and C17 group has a brass-plate with kneeling figures, usually set in a stone frame. The type originates in the Mede plate of c. 1475 already mentioned. Examples are at Burnett (N) 1575, Bishop's Lydeard 1585, Croscombe (N) 1606 and 1625, Shepton Mallet (N) 1649, etc. Another group, of the late C16, impressive in its restraint, has no figures at all, just a reredos architecture with columns and ornament (Ilminster 1580, Charlton Adam 1592, Curry Rivel 1593). Still, iconography in church monuments remained relatively static

S35

S35

---

* Other fireplaces of the C16 and C17 at Hetling House, Bath (N), Christon Court (N), Laverton (N), Long Ashton (N), Gournay Court, West Harptree (N), and Charlton House, Wraxall (N). For South Somerset, see p. 73.   See p. 73

until in the 1630s, noticeable all over the country though most strongly in London, a greater freedom was achieved. The Somerset examples of this have to occupy us later.

For the present it must first be established that this tendency towards innovations was not applied to CHURCH FURNISHINGS. On the contrary, where re-furnishing was done (and much was done even before the time when Laud became archbishop, which was in 1633), the style remained firmly Elizabethan and Jacobean. In pulpits, benches, screens and the like, the motifs are nowhere new: the usual broad blank arches, strapwork from the Netherlands, arabesques from France, etc. The only ornamental convention which belongs to the mid C17 and had not existed before is a kind of gristly forms in cartouches, instead of the harder leathery or fretwork forms of before. Examples need not be mentioned in much detail. Croscombe gives us without any doubt the N38b most complete picture of the refurnished village church (1616). C17 SCREENS are at Rodney Stoke (N) 1625 and Low Ham, both still Perp in composition, and at North Newton, with largish figures 1637, at Curry Mallet with figures and reliefs, at Thurloxton c. 1634, and Bridgwater, and finally as late as 1655 at Keynsham (N). A Jacobean REREDOS at Somerton with figures ought to be mentioned too. The vine-wreathed columns at East Brent are more probably of 1635 than of the C19. Jacobean and Laudian Pulpits have already been mentioned. BENCHES are less frequent. Sets are at West Coker (1633), and of one and the same simple type at Mells (N), Great Elm (N), Chilthorne Domer, and N38a Mudford. A grand DOOR was given to Bath Abbey in 1616. CHURCH PLATE is of course extremely plentiful. With the establishment of the Reformation under Queen Elizabeth cups and covers were needed everywhere, and what had been lost in the troubled years before was replaced. In the years 1572–4, one London maker, with the monogram I.P., supplied the cathedral and ninety-nine parish churches with plate. Of the C17 the most remarkable pieces, according to Bates, are the chalice of 1633 at Marston Bigott (N), five large standing cups of between 1611 and 1619 at Ilminster, Yarlington, Horsington, Odcombe, and Bath Abbey (N), two elegant small engraved tankards of 1605 at Binegar (N) and West Pennard, and domestic pieces of 1637 at East Lambrook, and 1640 at Barwick. Examples of other C17 METALWORK are the two splendid sturdy baluster-shaped LECTERNS, at St Mary Redcliffe Bristol of 1638, and at Wells (N) of 1660. In the latter the engraved decoration is already of the rich acanthus kind which belongs to the Restoration period. But

the most interesting pieces of interior embellishment of the years
with which we are concerned at the moment are the ROOFS of_{N30&}
Axbridge (N) and East Brent churches (1636 and 1637).* These _{S22a}
plain roofs with their ribbed patterns must of course be understood in conjunction with the Elizabethan tradition of ribbed
plasterwork patterns. But that does not explain the cusping,
especially at East Brent. The use of this motif was unquestion-
ably a self-conscious revival, a revival of a Bristol and Wells C14
and C15 speciality, and ought to be understood in conjunction
with the other instances already quoted of a medieval revival in
the late C16 and early C17.

A few CHURCHES built at the same time may also belong to it.
But it is difficult to decide here; for if a church was to be built in
the 1620s or 1630s, what other style than the Perp would have
been available? Inigo Jones's two London churches (one a Royal
chapel) were the only pattern for a classical style, and the Elizabethan style had never architecturally established itself in ecclesiastical architecture. So Wyke Champflower of 1623–4 has
purely Perp windows, Corston (N) in 1622 a purely Perp w window, Chapel Allerton has the date 1638 on a Perp window, Rod-
den (N) in 1640 panel tracery above round-arched lights; at
Kittisford in 1659 just one window has an architrave instead of a
hood-mould, and at Bath Abbey (N) fan-vaulting was continued
even as late as the early C17. The most interesting C17 church in
Somerset is Low Ham, begun in the 1620s and consecrated in
1669; for here the general impression is again entirely Perp, windows with two-centred arches, battlements and so on, but the
window tracery is an original paraphrase of Dec forms – again a _{S21}
revival in this case, it might be suggested, not a survival. A similar
case is the w tower at Keynsham (N) rebuilt in 1634, and the w
tower at Norton St Philip (N) altered in 1640.

The situation in provincial architecture and art in the second
third of the C17 is an interesting one everywhere. Low Ham and
the Keynsham and Norton towers are only one aspect of it. The
opposite aspect is the final establishment of classical architecture
in London. Inigo Jones in architecture, van Dyck and Rubens in
painting, Le Sueur and Nicholas Stone in sculpture had done
their decisive work in the 1620s and 1630s. They introduced into
English art the Grand Manner, formality on the one hand, an
easy and elegant fluency on the other. Concurrently, however,
there also appeared a greater appreciation of the Italian Baroque

* The painted roof of Muchelney church, folk-art entirely and probably as
late as the 1660s, may also be remembered.

as another version of the Grand Manner, rhetorical, sensational, and effusive. Now amongst English artists the Baroque could appeal to those who were used to the overcrowding of the Jacobean style, whereas the restrained Palladian classicism came as a complete reversal of all that had been practised before. The second third of the C17 is the period of conflicts between the three tendencies of classicism, Baroque, and Perp tradition. The process can be followed in all its variations in Somerset HOUSES.

N51   The first example is the most interesting, the new S front of Ashton Court (N), dated 1635. It has been attributed to *Inigo Jones*; on no sufficient evidence, but for reasons well understandable. For here suddenly the façade of a mansion was treated not as a surface to be decorated; the skyline was not punctuated by gables but given a balustrade, the windows were made upright and were rhythmically placed, and they received the alternatingly triangular and segmental pediments which are the hallmark of Palladianism. Yet the work of the 1630s at Ashton Court is not pure. There are oval windows in the attic as well, and the back has truncated gables with columnar chimney-stacks.

In architecture Ashton Court remained without echo for more than thirty years.* The usual domestic style remained Jacobean. In cottages and the like it remained so until deep into the C18, and it is interesting to record horizontal mullioned windows with arched lights as late as the Grammar School at Martock, 1661, mullioned windows with hood-moulds as late as 1682 (Wells), and 1689 (Blagdon, N), and without hood-moulds as late as 1738–40 (former Ridley's Almshouses) at Bristol, and as late as 1766 (Clapton-in-Gordano, N) and 1777 (High Williton, N) in villages. The form which follows it in the cottage and sometimes also in less visible places in major town houses is the upright two-light mullioned window (e.g. Dunkerton 1695, Newton St Loe 1698, Wells 1699, Ockhill 1723, Stanton Prior 1737 – all N). The form which Inigo Jones and his followers used, and which remained the classical form until sashing came in from Holland about 1690, is the cross-window, that is the upright window with a mullion-and-transom cross. This had existed in Elizabethan and Jacobean houses as well, but was not used systematically. Now we find it, e.g., at Stanton Wick Farm (N) in 1666, at Hassage (N) in 1677, and more grandly at Brympton d'Evercy before 1697. Concurrently the big segmental door pediment appears (Nynehead 1675) and just before 1700 the shell-hood.

* The oval windows in the attic were taken over at Cannington Priory as late as 1714.

The first examples of the grand evenly fenestrated façade without projections and recessions and without gables, such as Ashton Court had introduced, are Brympton d'Evercy (before 1697) and Hinton House, Hinton St George.

In the second half of the C17 great changes also took place in INTERIOR DECORATION. The simple oval or circular wreaths of Inigo Jones's plasterwork and the naturalistic treatment of the foliage of such wreaths and garlands which seems to have begun about 1650 – see Forde Abbey just across the Dorset border – is reflected in Somerset first rather humbly at Golden Farm, Poundisford Park, and Bournes, Wiveliscombe, and then in its most splendid form at Dunster Castle. The date there is 1681. In 1652 S52 at Taunton, in 1658 at Stringston plasterwork had still been in the Jacobean tradition, and in 1672 the same still applied to an overmantel at Christon (N).

Of an equally superb craftsmanship is the woodwork at Dunster. The staircase balustrade has gorgeously thick openwork foliage scrolls. The same craftsman may have carved the Wyndham Pew at Watchet (1688).* An earlier example of that style is also at Forde Abbey. There are interesting instances in the county to show how the staircase balustrade developed from the Jacobean type with turned or ornamented balusters, to the type of Dunster. The intermediate stage is cut-out panels, not with foliage, but with flat scrolls and such motifs as a shield or a fleur-de-lis – all in openwork treatment. That is the way the staircase is decorated at Tilly Manor, West Harptree (N) in 1659, at Farmborough (N) in 1667, and at King Charles' Bar at Wells (N). Stoke House Bristol of 1669 still has flat balusters, but they are decorated with garlands and swags now, and at Chedzoy, also about 1660–70, turned balusters are maintained, but they assume the generous outline and the sturdier girth which are characteristic of the late C17.

A motif popular in North Somerset in the last third of the century is the upright oval window keyed into a rectangular panel‡ (Farmborough 1667, Stoke House Bristol 1669, Batheaston 1670, Hassage 1677, Stevens Almshouses Bristol 1679, Deanery Wells, Dunkerton 1695 – all N). It is the typical example of a fashion. It comes and goes for no special reason, though the oval window as such has of course its explicable place in the semi-classical, semi-Baroque C17 architecture of England.

* Good late C17 woodcarving also on the Pulpits at Shepton Mallet (N), 1696, and at East Pennard. For early C18 work cf. below.
‡ The oval windows at Ashton Court and Cannington Priory are horizontal.

The most rewarding manner in which to observe in Somerset the development of style through the second and last thirds of the century is CHURCH MONUMENTS. The resolution to introduce new schemes of composition belonged to the thirties, *see* the two frontal demi-figures at Curry Mallet 1633, and the standing figure at Taunton 1635. The bust in an oval frame was a favourite with the London court sculptors at the time and is to be found more than once in Westminster Abbey. The Godolphin Monument at Bruton of 1636 may well be by *Le Sueur* himself, as Professor Webb has suggested. A conceit whose popularity also came from London, and in this case from *Nicholas Stone*, is the figure rising from the tomb in a shroud. Somerset paid tribute to this macabre fashion in monuments at Winsham (N) of 1639 and at Rodney Stoke (N) of 1651. At Rodney Stoke also is the earliest work of a stone mason who, down to the seventies, turned out gaily coloured monuments with whole figures or three-quarter figures in niches and the paraphernalia of the Court style used with happy ignorance (Rodney Stoke, N, 1657, Brent Knoll 1663, Keynsham, N, 1661, Bristol St Mark 1667, Axbridge, N, 1668, 1670, Cloford, N, 1676). A mystery remains the only really enthralling monument of these years in the county, the John Lord Poulett at Hinton St George. He died in 1649, but can these fluted tapering pilasters, can this thick garland of flowers, can this sphinx and this acanthus foliage really be so early? The sources of the pilasters are Italian and their appearance in England in conjunction with these motifs makes even Kenneth Wickham's proposed *c.* 1665 appear too early. His date was no doubt influenced by such equally Baroque performances as the porches of Chelvey Court (N), Wraxall Court (N), and Stoke House Bristol of 1669. In my opinion the Poulett Monument is still later, a very exceptional work of the end of the C17.

In architecture the most characteristic design of the end of the C17 is Halswell House of 1689. Here the Wren style is absorbed and given a higher pitch – a little provincially, similar rather to the way in which Sir William Wilson worked in the Midlands. The centre or frontispiece in particular is much dramatized. At Bristol the Wren style in its most unpretentious form makes its first appearance in the Colston Almshouses of 1691. Another set of Bristol Almshouses, those of the Merchant Taylors, were built two years later. The central entrance has a shell-hood now, a mark always of *c.* 1700, and the building material is brick.

The introduction of this material which has only a very limited regional justification in Somerset marks the end of Somerset art and architecture with a county character of its own.* If we now want to complete a summary of work of a higher than provincial standard, we have with few exceptions to keep to Bristol and Bath and their surroundings, a prosperous port and the first of the spas of England. The Bristol development does not form part of this Introduction, and readers can only be reminded of the city's regularized expansion which began in 1699 with the laying out of Queen Square, a square designed in conscious imitation of the N52b squares of London and larger than any built in London until then. Other squares followed, and soon Bath joined in to take the lead after a short time and become the pattern of English C18 town-planning.

The change, as will be explained in more detail in the Introduction to Bath, was due to John Wood. The expansion of Bath had begun a little earlier, thanks to Beau Nash's brilliant management of the spa. But what was built before Wood was not at all Palladian; it was rather Baroque in a free-and-easy way. But even this naive Baroque was at the time decidedly a modern style as against the gabled houses of the C17. Examples of c. 1720–30 survive here and there, with superimposed columns and pilasters or with giant pilasters. The wildest and the last is the façade of Rosewell House by *Strahan*. This is dated 1736. It has its N54b counterpart in a façade in Queen Charlotte Street at Bristol, as Bristol had also had its freely Baroque houses of about 1725 (Prince Street, St James's Barton). The only example in Somerset of the Baroque handled by an architect of genius also belongs to Bristol: *Vanbrugh*'s Kings Weston of c. 1710, etc. It had little N53 local influence.

Then, in 1727, came *Wood* and purity. The development of Bath in his hands and those of his son and their followers must again be described in detail in another place. What mattered to the county as a whole was the establishment of an exacting and not at all entertaining Palladianism for the town house, with Queen Square begun in 1728; for the public building in the town, N57 with the General Hospital of 1737 at Bath and the Exchange of N58b 1740 at Bristol; for the country house, with Prior Park of 1737 N55b – all by John Wood. And as the Circus and the streets around & 56 continue the town work and the Coopers' Hall at Bristol (by *Halfpenny*), the Guildhall at Bath (by *Baldwin*), and the Prison at

* The earliest example known to me is Gray's Almshouses at Taunton of 1635. Then follow for a more menial task the stables of c. 1670 at Barrington Court. The first use with pretensions to grand display is Ven House of 1698, etc.

Bath (by *Atwood*) continue the public work, so the many villas around Bath and Bristol (Redland Court 1735 by *Strahan*; Clifton Hill House 1746 by *Isaac Ware* of London; Titan Barrow Bathford 1748, Shockerwick c. 1750, Eagle House Bathford c. 1750, the latter three by the elder *Wood*; Royal Fort 1761 by *James Bridges*; Kelston Park c. 1770 by the younger *Wood*, etc.) continue the country work.

It took some time for this eminently urban style to reach the countryside, and it never quite reached the country town, though town-planning as such reached it in a small way. Four towns at least must be recommended: Shepton Mallet (N) because of its early C18 mostly still Baroque merchants' houses (proof of the continued prosperity of these small centres of cloth production – cf. Bradford-on-Avon over the Wiltshire border*), Wincanton because of its handsome stone houses and because we know a local architect-builder here, *Nathaniel Ireson*, Bridgwater because about 1720 the Duke of Chandos (Wood's first patron) began to build a handsome street of brick houses which might just as well be at Bristol, and because of one statelier but not purer individual house of about the same time (The Lions), and Taunton because of the stately assembly room which a local gentleman designed in 1770 and built in the centre of the town, and because of Hammet Street of 1788, another plain uniform brick street focused in this case spectacularly on the church tower.

Similarly in the country there was still work going on of quite a well-to-do kind which kept aloof from Palladianism and from Bath and Bristol. Good examples of the straightforward country-s53b house of c. 1700 are Ven House, Babington (N), and Nynehead. s54b Sandhill Park is of 1720, Crowcombe of the twenties and thirties. It is typical that for Crowcombe participation of *Ireson* and one of the *Bastards* of Blandford has been proved. More Palladian, N60a in the 1740s and 1750s, are Ston Easton (N) and especially Hatch Beauchamp. Ston Easton and Sandhill must also be mentioned for their Rococo interiors, together perhaps with Nettlecombe Court and Berkley (N). Nearer Bath and Bristol and yet not immediately dependent on them, it seems, are the very fine Early Georgian Widcombe Manor, Bath and Newton Park, which is of c. 1762–5 and offers with its curved links to outside pavilions one

---

* Defoe tells us much about these matters. Taunton made serges and druggets, Bristol druggets, Frome, Pensford, Norton St Philip, Bruton, Shepton Mallet, Castle Cary and Wincanton finer cloths, Wells and Glastonbury knitted stockings. Some wool had to be imported from the Midlands, Lincolnshire and Ireland – the latter via Bristol and Minehead.

of the finest C18 ensembles. For neither the name of the architect is so far known.

The refinement which Robert Adam had introduced is reflected in Somerset at Combe Hay (N), and Bailbrook Lodge near Bath (by *John Eveleigh*), and at Ammerdown (N) as it was originally built by *James Wyatt*. Here we have a new generation of architects led by *Robert Adam*. He himself designed Pulteney Bridge at Bath and made plans for the Bathwick estate which were not carried out. The execution lay in the hands of *Thomas Baldwin* who is also the architect of the Guildhall, the Cross Bath, and the Bath Street scheme, perhaps the most elegant pieces of design at Bath. The Guildhall and the *younger Wood*'s Assembly Room of 1776 are the most important public buildings of later C18 Bath. There were none of importance at Bristol, and in the smaller towns, though plenty of town halls and market houses were built, none were large or specially outstanding. Yet the C18 market house is quite a characteristic feature of the small Somerset town, starting from Somerton of *c.* 1700 and going via Langport of 1733, a plain quiet house in a terrace, and the freestanding market houses of Martock, Milborne Port, South Petherton to the stately Georgian town hall of Wells (N) of 1779, and the smaller Palladian town hall of Glastonbury of 1818. Specially successful as a focal point in an urban setting is the town hall of Bridgwater with its semicircular portico and that of Chard with its two-storeyed portico. But they date from *c.* 1820 and 1834 respectively, and we are not ready yet for the C19. S56a

There is first still ecclesiastical work of the C18 to be reviewed. Quite a number of CHURCHES were indeed built or repaired, though the most characteristic feature is now the proprietory chapel. A simple, not specially interesting new Early Georgian church is at Foxcote (N; 1721), and new W towers were built at Woodlands (N; 1712), Clutton (N; 1726), and Paulton (N; 1757). Woodlands is plain C18, Clutton Gothic Survival, Paulton with its ogee and quatrefoil motifs typical early Gothic Revival. The first of the proprietory chapels and the most important does not exist any longer, *John Wood*'s in the W vista of Queen Square, at Bath, a building with its Tuscan portico clearly reflecting Inigo Jones's at the W end of Covent Garden. Then comes the Redland Chapel near Bristol built close to Redland Court in 1740–3 by *Halfpenny*. The same relation exists between house and chapel at Babington (N) 1750, Berkley (N) 1753 (on a very interesting plan following the pattern of Wren's St Anne and St Agnes, and with fine stucco-work), and to a certain extent Redlynch of 1750. N32a

3—S.S.

At Cannington Priory inside the house in the 1720s a chapel was
built, also on an interesting plan, octagonal this time. When in
1767 the proprietory chapel in Milsom Street Bath was given an
octagon plan, however, the source was probably Nonconformist
architecture. The Milsom Street Chapel is by *Thomas Lightoler*.
N31b The *younger Wood* had built a church a few years earlier, in 1761
at Woolley, but it is certainly not better than the others. Particularly charming, just because frankly provincial, is the decoration of the chancel at Bruton (1743).

CHURCH MONUMENTS of the C18 and early C19 are of course
plentiful, though the majority are simple tablets, usually with an
urn or one or two allegorical figures and an urn. These tablets
were provided by sculptors' workshops from Bristol and Bath, and
their names occur all over Somerset, *Sidnell* of Bristol first, and
then the *Patys* and *Tyley* of Bristol, and *Ford, King, Reeves*,
and others from Bath. It is rare that a London stonemason was
commissioned (*Regnart, Physick*) or an Exeter stonemason (*Pierce,
Richards*) or one from Sherborne (*B. Bastard*). Of the major
names, men with a national reputation, few occur, and before the
N46a late C18 only one: *Rysbrack*. He, apart from his work at Bristol,
did the Sir John Tynte † 1742 at Goathurst, and the Lord
Poulett 1745 at Hinton St George, both with portrait busts at
the top. Otherwise there is (always excluding Bristol) *Nollekens*
twice (1785 Goathurst, 1793 Bath), *Flaxman* twice (one the
N46b delightful Dr Sibthorp, 1799, at Bath, the other of 1806 also at
S37a Bath), *Westmacott* twice or three times (Crowcombe 1807 or
1811, Frome, N, *c*. 1827, and probably Marston Bigott, N,
c. 1827), and *Chantrey* five times (Brockley, N, 1823, Selworthy
1828 and 1837, Wells 1834, Bath 1834).

As regards SCULPTURE other than monuments, Somerset
possesses the surviving fragments of a work of the first order, the
S31 altar by *Grinling Gibbons* and *Arnold Quellin* from the chapel in
Whitehall Palace. This was made in 1686 and found its home at
the end of a devious journey in the church of Burnham-on-Sea.
Also London work incidentally are the two wooden statues of St
Peter and St Paul from the organ at Bath Abbey 1702 (now at
Yatton), and probably the STATUE of Queen Anne at Minehead,
erected 1719. It may well be by *Francis Bird*.

CHURCH FURNISHINGS of the C18 and early C19 are not frequent but varied. Most of what is of more than local value again
belongs to Bristol. Otherwise Bath has a Sword Rest such as those
in Bristol churches, Newton St Loe (N) one of the earliest cast-
iron railings in existence. It belongs to a tomb of *c*. 1720 which

could be designed by *Gibbs*, who, we know, favoured cast-iron railings. There is a nice minor Rood Screen of 1729 at Crowcombe and a nice West Gallery on Doric pilasters of 1750 at Selworthy, a very pretty piece of Embroidery of 1720 at Axbridge (N), and an equally pretty Gothick Pew in a porch parvis at Selworthy, and there is a whole series of Brass Candelabra called at the time much more tellingly Branches. They were made in imitation of Dutch C17 pieces, and centres were certainly Bristol and Bridgwater. Dated examples are at Stogursey 1732, Batcombe, N, 1737, Lympstone 1744, Old Cleeve 1770, Burnham 1773, Backwell, N, 1786.

When dealing with religious buildings of the C18 NONCONFORMIST CHAPELS must for the first time be included. There are in Somerset a number of quite ambitious chapels, starting with the surprisingly large and self-assertive façade of the Congregational Church at Frome which was built as early as 1707. After that the buildings which matter most are again at Bristol. As a counter-example to the Friends Meeting House of 1747 there, which is again remarkably grand, the Meeting House at Claverham of 1729 (N) should be visited, which looks like a plain village house from the street and has its recessed façade at r. angles to it, a very modest piece of display. At Bath the only interesting chapel before 1800 is that formerly of the Countess of Huntingdon's Connexion. This is dated 1765 and purely Gothick of the most playful kind.

The sixties were the heyday of the EARLY GOTHIC REVIVAL in Somerset. Its place is mostly the gardens and grounds of country houses. Arnos Court near Bristol is a typical example. The house is really classical, in spite of ogee gables over the windows and battlements, but a fantastic Gothic of more than one mood pervades the Gateway, the Bath-house and the Stables and Offices, all of c. 1760–5. The architect was probably *Bridges*. A little earlier, about 1755, *Sanderson Miller* had designed for Ralph Allen Sham Castle on a hill near Bath, as an eye-catcher from N64a Allen's town house. About ten years later and probably immediately after Arnos Court, in 1766, Blaise Castle near Bristol N63 was built, as a triangular tower. In exactly the same year Henry Hoare (the Younger) of Stourhead in Wiltshire built Alfred's Tower on the crest of the hills between Stourhead and South Brewham. St Michael's Tower above Montacute dates from 1760, Conygar Tower above Dunster from c. 1765. In the 1770s Midford Castle near Bath (N) was built, a tower-like Gothic house N64b on a trefoil plan, and Enmore Castle, a much more ambitious castellated affair with thick angle and intermediate towers, was built shortly before 1779. Only a fragment of it survives, yet quite a sizeable residence. Willett's Tower near Brompton Ralph dates from 1820. Finally in 1805 the NW corner of Ashton Court (N) was gothicized, and about the same time, under the hands of *James Wyatt* and then *Sir Jeffry Wyatville*, much of Hinton House, Hinton St George. In connexion with these romantic and picturesque buildings and refashionings the creation of the COTTAGE ORNÉ must also be mentioned, because near Bristol N67 is Blaise Hamlet by *John Nash* of 1811 which is the most fanciful assembly of such cottages anywhere in England. The Bishop of Bath's *cottage orné* at Banwell (N) of 1827 has unfortunately been demolished, but Lympsham Rectory, probably of the 1820s, is a fine specimen of the romantically gothicized house.

Of GARDEN FURNISHINGS the best collection is again at Bristol, in the garden of Goldney House Clifton, mostly of the 1760s. Some picturesque towers are at Barwick near Yeovil, a rotunda stands near Halswell House, a lone survivor of a once larger assembly, another rotunda belongs to the Batheaston Villa (N). Much bigger and more demonstrative are the memorial columns erected at Burton Pynsent in 1765, at Butleigh (to Admiral Hood) *c.* 1815, at Ammerdown (N) *c.* 1825, and finally the Wellington Obelisk on the Blackdown Hills of 1817.

The development from these columns to the Wellington Monument is that from the Classical Revival of the C18 to the more specifically Greek Revival of the early C19. There are a few good examples of this in the county, the Commercial Rooms (by *Busby*) and the Council House (by *Sir R. Smirke*) at Bristol, the former Masonic Lodge of 1819 at Bath (by *Wilkins*), St George's church at Bristol (by *Smirke*), the Argyle Street Chapel at Bath (by *Goodridge*), Portis College at Weston near Bath (N, by *Page*), N70a and among Country Houses the excellent Leigh Court (N) of 1814 (by *Hopper*) with outstandingly good plasterwork, Cothelstone House of 1818, Claverton Manor (N) of 1819–20 (by *Wyatville*) which is considerably less severe, the Greek Doric porches of Barley Hall and Kingweston (by *Wilkins*), and the crazy Grecian paraphrase of Cricket Court *c.* 1820.* The Lansdown Tower, N69 built above Bath by *Goodridge* for William Beckford's old age in 1825–6, is also crazy in the extreme, a folly to live in. Its forms are ponderously, funereally Greco-Egyptian, but they are very freely treated. The design is really quite ahead of its time

---

* By *Soane* no more than two rooms at Cricket House, of *c.* 1804.

and has much that characterizes the change from Grecian to Victorian.

In the Gothic field a similar development can be traced. After the insouciant Gothic of the C18, there is, especially at Bath, a tendency towards a more scholarly handling of Gothic materials. The first example of this is St Mary Bathwick of 1814–20 by *Pinch*, a second Holy Saviour Walcot of 1829 by *Pinch* (?), a third St Mark Lyncombe of 1832 by *Goodridge*. But in other churches *Goodridge*, the architect of Beckford's house, could be as fanciful and crazy as the best. Combe Down church (N) of 1835 is an example of that with its absurd polygonal spires. The earliest of these excrescences, for which there was quite a fashion, is that of Holy Trinity Bath of 1820–2 (by *Lowder*). Rode Hill of 1824, a remarkable church, follows, and Holy Trinity Frome (N), and St Michael and St Stephen at Bath (N; 1835, 1840). *Sir George Gilbert Scott*'s first Somerset churches also are still closer to this tendency than to that archaeological accuracy which he discovered as his ideal early in the forties (Chantry (N) 1846, Nailsea (N) 1843 – the latter of the featureless Commissioners' type).

Of further VICTORIAN CHURCHES no more than a selection can be mentioned in this volume, and no more than a selection from that selection is needed here. *Richard Carver* is the local representative of the still pre-archaeological Gothicism of before 1840. At Blackford he built a Gothic octagon in 1823. *John Brown* of Norwich built St John at Bridgwater in 1843 in the E.E. style, not a popular style at that moment. The church is tall and impressive and not in the least overdone. By *Rickman* is a big church at Clevedon (N, 1839), and he did work at Bristol too. *Ferrey* was architect to the diocese of Wells and thus obtained several commissions for new churches. Corfe of 1842 is in that Neo-Norman fashion which in those years swamped the country.* West Lydford of 1846 is remarkably competent and sedate Gothic, Buckland St Mary of 1853 a noble incongruity in its rural position. *Sir Charles Barry* is credited with the design of the reredos at Wrington (N), 1832. *Scott* in his mature years built St John at Taunton (1863) and St Andrew at Bath (N; 1870–3), the latter now happily ruined. *Street*'s masterpiece in the area of these volumes was All Saints Clifton, unfortunately severely damaged. His other two Somerset churches are of little interest (Pitcombe 1858, Minehead 1880). *John Norton* had plenty to do in the county, in the ecclesiastical as well as the secular field. His chief

---

* The other neo-Norman churches of Somerset are East Huntspill 1839, Cleeve (N) 1840, Easton 1843, and Farrington Gurney (N) 1843. In addition there are Bristol churches of 1842 and 1848.

church is the large and townish West Quantoxhead of 1856. Others are at and near Bristol. *Butterfield* is not seen to advantage. Neither the Highbury Chapel at Bristol of 1843 (his earliest work) nor Gaer Hill of 1857 (N) nor St John Clevedon of 1876 (N) mean much. Nor is *Pearson*'s Oakhill of 1861 (N) worth a special visit. *Teulon*'s St Thomas Wells (N; 1856) has only a few of the oddities of which he was fond. By *Sir Arthur Blomfield* is the remarkably large and restrained, vaulted chapel of Tyntesfield (N; 1875). *Bodley* appears with a late work at Weston-super-Mare (N; 1899–1902), *Bodley & Garner* with the quite insignificant Peasedown St John (N; 1892–4), *Garner* alone at Camerton (N; 1891) and in the stupendous E part of Downside Abbey (N; 1902–5). He was followed here by *Sir Giles Gilbert Scott*, and if ever there was excuse for building in period forms in the C20, it is here. Both nave and tower (completed only in 1938) are nobly conceived. The whole of the abbey church has become the most splendid demonstration of the renaissance of Roman Catholicism in England.

But we must return to some Late Victorians who, stimulated by Norman Shaw, believed in a greater freedom in the handling of period forms. The Norman Shaw taste and the Arts and Crafts taste are pleasantly present in *Sedding*'s screens of 1888 at Axbridge (N)* and the House of Charity at Bristol of *c.* 1890, and in *Sir T. G. Jackson*'s churches of Hornblotton (1872–4) and Lottisham (1876). The interior of Hornblotton deserves special mention; for there are not many complete interiors preserved in the early Norman Shaw taste.

As regards C19 CHURCH FURNISHINGS the most interesting chapter is STAINED GLASS. Somerset has much, and it ought to be noticed – from *Eginton* (Wells 1813) to *Willement* (Wells 1843, Butleigh), to *O'Connor* (window with the portraits of the Stephenson family, Lympsham 1863) and the other High Victorians, and so to *William Morris*. The glass of *c.* 1864 at Winscombe (N) must be by him or his firm. Early also is the Morris glass at Over Stowey (1870, 1874), late that at Holy Trinity Frome (N) 1886, etc. Strongly influenced by Morris is the stencilled decoration of the chancel at Stogumber. Early *Kempe* glass is at East Lydford (1879) and Badgworth (1879), and whole series of windows by him can be seen obscuring the churches of Barrow Gurney (N; *c.* 1890) and Wraxall (N; 1896, etc.).

With a Font at Norton-sub-Hamdon by *Henry Wilson*, Sedding's principal pupil, we pass into the TWENTIETH CENTURY.

* The church at Wincanton of 1889 is less personal.

Here the most noteworthy piece of work is a chapel added by *Lutyens* to Brushford church in 1926. *Voysey* in his last years did a S22b reredos for Culbone church (1928). He did more work for Lady Lovelace in the neighbourhood, but that was secular, and we have not yet caught up with the secular architecture of the Victorians.

There are no VICTORIAN PUBLIC BUILDINGS worth noting, except perhaps the skilful work of *Brydon* at Bath in the 1890s. There are a number of large Gothic schools at Taunton and Bath, and of course at Bristol, and the excellent school buildings of *c.* 1912 by *Stokes* for Downside (N).

What COMMERCIAL AND INDUSTRIAL ARCHITECTURE has to contribute is confined to Bristol, except for a few early MILLS at Shepton Mallet (N; before 1800) and at Chard (iron staunchions and iron girders), and a little early factory housing outside Wellington called Five Houses.

The rest is DOMESTIC ARCHITECTURE. The terraces of Clifton kept up an extremely creditable Grecian into the forties. Then Italianate, Tudor, Jacobean forms break in. Tudor in the country appears at a startlingly early date at Warleigh House, Bathford (N): in 1814–15. One does not expect a domestic Tudor Revival before 1825 or 1830. High Victorian Tudor is the style of *Clutton*'s Quantock Lodge, Over Stowey (1857). Gothic in the most ambitious High Victorian fashion is *John Norton* at St Audries, West Quantoxhead, and at Tyntesfield near Wraxall (N)N71b in 1862–4 and at Chew Manor (N) in 1864. *T. H. Wyatt* at Orchardleigh (N) in 1855–8 uses a mixed Elizabethan style. *Owen Jones* at Abbotsfield *c.* 1872 is disappointing.

That is all that needs comment, and there is rather less for the C20: *Voysey*'s Lilycombe near Porlock of 1912, *Lutyens*'s remarkably restrained Mells Park (N; of 1923) and *Lutyens*'s gardens at Ammerdown (N) and Hestercombe. S56b

It would be gratifying if this survey could be ended by a list of buildings erected in the last twenty years in the architectural idiom of today. But they are all but absent, or least on an aesthetic level worth study. There is little need for flats outside Bristol, council housing is indifferent, and sometimes painful. Factories are coming on, but results which deserve mention here have so far only been obtained in a few SCHOOLS built in the last few years by *R. Oliver Harris*, the county architect.

But it may well be that the absence of modern building is the price one has to pay for still being able to enjoy most of Somerset as a rural retreat. It may well be that its peace and serenity would go, if it were attacked not so much by the crisp precise forms of modern architecture as by what they stand for.

Finally, as usual in these volumes, a survey of what the following pages have been compiled from, or, from the user's point of view, what qualifies as 'Further Reading'.

Somerset is uncommonly well provided for. The *Proceedings of the Somerset Archaeological and Natural History Society* are amongst the best of the archaeological journals in the country. The late Francis C. Eeles's contributions in particular are invaluable.* He has also written a number of excellent guides to individual churches. In addition there are three outstandingly good monographs, all three published within the last few years. For the medieval parish churches we have the late Kenneth Wickham's book *Somerset Churches* (London 1953). This is so carefully prepared and so beautifully written that I would have wished to be able to reprint it *in toto* as an introduction to my gazetteer. I would also have wished that Fate had allowed Kenneth Wickham to write his own gazetteer. His experience and his enthusiasm would have achieved something better than is within my power. Even as it is I feel in need of an excuse for competing with his book. My excuse is that I include Wells and Glastonbury and he does not, and that I include all secular architecture as far as I am able to.

For Georgian architecture, which is after all chiefly secular, my book is indebted as much to Mr Walter Ison as it is to Kenneth Wickham for churches. Mr Ison's *Georgian Buildings of Bath* (London 1948) and *Georgian Buildings of Bristol* (London 1952) are both scholarly and interesting to read. They contain much unpublished material and present it in such a form that all I had to do was to re-group it according to the system of *The Buildings of England*. In addition I used for the history of Bath and Bristol Mr Bryan Little's two books of 1947 and 1954, and for Victorian churches at Bristol G. D. & G. F. Hake's type-written *List of Bristol Churches* at the Bristol Central Library. Mr Rupert Gunnis's *Dictionary of British Sculptors, 1660–1851* (n.d.), has already become a standard work, and I have made full use of it. Mr Howard Colvin's admirable *Biographical Dictionary of English Architects, 1660–1840* (London 1954), was published a little later and could only be used at proof stage, not on the journeys.

On individual aspects of the architecture and antiquities of Somerset the following books and papers ought to be consulted:

---

* An index to Vols 1–80 was published in 1937, an index to papers on effigies in 1932.

Prehistoric and Roman Remains: D. P. Dobson: *The Archaeology of Somerset* (London 1931); A. Bulleid and H. St G. Gray: *The Lake Villages of Somerset* (London 1924); E. J. Burrows: *Ancient Earthworks and Camps of Somerset* (London 1924).

Wells Cathedral in the C12 and C13: *Trans Som. Arch. & N.H. Soc.*, 1863 (Willis), and *Archaeological Journal*, 1928 (Armitage Robinson and John Bilson). – Glastonbury: There is nothing more recent than F. Bligh Bond's *Architectural Handbook of Glastonbury Abbey*, Glastonbury, 3rd ed., 1920. – Dunster: Sir H. C. Maxwell Lyte, 2 vols, 1903. – Plate: *Proceedings*, 1897–1913.

FINAL ADDENDA
(DECEMBER 1957)

PAGE	LINE	
27	37	Of the late C13 probably also the oaken archways at Stoford Farm, Halse.
34	3	[Somerset Towers.] It will make an understanding of the following pages easier if the reader can gain access to a copy of F. J. Allen, *The Great Church Towers of England*, Cambridge, 1932.
46	34	The abbots of Glastonbury were busy not only at their abbey but also in parish churches and manor houses. Abbot Selwood's initials appear at Ashcott, Ditcheat, East Brent, High Ham, Ivy Thorn Manor, Kingston, Meare, and Norwood Farm; his successor Abbot Bere's, the last abbot, at Bruton, Chedzoy, Glastonbury St Benedict, Othery, and Weston Zoyland.
57	foot-note	C16 and C17 fireplaces in South Somerset are at Cothay, Marshwood Farm Carhampton, Montacute, Nettlecombe Court, Newton Surmaville, Poundisford Lodge, Flook House Taunton (as late as 1652), Wayford Manor, Wigborough.
130	23	[Combe St Nicholas.] Remains of a C15 ROOD SCREEN.
235	26	[Merriott.] SCULPTURE. Stone Crucifix said to be the head of the former village cross.
238	13	[Milborne Port.] Fine panelled Perp ceiling in the crossing tower; Perp also the N chancel chapel of two bays.

SOUTH AND WEST SOMERSET

*

ABBOTSFIELD *see* WIVELISCOMBE

ADSCOMBE *see* OVER STOWEY

AISHOLT

ALL SAINTS. In an almost inaccessible position in a fold of the
Quantocks. The W tower is remarkable for being, it seems,
unrestored. Humble two-bay arcade inside with standard
piers (four hollows). The chancel arch is probably older. It is
triple-chamfered. The two outer chamfers run continuous
into the inposts. The middle chamfer stands on octagonal
responds of red sandstone with plain capitals. All this looks
early C14 except for the Perp tower top. – PLATE. Set of 1844.

ALCOMBE
1 m. NW of Dunster

ST MICHAEL. 1902–3 by *C. Samson* (GR). Chancel 1937.
C15 doorway from Dunster, where it was erected inside the
Norman portal. – PULPIT. C18, also from Dunster.

ALFORD

ALL SAINTS. A fine position away from the village and against
the screen of the grounds of Alford House which extend to the
river Brue. The building is an uncommonly complete example
of a Perp church, not substantially restored or freshed up, and
still provided with its screen and benches. Modest W tower
with old pyramid roof. Embattled aisles with much-cusped
three-light windows. Chancel with two-light and three-light
windows. All this is clearly Perp. – The chancel roof is Somerset timber-work at its best, even if on a small scale. Tie-beams,
king-posts, and some tracery. – ROOD SCREEN. A curious
design, three-light sections with an arcaded band across,
transom-wise. Not in its original state. – PULPIT dated 1625.

– BENCHES, with poppy-heads, plain tracery, and such motifs as a pelican, a dragon, the lamb with the cross. – STAINED GLASS. Large figure of the Magdalen, early C16. In the same window fragments of angels, canopies, etc. – PLATE. Chalice and Paten by *Richard Orenge* 1574; Flagon and Paten 1824.

ALFORD HOUSE. A Late Georgian house remodelled in an insensitive neo-Elizabethan by *Penrose* in 1877. Symmetrical façade with two porches, both with slated pyramid roofs.

BRIDGE (river Alham). Packhorse bridge on the track to Hornblotton (Jervoise).

ALFOXTON PARK *see* HOLFORD

₃₀₂₀
ALLER

ST ANDREW. Late Norman S doorway; the zigzags of the arch are placed at 45 degrees to the wall. Then comes the C14 work, an interesting and somewhat puzzling contribution. The W tower on the ground floor opens towards the nave with responds of the standard four-hollows design, but the members are treated so broadly and the capitals are so large and simple that the date is certain. In addition the same arches are repeated N and S so as to lead into former embracing aisles or indeed projected transepts. There is no W doorway. The upper parts of the tower are Perp, and the junction can be seen inside where the buttresses are started high up on angel brackets. The tower is not high. The higher stair-turret has a spirelet. N aisle and chancel rebuilt 1861. – FONT. Small and flat octagonal bowl, with very simple ornamental motifs; dated 1663. – PULPIT. Jacobean, daintily detailed. – PLATE. Chalice and Cover 1630; Paten 1710 by *Richard Bayley*. – MONUMENTS. Defaced Effigy of a cross-legged Knight, *c.* 1310. – Defaced Effigy of a Knight, *c.* 1375, in a many-cusped recess in the chancel, with an ogee arch at the top.

COURT HOUSE. An outbuilding behind has two doorways with four-centred heads and two cusped straight-headed two-light windows. The date is thus probably *c.* 1500.

<sub>9040
inset</sub>
ALLERFORD
½ m. SE of Lynch

PACKHORSE BRIDGE. Two arches; very picturesque.

ANGERSLEIGH   *1010*

ST MICHAEL. W tower C14 with Dec two-light bell-openings
and buttresses only at the foot. Nave Perp, embattled, and
with straight-headed windows. – Inside much elaborate
WOODWORK. Some of it may be original, but most of it was
carved by *A. E. Eastwood* of Leigh Court within the last
fifty years. – PLATE. Chalice and Cover by *Ions* of Exeter
1574; Plate 1676.

LEIGH COURT. Built shortly before 1829. Five by five bays.
Canted porch with unfluted Ionic columns. Canted bay-
window on the S side.

ANSFORD   *6030*

ST ANDREW. Simple Perp W tower. The rest mostly by *Giles*,
1861 (GR). Of that date also the Crucifixion in STAINED
GLASS inside. – PULPIT. Jacobean. – PLATE. Chalice 1573;
Chalice 1574; Paten C18.

ASH   *4020*
3 m. SW of Ilchester

HOLY TRINITY. 1840 by *Kempthorne*. Chancel 1887; W tower
C20. In the lancet style; poor.

ASHBRITTLE   *0020*

ST JOHN BAPTIST. Tower and chancel rebuilt 1874. Large
six-light S window, Perp, divided into two three-light sub-
arches. Aisle arcade of three bays with piers of the four-waves
type. Capitals with leaf bands; depressed pointed arches. The
S porch doorway also has capitals with leaf bands. – PLATE.
Chalice and Cover by *Ions* of Exeter 1574; Flagon 1683;
Saucer 1717; Paten 1726.

ASHCOTT   *4030*

ALL SAINTS. Perp W tower with higher stair-turret. The
initials of Abbot Selwood of Glastonbury on it, but no
significant work, except perhaps the pierced parapet with
pointed quatrefoils in lozenges which appears at Meare also
with Selwood's initials. Perp windows. All over-restored. In
1831 the aisles were taken out and the nave made as broad as

the age liked it. – STAINED GLASS. Chancel s window by *Kempe* 1889; E window by the same, 1898. Is it delusion to find the earlier window more intense and concentrated? – PLATE. Chalice and Cover 1635; Paten 1728.

ASHILL
3010

ST MARY. Norman N and s doorways. The N doorway has octagonal shafts and zigzag. Zigzag also above the somewhat altered chancel arch with its two blocked recesses for side altars. Near the E end of the N side of the nave a late C13 window with cinquefoiled rere-arch. Dec chancel with Perp E window. Its inner shafts and the inner rere-arches are Dec. Dec also the two tomb recesses in the N wall of the nave. The larger is of *c.* 1300, the EFFIGY that of a lady wearing a wimple. She lies below a trefoiled gabled arch and has two small attendant figures by her head. The EFFIGY in the smaller recess represents a Knight and is of *c.* 1380. The recesses are both cusped, the later one with ogee cusping. – FONT. Octagonal, Perp. Stem with blank arches, bowl with shields, etc., in sexfoils. – PULPIT. Jacobean. – PLATE. Chalice and Cover 1574; Salver 1769.

ASHINGTON
5020

1 m. SE of Limington

ST VINCENT. Small. Nave and chancel; no tower. Basically E.E.; see a former w lancet visible only from inside, and the chancel windows. On the E side a group of three stepped lancets, on the N and s single lancets. They all have rere-arches, trefoiled on the N and s, cinquefoiled on the E side. Perp nave windows. Later still the lantern-shaped projecting bell-cote supported on a heavy buttress up the middle of the w side (cf. Brympton d'Evercy and Chilthorne Domer). – Very complete Jacobean FURNISHINGS. Box-Pews with shell-tops, the two larger pews in front for the squire's and the rector's families, the Reader's Desk attached to one of these, and a Pulpit with back and tester. The pulpit is dated 1637. – PLATE. Chalice and Cover 1571; Patens 1717 and 1727.

MANOR HOUSE. Fragmentary, but interesting. Testimony of a C15 house is the doorway which forms the present front entrance, the back doorway which led into the screens passage and the small two-light window above, a diagonal buttress at the sw end, and a spiral staircase in a turret at the NW end. This house was altered and enlarged about 1600. It had then a s front with the present large two-storeyed canted bay-window, and a gable over, a second gable corresponding to the first, beyond the present E end wall of the house, and a square tall porch corresponding to the C15 back entrance. Of the three gables of the front only that over the bay-window remains. The Jacobean work has large mullioned and transomed windows.

ASH PRIORS

HOLY TRINITY. W tower with diagonal buttresses and battlements. Two-light bell-openings and Somerset tracery. Square higher stair-turret. Nave and aisle with three-light Perp windows. Humble two-bay arcade with standard piers (four hollows). Small N and S chapels. Much restoration in 1874. – PLATE. Chalice by *Bayley* 1737.

PRIORY. Of a pre-Reformation house the two-storeyed porch survives. The '1529' in one of the spandrels of the four-centred head of the doorway is a credible date. At the back of what must have been the dais end of the Hall remains of what was probably the outer wall of the spiral staircase.

ASHTON
½ m. E of Chapel Allerton

(WINDMILL. Derelict, but with machinery and remains of the sails. It had originally a thatched cap – a feature almost unique in England. R. Wailes.)

ATHELNEY *see* LYNG

BABCARY

HOLY CROSS. Perp, consisting of W tower, nave, and chancel. The tower arch seems to indicate an earlier date for the lower part of the tower. N aisle added by *Ferrey* in 1876. – FONT. Octagonal, Perp, with panelled stem, panelled underside of the bowl, and quatrefoils on the bowl. – PULPIT. 1632, with the usual blank arches and plenty of flat arabesque decoration. – PLATE. C15 Paten; Chalice and Paten by *T. Mason* 1730.

3050

BADGWORTH

ST CONGAR. A rare dedication, but cf. Congresbury about 7 miles N. Early C14 chancel, rebuilt in 1864. Original the chancel arch, double-chamfered in a continuous moulding. In the N wall a tomb recess, largely restored, but with a big ogee-arch which can be trusted and a fine original head as a label-stop. Also C14 the nave, *see* its doorway with quadrant mouldings and the original DOOR with Dec tracery. Contemporary with the doorway perhaps the lower parts of the W tower. Tower arch with three continuous quadrant mouldings and angle buttresses stopping not very high up. The W door is of 1709, the upper parts of the tower with a parapet pierced in the form of quatrefoiled lozenges and with pinnacles is, of course, Late Perp. So are the S windows of the nave. There is however a short N aisle attached to the nave, and this takes us back again to the C14, as witnessed by its slightly pre-Perp two-light window on the S side (the W window is blocked) and by its cinquefoiled rere-arch. The W doorway into the chapel also has a cinquefoiled arch, a most unusual thing. The arcade to the aisle on the other hand has details which cannot be accepted as medieval. The most likely date is the C17, and that would accord with the panelling. – PULPIT. Jacobean, with the usual low blank arches filled with plants, etc. But the wooden pulpit stands on a stone foot which is clearly Perp and belongs to a previous pulpit. There are plenty of Perp stone pulpits in this part of Somerset, although none with a foot decorated in the costly way in which it is done here, by figures of the four Latin Fathers. The sculptural quality is indifferent. – BENCHES. Plain, with plain, rather thin, poppy-heads. – STAINED GLASS. In a nave N window *Kempe* glass of 1879, remarkably good, with a dark leafy background. The E window, also by *Kempe* and dated 1886, is more conventional and rather in the colours of Clayton & Bell. – PLATE. Chalice and Cover 1573; Paten by *Joseph Clare* 1723; Flagon by *Robert Cox* 1755.

BADGWORTH COURT. Early Georgian five-bay two-storey S front of stone with three-bay pediment. Square cupola. To the N nine-bay brick wing of 1820 with two bow-windows at the sides. To the E early C19 Tuscan four-column porch. Staircase hall with a screen of two Tuscan columns and an open-well staircase. Finely turned balusters and carved tread-ends.

BALTONSBOROUGH

5030

ST DUNSTAN. Perp and of no special architectural interest. The most handsome touch is the weather-vane on the W tower, with very large scrolly iron-work made by the local blacksmith early in the C19. It stands on a pyramid roof rising behind the battlements of the tower. Nave with ceiled wagon roof, no aisles. In the chancel at the back of the Sedilia two shields in cusped panels. The Sedilia had probably been replaced later by a monument. – FONT of the usual Perp type. – PULPIT. Perp, of stone, with blank castellation at the top. – BENCHES. Perp and plain. Hinged on to one of them a baby seat, on Jacobean legs. – S DOOR Perp, traceried, with original knocker. – CROSS in the churchyard, with original 25a badly defaced Crucifixion in the head.

GATEWAY into the churchyard from the W, a pretty feature. The date is almost illegible; it seems to be 1826.

GATEHOUSE. E-shaped front with mullioned windows carrying hood-moulds. The porch has Ionic pilasters, a fluted frieze, and a gable. To the l. of the porch the former Hall (window with a transom as well as mullions). At the back a second porch with a fancy-shaped gable on Tuscan columns and the date 1637. This as well as a pedimented fireplace inside with the same date seem to have been brought in from another house.

BARLINCH ABBEY
1 m. NW of Dulverton

9020
inset

ST NICHOLAS'S PRIORY was a late C12 foundation for Augustinian Canons. Not an abbey, but a priory. The position in the narrow valley is eminently picturesque, but the ruins are too scanty to allow a mental reconstruction of the premises of the small establishment. From S to N there is first, W of the farmhouse, the most substantial fragment, a wall with two buttresses, remains of window surrounds, and two projections at the W end. In the barn of the farmhouse tracery of one window. N of the farmyard a four-centred arch, further N two more walls running E–W.

BARRINGTON

3010

ST MARY. A picturesque sight from the village, with its group of N transept, N porch, and crossing tower. Essentially C13.

To this belongs the crossing tower, *see* its inner arches (double-chamfered, no capitals or imposts) and its lancet windows. The top parts added in the C15 (two-light bell-openings and battlements). C13 also the transepts (*see* e.g. the corbel-table). The S transept S window has typical late C13 tracery (three lights, the first and third lancets, the middle one lower with a large circle above which is six-foiled). Inside the S transept a Piscina with some late C13 detail and inner shafts to the windows. Perp nave. Perp N porch with ogee gable to the doorway and several thin triangular shafts above. Well moulded doorway. S aisle of 1860. – STAINED GLASS in the chancel by *Kempe*, *c.* 1897. – PLATE. Chalice and Cover 1573; Paten 1723; Flagon 1724.

VILLAGE. An extremely attractive village of stone-built cottages, many of them thatched. No single house need be pointed out specially.

46b

BARRINGTON COURT was built by Lord Daubeney shortly after he had got married in 1514. The house is, considering its date, of exceptional historical interest, and it is in addition, with its warm Ham Hill stone walls covered with lichen and its triangular gables and twisted finials, extremely attractive. The most remarkable thing about Barrington is the almost complete symmetry of its S front, which is designed on the E-scheme, a scheme usually considered by laymen a creation of the Elizabethan age. The house is of two storeys with a third in the gables and dormers. The porch has three storeys and a fourth in the gable. On the gables are the twisted finials already referred to, and the chimneys also are twisted. The main front, which is in this case the S front, the least usual amongst Tudor houses, seems at first entirely symmetrical – a feature which heralds the Renaissance even where, as at Barrington, it appears without any Italian motifs. There are only slight deviations from symmetry; the chief of them is that to the r. of the porch the Hall has two four-light windows and then, in the angle between centre and r. wing, a small square projection now simply a bay, but originally a staircase, whereas to the l. of the porch there is only one four-light window and a larger staircase projection. But both projections faced the porch with a three-light window and the S with a three-light window. All the original windows at Barrington are mullioned and hood-moulded and have four-centred heads to the individual lights. All the principal windows in addition have transoms and four-centred heads below the transom as

well. The porch and the fronts of the wings are strengthened
by thin diagonal buttresses. The N front is now the entrance
side; originally there was here only the back exit from the
screens passage. This side is only fragmentarily symmetrical.
The ends have cross-gables of identical size, and above the
centre and the doorway is a smaller dormer. But there are
two projecting chimney-breasts l. and r. of the doorway, and
these differ considerably in thickness.

The interior is also of interest, but thanks to bought
rather than original furnishings and fittings. The Hall has
linen-fold panelling, genuine but not belonging to the house,
the staircase a timber roof which comes from Hereford, and
the so-called Small Dining Room is made into the most
spectacular apartment of the house by an early C16 screen
which was part of the outer wall of a house at King's Lynn,
and a contemporary ceiling of honeycomb-carved wooden
ribs in star patterns, from the same house.

W of Barrington Court about 1670 a square block was
added independent of the old building. It contained STABLES
and offices and was originally open to the N. It is two-storeyed,
of brick, with quoins and hipped roof. It was altered about
1760 and again about 1920–5, when the block became part of
the living quarters of the house. The W front was then given
its arched French windows and terrace. The architects were
Forbes & Tate.

They also built the large group of farm buildings, N and NW
of the house at some distance from it and connected with it
by avenues.

BARTON GRANGE see CORFE

BARTON ST DAVID　　*5030*

ST DAVID. Small with a tower, octagonal from the foot, in the
angle between N transept and chancel. This is an East English
feature, unique in Somerset. The tower seems entirely Perp,
but the church is much older. Norman N doorway with one
order of columns and, in the arch, a trellis of bands of zigzag.
This doorway is C12; C13 must be the plain low arches
from the nave to the chancel and the transepts. (The S
transept was rebuilt in 1894.) They have demi-shafts with
plain moulded capitals and single-chamfered arches. The
chancel is much renewed, but the cusped lancet windows and
the E window of three cusped stepped lancet lights, all with

cinquefoil rere-arches inside, may well represent original work of *c.* 1300. The Perp style, apart from the tower (which perhaps replaced, in a safer position, a former crossing tower), provided a number of new windows. – PLATE. Paten 1633; Chalice 1756. – CHURCHYARD CROSS with the defaced figure of St David on the shaft.

EBENEZER CHAPEL, 1804, altered 1871. To 1804 one would attribute the plain oblong plan and the Y-tracery and quatrefoil, to 1871 the elaborate picturesqueness of the asymmetrical little spire.

BROADSTONE FARMHOUSE, Silver Street. Remarkable only in that it is dated 1692 and yet shows nothing essentially beyond the Jacobean conventions. Symmetrically placed mullioned windows, two gabled dormers.

BARWICK

₅₀₁₀ placed in margin

ST MARY MAGDALENE. A small church close to a small sandstone cliff. C13 transeptal N tower, unbuttressed, with lancet windows and parapet. The church is Perp. The show side is the N, with an aisle enriched by three-light windows, gargoyles, and battlements. Also good roof inside this aisle. The building of the aisle may be datable *c.* 1489 (subscription of money by the nuns of Syon Abbey which was the lord of the manor). The S aisle arcade seems older, and it was gained by cutting through a yet older wall. Single-chamfered piers and single-chamfered arches. Chancel rebuilt in 1885. Into it leads a C13 doorway from the tower. Two of the wedge-stones are parts of an earlier C13 foliated cross. – FONT. Circular, Norman, with broad flutes and a cable moulding. – STALLS and PEWS with coarse Renaissance ends and fronts. One bench-end is dated 1533. On one a man shooting a bird, on another a man climbing a tree, also fox and goose, and dogs hunting a rabbit. Arms on the chancel stalls refer to *c.* 1530–50. – PULPIT. 1619. With one tier of blank arches and ornamental panels above. – PLATE. Chalice 1628; Saucer 1640; Flagon inscribed 1709; Paten 1714. – MONUMENTS. Nice minor monuments from 1681 to the early C19.

In the village street E of the church cottages of 1811 which, with lancet windows with Y-tracery, look like a Nonconformist Chapel. Higher up to the E COURT FARM HOUSE, late C17, with characteristically moulded door surround and large two-light mullioned windows.

BARWICK HOUSE. The house itself is probably Georgian, but was given a Victorian fancy-Jacobean appearance *c.* 1830. In the grounds three FOLLIES of *c.* 1830. Just E of the house a Gateway, Gothic, of rough stones and crowned by a small spire. By the NW entrance to the grounds a Spire with ball finial, standing on an open Gothic 'umbrello'. Near the NE corner a column of rough stones or a thin round tower. (Also a circular Grotto. B. Jones.)

BATHEALTON
0020

THE CASTLES. Prehistoric earthwork above Venn Cross Viaduct in the Tone Valley. The camp is an irregular oval, 230 by 140 yards. The E end has a steep bank with an entrance; elsewhere the builders made use of the scarp of the hill.

BATHPOOL
2020

(HYDE COTTAGE. With a good plaster ceiling of the early C17.)

BAT'S CASTLE see DUNSTER

BATTLE GORE see WILLITON

BAWDRIP
3030

ST MICHAEL. Still essentially a C13 church, cruciform with crossing tower. The crossing is marked impressively inside by low double- and triple-chamfered arches. The arches are of Ham Hill stone, the plain piers of lias. The E and s arches rest on small heads carrying stiff-leaf capitals, the W and N arches on larger heads. Those of the W arch are of great perfection. The tower outside is square and rather tall. To the S a two-light Dec window. The top has battlements only and no pinnacles. An extremely odd feature of the interior is the exposed staircase climbing up the wall above the E arch of the nave to connect the outer staircase in the angle between nave and N transept with the upper storey of the tower. The nave is aisleless and like the transept belongs to the C14. Most of the windows are unfortunately C19 restoration (1864–7 by *Giles*). But the three-light reticulated W window is reliable, and so are the S transept Piscina (with an ogee arch) and the large recess in the N transept with openwork cusping, the cusps being carved as heads. – PLATE. Set of 1763 by *Fuller White*. – MONUMENT. Defaced later C13 effigy of a Knight in armour.

BEERCROCOMBE

3010

ST JAMES. Smallish. C13 nave, *see* one uncovered lancet window on the N side. Early C14 W tower, *see* the renewed W window and the curious arch towards the nave, which rests on two little men or monsters with three-clawed feet. Rere-arches on angels for the S windows inside. – PULPIT. Jacobean. – PLATE. Chalice and Cover 1573.

BERROW

3050

ST MARY. Among the dunes near the sea. Of carboniferous limestone with Doulting stone dressings. Essentially a C13 church. C13 chancel arch on corbels with moulded capitals. The S doorway is C13 too, with a continuous roll-moulding. The tower arch moreover, which is double-chamfered, has its inner arch again on moulded corbels. The chancel windows appear Dec but are all renewed or new. The W tower has a Perp top with two-light bell-openings with Somerset tracery. Heavily embattled top without pinnacles. The S aisle is embattled and has three-light Perp windows. The aisle arcade is low, of five bays, with standard piers (four hollows). – FONT. Discovered in 1926. Of an unusual shape, a heavy quatrefoil, apparently of the C13. – SCULPTURE. At the same time a C15 cross head was found, with the Crucifixion on one side, the Virgin between two praying figures on the other (cf. Stringston, Wedmore). – WEST GALLERY. The cornice with an inscription of 1537 is all that is left of it. – PULPIT. Jacobean. With the usual short blank arches in two tiers. – READER'S DESK. Of the same style, dated 1631. – PLATE. Chalice and Cover 1573; Tankard 1764. – MONUMENTS. Two badly defaced late C13 effigies of a Knight and Lady; in the churchyard.

BERRY CASTLE *see* PORLOCK

BICKENHALL

2010

ST PAUL. 1849 by *P. C. Hardwick* (GR). – PLATE. Electroplated Set of 1841.

BICKHAM *see* TIMBERSCOMBE

BICKNOLLER 1030

St George. Evidence of a Norman church the Pillar Piscina in the chancel with a cable-moulding. The rest is Perp, the tower probably earliest. It is modelled on that of Stogumber, with diagonal buttresses, battlements, and a higher square stair-turret. The tower arch towards the nave is triple-chamfered. Chancel E window of five lights. The lights are blocked at the foot, no doubt because of a former reredos. The blocking stones externally decorated with quatrefoils containing shields and roses. The finest Perp is on the s side. Battlements also with pierced quatrefoils. Two-storeyed porch. Delightful tracery, especially in one window in the nave s side, with the little mannered details of the workshop which also provided windows for Watchet. Late Perp N aisle arcade of five bays. The piers of the four-wave section; well carved capitals. Three-light windows and battlements with pierced quatrefoils. In the chancel two identical recesses with four-centred arches and large tracery in the spandrels. – ROOD SCREEN. Of the Devon and Dunster type, with four-light sections (the arch divided into two sub-arches of two lights each), panelled ribbed coving, and carved cornice. – BENCHES. Of the Crowcombe, etc., type, straight-headed and excellently detailed. The motifs are mostly close tracery and branches with leaves and flowers or leaves and fruit. The date no doubt *c.* 1520–30. – PLATE. Elizabethan Chalice by *J. Ions* of Exeter; Paten 1704.

Gatchells, much restored C15 farmhouse.

Trundle Ring Camp. Prehistoric earthwork $\frac{1}{2}$ m. above Bicknoller Church. It is circular, about 100 yards across, and consists of an earth-and-rubble bank with exterior ditch. It is perched – precariously and inaccessibly – on the sheer slope of the hill. There are minor fortifications of prehistoric date in the district at Newton Camp and on Tet Hill.

BIDDISHAM 3050

Church. The small w tower without buttresses and with an unmoulded tower arch might be C13 or simply minimum work of the C14 or C15. Perp two-light bell-openings; parapet. – s door. An interesting piece of the late C16 or early C17. –

FONT. Square, Norman, with three scallops on the underside.
– PULPIT. Jacobean, similar to Weare.

BISHOP'S HULL

ST PETER AND ST PAUL. The remarkable thing about the
church is its N porch tower. It dates in its lower parts from
the C13 (doorway with continuous double-chamfer). Above
the lowest stage it turns octagonal (cf. Ilchester, etc.). Lancets
with later Somerset tracery. Later two-tiered bell-openings
and battlements. The rest modest Perp except for one C13
window now re-set in the Vestry, and the W front, which in
1826 *Carver* made Gothic in the taste of his time. Three-bay
porch with four-centred arches. The interior of the church is
striking if not beautiful. The architect of 1826 tore out the
aisle arcades to make of the church the barn which the age
favoured. But he left the Perp chancel and the N chapel of two
bays, a lopsided appendix. Two S windows, of three lights
with nice cusping, were also allowed to remain. The Perp
parts are standard (four-hollows piers). The N chapel capitals
with busts of angels (à la Taunton). – PULPIT. Made up of
parts of the rood screen. – BENCHES. A number of the early
C16 contrasting with the box-pews of 1826. The old set has
the characteristics of West Somerset, straight-headed with
tracery or plant motifs, also a night-watchman, and a Resurrection of Christ with the Pelican below. – PLATE. Flagon and
Paten by *Robert Timbrell* 1699; Spoon mid C17. – MONU-
MENTS. George Farewell † 1609. Alabaster, with effigy
reclining on elbow. Shallow coffered arch. Broad strapwork
surrounds the inscription plate. The group of the kneeling
children against the tomb-chest is carved quite exceptionally
beautifully. – Opposite small monument to three of Edmund
Farewell's children who died as infants. Niche with the three
babes piled rather on top of each other. Very naive.

MANOR HOUSE. Dated on the porch 1586. E-plan. The porch
entrance a round arch flanked by good Ionic columns. Very
good original door. The windows of the house mullioned and
mullioned and transomed.

BISHOP'S LYDEARD

ST MARY. A red sandstone church with a swagger W tower,
tall and yet sturdy. This forms one group with Ile Abbots,

Kingston, and Staple Fitzpaine. The group is a slightly simpler
version of Huish and Kingsbury. Set-back buttresses and
higher NE stair-turret. The buttresses have two tiers of
attached pinnacles and pinnacles at the top. The angles themselves also sprout out in pinnacles a little lower down. In
addition the tower has pierced battlements (quatrefoils and
in the merlons arcading) with pinnacles and corbelled-out
intermediate pinnacles. Above the w door a five-light window.
On the second stage windows with Somerset tracery, and
again on the third. These latter are flanked by statue niches.
Finally the bell-openings, two of three lights on every side,
with transom, tracery, and Somerset tracery. The rise from
plainness to exuberant decoration is masterfully handled. The
arch between tower and nave is moulded, not panelled.
Embattled s aisle, no battlements on the N aisle (exterior C19).
Rood-turret. The chancel, compared with all this display,
appears low and, as it were, a little left out. The whole interior
also strikes one as low after the tower. Four-bay arcades with
standard piers (four hollows). The piers are lower on the N
than on the s side. Chancel arch taller and of the same section.
The same section also for the chapel arches N and s. Ceiled
wagon roof with 'ceilure' over the rood screen.* – FONT.
Octagonal, Perp (or C17?), with panelled stem and complicated quatrefoils, rosettes, crosses, etc., on the bowl. – ROOD
SCREEN. All across nave and aisles, with four-light sections,
the tracery arranged in two two-light sub-arches. Ribbed
coving, an inscription (the Creed), and carved cornice. –
PULPIT. Jacobean, with the usual short blank arches and
foliage, etc., decoration. – BENCHES. A remarkably complete
display of ends, backs, and fronts. Early C16. The motifs
include a windmill, a ship, a stag, and the marks of the Passion. 25a
– PLATE. Chalice and Cover 1617; Chalice turned into a
Flagon 1753 by *William Grundy*; Paten 1753. – MONUMENTS.
Brass plate to Nicholas Grobham † 1585 and wife, w end s
aisle. Kneeling figures and inscriptions above and below. –
Thomas Slocombe † 1801, by *Thomas King* of Bath. Oval grey
marble back-plate and two standing white women by an urn
(cf. Langford Budville). – In the Churchyard a CROSS
with a decorated base and a figure on the shaft.
ALMSHOUSES. Founded 1616, much restored. Doorways with
cambered heads. Mullioned windows.

* The chancel decoration is the work of *Sir Ninian Comper* and was
carried out in 1923.

LYDEARD HOUSE, NW of the church. Probably mid C18. Five bays, two storeys. The centre bay projects and has a pediment with an oval window. Quoins. Ground-floor windows with pediments. Four-column Ionic porch. Stables on the l.

1010

BLACKDOWN HILL

WELLINGTON MONUMENT. Obelisk, intended for a cast-iron statue. By *Thomas Lea Jun.*, 1817–18.

6020

BLACKFORD
3 m. E of Sparkford

ST MICHAEL. Humble Perp W tower. The rest much renewed. Norman S doorway. Two colonnettes, one with horizontal zigzag carving, the other with spiral fluting. Fluted capitals, zigzag in the intrados of the arch. Perp chancel arch. – SCULPTURE. Two pieces of an alabaster reredos: parts of a St Michael and a Crucified Christ. – PLATE. Chalice and Paten by *Orenge* 1574.

At the E end EAST HALL FARM HOUSE with regular mullioned windows, late C17.*

4040

BLACKFORD
2 m. W of Wedmore

HOLY TRINITY. 1823 by *Richard Carver*. An octagon, with an ogee-capped lantern. Slightly projecting transepts and chancel. Eight-ribbed ceiling. Thin, shallow porch with four-centred arches. The windows have Y-tracery and also four-centred arches. – PLATE. Set of 1823.

2030

BLACKMOOR FARM
1 m. SW of Cannington

An extremely rare and fortunate survival – the manor house of a distinguished man who made his will in 1508 (Sir Thomas Tremaill),‡ kept externally in almost exactly the state in which it was at his time. Most of the windows are of *c.* 1500, straight-headed, of two or three lights with ogee-heads to the

---

* The MHLG mentions a C16 house of stone, thatched, with a stair-turret and a four-centred doorhead.
‡ This information was generously given me by Mr A. W. Vivian-Neal.

lights, smaller or larger, and with or without transoms. The E front has its original porch with the original outer and inner doorways. The side windows have been blocked. In the Hall are the original beams (it was a one-storeyed hall) and the original fireplace. Even the spiral staircase off the back end of the screens passage is still there. At the N end of the E front projects the chapel wing. The chapel has a three-light E window and one-light N and S windows. More original windows on the sides and at the back.

BOSSINGTON see LYNCH

BOWER HINTON see MARTOCK

BRADFORD-ON-TONE

1020

ST GILES. Three-bay arcade of circular piers with double-chamfered arches, about 1300. The chancel arch also was originally of about that date. In the chancel one S lancet. The N chapel is C19, the S chapel Perp. Piers with the Devon band of leaves as capitals. The exterior Perp, embattled aisles, W tower with stair-turret placed in the centre of one side (cf. Wellington, West Buckland, and Devon). Diagonal buttresses, heavy diagonal pinnacles. Simple two-light bell openings. – PULPIT. Early C18, with rich carving. – PLATE. Chalice and Cover 1662. – MONUMENT. Knight wearing a pointed bascinet, c. 1375.

(BRIDGE. May be C15. Repaired 1698. Two pointed arches, chamfered ribs in two orders. Jervoise.)

BRATTON COURT

1 m. W of Minehead

9040
inset

A remarkable survival of parts of a C15 manor house. Of the Hall the position and the dimensions (37 by 25 feet by 28 feet high) are clear, and arched braces of the roof can still be seen. The chapel wing, at r. angles to the Hall at its High Table end, still has several windows with and without transom and with a little tracery. They are all of oak. The Chapel roof also has arched braces and in addition wind-braces. Of the king-posts one with its four-way struts has been re-erected in the (new) dining room. – Gatehouse with original oak gate.

BRATTON SEYMOUR

HOLY TRINITY. Low Perp w tower with tiny pinnacles. The
rest mostly renewed in 1830. The s porch has an outer arch
with curiously decorated wedge-stones. Norman s doorway,
the imposts with zigzag, the arch with double zigzag. In the
chancel an early C14 (pre-Dec) window which looks historically trustworthy.

THE HALL SCHOOL. 1868 and 1888. Built for *Charles Pen-
ruddocke* to his own design. The kitchen is a replica of the
Abbot's Kitchen at Glastonbury.

BREANE

ST BRIDGET. A rare dedication in Somerset. The church stands
in a long scattered village nowadays of far more caravans than
houses. Much renewed. Short s porch tower with saddleback
roof, perhaps in its masonry C13, as the rest of the church
walls may also be. – FONT. Perp, octagonal, panelled stem and
panelled under-side. No quatrefoils. – PULPIT. 1620. Plant
motifs. No blank arches. – PLATE. Chalice 1772.

IRON AGE CAMP. Remains on a promontory above the sea.
The downs are also dotted with prehistoric huts and hut-
circles.

BRENT KNOLL

ST MICHAEL. The oldest part of the church is the s doorway,
Norman, with a zigzag frieze at r. angles to the wall in the
outer arch moulding. The actual opening was heightened and
made pointed at a later date. In the N aisle is a Pillar Piscina
on a decorated shaft and with a scalloped top. This is clearly
also Norman and must have been removed to its present place.
The s porch and s transept follow in order of *ancienneté*.
They are early C14, as witnessed by the triple-chamfered porch
doorway with one order of shafts, the ogee-headed w lancet of
the transept, its triple-chamfered small w doorway, and the
cinquefoiling of the windows inside. The rest is Perp. w
tower with set-back buttresses, a pierced parapet with quatrefoils in lozenges, pinnacles, and a higher stair-turret. w doorway flanked by niches, renewed five-light w window, two-
light bell-openings flanked by identical blank two-light
windows. N aisle of six bays with buttresses and pinnacles and
a pierced parapet exactly like that of the tower. No s aisle.

Tall thin N aisle arcade with piers of four-waves moulding. Good panelled aisle roof, wagon-roof in the nave. Tower arch 19 on responds of a broadly treated four-hollows section, i.e. no later than *c.* 1400. – BENCHES. They are the most interesting piece of furnishing in the church, for iconographical reasons. They have the usual tracery and poppy-heads of lozenge shape, but in addition to the usual representations of the Pelican, Lamb and Flag, and Signs of the Evangelists, they show a bit of animal fable with a polemical meaning which must have been patent at the time to everybody who saw it. On the first Reynard the Fox is seen disguised as a mitred 26b Abbot. He is paid respect to by three monks in cowls who have the heads of swine. At the foot two monkeys roast a pig on a spit. On the second the fox is foot-cuffed and below put into the stocks, and a monkey guards him. His mitre hangs on the wall. On the third he is hung by the triumphant geese. What does this imply? A general hatred of the parishioners or some wealthy donor for monasteries and Glastonbury in particular? Or a topical reference which escapes us? There is no evidence to prove that at that time Glastonbury tried to recover South Brent which had gone to the Bishop of Wells in the C12. Whatever the immediate meaning, the outspokenness of the statement remains memorable. – PULPIT. 1637, with the familiar short blank arches in two tiers. – MONU-MENT. John Somerset † 1663. In the centre of this big and naive monument is John Somerset, a three-quarter figure in an oval niche. To his r. and l. his two wives, sweet figures, also in niches, the younger one with a large and becoming hat. Two reliefs below. In one kneels his family. In the other he is seen rising in his shroud from his tomb, just like George Rodney at Rodney Stoke in the monument of 1651, done probably by the same workmen (cf. as an even closer parallel Sir Edward Rodney † 1657). Twisted columns between the three niches (cf. Sir Thomas Bridges † 1661, Keynsham), and open segmental pediment at the top. The inscription below reads as follows:

His county gave him name, and 's name exprest
In what his ancestors and 's selfe were blest:
Hence his first years the best improvements knew,
Which happily what's great and good pursue.
Nor did his thinking age shame his first years,
He knew noe mean delight, noe sordid cares;
In short, his hopeful offspring ordered hence

To heaven in their baptismal innocence;
The needy here on earth he chose to be
His care, even his adopted progenie.
Such were his thoughts, and thus his actions strove,
While he remained below, to live above;
And when the Almighty found him fit for bliss,
He call'd him to his proper happiness.

MANOR HOUSE, ¼ m. NE of the church. 1862–4 by *John Norton*.

BRENT KNOLL CAMP. An impressive Iron Age fortification on Burnham flats, 6 m. S of Weston-super-Mare. It is one of the finest camps in North Somerset. The knoll soars suddenly out of the plain to a height of nearly 550 ft above sea-level; tradition has it that the Devil threw down at this spot a shovelful of earth while he was digging Cheddar Gorge. The oval camp, with its great rampart, commands the whole district. Tradition has it that a great battle was fought under Brent Knoll once upon a time; it may have been the battle recorded in the Anglo-Saxon Chronicle for the year A.D. 847, when the men of Dorset and Somerset banded together and beat the invading Danes.

BREWER'S CASTLE *see* DULVERTON

3030

BRIDGWATER

11b ST MARY. A large, low, and spreading church. Its stone spire is tall and exceedingly elegant, but the tower on which it stands is too short to allow the spire to dominate the town. The tower is of red sandstone; so is the chancel; the rest is grey, the S aisle and S transept rebuilt in a light, silvery stone. The tower is early C14 work. It has big diagonal buttresses and towards the nave a low arch of three continuous chamfers. The bell-openings have Dec tracery and Somerset tracery. The square stair-turret rises higher than the battlements of the tower. Big Perp doorway with large leaves in the spandrels and above it a Dec two-light window. The spire was begun in 1367. It is tall, fine, and sheer without any fussy dormers. It was probably designed by *Nicholas Waleys* (J. Harvey). The N and S sides of the church are complicated in their external appearance by the existence of transepts with E chapels, and by chancel chapels. The transept fronts, though apparently much restored, yet seem reliable in their curious features, Dec work of the mid C14, more florid and inventive than the Dec style usually is in Somerset. Especially odd the tympanum of the N doorway and the oculus window above it, with a straight-sided star pattern. The oculus above the S doorway has a double-cusped quatrefoil. The capitals of the colonnettes of the N doorway must remain from the C13 (*see* below). They have stiff-leaf very different from the leaves in the tympanum above. Niches l. and r. of the N oculus. Elaborately traceried five-light window to the l. of the N doorway. Perp parapet with trefoiled pierced triangles. Below the N transept is a crypt. Its single-chamfered small doorway, and the two recesses for tombs l. and r. of it, must belong to *c.* 1300. The recesses have arches with seven cusps each. In the recesses are almost unrecognizably defaced monuments. The E end including the chancel chapels has a parapet of pierced pointed quatrefoils. Large windows everywhere. In the S aisle they are reticulated but all C19; otherwise they are Perp, mostly of four and five lights. The aisles are separated from the nave by arcades of six bays with piers of standard four-hollows section and little circular capitals only to the shafts – an uninspired treatment. The clerestory dates from the C19. The E arches of the crossing are different, plain, massive, and polygonal. They belong to the pre-Perp building of which other evidence has already been mentioned. The arches of the chancel chapels die into the imposts. The arches from the aisles into the transepts have standard responds. The most original motif inside the church is the balconies opening from the upper storeys of the porches. In the aisle walls are tomb recesses. In the N aisle one has open cusping, the other cusping and sub-cusping. In the S aisle they seem all Dec (with ogee arches and very big leaf cusps) and are all Victorian. The nave roof is Victorian, the chancel roof can be dated by a boss with the name of a man who died in 1422. It has cusped principal braces, a highly successful motif. – SCREENS. S and N chancel chapels, with one-light sections. – S transept: a splendid Jacobean piece which served in the C17 as rood screen. Dado with rusticated columns and two tiers of arches between. One-light divisions with thin ornamented columns. Strapwork and obelisks on the top. – The BENCHES behind the screen (Civic Pew) are of the same date. – PULPIT. A fine Perp piece, with delicate tracery panels. – COMMUNION TABLE. Elizabethan or Jacobean. –

STALLS. The remains of the original stalls are used as Sedilia. – PAINTING. Mourning over the dead Christ, large, given to the Church in the C18 by 'Mr Pawlet of Hinton St George' (Shaw's *Tour*, 1788), looks Bolognese, second half of the C17. – PLATE. Chalice and Cover 1640; Flagon by *James Wilkes* 1724; two Dishes by *Robert Lucas* 1727; Chalice and Paten by the same 1723; Funnel 1811. – MONUMENTS. Francis Kingsmill † 1620. Big hanging wall-monument. He is represented semi-reclining on his elbow. Behind him, of equal size, kneel his sons † 1621 and † 1640, both facing E. – John Dunning † 1821 by *Reeves* of Bath.

ST ANDREW. 1870 by *John Norton*. (Ian Nairn.)

ST JOHN BAPTIST, Eastover. 1843 by *John Brown*, surveyor of Norwich Cathedral. The seven years after Holy Trinity have made much difference. St John is, at least in its details, a much more knowledgeable job. Neo-E.E., and with nothing of the leanness of the Commissioners' Churches. On the other hand in composition and proportion the church is far from the spirit of the C13. Strong W tower intended to carry a spire; nave and narrow chancel, both very tall and remarkably impressive [in their excessive height. – STAINED GLASS E window by *Douglas Forsyth*, 1916. – PLATE. Two Flagons and two Patens 1844.

HOLY TRINITY, Taunton Road. 1839 by *Carver*. Nave, chancel, and bell-cote, and lower polygonal W porch. Whitish-grey stone. The gables of a pitch as if they had been conceived as pediments. Perp tracery in windows of a proportion as though they had started as 'Commissioners'' lancets. Interior without aisles but with three galleries, W, N, and S. Open timber roof with tie-beams and lots of thin tracery above them.

BAPTIST CHURCH, St Mary Street. 1837 by *Edwin Down*. Three-bay front with giant unfluted Ionic columns *in antis* flanking the entrance. Pediment across the whole front.

UNITARIAN CHAPEL (originally Presbyterian), Dampiet Street, 1688, re-modelled 1788. Mentioned by Defoe as 'a fine meeting house'. Red brick. To the first date belongs the heavy shell-hood of the door, to the second the rest of the façade, especially the Venetian window above the door.

METHODIST CHURCH, King Street. 1816, with a portico added. Plain red brick front.

PUBLIC BUILDINGS

(Town Hall, Market Hall, Rural District Offices, County Court, Infirmary) *see* Perambulation.*

PERAMBULATION

We start by the church. ST MARY STREET winds its way along from the Taunton Road entrance into Bridgwater, past the churchyard, to end near the w end of the High Street. Several nice houses, though none of special merit. w of the churchyard the RURAL DISTRICT OFFICES (The Priory), much modernized in the front, but with its Late Georgian garden side (two storeys, five bays). The Venetian window may originally have belonged to the front of the house (suggests the MHLG). Then, facing the church, No. 47, the remains of a Chantry House, much altered, but preserving its chimney-breast. The Baptist Chapel (*see* above) is recessed and turns a cold shoulder to the old church. No. 41, six bays, two-and-a-half storeys, with segment-headed windows, older than its charming early C19 shop-front. To continue this side of the street as it turns s from the churchyard: the TUDOR CAFÉ, with a sham half-timbered front, has plasterwork of *c.* 1600 inside. Off on the r. FRIARN STREET has a few good houses, especially No. 15 of *c.* 1700, with a big shell-hood over the doorway. Friarn Street is called after the Franciscan Friary which was here. Of this nothing survives above ground. From Friarn Street one can go back to St Mary Street by SILVER STREET where the stone wall and large chimney-breast and the oaken doorway of one house certainly belong to a pre-Reformation building, though hardly to any connected with the Friary.‡ On the other side of St Mary Street, facing the churchyard from the E, Nos 38–40 are the best house, late C18, with three storeys and four bays. Two nice doorways.

At the NE corner of the churchyard the Market Hall starts, the urban centre of Bridgwater. The church lies back and out

* On the Sydenham Estate, at the s end of PARK WAY a group of two SCHOOLS has recently been completed, one Infants, the other Junior. They are of brick in the modern style, with flat roofs and an informal plan. The architect is the County Architect *R. Oliver Harris*. Another good new school the BRIDGWATER DAY SPECIAL SCHOOL, Hamp Street.

‡ Excavations have however revealed the bases of six Perp piers of usual section (four hollows) across New Road to the w of the house called The Friars.

of the way. At CORNHILL, the triangle which the Market
Hall faces, the three main streets converge. The MARKET
56a   HALL was designed by *John Bowen*, who was an India
merchant (that is, an amateur), and built in 1834 (date-stone
found). It faces Cornhill with a more than semicircular portico
of heavy unfluted Ionic columns. This is crowned by an attic,
a drum, a dome, and a lantern. The whole seems just right in
scale and modest formality for a country town of some pride
and traditions. Behind the rotunda is the Market Hall proper
displaying to St Mary Street and the High Street entrances
with Ionic columns *in antis*. In the HIGH STREET otherwise
the Royal Clarence Hotel and the Town Hall deserve notice.
The ROYAL CLARENCE HOTEL is probably by *Benjamin
Baker* and of about the same date as the Market Hall. It has
a porch of four unfluted Ionic columns and is three storeys
high. The TOWN HALL has a nicely restrained classical
front of nine bays, with two pillared porches and a five-bay
centre with panelled pilasters. Its date is remarkably late:
1865. The architect was *C. Knowles*.*

The principal part of this perambulation starts facing E from
the Market Hall. In the middle of Cornhill a STATUE of
Admiral Blake by *D. W. Pomeroy* 1898–1900. Next to the
Royal Clarence Hotel at a corner the WESTMINSTER BANK
peeps through, a pretty, low neo-Baroque façade of 1904, with
a concave corner entrance, big Ionic columns, and garlands
over the ground-floor windows. Opposite, on the S side of
Cornhill, two four-storeyed office buildings in the sober
Italian High Renaissance style of *c.* 1860, as if they stood somewhere in Bishopsgate or Gracechurch Street. Next to them
on the r. a nice Georgian front of five bays with Venetian
window.

To the E FORE STREET runs towards the river Parrett. Several
acceptable Late Georgian and Early Victorian houses, interrupted by the recessed Gothic front of the Congregational
Chapel. On the other side a glimpse up a side-street to the
axially placed façade of the COUNTY COURT in Queen
Street, an early C19 façade of five bays and two storeys with
a three-bay pediment. Blank segmental arches on the ground
floor. On the first floor attached Ionic columns in the middle,
tall tripartite windows on the sides.

So the river and the quays are reached. It is here that Bridgwater displays its individual character, a character curiously

* Three MACES of the mid C17, silver repoussé.

East Anglian with the red brick houses and the estuary close at hand. The bridge is unfortunately no longer that made of cast iron at Coalbrookdale in 1795. The quays are a minor edition of Wisbech, minor indeed in terms of good architecture. There is really only one house facing the river which is worth special notice. We start first to the sw. At the end of Binford Place the PUBLIC LIBRARY, a nice version of the Market Hall rotunda, with a real rotunda portico and a dome behind. It is by *E. Godfrey Page* and was built in 1905. It stands at the entrance to BLAKE GARDENS. In these an archway at the head of which is the top part of a four-light Perp window, no doubt from St Mary's Church, when new tracery was substituted for old. Then SE, SALMON PARADE to the INFIRMARY, with a six-bay façade of probably *c.* 1840. Specially characteristic the heavy sanserif lettering. Four-column Ionic porch. Along the NE quay, called EAST QUAY, only one house of note, No. 4, Early Georgian, with a Gibbs surround of the doorway and segment-headed windows.

WEST QUAY, the NW of the four quays, is the most important; for here, after the nice FOUNTAIN INN (Messrs Starkey's deserve much praise for the black and white of their pubs) and a six-bay Early Georgian house with regrettable shop-front, one reaches the corner of Castle Street* and soon the best house of Bridgwater, THE LIONS, an ambitious mansion of *c.* 1730, built for himself by *Benjamin Holloway*, a carpenter and builder. Yellow and red brick chequer, five bays and two storeys on basement, with one-storey projecting pavilions. The pavilions have Venetian windows to the street and pyramid roofs. They are connected by a stone balustrade with the lions flanking the entrance to this little forecourt. Up a flight of steps to the main entrance, which has attached Tuscan columns and a metope frieze. The middle window above is arched and flanked by a kind of fluted pilasters with no capitals. Above these, separate corbels carry a segmental pediment. The other first-floor windows have aprons. They are, like the ground-floor windows, segment-headed. All these motifs are far from correct, and the whole is in a robust provincial Baroque taste. Some nice panelling and fireplaces inside.

If The Lions is the best house at Bridgwater, CASTLE STREET is the best street. It was projected by the Duke of _{54a}

* For No. 12 *see* in the text below.

Chandos in 1721, and begun in 1723. It is not quite certain who designed the houses. The Duke's surveyors and masons from Canons and London, *Fort* and *Shepherd*, appear in the story as unravelled by Mr Collins Baker. But the most likely designer is *Holloway* of The Lions who was certainly the builder employed by the Duke. According to the MHLG only the N side was at first built; the S side is a late C18 copy. The houses are of brick with quoins and the delightful motif of parapets curving up, as the street rises. Each house is of five bays, and all have segment-headed windows. The doorways vary widely, Ionic pilasters, Ionic pilasters outside an arched Gibbs surround, Corinthian pilasters, and – the spirit of The Lions – Roman Doric pilasters placed at an angle and carrying a metope frieze. The S side is simple in its details. The street leads to KING SQUARE which, though of plainer late C18 brick houses, would as a whole have been a match for Castle Street if it had been completed. But only two-and-a-half sides were built. The rest is scrappy in plan. In the middle of the square STATUE by *John Angel*, 1924 – a World War memorial. Seated bronze statue of a mother with children intended to represent Civilization. Under her feet Strife, Bloodshed, Corruption, and Despair; tiny figures. In her lap the Book of Law. She holds up an orb, the World.

King Square stands on the site of the centre of BRIDG-WATER CASTLE, a stronghold built in 1216 and slighted in the Civil War. The only surviving part is the WATER GATE, adjoining No. 12 West Quay. The arch is segment-headed and has single-chamfered ribs. The wall is 12 ft thick.

EARTHWORK. On the road to Cross. Allegedly prehistoric. However, it appears to approximate more closely to the lay-out of a medieval motte and bailey.

3010
BROADWAY

ST ALDHELM AND ST EADBURGA. Chancel and transept of the late C13 to early C14. Three stepped lancets at the E end. Cinquefoiled rere-arches to the E and the N transept N windows. Perp nave and W tower. Original chancel roof. – FONT. Octagonal, Perp. On each side a small figure flanked by slim panels l. and r. – PULPIT. C16; rediscovered c. 1900. – PLATE. Chalice and Cover 1572; Salver 1705 by *Benjamin Pyne*. – CHURCHYARD CROSS. The shaft has two figures on top of each other. The head is missing.

CONGREGATIONAL CHAPEL, 1739. The arched windows with two mullions and a transom at the height of the springing of the arch go with that date.

EVERY'S ALMSHOUSES. Founded under a will of 1588. With mullioned windows and cambered door-heads.

BROMPTON RALPH

ST MARY. Quite a big tower; in a prominent position. Thin diagonal buttresses, battlements, square NE stair-turret, two-light bell-openings with Somerset tracery. Tower arch tall and single-chamfered. No original work outside the rest of the church, and hardly anything inside (restoration by *H. Parsons*; 1881–2; GR). – FONT. Perp, octagonal, with flower and leaf motifs, a quatrefoil, and also a chalice and two flagons. – ROOD SCREEN. Fragmentary. The sections of three lights, cusped with intersecting arches. A Welsh, not a SW English type. Remains of original colour. – BENCHES. Plain, straight-headed. – COMMUNION RAIL. Important, because dated: 1677. The balusters turned and quite sturdy, but already of a certain elegance in outline. – PLATE. Chalice and Cover 1573; Paten by *Henry Chawder* 1790. – MONUMENT. T. Camplin † 1780. Draped urn on an oval grey back-plate. By *King* of Bath.

Brompton Ralph faces just across the valley WILLETT'S TOWER, a folly tower erected in 1820 (by Mr Belmerton, probably in connexion with Willetts, a house further NE). The tower is pretty well a copy of a ruined Somerset church tower, and an attached piece of the ruined church has also been specially erected to reinforce the effect. Large pointed arch, two-light windows, battlements, higher stair-turret, diagonal buttresses only at the foot.

BROMPTON REGIS

ST MARY. Much restoration of 1853, in the Geometrical style. Good Late Perp N aisle with windows of the attractive Dunster type. Small W tower assigned to the C13 on account of its coupled lancets as bell-openings. The interior surprisingly spacious, with a five-bay arcade. The piers are of the four-wave type. The capitals are leaf-bands. – PULPIT. Jacobean. – ORGAN CASE. Handsome piece in the Arts &

Crafts style, black, with pretty golden flowers and other small-scale motifs. – STAINED GLASS. E Window, 1896, no doubt by *Kempe*. – PLATE. Chalice and Cover of *c.* 1574 in contemporary leather box; Paten inscribed 1635; Almsdish by *Ebenezer Coker* 1767.

2030   BROOMFIELD

ALL SAINTS. Beautifully situated, with two yew trees S of the church, and a screen of majestic elms and beeches against N and E winds. The usual modest W tower of the district. The chancel must be early C14, *see* the prettily cusped door-head on the S side. Early C16 N aisle embattled with pierced quatrefoils. The arcade of four bays with piers of the four-waves section. The capitals have leaf bands (but on one the Instruments of the Passion can be recognized), the arches are four-centred. The chancel arch is of the same section as the arcade, but with a small capital only to the shaft. Leaf bands on the capitals of the arch to the N chapel. Original wagon roofs, on angel figures in nave and chancel. – FONT. Octagonal, Perp, with the familiar quatrefoils. – BENCHES. A very complete set, square-headed, with tracery, big plants, etc. One bench
25b front has been made the front of the family pew in the N aisle. On one bench-end the name *Simon Werman* is inscribed. That name also appears at Trull, with the date 1561. – STAINED GLASS. In the chancel S window divers C15–C16 fragments, architectural canopies, two angels recommending two kneeling figures, two angels' heads, etc. – The E window is of 1913 and clearly by *Morris & Co.* – PLATE. Chalice and Cover of 1635; two Patens 1709 by *William Gamble*; Flagon 1721. – MONUMENTS. Brass to Richard Silverton † 1443, chaplain, holding a chalice. The head is missing. 20-in. figure. On the tower floor. In the inscription he is said to have 'sumptuously repaired and magnificently decorated' the church. – Two minor wall monuments with draped urns, one († 1788) by *Reeves* of Bath, the other († 1790) by *King* of Bath.

RUBOROUGH CAMP. An Iron Age camp near the Traveller's Rest Inn. The banks are still 20 ft high. The shape is triangular: 230 yards from base to tip, 170 yards across the baseline. It is a fine monument.

BROWN DOWN *see* OTTERFORD

BRUSHFORD

9020
inset

ST NICHOLAS. Two-storeyed W tower with diagonal buttresses
with many set-offs, nave and chancel. Nice early C16 S windows. The only piece of architectural interest is the N chapel 22b
built by *Lutyens* in 1926. Its odd cross-window on the E side
and especially its decoration by plain raised squares and
circles betray at once Lutyens's fascination with geometry. –
Inside MONUMENT to A. N. H. Molyneux Herbert † 1923.
Recumbent effigy by *Cecil de Banquière Howard* of Paris,
under a wooden canopy. – FONT. Square, Norman, of Purbeck marble, with six shallow blank arches on each side. –
ROOD SCREEN. Perp; no tracery left, but the ribbed coving
is preserved. – STAINED GLASS. Seated Virgin (Chancel S
window), French, early C16. – Luard window † 1891 by
Morris & Co. The three square storeys below the three single
figures are particularly fine. – PLATE. Chalice 1653; Paten late
C17; Flagon by *John Elston* of Exeter 1727.

BRUTON

6030

ST MARY. One of the proudest churches of East Somerset.
Built of Doulting stone, as is most of the town. The building
history starts with the Crypt below the chancel. This is early
C14 work with two octagonal piers and plain chamfered ribs.
The N porch tower looks late C14. It has diagonal buttresses
and battlements. Plain two-light bell-openings. Of the same
date the N aisle with battlements and three-light windows with
Perp tracery.* The same tracery in the S aisle, but here the
parapet must have been altered when the clerestory was added
early in the C16. Early C15 is the date attributed by Mr Eeles
to the nave. It is of five bays, the piers slim and of standard
section (four hollows). The arches are four-centred, but only
slightly depressed. In the late C15 the splendid W tower was
added. This is $102\frac{1}{2}$ ft high, and has set-back buttresses connected by a diagonal across the angle of the tower which thus
disappears. The buttresses carry long shafts set diagonally and
crowned by pinnacles quite detached from the wall, and the
main diagonal is continued into the main pinnacles, also set
diagonally. Large W door with W window of five lights over.

* The monogram of Abbot W. Gilbert (1511–33), the shield of Bishop
Fitzjames of London (1506–22), and the monogram and punning beer-barrel
of Abbot Bere of Glastonbury (1493–1524) can only refer to internal alterations – *see* below.

Two niches by its sides and one above it. The next stage has a two-light window with niches on shafts to its l. and r. The bell-stage has three tall two-light windows with transoms and Somerset tracery. They are flanked by shafts with pinnacles. On the N side this arrangement is modified, because the stair-turret interferes. The battlements have shields and quatre-foils but are not pierced. The tower arch towards the nave is tall and has an elaborate continuous moulding. The ground storey of the tower was fan-vaulted inside in the C19. Between 1506 and 1523 the nave received a clerestory of uncommonly wide, not very high four-light windows. The clerestory para-pet of pierced trefoiled triangles is repeated over the aisles. The nave roof was put on at the same time. It is of Somerset type, richly detailed, with tie-beams and king-posts and tracery above the tie-beams. The beams rest on shafts with elegantly decorated stone niches. These contain C19 statues. The aisle roofs are contemporary with the nave roof. All this work can be dated by the occurrence of the shields etc. already referred to in the N aisle parapet and by the shield of Bishop Fitzjames on the nave roof. In 1743 the chancel was rebuilt. It is a handsome piece of its date. There is no E window but a pediment with the Berkeley arms. The N and S windows are of two lights with round heads and a circle above with pediment, Corinthian columns and pilasters and Rococo decoration. The roof is a plaster groin vault with garlands of leaves as ribs.

FURNISHINGS. COMMUNION RAILS and STALLS con-temporary with the chancel. – PULPIT. Jacobean type with the usual short blank arches. – CHANCEL SCREEN, neo-Georgian, 1938. – SCREEN now under the tower. Dated 1620, decorated with foliage scrolls rather than strapwork. – BENCHES. Partly Jacobean. Ends with shell-tops and elon-gated panels below them, similar to those of the Pulpit. – ROYAL ARMS of Charles II. – ALTAR FRONTAL (or Cope?), fragmentary, embroidered on velvet, probably C15. – PLATE. Two Chalices with Covers, Paten and Flagon, given 1706; Flagon and Almsdish 1744; Candlesticks 1744. – MONU-MENTS. Sir Maurice Berkeley † 1581 and his wives † 1559 and 1585. Recumbent effigies on a tomb-chest with strapwork panels. The monument is in a deep niche in the chancel as if it were (or replaced) an Easter Sepulchre. Front with columns carrying two arches. Back with cartouches. All stone. – Oppo-site William Godolphin † 1636. Bronze bust in oval niche

below a broken segmental pediment ending in incurved
scrolls. The bust might well be by *Le Sueur*. – Captain William
Berkeley, 1749 by *P. Scheemakers*. Tablet of modest size and
design. – In the nave s arcade big tomb-chest with quatrefoils.
No effigy. Doubtfully connected with Abbot Gilbert, prior
1494, abbot 1511–33. Badly preserved.

To the W of the church in the street called PLOX remains
survive of the ABBEY WALL, with a long row of buttresses.
This belonged to the Augustinian Priory founded in 1142 and
made into an abbey in 1511. Attached to the wall is the
stately VICARAGE, dated 1822. On a hill to the S the prominent tower-like four-gabled DOVECOTE of the abbey.
Some mullioned windows. Is it C16? Opposite the abbey wall
KING'S SCHOOL. This was founded in 1519 by Bishop
Fitzjames of London, Abbot Gilbert, and Dr Edmunds,
chancellor of St Paul's Cathedral – perhaps stimulated by
Colet's foundation of St Paul's School in 1510. The buildings
of the school are mostly C19, but include C16 work in Old
School. This was a small separate building – as most C16
schools were – and nestled in the shadow of the abbey wall.
Mullioned windows with arched lights, and a central doorway,
remade with heavy Tuscan pilasters and pediment. It leads
into the former screens passage. Originally the Hall would
have been on the r., the parlour on the l., the kitchen, etc.,
where the housemaster's hall now is, and the school-room in
the place of the changing-room on the r. The dormitories
were on the first floor. The heavy undecorated Hall Screen
survives. At the back a wing was added early in the C18. To
the r. of the old house a taller addition of 1834. In this an
Elizabethan timber lobby, brought in from outside.*

The church, abbey, and school lie on the S side of the river
Brue, the town on the N. One of the bridges, W of the main
bridge, is a handsome one-arch PACKHORSE BRIDGE (C15?).
Over the main bridge PATWELL STREET climbs up towards
the main crossing of the town. Facing into Patwell Street at
its S end a Late Georgian stuccoed façade with giant pilasters.
In Patwell Street the OLD BULL INN with an elaborate
wrought-iron sign bracket.

The main crossing is of that ingeniously warped kind which
old towns always seem to prefer to a straight rectangular

* New House was built in 1870–2 and added to in 1878 and 1913 (Dining
Hall). The Laboratory Block dates from 1902, the Gymnasium from 1921,
Memorial Building from 1919–24.

layout. From the sw a nice c18 façade looks into it diagonally
(with a Venetian centre window). To the n of the crossing
COMBE STREET with the Georgian ASSEMBLY ROOMS in
the yard of the Blue Ball Hotel. To the e QUAPERLAKE
STREET with a number of pleasant Georgian houses with or
without pedimented doorways. The HIGH STREET runs w.
Here the CONGREGATIONAL CHAPEL of 1803, a broad
symmetrical five-bay front with angle pilasters, and windows
exhibiting the usual Y-tracery. Then Nos 34–36, the former
ABBEY COURT HOUSE, mid c15, with timber-framed upper
storey. Large carved stone brackets. All much renewed.
Moulded beams inside. – After that SEXEY'S HOSPITAL
founded in 1638. It consists of two courts, of which the w
court is original. Three ranges, two with wooden gallery of
access to the upper tenements, and Chapel and Hall. The
Chapel has excellent original woodwork, stalls and pulpits,
and three-light Perp windows with the centre light raised so
as to give a stepped top to the window and with hood-moulds.
In the Hall the lower part of the Screen survives, with Ionic
columns. Above the Hall entrance late c17 bust of the founder
surrounded by garlands. Signed by *William Stanton*. The e
court was rebuilt in 1820. – w of Sexey's Hospital another
good house which must be Jacobean or a little earlier.

SEXEY'S BOYS SCHOOL, Yeovil Road. 1891 by *E. J. & F. W.
Skipper*. Partly neo-Tudor, with cupola.

BRYMPTON D'EVERCY

12 The *ensemble* of the house with its garden and outbuildings,
the chantry house, and the church is of exquisite beauty, one of
the most perfect the county has to offer. The stone used is Ham
Hill, and its lovely colour can nowhere be seen to greater
advantage.

ST ANDREW. Low and rambling and extremely attractive. The
s transept seems the earliest part. Its s window has Late
Geometrical tracery of c. 1300. The nave has a trefoil-headed
s doorway of about the same date. The n transept is later c14,
the chancel without chancel arch of c. 1400, the n chancel
chapel mid-c15. It is called the 'new Ile' in the Will of
Walter Sydenham of Brympton House. The w end has a
picturesque heavy bell-cote like a big lantern. Mr Eeles
suggests the mid c15 as its date. Inside, the s transept bears

out the evidence of the exterior. The entry from the nave is by a cusped arch on corbels, the windows have rere-arches and that on the E nook-shafts. In the N transept a piscina, a small fireplace, and a squint towards the chancel. From the transept a doorway and a window lead into the Perp N chapel. This has niches for statues l. and r. of the E window. – FONT. Early C14 with cinquefoil-headed panels. – PULPIT. Jacobean. – CHANDELIERS. Three brass chandeliers, probably regionally made (Bridgwater? Bristol?). – ROOD SCREEN. Stone. For the type cf. Nether Compton, Bradford Abbas, and Thornford in Dorset. Heraldry indicates a date in the second quarter of the C15. Simple. The doorway has in its spandrels on the E side two dragons. – STAINED GLASS. Bits of the C14 and 15 in the W window and the N chapel. – PLATE. Chalice and Cover 1629; Flagon 1619; Paten 1699. – MONUMENTS. Knight, c. 1275 or a little later; cross-legged with mail coif, much restored (chancel chapel). – Priest, early C14 (N transept). Under a low Perp canopy with, in the spandrels, scenes of the Annunciation and the Adoration of the Magi. – Lady wearing kerchief and wimple, c. 1325 (N transept). – Lady, c. 1440 (chancel chapel), uncommonly big, with horned headdress. – John Sydenham † 1626 (chancel). Canopy on four columns. Inside the tomb-chest which is open by an arcade of low arches lie scattered bones.

BRYMPTON D'EVERCY HOUSE. The property was given in 1434 by John Stourton of Preston Plucknett to his daughter who was married to John Sydenham. Nothing of the house dates back further than the C15, and it is indeed doubtful if anything, except a four-light window on the S side of the SW corner, is earlier than c. 1520. Of that date and later dates is the enchanting façade. It consists of the Hall, which no doubt originally reached up to the roof but was divided and provided with mullioned and double-transomed windows on the ground floor and cross-windows on the upper floor at the time of Elizabeth I, and of the earlier staircase turret and parlours to the S of it. The whole makes an admirable group, especially as, to add yet more variety, a new porch was placed in front of the hall in 1722, consisting it seems of a mixture of early C16 with imitation Gothic pieces. The porch has a quatrefoil frieze and battlements presumably originally at first-floor level. The staircase turret is given a frieze of pointed quatrefoils in lozenges and battlements with a frieze of quatrefoils in roundels, the parlour carries on that top motif, but has below a very elaborate frieze of much larger cusped lozenges with shields. The windows of that period are all mullioned and have four-centred heads to the individual lights.

Apart from this front not much can now be seen of Tudor work. The whole s range was rebuilt shortly before 1697, its N side altered when the staircase was given its present form which can hardly have been before the second half of the C19, and the Kitchen, projecting N from the E end of the s range, while it may well contain C15 or early C16 masonry, is in its present appearance also not earlier than the later Elizabethan Age. The s front is, side by side with that of Hinton House, the most important example in Somerset of the late C17 style on a palatial scale. It is classical architecture not yet in the sense of Inigo Jones's purity nor, of course, of Christopher Wren's grandeur, but rather of the Old Ashmolean of Oxford and other such provincial mid-C17 buildings. The windows are strictly symmetrical, ten on the ground floor and ten on the first floor, they are broad, but upright and of cross-type and all the way surmounted by alternatingly triangular and segmental pediments. The roof is hipped and hidden by a balustrade. – Not much need be said about the interior. The Hall has an Elizabethan fireplace with an C18 relief. Along the s front are rooms with late C17 fitments and Georgian fireplaces, mirrors, etc.

CHANTRY HOUSE, or rather, according to Mr Hussey, the Dower House of Joan Sydenham née Stourton. It is a separate oblong house between the Manor House and the Church and adds considerably to the picturesqueness of the whole group. On its N side, asymmetrically placed, is a polygonal embattled stair-turret with ample windows in groups of two on each side on the first floor. For, unusual as this is in the C15, the Hall was here on the first floor, with collar beams and cusped windbraces, as at Lytes Cary. The windows are tall and a little narrow, of two lights, with transoms and cusped heads. To the E is the Chamber, and in this is a fireplace with a frieze of large quatrefoils (early C16) and an Elizabethan plaster ceiling with thin curved as well as straight ribs and a pendant.

ALCOVE, NW of the house. Built in 1723, but clearly out of existing parts and with a view to romantic picturesqueness. The archway must be late C16 or early C17, and the bell-cote may be of the later C17. In any case it cannot be of 1723.

STABLES, NW of the house. A one-storeyed building of c. 1680–90, with big hipped roof, quoins and cross-windows, and a doorway with a pediment on brackets, very handsome in itself and providing yet another note in the wide variety of the approach to the house.

BUCKLAND ST MARY

St Mary. 1853–63 by *Benjamin Ferrey*. A noble incongruity, due to the rector, the Rev. J. E. Lance. Large with a substantial sw tower and in a style not at all *du pays*. Moreover far too large for a small and scattered congregation. Yet everything done with utmost care and lavishness. Capitals and corbels carved with naturalistic foliage. Pulpit (by *Forsyth*) and Font with much figure carving. Carved statues of the apostles on the upper walls of the nave (by *Earp*). Reredos with much marble and alabaster (by *Forsyth* 1888). The chancel walls elaborately diapered. In the N wall MONUMENT to the rector's wife who had died young in 1839. She is seen rising with her baby son from the grave, having broken the lid. By *Forsyth*. – Plenty of STAINED GLASS from divers makers (w window by *Clayton & Bell*, chancel windows by *O'Connor*, s and E and N aisle w windows by *Kempe & Tower*). – PLATE. Silver-gilt Chalice and Paten; Flagon by *Gabriel Sleath* 1721.

BURNHAM-ON-SEA

St Andrew. Of dark grey decaying stone, close to the sea. Early c14 s transept with two cinquefoiled recesses inside the s wall and a cinquefoiled two-light window. Late c14 w tower with set-back buttresses, battlements, a higher stair-turret, and no pinnacles. Two-light bell-openings. Tower arch inside with a characteristic moulding and capitals and abaci following it (cf. North Curry). The rest of the church also Perp, except for the five-bay N aisle. This must be heavily restored and partly remodelled. Embattled outside; inside five piers of standard (four-hollows) section, but quite excessively flat four-centred arches and besides a gallery squeezed in under them. An inscription records the repair and enlargement of the church in 1838. – What the church must be visited for is, however, not its architecture, but the remains of the WHITEHALL ALTAR, i.e. the altar commissioned in 1686 by James II from *Grinling Gibbons* for the chapel of Whitehall Palace. It was a splendid chapel (*Verrio* was paid

£1210 for painting it), and a splendid altar. This was designed by *Wren*, and the sculpture, four large figures (now lost), two large kneeling angels, reliefs, and ornament, was commissioned from *Grinling Gibbons*. He made them in collaboration with *Arnold Quellin*, and the two received £1875 for their work. The angels worshipping the sacrament are not a traditional English feature, but one characteristic of French altars of the c 17. They are noble figures, rhetorical and yet in attitude and expression not too melodramatic. Of far greater charm *Gibbons*'s own contribution, the many cherubs. Four reliefs, two with praying cherubs, one with a censing cherub, one with a cherub carrying a chalice and flagon. Finally a panel with ten delightful cherubs' heads surrounding the Lord's name in Hebrew letters. It would be well worth while to try and re-assemble the scattered parts in something like their original context. The altar was taken to Hampton Court in 1696 and from there by Queen Anne to Westminster Abbey, where it remained until it was in 1820 disposed of to Bishop King of Rochester, Vicar of Burnham. – PULPIT. Jacobean or a little later. With one tier of panels with blank arches and one of oblong panels within the panels. – CHANDELIER. Brass, of three tiers; 1773. – PLATE. Set of 1768.

The development of Burnham-on-Sea need not detain us long. There are clear traces of the village before it became aware of the sea. Cottages to the E and S of the churchyard and extending into the streets further S, at the Manor House and Burnham Hall a little inland, all Late Georgian to Early Victorian. Further N and outside the village a landmark, the tall white lighthouse (with two adjoining villages). The effort to establish something on a par with Weston-super-Mare comes with the two quadrant terraces N of the church, and they probably date from 1855.

BURROWBRIDGE

The feature conspicuous here for miles around is BURROW MUMP, a natural eminence and perhaps the place of King Alfred's fort or camp in 879. Its military importance in the midst of this flat marshy land is patent (Sedgemoor, Zoyland, that is Sealand, etc.). There certainly was a castle here in the c 12. What remains now is also partly medieval, the tower of a church, dedicated, as was usual for churches on hills and rocks, to St Michael. The details of the tower were altered in 1724, when a new church was begun attached to it. This was to have nave, chancel, and s porch, but was never finished.

Below the Mump a new church of St MICHAEL was built in 1836 by *Carver*, a poor lancet job with pediment-like gable and bell-cote.

BURTLE (EDINGTON BURTLE)   4040

St PHILIP AND St JAMES. 1838–9 by *R. Carver* (GR). Nave and lower chancel, and square stone bell-turret with pyramid roof. Inside the foundation INSCRIPTION, all in black letter, including important words in black-letter capitals, very pretty and quite illegible. – PLATE. Chalice and two Patens 1839.

BURTON PYNSENT   3020

Burton Pynsent was a large Elizabethan mansion when in 1765 Sir William Pynsent left it to William Pitt as a token of his enthusiastic esteem. Pitt, then out of office, retired to it and added a more commodious range of moderate size. This is the only survivor of the house. The rest was pulled down in 1805. The Pitt addition is seven bays wide, two storeys high, and of brick with a quoined three-bay centre. This is given a pediment and a lantern turret. Shell-hood over the doorway. The entrance side was remodelled *c.* 1910. In the grounds to the E a COLUMN erected by *Capability Brown* in 1765 to the memory of Pynsent. It is a Tuscan column with the usual drum above the capital and an urn on top.

BURY BRIDGE *see* DULVERTON

BURY CASTLE *see* DULVERTON and SELWORTHY

BUTLEIGH   5030

St LEONARD. Nave, chancel, and crossing tower, early C14, but all much restored (by *Buckler*). Transept of 1851, N aisle of *c.* 1859. The embattled crossing tower has no buttresses. It stands on low arches with complex mouldings. Vault inside with ribs and ridge-ribs, on corbels. The windows mostly two-light Dec. One on the s side near the w end looks reliable.

Only the w window of six lights is Perp (and trustworthy). – FONT. Octagonal, Perp, with, on the panels of the bowl, the lamb and cross, the lamb and flag, and two birds. – BENCHES. A few are original. – STAINED GLASS. Nave s window of 1851 by *Pugin*.* – s transept 1853 by *Ward & Nixon* (TK). – E window 1829 by *Willement*. This is specially interesting as no longer painted in the Georgian way, and not yet Victorian at all. Pugin does here in no essential way go beyond Willement. – PLATE. Two Patens, one perhaps of 1686, the other of 1725. – MONUMENTS. Three kneeling figures from an Elizabethan tomb. – Three brothers Hood, including Admiral Hood. Large wall monument by *Lucius Gahagan* of Bath, undated. At the foot relief of a sea-battle. On the sides Gothic shafts, at the top richly crocketed ogee arch.

BUTLEIGH COURT is large, neo-Henry VIII, and abandoned. It was built in 1845 by *Buckler*. Eastlake says that 'the elevations are varied in design, and embellished with buttresses, turrets, battlements, and other features suited to the style'.

In the HIGH STREET No. 29 is dated 1673. It is a symmetrical three-bay cottage with mullioned windows under hoodmoulds and two gables.

HOOD MONUMENT, on Windmill Hill, connected with Butleigh by a magnificent long avenue of cedar trees. The monument is a Tuscan column, with drum (circular heavily framed openings), and at the top a glass dome and big stone shields. Admiral Hood died in 1814.

OBELISK in Copley Wood. To the memory of Lord Roundway, *c.* 1830. Red granite.

WOOTTON HOUSE, Butleigh Wootton. C18 house of seven bays with raised five-bay centre. Iron veranda along the whole front.

CADBURY CASTLE *see* SOUTH CADBURY

CANNINGTON

ST MARY. A large church, of red sandstone, with one large roof covering nave, aisles, and chancel. Powerful w tower. The church is entirely parochial in appearance. It cannot be the former church of Cannington Priory, a house of Benedictine

* Information received from Mrs Stanton.

nuns, founded *c.* 1138 (by Robert de Courcy of Stogursey). Its position in relation to the priory must have been similar to that at Muchelney. Of the parish church of the C12 one composite pier with a strong attached shaft remains, now in the vestry. If it is *in situ*, the Norman church was not in line with the present chancel. But an irregularity of this kind is to be expected, as the present Perp tower is not in line with the rest of the later Perp building either. The tower is probably of the later C14. It is tall, of four stages, and lavishly detailed. Set-back buttresses, battlements, no pinnacles. Doorway with leaf-scroll along one moulding between pairs of niches l. and r., and additional niche in the SW corner between the buttresses. Four-light W window with niche above. Bell-openings of two lights. The W ends of both aisles, partly embracing the tower, have three-light windows with transoms and tracery also below the transom, of the pattern familiar from Cleeve, Dunster, Crowcombe, etc.* Both aisles are embattled. Rood-stair-turret on the N. Tall gabled porch on the S with panelled doorway. The side windows also of the ambitious variety with transoms. The E window, of the same type, has five lights. The N side of the church must almost have touched the priory buildings. Inside, the E side of the tower proves that it existed before the nave. Moulded arch, lower than the arcade arches. The former roof-line of the nave is clearly visible. Extremely tall arcades of five bays. The red sandstone is exposed internally, certainly not in accordance with the original state. The piers, in spite of their great height, are of the standard four-hollows section and have thin capitals to the shafts only. There is no chancel arch. One outer roof covers the aisle roofs and the wagon-roof of the nave. – ROOD SCREEN. Partly original; of four-light sections, the Dunster type. – GATES to the N chapel, of wrought iron, with the Clifford arms, early C18, and very swagger; no doubt from the house. – PULPIT. Incorporating Perp bits. – REREDOS. Made by *Powell's* in 1893 for Philip and Joanna Pleydell Bouverie. The two patron saints have their faces. – STAINED GLASS. The SE window by *Kempe*, 1888. – PLATE. Chalice and Cover 1632; Salver 1725; Flagon by *Robert Lucas* 1729; Dish C18. – MONUMENTS. Nothing of much value. One minor wall monument by *King* of Bath († 1792).

CANNINGTON PRIORY, now the Somerset Farm Institute. A large Elizabethan mansion, lying to the N of the church.

* In the spandrels little trefoils instead of the more usual quatrefoils.

The buildings are said to represent the buildings of the nunnery. The premises were granted in 1538 to Edward Rogers and remained in the Rogers family until in 1672 they came to the first Baron Clifford of Chudleigh. The house is of red sandstone, built round an irregular inner courtyard, which can thus not represent the cloisters of the nunnery. The outer E wall shows signs of pointed arches, otherwise all seems later C16. The w wall, not quite in line with the w end of the church, is three-storeyed. The gateway has thin pilasters of ignorant design. A four-light window above. The windows to the l. and r. are regularly arranged, except that the r. side is shorter than the l. The second floor with broad four-light windows with segmental heads and horizontally placed ovals at the angles is clearly later. A rainwater head in the courtyard, with the date 1714, may represent the date of the heightening. The E range of the house, opposite the archway, contained the Hall. It is on the first floor, a reflection perhaps of where the large room – the nuns' dormitory – was in this range in monastic times. The outer staircase has gone, but the big doorway remains, and two large three-transomed windows to its s. Next to the Hall on the s is a projecting stair-turret. The internal arrangements have all been changed, and the only room of interest is the outcome of one such change, the former CHAPEL, now lecture room, an octagon of c. 1720 or 1730 with a projecting lower chancel. This has still its plaster ceiling. The chapel is articulated by giant Corinthian pilasters with capitals of a fan shape. At the w end formerly three boxes, for the family.

In the village, especially NE of the church and priory, some good Georgian houses. One of them faces the traveller as he arrives from the w. Five bays, two storeys, quoins and parapet. Gibbs surround and pediment to the doorway. The ROGERS ALMSHOUSES, founded in 1672, are quite plain, of seven bays with a small lantern.

GUERNEY STREET FARM. A gabled late C16 front with porch and two projecting wings. To the r. of this range at r. angles one of pre-Reformation date. This has at its back a small chapel and a newel staircase. Older than the front also the back range with the large former kitchen. The various ranges form a small irregular court. The early windows are of two lights, straight-headed, with cusped lights, and two have transoms. The house deserves closer study (*see* e.g. the illustration of 1845 in Braikenridge's Collinson).

CYNWIT'S CASTLE. The hill NW of the village has been scarped for defence and walls were thrown up in the Iron Age. Here took place, in 878, a battle in which the Saxons under King Odda defeated a force of Danish sea-raiders under Ubbe. From the nearby quarry a thousand hacked and hewn skeletons were recovered – casualties of the affray. This number tallies with that given in the Anglo-Saxon Chronicle.

CARHAMPTON

ST JOHN BAPTIST. Red sandstone. The W tower with its heavy pinnacles was rebuilt in 1870. It has diagonal buttresses and three-light bell-openings. The stair-turret has a steep crocketed octagonal roof. The rest of the church was restored in 1862–3. The church has nave and chancel without division and a S aisle running as far E as the E end of the chancel. The exterior is Perp with prettily cusped tracery in the three-light windows in the special style of this part of Somerset. The aisle arcade is of six bays with piers of standard section (four waves). Capitals small and circular for the aisles, polygonal for the chancel chapels. The arcade arches are four-centred. Remains of the original wagon-roof with carved wall-plate and bosses in the S aisle. – SCREEN. Of the type of Minehead and Dunster, with four-light sections, the tracery divided by sub-arches into twice two lights. Ribbed and panelled coving. Five carved friezes in the cornice. But the distinguishing feature of the Carhampton Screen is the fact that it has been repainted in such a way as to represent the original appearance of all these screens. We may like the dark wood and the flickering highlights on it, but the C15 and C16 never saw them like that. They were coloured all over in red, blue, green, white, and gold, and a very pleasing, cheerful harmony it is. – PULPIT. Nicely and sparingly carved, C18. – PLATE. Chalice dated 1634; Flagon 1746; Paten 1810. – MONUMENT. Brass inscription to two members of the Escott family, † 1755 and 1763, with a long text, handsome lettering and elegantly drawn scrolls round the coat of arms above; signed by *C. Sherborn*, Gutter Lane, London.

MARSHWOOD FARM, a former Luttrell residence. Perp porch, the entrance remodelled Elizabethan. In the porch, re-set, two former overmantels with bold coarse strapwork, enclosing the Stoning of St Stephen and the Sacrifice of Isaac. In the back Drawing Room another Jacobean overmantel. In the room to the l. of the porch moulded beams. The overmantels by the same craftsman as those at Dunster.

CASTLE CARY

6030

ALL SAINTS. Large Perp church on a hill to the S of the town, largely rebuilt by *Benjamin Ferrey* in 1855 (GR). The old church had a spire, an unusual feature in Somerset, but Ferrey made it far more florid than it had originally been. Arcade of five bays with standard piers. Clerestory with three-light windows. – FONT. Octagonal, Perp. A frieze of very large leaves between shaft and bowl. – DOOR, S doorway. Original, with tracery. – STAINED GLASS. E window, twelve figures in three tiers, by *O'Connor*, 1855 (TK). – W window by *Powell & Sons*, 1864. – PLATE. Chalice 1640; Flagon 1783; Paten 1788. – MONUMENT. John Russ † 1758 by John Ford. Wall-monument with an amply draped standing female figure, her elbow on an urn.

The CASTLE from which Castle Cary derives its name stood on a hill to the NE of the church. The size of the large keep, *c.* 78 ft square, but not strictly rectangular, is marked out. Nothing else is visible.

In the middle of the town the MARKET HALL by *Penrose*, 1855, the replacement of one of 1616. From this perhaps the Tuscan columns of the ground floor. The rest a High Victorian mixture of coarse Gothic and Jacobean details. Behind the Market Hall in BAILEY HILL the circular LOCKUP of 1779 and the Post Office, a good five-bay C18 house with central Venetian window.

Behind SOUTH STREET the CONGREGATIONAL CHAPEL, a plain brick parallelogram of 1816 with quoins and arched windows provided with Y-tracery.

The best houses are in the HIGH STREET and its continuation NORTH STREET (e.g. Beechfield and The Pines). Also in North Street the METHODIST CHAPEL. This is of 1839 and has a front with arched windows in two storeys, a Tuscan porch, and a fanciful pediment.

CATCOTT

3030

ST PETER. Externally of no interest, but internally well preserved in its early C19 state. Plain heavy BENCHES, thin early C19 WEST GALLERY, plain Jacobean PULPIT and Reader's

DESK, Jacobean COMMUNION RAIL with vertically symmetrical balusters. Ceiled wagon roof in the chancel. The Lord's Prayer is painted on the wall inside a painted frame of wavy scrolls. A second inscription is: 'Aged men, be sober, grave, temperate, sound in faith, in charity, in patience. Young men likewise exhort to be sober minded.' Titus II, 2 and 6. – PLATE. Chalice and Paten 1635; Pewter Flagon 1732.

CATHANGER see FIVEHEAD

CHAFFCOMBE
3010

ST MICHAEL. W tower with set-back buttresses and two pinnacles above them on the corners of the battlements. Higher stair-turret. The church was rebuilt in 1860 by *J. M. Allen* (GR). – Much STAINED GLASS of about that date. – PLATE. Chalice and Cover 1574.

CHALTWAY MANOR see CROWCOMBE

CHAPEL ALLERTON
4050

CHURCH. Probably late C13: *see* the nave S lancet with pointed trefoiled rere-arch, the single-chamfered S doorway, and the chancel N lancet now opening into the vestry, and also the renewed chancel S lancet. On the whole much too restored to be of value. Interesting nave S window, quite a normal Late Perp window, straight-headed with pointed-arched lights, small leaves in the spandrels and on the hood-mould, but dated 1638. N aisle and chancel arch of 1860. – FONT COVER Jacobean. – PLATE. Chalice and Cover 1573.

CHAPEL CLEEVE see OLD CLEEVE

CHARD
3000

ST MARY THE VIRGIN. A large, solid, stately church, without flights of fancy. Perp throughout, except for an uncovered half of a Norman arch in the chancel S wall. Uncommonly low W tower with set-back buttresses, higher stair-turret, battlements, and pinnacles. Two-light bell-openings with

Somerset tracery. The aisles have three-light windows, and
battlements. The N transept has a stair-turret. Two-storeyed
N porch with crocketed ogee gable and niche over. The reliefs
above are of 1882. One-storeyed S porch. At the E end the
chancel projects one bay. The buttresses carry pinnacles here.
On both sides the transepts and porches are pinnacled. The
interior is not high. Six-bay arcades with standard piers
(four hollows). The panelled wagon roof starts immediately
above the two-centred arcade arches. Cut into it charming
Jacobean dormer windows. Moulded tower arch. The N transept arches are of the same type, the S transept arches are
panelled. Niches l. and r. of the chancel E window. – FONT.
Octagonal, Perp, with quatrefoils. – MONUMENT. William
Brewer † 1614. Simple epitaph with kneeling figures. –
CHURCHYARD GATES, cast-iron and Gothic, probably of
c. 1825, the time of the CHURCH ROOM to the W (dated 1827).

PERAMBULATION

The tour starts at the TOWN HALL, an impressive building
in Fore Street. It does not stand free, but projects into the
wide, market-like street with a two-storeyed portico. Both
storeys have coupled Tuscan columns. Pediment and wooden
lantern. The building was erected in 1834. In FORE STREET
E of the Town Hall three Nonconformist chapels. CONGRE-
GATIONAL, with the hideous mid-Victorian details often to
be met in the county and also the characteristic asymmetrical
spirelet. The date is 1867, the architect was a *Mr Stent* of
Warminster. METHODIST, 1895 by *R. Curwen*, red brick and
stone dressings, Geometrical style, undistinguished. The
third chapel is older and now disused. With its three lancet
windows in the front, it dates from 1859. Near the E end on
the N side the GRAMMAR SCHOOL, dated 1583. It was a
private house then and became a school in 1671. Faced with
square flint. Central three-storeyed porch, symmetrically
arranged six-light and four-light windows. Some original
internal features (fireplaces, spiral stair). A little higher up
on the same side Georgian houses and LLOYDS BANK, a
handsome Early Victorian seven-bay house with tripartite
windows in the centre. It was built as a hotel in 1849. Opposite
the Town Hall the GEORGE HOTEL with a four-column
Tuscan porch, and then a little further W the most interesting
house in Chard, the so-called COURT HOUSE. It is a group

48b

of several Late Elizabethan houses; two storeys and dormers. Built mostly of squared flints. Two porches (one of three, the other of two storeys), four gables, three canted oriels – all picturesquely uneven. At the back the Court Room, a room of 30 by 20 feet with ten-light windows to N and S (still four-centred heads to the lights) and a plaster tunnel-vault inside, very crudely done. On one tympanum a crest and caryatids in profile, on the other Justice, another figure, and small scenes in strapwork surrounds. Plaster ceilings in front rooms also. W of this house the CROWN HOTEL with nice Egyptian lettering.

FORE STREET is continued in HIGH STREET. THE CHOUGHS is of c. 1600 with a seven-light mullioned window under one of its two gables. Then HARVEY'S HOSPITAL, rebuilt 1841 in a neo-Tudor style, with pretty black-letter inscriptions in gables and parapet. Several Georgian houses with column porches.

At the meeting of Fore and High Streets HOLYROOD STREET turns S. The SE corner is rounded and marked by a digni-fied urban house in a classical style of c. 1845. Then the BAPTIST CHAPEL, dated 1842, with Grecian detail and extremely elongated Doric pilasters carrying a pediment. Further on on the same side, two factories with buildings of c. 1825. They are both five-storeyed and of brick, the first (Messrs Gifford Fox & Co.) is ten windows long and has straight-headed windows, the second (Sterling Instrument Co.) is fifteen windows long and has segment-headed windows. Iron staunchions and girders and flat brick arches in both. In the first a beam engine is still preserved.

SOUTH CHARD 1 m. SE. Scattered tesserae and building material indicate the former presence of a ROMAN VILLA.

WADEFORD, 1½ m. NW. A ROMAN VILLA with seven mosaic floors is recorded.

CHARLINCH

2030

CHURCH. Over-restored in 1886. Norman S doorway, much defaced. One order of colonnettes, segmental arch with hood-moulds originally with small heads at its ends. No decoration left otherwise. The chancel arch inside is Norman too, at least in its responds. The double-chamfered arch which does not quite fit probably belongs to the C13. – FONT. Norman. Circular, fluted. – PAINTINGS. On the altar copies after

Francesco Francia. – STAINED GLASS. S Transept E window, four C15 figures in the heads of the tracery. – PLATE. Chalice 1630; Salver 1744; Flagon by *Francis Crump* 1766.

CHARLTON ADAM

5020

ST PETER AND ST PAUL. Structurally, it seems, C14, *see* chancel arch and tower arch. The external appearance of the church however entirely Perp. The S porch is attached to the S transeptal chapel. Restored 1892 by *H. Wilson.* – PULPIT. Jacobean; simple. – PAINTINGS. Trecento Crucifixus with angels in the trefoiled ends of the cross. Copy of one in the Accademia at Florence. – Virgin and two Saints, whole figures, Venetian, *c.* 1500 (from the Zouche Collection at Parham, Sussex). – PLATE. Chalice of *c.* 1573; Paten by *Richard Bayley* 1718. – MONUMENTS. Thomas Basket † 1592; no effigy. Standing wall-monument, strap cartouche with inscription between short columns; pediment. – Two C17 Strangways monuments, slate plates with inscriptions, as they are often to be found in this part of Somerset.

THE ABBEY. E of the church. Late Elizabethan house probably incorporating earlier masonry. The buttressing of the w and s walls especially indicates a pre-Reformation date. Mullioned windows with hood-moulds, except for the Drawing Room on the first floor which has cross windows. The room is panelled and has an overmantel, also of wood, with three pairs of colonnettes.

CHARLTON HORETHORNE

6020

ST PETER AND ST PAUL. Perp w tower, not large, but with some ambition. Set-back buttresses with tiny pinnacles. Statue niche above the w window, two-light bell-openings with Somerset tracery. Gargoyles, battlements, pinnacles. Higher NE stair-turret. The church is much renewed (1863), but there is evidence of the C12 (s aisle) and of an early C14 enlargement to take a low ogee-headed recess. Early C14 also the chancel E and S windows. The S arcade is certainly C19. The N arcade is later C14. It has low octagonal piers and double-chamfered arches. There are also in this aisle two large twin recesses with ogee gables carrying finials. E of these, in the corner, two fine statue niches on ornate corbels. One is of the C14, the other of the early C15. The latter with a woman's head (horned head-dress) and two small figures is specially good. Remains of original colouring in them. – PLATE. Chalice and Cover by *Orenge*, dated 1603; Paten 1634.

MANOR HOUSE. Large early C17 building with mullioned and transomed windows. Symmetrically arranged gabled W front. E side with a semicircular stair-turret. N façade with central porch. The garden in front of this side has good piers and faces the pretty triangular village green.

On its N side MONKS PLACE, smaller, but also with mullioned windows and a central porch, and VINE COTTAGE, dated 1634. The front windows are deprived of their mullions.

WATERLOO CRESCENT, $\frac{1}{2}$ m. S. Plain and urban-looking crescent (cf. Compton Pauncefoot). The name dates it.

CHARLTON MACKRELL

5020

ST MARY. Nave, transepts, chancel, and crossing tower. So much restored *c.* 1847 that it is now almost entirely a C19 church. Crossing tower on Perp piers of the standard four-hollows section, but treated so broadly that a C14 date is likely. The tower has two-light bell-openings, battlements, and a higher stair-turret with spirelet. The N transept N window is the only valid piece of information on the medieval fenestration of the church, a fine and fanciful design of *c.* 1330–40. Five lights with a large circle at the top divided perversely by means of reticulation. Flowing tracery of a simple kind in the two-light side parts. – BENCHES. Straight-headed, of the early C16, but also some with poppy-heads. – STAINED GLASS. The W window an exceptionally complete display of pre-archaeological, still painterly, early C19 glass. Ten figures. The chancel glass would fit the date 1847. – PLATE. Chalice 1570. – MONUMENTS. Two mutilated and defaced effigies, husband and wife, carved of one block of Purbeck marble. Late C13; said to be William le Lyt, the first Lyte of Lytes Cary.

THE COURT. Built as the rectory, probably in 1792 (date on a gable in the stable-yard). Embattled S front with sash-windows and Gothick porch. Inside a tripartite screen in Gothick forms between hall and staircase. The staircase is elegantly curved in the Georgian fashion, but has an iron handrail with thin Gothic details. Indications of an earlier part at the back.

MANOR FARM, at the end of the parish. The former manor

house of Charlton Adam. Medieval house with hall in the middle, solar at one end, and kitchen and offices at the other. In the present drawing room the medieval fireplace surrounds and behind the drawing room, at its w end, the spiral staircase. Much altered *c.* 1710–20, when the hall was divided into a dining room and a vestibule, and a suite of rooms was added on the N side. In the dining room attractive wall paintings of landscape. Most of the motifs are imaginary, but on one is Glastonbury Tor and on another the Eddystone lighthouse in the shape in which it was rebuilt in 1709.

ROMAN CEMETERY. Discovered in the 1930s and ruthlessly quarried away.

HURCOTT. Remains of a defensive Earthwork that may be part of a destroyed prehistoric camp.

CHARLTON MUSGROVE
7020

ST STEPHEN. Humble w tower, but complete with two-light bell-openings, battlements, gargoyles, and pinnacles. Nave and chancel, low and panelled chancel arch. – FONT. Octagonal with carved flowers, cross, etc., on square panels. It might be of *c.* 1660–70, re-tooled. – PLATE. Chalice Cover 1573; Saucer 1633.

CHARLTON HOUSE. Built *c.* 1810. The Jacobean-looking porch is a copy of that of the House at Charlton Horethorne.

CHEDDON FITZPAINE
2020

ST MARY. Thin unbuttressed w tower of the C13: *see* the lancet openings and the small size of the arch towards the nave, even if this was later given Perp details. Perp pierced arcaded parapet. s aisle with pierced quatrefoiled parapet. The church was over-restored in 1861. Three-bay arcade with standard piers (four-hollows), on the N side with capitals with leaf bands, on the S side with angels, as at Taunton near by. Four-centred arches. – BENCHES. Straight-headed, with tracery, flowers, a double eagle, etc. Unusually broad frames to these motifs. – PLATE. Paten 1712.

CHEDZOY
3030

ST MARY. Historically the aisle arcades come first. They are of five bays with circular piers, simple moulded capitals, and

double-chamfered arches; clearly C13 work. Then follows the
chancel. N lancets with pointed trefoiled rere-arches, s window
of two lights with Y-tracery now, but the broad trefoiled arch
apparently original, Sedilia with shafts and pointed trefoiled
arches. A s chapel was attached to the chancel, but has disappeared except for the circular pier with four attached shafts,
which is visible outside, and the chamfered arches of the two
bays of the chapel. The E window is now Perp, but the chancel
must be late C13. Contemporary perhaps the s aisle with its
doorway, the s porch, and one two-light window with bar
tracery. The Perp work is more in evidence. The w tower is
of three stages, not too grand, with set-back buttresses ending
in long shafts for former pinnacles, with w doorway (leaves
in the spandrels), a four-light w window, two-light windows
on all sides above, and then the twin two-light bell-openings
flanked by thin shafts with pinnacles. Top battlements with
quatrefoils and inconspicuous pinnacles. The N aisle is
narrower than the s aisle. Both are quite straightforward. On
the s porch the initials of Abbot R. Bere of Glastonbury
(1493–1524), but also a date 1579. Inside, a Perp clerestory
rises above the C13 arcade. The tower arch is panelled; so
are the four arches into the transepts.* Handsome ceiled
wagon-roof in the chancel with carved wallplate and bosses.
– PULPIT. With tall linen-fold panels; is it Early Elizabethan? –
ORGAN SEAT. Made up of a panel dated 1620 and filled with
the typical blank arches in two tiers. – LECTERN. The
stand is a big baluster. – BENCHES. With broad tracery, and
also leaf motifs, mostly in geometrical patterns. On one end
an M with a crown, that is Queen Mary (1554–9). – s DOOR.
Excellent C16 work with oblong panels with vigorously carved
lozenges in them; heavily studded. – Badly treated remains of a
COPE of c. 1500, transferred to modern silk. The figures are
the Virgin and Saints under canopies, and wheeled cherubim.
– PLATE. Chalice and Cover 1573; Flagon 1758. – BRASS to
Richard Sydenham. In armour, c. 1490, a 4 ft 3 in. figure;
nave floor.

CHILLINGTON

3010

St JAMES. Small, Perp, with bell-cote, s porch, and panelled
chancel arch. The s transept was added in Victorian times. –
PLATE. Chalice and Cover 1575; Chalice 1800.

* But above the w arch into the N transept is an inserted Elizabethan arch
with much pretty leaf decoration.

CHILTHORNE DOMER

St Mary. Nave and chancel. No tower, but one of the heavy, lantern-like corbelled-out bell-cotes (cf. Brympton, Ashington, etc.). The chancel is of *c.* 1300, *see* a cusped lancet window, with pointed cinquefoiled rere-arch inside (E window 1883) and the chancel arch, double-chamfered on big head corbels. Nave Dec (see two N windows). There is no W window. The nave is embattled, even up the slopes of the W gable. S porch with unribbed pointed tunnel-vault. – FONT. Octagonal, Perp, with quatrefoil frieze. – PULPIT. Jacobean, complete with back and tester. – PEWS, also Jacobean. The ends have shell-tops with finials. – PLATE. Set of 1817. – MONUMENT. Knight with mail-coif and shield; *c.* 1275.

CHILTON CANTELO

St James. 1865 by *Sir Arthur Blomfield* (GR), but with none of the robustness of some other earlier buildings of his. Original Perp W tower with set-back buttresses ending in attached pinnacles below the battlements. Further pinnacles on the battlements, and corbelled-out intermediate pinnacles in the middle of the sides. Higher NE stair-turret. Three-light bell-openings with Somerset tracery. Quatrefoil frieze below them. Panelled tower arch inside. – PLATE. Chalice and Cover 1573; Paten early C18.

CHILTON POLDEN

St Edward. 1888–9. – PLATE. Chalice and Cover early C18; Salver 1775. – MONUMENT. Tablet with a draped urn, 1776 by *James Allen* of Bristol.

Chilton Priory, ½ m. S, on the main road. Built in the first half of the C19 for Stradling, the antiquary and collector, it is said by a self-taught craftsman, *William Halliday* (see Othery). The house is built in the likeness of a medieval church, with W tower and S porch. The ground falls so steeply to the N that from the road one can hardly see the castellated two-storeyed house below.

CHILTON TRINITY

Holy Trinity. Small, Perp, of no interest. – PULPIT. Jacobean, and of a specially pretty design, with two blank arches on top of each other in each panel, each arch filled with a big flower. – PLATE. Chalice and Cover by *Ions* of Exeter 1574.

CHIPSTABLE

ALL SAINTS. 1869 by *Ferrey* (GR) in the Geometrical style. In a small village deep in the hills. What remains of the old church is the W tower with set-back buttresses and battlements, and the handsome capitals of the three-bay arcade, with demi-figures of angels on all four sides. – BENCH ENDS. Square-headed, of *c.* 1530. On one of them a pestle, on another a huntsman. – STAINED GLASS. By *Clayton & Bell* (MHLG). – PLATE. Chalice 1792.

CHISELBOROUGH

ST PETER AND ST PAUL. E.E. crossing tower, *see* three of the four arches inside, and some lancets outside, plain and with moulded frame. The double-chamfered arches inside start almost from the ground; no responds, no capitals. The tower, behind a plain parapet, is surmounted by a fine Perp spire, with considerable entasis. It is decorated by a band of pointed quatrefoils. The nave has big lancet windows with buttresses between and is not divided by arcades inside. It is of 1842 (architect *E. L. Bracebridge*; GR), the chancel is C17. But between nave and crossing slight Norman evidence appears – a capital and two bases of colonnettes. This in 1911 was blown up into a full Norman arch. Inside the crossing a star-vault on moulded corbels, put in perhaps as a strengthening when the spire was added. – PLATE. Chalice and Cover 1571.

(STRAP FARM HOUSE. 1576. With mullioned windows and cambered door-head. MHLG.)

CHURCHSTANTON

ST PETER AND ST PAUL. A Perp church, except for the plain unbuttressed W tower which in its lower parts looks *c.* 1300, *see* the mouldings of the W doorway and the lancet window above. Perp nave and S aisle windows. The S aisle arcade is uncommonly ornate, more Devon than Somerset. Piers with a section with four main shafts and, in the diagonals, a wave moulding and another shaft. Capitals and broad horizontal

bands of leaves. Finely moulded arches. s chapel divided
from the chancel by an arch which clearly contained a tomb
originally. The capitals again have leaf-bands. – FONT.
Norman, square, and roughly hewn at the angles for heads to
be carved. The intended design is of the Cornwall type of
Bodmin. – PULPIT. Jacobean. – West Gallery made up of
BENCH ENDS. – BOX PEWS 1830. – STAINED GLASS. Fragments in N windows.

0030   CLATWORTHY

ST MARY. Whitewashed. Plain w tower with diagonal buttresses
and battlements. s porch with wagon-roof. – PULPIT. Late
Georgian; plain. – ORGAN CASE. Pretty, simple Late Georgian
Gothic. – STAINED GLASS. Chancel; of the time of the
restoration of 1865. – PLATE. Chalice 1757; Almsdish by
Robert Sharp 1797.

CLATWORTHY CASTLE. An Iron Age camp w of the village
on the wooded slopes of the Brendon hills. Its form is a rough
triangle, about 260 by 420 yards. The bank still rises in places
15 ft above the foot of its ditch.

0040   CLEEVE ABBEY

Cleeve Abbey was founded in 1198 by William de Romare
for Cistercians. It was colonized from Revesley. Of the buildings erected from the end of the C12 to the later C13 a good
deal survives or can be traced, but the most remarkable
survival at Cleeve is the Refectory, sumptuously rebuilt in
the C16. The group of buildings as it is now kept by the
Ministry of Works gives an impressive experience of life in a
small Cistercian house just before the Reformation.

   The CHURCH has to be traced from exposed foundations
to the N of the principal remaining buildings. Only the s wall
of its s aisle, pale rose-coloured, as are the other buildings,
stands high up, but as it bordered on the cloister it has no
windows nor indeed any other details except for a small
trefoil-headed blocked doorway. The s transept s wall also
stands, being the N wall of the adjoining monastic buildings.
The church was of what can be called the standard Cistercian
plan, nave and aisles (of six bays), crossing and transept, and
a straight-headed chancel flanked on either side by two also
straight-headed but shorter and narrower chapels giving on

to the transepts. That is the same as existed at Fontenay, the earliest surviving house in France, and constitutes the basic plan for Cistercian houses of some ambition about 1135–75 (cf. in England e.g. Tintern and Roche).

Adjoining the s transept on the s is the former Sacristy, a small room with the Cistercian feature of an oculus window to the E. Then follows another small room and then the well-preserved VESTIBULE to the CHAPTER HOUSE. The usual windows l. and r. of the entrance with their plate tracery date this part to the second half of the c13. The doorway is double-chamfered with a continuous moulding. The Vestibule is vaulted in two low broad bays with single-chamfered ribs on short corbels. The Chapter House itself was higher. It had vaults of the same kind, and only one square bay. Next follows the stone-stair to the monks' DORMITORY. This is at Cleeve preserved in an exceptionally complete form, though its roof is reconstruction. It stretched all along the E range of the Cloister and beyond the s wall of the s range. It has plain small single-chamfered lancet windows. The stairs into the church are at its N end, close to its s end on the E side is a large door-way which is said to have led to the Infirmary.* Below the E end of the Dormitory was the vaulted Day Room (see the springers of the vaults). It has two handsome s windows, tre-foiled with a quatrefoil in plate tracery above. Otherwise, what still represents the c13 is in the s range one doorway, with one order of colonnettes. This now is the entry to the Refectory stairs, but the c13 REFECTORY was on the ground floor and oddly enough at r. angles to the s range. It came out as far as the s end of the Dormitory, and its extent is known from the extremely interesting TILED PAVEMENT which has been found and exposed. The tiles are similar to those of Salisbury Chapter House and Clarendon Palace and contain, besides foliage and combat scenes, the arms of England, of Richard Plantagenet, son of Henry III's brother Edmund, of the same as Emperor (i.e. after 1257), and of his wife (a de Clare) whom he married in 1272.

The s range was drastically remodelled by William Dovell, the last Abbot (1507–37). He subdivided the room on the ground floor into kitchens, etc. Two of the rooms here have garderobes in the thickness of the wall, as a flushing stream

---

* Where was the Rere-Dorter or the principal lavatories? The Infirmary and its chapel were partially excavated by the late St John Hope, but the results are unpublished.

runs underneath this range and comes out of the E wall of the
Dormitory. The new REFECTORY above is one of the finest
rooms in Somerset. It has five large and wide regularly
spaced three-light windows with depressed pointed heads to
the cloister garth and to the S one plus the main fireplace plus
three. The windows are finely detailed with the crisp cusping
characteristic of the Dunster workshop which must have
made them (cf. also Selworthy, Luccombe, etc.). Another
window of the same style with a transom is to the S of the five
on the N side, a little higher up. Inside, next to the (C19) fireplace, is the Reader's Desk, a stone niche in the thickness of
the wall, up some steps. The Refectory is not only a light, it is
also a lofty room. It possesses one of the best wagon-roofs in
Somerset, with angels supporting principals and sub-principals. To emphasize the principals the angels come forward as
if the roof were a hammerbeam roof, which it is not. Pierced
arcading above the principals. By this means a clear articula-
tion is introduced in a roofing system which otherwise tends
to be a little uniform.*

The CLOISTER walls survive in only one place, though
beam-holes indicate their height everywhere. In the W range,
which has been altered more than the others, a stretch of
cloister was renewed by Dovell. This has four-light openings
with Tudor arches. The Abbot's quarters lay in this range
or projected from it.

Finally the GATEHOUSE to the NW of the church. It was
built in the C13 and altered by Dovell and shows his arms and
an inscription over the entrance which runs as follows: Porta
patens esto/ Nulli claudaris honesto. Large two-centred archways with continuous double-chamfers. No separate entry for
pedestrians. A four-light straight-headed window above to
the outside and inside. Above this niches for sculpture. On
the inside a Christ Crucified in shallow relief, on the outside a
small Madonna. The archway was originally divided into two
bays by attached piers and vaults. In the walls three broad
blank arches. What was their purpose?

CLOSWORTH

ALL SAINTS. Perp, much restored in 1875. W tower with
diagonal buttresses and large two-light bell-openings filled

---

* Mr E. Tompkins comments that the roof is not a wagon-roof either. It
ought to be called a half-hammerbeam roof.

Scenery: Luccombe

(a) *Scenery:* Dunster

(b) *Scenery:* Porlock Bay

(a) *Scenery:* Exmoor

(b) *Prehistory:* Ham Hill, fortified settlement

Early Norman: Milborne Port, capitals

4

(a) *Early Norman*: Milborne Port, transept arch

(b) *Norman*: Stogursey

Norman: Stoke-sub-Hamdon, tympanum with Tree of Life, Lamb and Cross, Leo, and Sagittarius

6

Norman: Langport, tympanum with Lamb and Cross, two angels, and two saints

Norman: Culbone

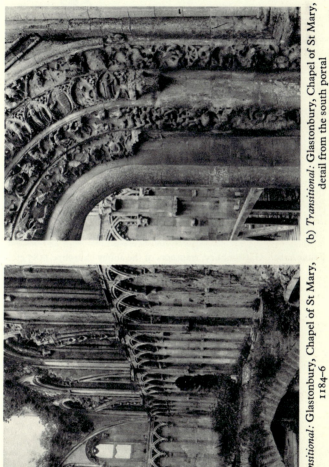

(a) *Transitional*: Glastonbury, Chapel of St Mary, 1184–6

(b) *Transitional*: Glastonbury, Chapel of St Mary, detail from the south portal

9

Transitional: Glastonbury, transepts of the abbey church, *c.*1185 etc.

(a) *Early English:* Bawdrip, detail from the tower arch

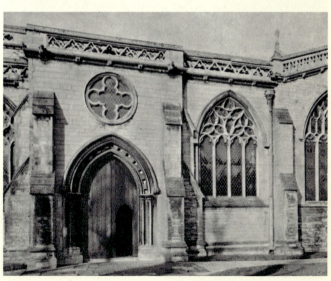

(b) *Decorated and Perpendicular:* Bridgwater

Perpendicular: Brympton d'Evercy, church, and, on the left, house (mostly *c*.1520)

(a) *Perpendicular Exteriors*: Crewkerne, west front

(b) *Perpendicular Exteriors*: Ilminster, crossing and south porch

13

Perpendicular Exteriors: Yeovil

Perpendicular Exteriors: Crowcombe

(a) *Perpendicular Towers:*
Evercreech

(b) *Perpendicular Towers:*
Huish Episcopi

Perpendicular Towers: Taunton, St Mary

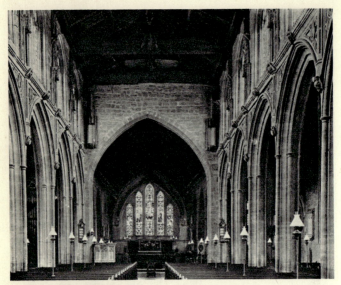

(a) *Perpendicular Interiors:* Martock

(b) *Perpendicular Interiors:* Stogumber

18

Perpendicular Roofs: Brent Knoll

Perpendicular Roofs: Weston Zoyland

Seventeenth-Century Gothic: Low Ham (*c.*1620–69),
west window

(a) *Seventeenth-Century Gothic:* East Brent; the ceiling is of 1637

(b) *Twentieth-Century Gothic:* Brushford, Herbert Chapel by
Sir Edwin Lutyens, 1926

22

Church Furnishings: Reredos from Wellington,
now at Taunton Castle, *c.*1380

(b) *Church Furnishings*: Meare, south door, probably early fourteenth century

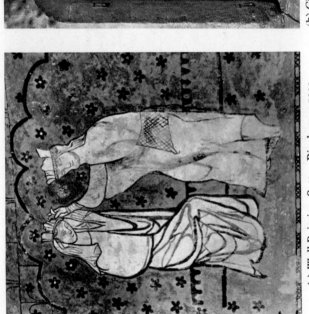

(a) *Wall Painting*: Sutton Bingham, c.1300

24

(b) *Church Furnishings*: Broomfield, bench end

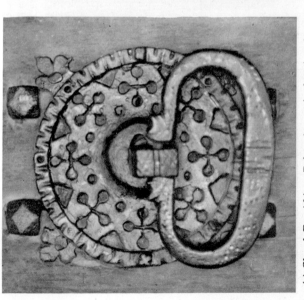

(a) *Church Furnishings*: Baltonsborough, door knocker, probably fifteenth century

(a) *Church Furnishings*: Bishop's Lydeard, bench end with windmill

(b) *Church Furnishings*: Brent Knoll, bench end with the fox as an abbot preaching to birds. Below, two apes roasting a pig

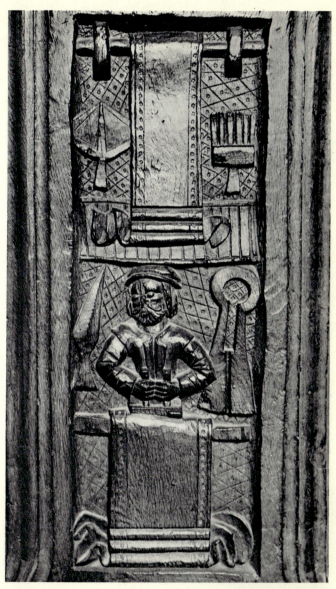

Church Furnishings: Spaxton, bench end with a fuller and his tools

(a) *Church Furnishings*: Crowcombe, font

(b) *Church Furnishings*: Trull, pulpit

28

Church Furnishings: Carhampton, rood screen

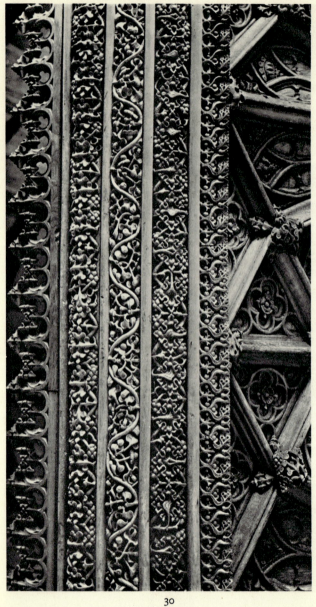

Church Furnishings: Halse, detail from the rood screen

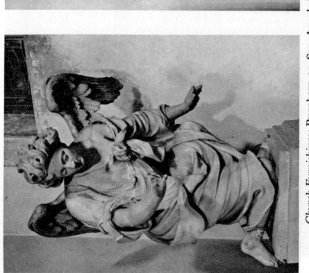

Church Furnishings: Burnham-on-Sea, Angels from the former altar of the chapel at Whitehall Palace. 1686, by Grinling Gibbons and Arnold Quellin

Church Furnishings: North Petherton, stained glass by
C. E. Kempe, 1896

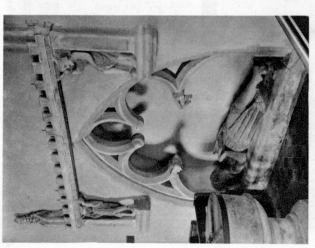

(a) and (b) *Church Monuments, fourteenth and fifteenth centuries: Pendomer, c.1320, and Porlock, c.1460*

33

(a) and (b) *Church Monuments, fourteenth and sixteenth centuries:* Withycombe, *c.*1300, and White Lackington, before 1583

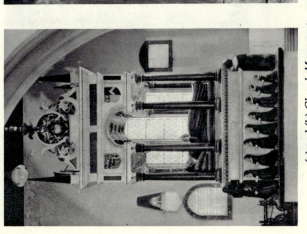

(a) and (b) *Church Monuments, seventeenth century*: Sir John Popham † 1607, Wellington, and George Farewell † 1609, Bishop's Hull

Church Monuments, early eighteenth century: John Baron Poulett
† 1649, Hinton St George

(a) *Church Monuments:* Detail from the monument to James Bernard
† 1805, Crowcombe. By Sir Richard Westmacott

(b) The Mace of the Town of Ilchester, thirteenth century.
The head is 7½ in. long and of brass

(a) *Secular Architecture:* Lytes Cary, the chapel on the left *c.*1343, the rest mainly *c.*1515–20 (*Copyright Country Life*)

(b) *Secular Architecture:* Lytes Cary, Hall roof (*Copyright Country Life*)

(a) *Secular Architecture:* Cothay Manor House
(*Copyright Country Life*)

(b) *Secular Architecture:* West Bower Manor House, near Durleigh

Secular Architecture: Glastonbury, George Inn

Secular Architecture: South Petherton, King Ine's Palace,
bay-window

(b) *Secular Architecture*: Preston Plucknett, Abbey Farm, kitchen chimney

(a) *Secular Architecture*: Porlock, Doverhay Manor House, window

42

Secular Architecture: Preston Plucknett, Abbey Farm, the Great Barn

Monastic Architecture: Glastonbury, the Kitchen,
probably later fourteenth century

Monastic Architecture: Muchelney, fireplace in the Abbot's Lodgings, early sixteenth century

(a) *Monastic Architecture:* Cleeve Abbey, Refectory, early sixteenth century. On the left the thirteenth-century Dormitory

(b) *The time of Henry VIII:* Barrington Court, begun *c.*1515

The time of Henry VIII: Montacute, porch from Clifton Maybank (Dorset), *c.*1535

(a) *Elizabethan:* Cothelstone, perhaps *c.*1560

(b) *Elizabethan:* Chard Grammar School, 1583

Elizabethan: Montacute, *c.*1590 (*Copyright Country Life*)

(a) *Elizabethan:* Montacute, the Library

(b) *Jacobean:* East Quantoxhead, overmantel (*Copyright Country Life*)

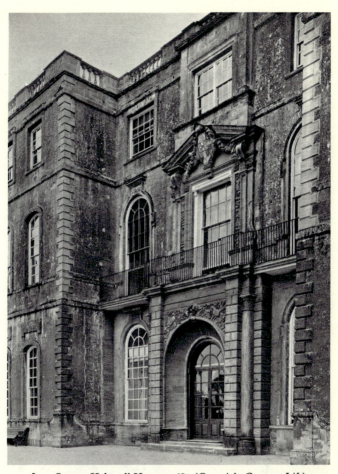

Late Stuart: Halswell House, 1689 (*Copyright Country Life*)

Late Stuart: Dunster Castle, plaster ceiling of the Dining Room, 1681
(*Copyright Country Life*)

(b) *Queen Anne*: Ven House, *c.*1700–20
(*Copyright Country Life*)

(a) *Late Stuart*: Dunster Castle, staircase,
*c.*1680

53

(a) *Georgian:* Bridgwater, Castle Street, begun in 1723

(b) *Georgian:* Crowcombe Court, begun probably in 1725
(*Copyright Country Life*)

Georgian: Crowcombe Court, staircase, *c.*1740
(*Copyright Country Life*)

(a) *Georgian:* Bridgwater, Market Hall, *c.*1825. By Benjamin Baker

(b) *The Twentieth Century:* Hestercombe, the Gardens.
By Sir Edwin Lutyens (*Copyright Country Life*)

with Somerset tracery. Higher stair-turret. Gargoyles, battlements, pinnacles. To the s and n on the lowest stage statue niches (n blocked). On the s side, on the second stage, a small window with, above its apex, a relief of three praying figures. This cuts across the string between the second and third stages. Towards the w on the third stage a statue niche. Panelled tower arch to the nave. No aisles. Porch with pointed ribbed tunnel-vault. In the chancel one original lancet window (drawing in Braikenridge's Collinson). This dates the chancel back to the c13. – PULPIT. Jacobean, with tall blank arches and panels containing lozenges. – PLATE. Chalice 1685.

COCKWOOD see STEYNING MANOR

COLE see PITCOMBE

COMBE FLOREY

1030

ST PETER AND ST PAUL. Red sandstone, even the window tracery red. The (rebuilt) n aisle wall contains what is now the oldest work. It dates from c. 1300. Cinquefoiled rere-arches to windows which were considerably widened and provided with Y-tracery in the early c19. In one window the remains of the original jambs can be seen. Perp w tower with diagonal buttresses, battlements, and pinnacles. The chancel was rebuilt c. 1850. Three-bay n arcade with piers of standard section (four hollows) and handsome capitals with angel-busts. In the tower arch also two angels at capital height. – PULPIT. Perp. The panels carved with the same motifs as in dados of rood screens. – BENCHES. Of the type of the district, straight-headed, with much intricate tracery. – PLATE, Chalice and Cover 1573; Set by *William Fawdery* 1727. – MONUMENT. Life-size effigies of a cross-legged Knight and two ladies, probably his two wives, early c14, with subtle differences in the drapery of the two female figures. – Brass to Florence Fraunceis c. 1550, the figure 12 in. long (behind the organ). The brass must have been made when her husband died in 1485. His brass is lost. – Brass to Nicholas Francis † 1526, the figure 28 in. long.

MANOR HOUSE. The Gatehouse is of 1593 and was originally four-storeyed. Four-light transomed window above the archway. More mullioned windows. Gable. Stair-turret on what

5—s.s.

is now the outside. (Original fireplace, frieze, and ceiling inside.) The original house was between the gatehouse and the church. The present house is up the hillside. It was built *c.* 1675 and received a new front in 1730. Five bays and two storeys, with pedimented doorway and ground-floor windows with Gibbs surrounds. (Nice staircase of *c.* 1735.)

COMBE ST NICHOLAS
3010

St Nicholas. Evidence of a Norman church is the fragment of a N doorway now part of the N aisle arcade of the present church. The doorway had two orders of columns. The stone was grey, not brown like the arcade. To the C13 or early C14 belongs the lower part of the W tower with a triple-chamfered E arch dying into the imposts and with cusped lancets and rere-arches. Perhaps contemporary with this are the chancel side windows with rere-arches and the chancel Piscina with a continuous roll-moulding. The rest is Perp: upper part of the modest W tower, the not very high aisle arcades of five bays with standard piers (four hollows), the aisle walls, porch, and chapels, partly embattled, and the two rood-stair turrets. The N arcade accommodated the fragment of the Norman doorway in spite of the irregularities which that enforced – a sign of remarkable piety towards a distant past. The N and S chapels have panelled arches towards the chancel, the S chapel a depressed four-centred arch towards the aisle.

See p.73 Northay Barrow. A Bronze Age barrow that yielded funerary relics of its age. Further Bronze Age remains were found on Combe Beacon.

COMBE SYDENHAM
0030
2 m. W of Stogumber

Mainly Elizabethan, but incorporating substantial remains of a medieval house. In the W front buttresses and two-light transomed windows with cusped pointed lights. Nearer the N end on the upper floor five large Elizabethan windows with three transoms. Originally there were more to the S. They are now blocked. The S front has an Elizabethan porch with arched entrance on pilasters. Vault inside with Sydenham initials and the date 1580. The windows of the S front are all later and uninteresting. Inside, behind the porch, remains of the medieval Hall range, a vast partly uncovered fireplace, and the remains of a newel staircase between it and the screens passage. The hall originally reached up to the roof, where the timbers still remain. It was horizontally divided in Elizabeth's time. In the Drawing Room w of the Hall good Elizabethan plaster ceiling and frieze. Another in the room above the drawing room. A larger staircase was built into a square projecting tower in the re-entrant angle between the s and w blocks. It is said that more towers existed in the Middle Ages. The staircase itself seems early c19.

COMBWICH
2040

The village lies on the river Parrett in the flats of its estuary. The character of the landscape here is not Somerset, but rather East Anglian or even Dutch.

St Peter. By *J. Knowles*, 1870. The s porch tower is such as only the sixties could design. Gables cut off at half their height and broaches in the diagonals lead from square to octagon. Then eight steep gables and a spire. Dec detail. Inside the polygonal apse thick gabled arcading. All foliage naturalistic. – The Stained Glass is of the period.

COMPTON DUNDON
4030

St Andrew, Dundon. A remarkable early c14 chancel, with an original treatment of the five-light e window. In the head a kind of irregular clover-leaf. Sedilia with three ogee arches. Perp w tower with battlements and low tiled pyramid roof. Perp nave windows. Original wagon-roofs. – Pulpit 1628, tucked extremely prettily into the upper opening of the roodloft staircase, and with two-tiered balustrading to its r. – Stained Glass. Many original fragments in nave windows and one chancel window. – Plate. Chalice and Cover 1570.
Trays Farm, Compton. The projecting wing on the l. has buttresses and on the e side a small circular window with a wheel of mouchettes; c14 work probably, although there was a revival of the motif, especially in wood, in the early c16.
Compton Dundon Camp. Iron Age camp on Dundon Hill. The Hill rises nearly 300 ft above the plain, and the whole of the hill-top is crowned with a wall of earth and stones, in places 10 ft high. It is sited in a position that is impregnable. At the southern tip of the camp is a mound 20 ft high known

as DUNDON BEACON. It may have been thrown up as a primitive watchtower with spoil from the ditch. The camp may have served as an outpost for the settlement at Glastonbury.

On Winsford Hill stands the LONGSTONE. This is a standing stone, 3 ft 6 in. high and 14 in. wide, with the rough inscription: *Carataci Nepus* (The Nephew of Caratacus). It is thought to date from the C5 and may be either a gravestone or a boundary-mark.

COMPTON PAUNCEFOOT
6020

ST ANDREW. Low Perp W tower with diagonal buttresses and plain parapet. Stone spire with band of ornament. Nave and aisles under separate roofs. S porch doorway with big foliage spandrels. Much renewed. Ten marks were left in 1485 by Sir Walter Pauncefoot for the building of the church and £20 for 'the making of myne ile there'. Inside three-bay arcade with standard piers (four hollows). Panelled chancel arch. In the S aisle E bay below the S window frieze of cusped quatrefoils with shields and part of a stone inscription to Anne Whitney † 1535. – STAINED GLASS. Five windows by *Capronnier* of Brussels, 1860s and 70s. – W window clearly by *Kempe*; 1896. – PLATE. Paten 1697; Chalice and Paten by *Thomas Tearle* 1728.

Opposite the church to the SW the OLD RECTORY, Georgian, and behind this a little to the W THE CRESCENT, a quarter-circle of five cottages, quite big and placed with wooden porches. The date 18.. is illegible (cf. Charlton Horethorne).

COMPTON CASTLE. Built about 1825 for Mr Hussey Hunt. A delightfully situated Gothick castle, the E front overlooking small hills and lawns and a serpentine lake with a small waterfall at its S end. The E front is not broad. It is castellated and has round angle turrets, two bay-windows, and a tall porch with two-centred arch. Behind the façade and the lake a semi-circle marked out by slim round and square towers. The back of the house with a deep courtyard between two wings is older, probably C17.

SIGWELL'S CAMP. An Iron Age Encampment, now largely ploughed-out. It was triangular in shape.

CONYGAR HILL *see* DUNSTER

COPLEY *see* KINGWESTON

CORFE

2010

St Nicholas. Neo-Norman, 1842, with tower and aisle of 1858. The older part by *B. Ferrey*, the newer by *Giles* (GR). – FONT. Circular, Norman, with interlaced arcading. – PLATE. Chalice and Cover 1573; Plate 1768.

BARTON GRANGE. Big and now rather shapeless. It is the remains of the kitchen and office wing of a large C16 mansion. The mansion had big four-light mullioned windows with arched lights. A model is at the Taunton Museum.

CORTON DENHAM

6020

St Andrew. 1869–70. By *Charles Baker Green*. – PLATE. Chalice and Cover by *Orenge* 1573; Paten 1677.

COSSINGTON

3040

St Mary. Mostly Perp, blue lias, simple, and much renewed. In the chancel a N recess which is cinquefoiled, also the remains of a small N window and the rere-arches of S windows. All this is of the C13. Remains of a S transept arch. Porch entrance C14. – PLATE. Chalice and Cover 1573; Chalice and Paten 1704. – MONUMENTS. Outside the porch effigy of a Lady, *c.* 1375; in a decaying state. – John Brent † 1524 and wife; brass in the chancel floor; good 2 ft 9 in. figures.

COSSINGTON HOUSE, Neo-Tudor, 1863.

COTHAY

0020

Cothay is one of the most perfect smaller English manor houses of the late C15. It is not large, looks warm and comfortable in its reddish brown stone, and has all the picturesque informality of plan and elevation which the Renaissance was so anxious to get rid of.

The house is approached through a GATEHOUSE and a forecourt. The gatehouse is heavily buttressed and embattled. On the inside it has a higher embattled stair-turret. Rooms on two storeys lie to the N of the gateway. This has a four-centred head. Above the gateway to the outside is the coat of arms of Walter Bluet and his wife, the owners from 1481 onwards. Cothay had belonged to the Bluets from the middle of the C14, but not been inhabited by them until 1457.

The front of the house, that is the E side, appears with two cross-gables at the ends and attached to the l. of them the smaller gable of the two-storeyed porch. The wings as well as the recessed centre are buttressed. The windows are upright and mullioned with four-centred head to each light – the typical form of c. 1500. To the r. of the porch the two windows are transomed, the sign of the Hall behind them, and on the first floor of the r. (N) wing is another transomed window, the sign of the Solar behind. The window below this is Elizabethan, of timber and mullioned and transomed. The W elevation is even less regular, owing to the addition in the early C17 of a Dining Room where originally the back door out of the screens passage had been. This projection lies now immediately by the side of the big hall chimney. The S wing of the C15 house projects almost as far as the Dining Room, the N wing has the transomed back window of the Solar and above it in the gable a pretty oculus window with a wheel of three mouchettes. In the middle of this wing, facing N, is a projection for a spiral staircase. Another staircase, probably inserted later, leads up from the middle of the screens passage. The passage is entered from the porch by an original door. The Hall screen is preserved, a simple structure of boards and muntins. Above it on projecting beam ends is the gallery, closed in, it seems, from the beginning and only opened towards the Hall by a mullioned window. The gallery leads to the chapel which is above the porch. The Hall has a fine strong timber roof, with moulded arched braces supporting collar-beams and three tiers of curved wind-braces. At the dais end early C17 panelling. The large and somewhat sombre Solar has a roof just like that of the Hall. Below it are the Parlour with moulded beams and early C17 panelling and the Library, once a store-room. Early C17 also the panelling of the Dining Room behind the Hall. Here is the only more ambitious fireplace in the house, strapwork and arabesque decoration and four small standing figures in the overmantel. In the S wing on the upper floor are two more rooms, and in these interesting wall-paintings have survived. They date from the late C15 and are among the earliest remaining in English houses. In the Gold Room the principal survival is a standing figure of the Virgin within a large roundel. Sun and Moon and some architecture behind the figure. The Green Room has moulded beams, a frieze of painted parchment scrolls with inscriptions, and figures below. One of them is the Virgin standing and the infant Christ travelling towards her, very small, along a bunch of rays emanating from the hand of God. So the scene represents the Immaculate Conception. Another figure is a man in modish clothes.

COTHELSTONE
1030

ST THOMAS OF CANTERBURY. Immediately behind the manor house. Red sandstone. Mostly Perp. The w tower with Victorian top (1864). Inside, the s chapel earlier than the rest. Two bays, divided by a circular pier. The w respond a moulded corbel, c. 1200. – PULPIT. Jacobean. – BENCHES. Of the type of the district, straight-headed, with motifs chiefly of intricate tracery and intertwined branches and foliage. – STAINED GLASS. Good small C15 figures in the heads of N chapel windows. – MONUMENTS. Knight and Lady of the late C14. Angels by her head, two squirrels under her feet. – Sir John Stawell † 1603 and wife. Alabaster effigies, well carved.

COTHELSTONE MANOR. Cothelstone is easier to like than to understand. The house is not large and consists of a centre 48a and two projecting wings. In front of the house the gatehouse survives and the two together, in their red stone, form an enchanting whole. The aesthetic appeal is not lowered by the fact that the r. half of the house is largely reconstruction of the C19. Earlier illustrations show that part in ruins. Inside also nothing remains now of special architectural interest. But the exterior of house and gatehouse is fascinating in the details. Whoever designed the house had a passion for baluster and candelabra shapes. They occur everywhere, in the window mullions outside and inside, as colonnettes flanking the doorway, and also for no good reason attached to the middles of the centre and projecting wings. The wings carry big end-gables, the centre has two gabled dormers. The gatehouse also uses the candelabra motif. The centre of the gatehouse is raised and castellated. To the l. and r. of the gateway is a three-light window on the first floor, but on the ground floor a curious composition in which the centre of the three-light window is replaced by a blank shell-headed niche. How should all this be dated? There are no records in existence to suggest a date. Balusters and candelabra are on the whole an early fashion, before 1560 rather than after. The house is in fact called ancient in Thomas Garard's book of 1633. Or could it be later than 1633? The position of Sir John Stawell, the owner of the house, in the Civil War makes that improbable. For the usually accepted date *c.* 1600 there is in any case no documentary support.

To the NE against the hillside a SUMMER HOUSE with canted bay-window. The second bay-window is a C19 duplication. Close by a LOGGIA of three arches at the top of the bowling green. The arches and the pillars supporting them have intermittent rustication.

COTHELSTONE HOUSE. 1818, in the neo-Greek style, ' correct and chaste' as Neale calls it. Three-bay front; the centre bay with giant Ionic columns *in antis*, the sides with tripartite windows flanked by coupled Ionic giant pilasters. Excellent interiors; especially the Drawing Room with original plasterwork and wallpaper, the elongated octagonal Hall, and some Grecian fireplaces. – LODGE with short Tuscan columns to flank the doorway and divers curved projections.

COTTAGES. (In cottages N of Cothelstone House plasterwork of the Elizabethan or Jacobean period is preserved.)

COTHELSTONE BEACON, on Cothelstone Hill, a tower erected in the early C19 as a folly. It is now a ruin and as such a more convincing folly than at the outset.

COW CASTLE *see* SIMONSBATH

CREECH ST MICHAEL

ST MICHAEL. An uncommonly interesting church. The S doorway has an order of colonnettes and a double-chamfered arch. That must be C13. The continuous moulding of the chancel piscina can hardly be later. So a nave and a chancel were in existence when late in the C13 a N tower was built, a fine piece to judge from the sturdy arches which lead into the nave and also into a contemporary N chapel E of the tower. The arches of the tower have three powerful shafts each and there is in addition one intermediate one in the one completely surviving corner. Similar simple shafts between nave and chapel. The rest is Perp (except for the C19 E window), i.e. the upper parts of the tower, the handsome W front with doorway, four-light window, and three niches, the S transept or chapel, the N aisle of one bay, and the one-bay chapel lengthening that of c. 1300. The S transept arch is panelled between thin shafts. The other internal details are also familiar, but the designer has had a special liking for niches. One is in the chancel arch on the N side, two are above each other on the E side of the transept arch, one is in the E respond of the Perp N chapel. Fine wagon-roof in the nave, with broad carved wall-plate; simpler wagon-roof in the chancel. In the S transept some modest plasterwork of c. 1700. – FONT. The typical octagonal type of the Perp style. – BENCH ENDS made up into a reader's desk. The date 1634 may come from a pulpit or communion-table. – ROYAL ARMS, prettily carved, c. 1710. – PLATE. Chalice 1573; two Salvers 1762 and 1791. – MONUMENT. John Keyt † 1739 and his wife † 1757. With a fine completely asymmetrical Rococo surround for the coat of arms.

COLD HARBOUR FARM, Ham, at the extreme E end of the hamlet. Plaster ceiling of 1679 in the sitting room with the Sacrifice of Isaac.

CREWKERNE

4000

ST BARTHOLOMEW. The large parish church of a prosperous town, mostly of the later C15 and early C16. From the E it appears low and spreading below its dominant crossing tower, but from the S and N the surprise is the nave with its tall clerestory and its W front flanked by two polygonal turrets, 13a like the front of Bath Abbey or the Tudor Royal Chapels. Total length 167 ft, height of the tower 80 ft, of the nave 50 ft, total width across the transepts 146 ft. The transepts appear indeed unusually long, and on the N side to the E of the transept there is not only a three-bay chancel chapel, but in addition an outer chapel, in the angle between transept and chancel chapel. Yet the transept projects by one more bay. The whole church is embattled, there are plenty of gargoyles, mostly small, and the windows are all very large, of four lights in the chancel, five in the S transept (S), and – a most unusual lavishness – six in the nave aisles. Six-light windows also in the N transept, seven in the W front. The window here has an embattled transom. The W front also has a large doorway with an ogee gable, quatrefoils in the spandrels, triangular shafts to the l. and r., niches to the l. and r. of these, and busts on top of the niches. One of the two at least seems original. The composition of the W window under its two-centred head is of two side arches and a middle arch of three lights, with the two main mullions running up into the main arch. The source of this composition is Gloucester. The aisle windows, also two-centred, group their six lights into twice two arches of three lights each. Altogether the tracery at Crewkerne is of an unusual variety of designs. The aisles are only three bays long, but the bays are wide. The clerestory windows, having only three lights, are five in number, i.e. they do not correspond to the arcade below. The S porch is two-storeyed. Its doorway has triangular shafts to the l. and r. and blank panelling above with a niche in the middle. Fan-vault inside. The N transept is distinguished from the rest by a quatrefoil frieze below the windows, the S transept by that eminently curious motif, an outer covered seat in the angle between the buttresses at the SE corner. The N and S aisles have pinnacles on the battlements. The crossing tower has set-back buttresses, a SE stair-turret, and coupled corner pinnacles. The bell-openings are of two lights and very long. They descend into the stage below the bell-stage and nearly fill the total height of the tower. They have a transom ranging with the string course between the two stages, and tracery in the head, as well as below the transoms, in addition to the familiar Somerset tracery. The type ought to be compared with Hinton St George and Norton-sub-Hamdon.

Now the inside. The massive crossing-piers, much too heavy for their Perp detail, prove that the crossing is a survival from an earlier church. There is indeed above in the N wall a blocked C13 window. But the most felicitous effect of the interior is the picturesque grouping of chapel behind chapel in the NE corner. There are, in fact, as has been pointed out, a N aisle, a long N chancel chapel, a long N transept, and a one-bay outer chancel chapel, off the transept. Nave of three wide bays with tall, very thin piers of an original design combining the two standard Somerset types. There are four shafts, but in the diagonals specially deep hollows flanked by wave mouldings. The same section repeats in the chancel chapels. The arches are two-centred, the piers answered in the aisles by wall-shafts. The arches of the crossing have broader mouldings. Inside the tower a fan-vault. There is a joint between the tower and the nave indicating a break in the building history. In the NE parts of the church the arches are four-centred. The E wall of the chancel has two doorways l. and r. of the altar. These led into a former sacristy the extent of which is marked by a railing outside. The nave roof is a depressed wagon-roof on angel figures. The N transept has an uncommonly rich panelled ceiling. A similar ceiling over the chapel between transept and chancel aisle. Two early C19 W GALLERIES. – FONT. Square, Norman, of Purbeck marble, with six blank flat arches with segmental heads on each face. – PLATE. Exeter-made Chalice and Cover renovated 1607; Chalice and Cover inscribed 1609; Dish 1683. – BRASS. Chancel S wall, Thomas Golde † 1525, kneeling figure of a Knight.

TOWN

A perambulation of the town will start in the MARKET SQUARE. VICTORIA HALL is free-standing on all sides. It is in a Jacobean style and dates from 1899 and 1901. Along the square several nice Late Georgian houses, especially Nos 7–11, five bays, of remarkable elegance in the proportions, and the George Hotel. From the Market Square to the E EAST STREET. Here MEREFIELD HOUSE of 1810–11 with Greek Doric doorway and excellent C18 wrought-iron gates. To the W CHURCH STREET rising gently, with a good row of Georgian houses on the S side, especially Nos 3 and 9 (9 has a central Venetian window). At the end of Church Street is the church and round at its N side the back of the former GRAMMAR SCHOOL. The building is Jacobean. The front is in Abbey Road. The building has a five-bay front with a gabled central entrance and mullioned and transomed windows. A gable also at the back overlooking the churchyard. To the W of the School ABBEY HOUSE, an Early Victorian house which has preserved one C15 window from the former Clergy House which stood on this site. It is built into the S front.

Back to the Market Square, and now S. MARKET STREET is as wide as a market and has a good classical Early Victorian building on the W side, the WESTMINSTER BANK. On the other side the ST MARTIN'S SCHOOL, with a good five-bay Georgian front. From the top end of Market Street to the E SOUTH STREET with a small house of 1687 with mullioned windows, to the S HERMITAGE STREET with the UNITARIAN CHAPEL. The windows of this might well be those of

the year when the chapel was first built: 1733 (two arched
with mullion and transom, one semicircular and tripartite).
To the w WEST STREET with the over-restored CHUBB'S
ALMSHOUSES, originally of 1644, and the most attractive
DAVIS'S ALMSHOUSES of 1707. One storey with nine bays:
three doorways and six flanking windows. The centre has a
pediment of three bays, on Tuscan pilasters. At the back two
projecting wings.

GRAMMAR SCHOOL, at the entrance to Crewkerne from Yeovil.
1876–82 by *Giles & Gough*. Tudor style, with a picturesque
central tower.

CRICKET MALHERBIE
3010

ST MARY MAGDALENE. 1855 by *J. M. Allen* (GR).

CRICKET COURT. Built *c.* 1820 by Admiral Pitt, it is said to his
own plan. The appearance of the house makes that probable.
Entrance porch of heavy Tuscan columns. Doorway with
tapering sides in the Greco-Egyptian fashion. Windows with
metope frieze over. Upper windows with Baroque ears. Balcony with iron railing running all round at the level of these
windows. Entrance Hall with oval dome on the oddest curved
coving. Ionic order below. Doorways with Ionic half-pilasters
left and right. The capital has one volute to the l., one to the r.
of the door, that is it stretches all along the lintel, a painful
sight. The basement shows the mullions and four-centred
arched lights of the fenestration of an Elizabethan house which
preceded Admiral Pitt's.

CRICKET ST THOMAS
3000

CRICKET HOUSE. Rebuilt in 1801–4 for Admiral Hood, later
Lord Bridport, by *Sir John Soane*. Seven by six bays with
one-storey Tuscan porch and with colonnades on two of the
other sides. Only minor features remain of Soane's work,
especially in the small rooms above each other in the SW
corner. The centre of the house is the excessively spacious
staircase, put in within living memory, with Soanian detail.
Remains of the preceding Tudor house in the kitchen garden.
ORANGERY with glazed walls between Doric pilasters.

ST THOMAS. Largely rebuilt in the C19. – PLATE. Salver 1674;
the rest early C19. – MONUMENTS. Viscount Bridport † 1816.
By *Soane*.* Spiral-fluted base and two heavy unfluted Ionic

---

* Information kindly provide d by Dorothy Stroud.

columns carrying a top-heavy pediment with massive oddly-detailed acroteria. – Countess Bridport † 1831 by *Lucius Gahagan*. – Rev. William Earl Nelson, Duke of Bronte, † 1835, with semi-reclining figure and above this angel in relief carrying up two children. Unsigned.

CROWCOMBE

1030

HOLY GHOST. Red sandstone. C14 W tower with reticulated tracery in the W window, and two-light bell-openings with a transom. On the S side a similar window below. On the tower originally stood a spire nearly 80 ft high. It was struck by lightning in 1725. The tower arch is very tall and moulded. Nothing specially remarkable about the chancel and N aisle. But the S aisle and especially the view from the S W are perhaps more sumptuously Late Perp than anything in the county. The W gable of the aisle and the gable of the two-storey porch with the stair-turret in the re-entrant angle are the elements of the composition. Quatrefoiled battlements and pinnacles, and finely detailed tracery of the three-light transomed aisle windows. The porch on the upper floor has a three-light window too. Fan-vault inside the porch. All this was probably no sooner completed than benches were ordered for the church, and their date (cf. below) is 1534. The arcade piers inside are very tall. They have the familiar four-waves moulding and poor small capitals to the shafts only, decorated with bits of foliage, an awkward compromise between the type of piers with only four capitals and the other with bands of foliage. Chancel arch and N chapel arch are similar, but have un-decorated capitals. An arch also separates the S chapel from the S aisle. – FONT. Octagonal, Perp, with panelled stem and seated figures in panels on the bowl, e.g. Christ showing his wounds, the kneeling donor, St Anne teaching the Virgin to read. – REREDOS. Rich C19 carving with side parts painted on tiles and glazed. – ROOD SCREEN 1729. Nicely carved with pierced foliage in the segmental heads of the sections. – PULPIT. Perhaps contemporary with the Screen. – BENCHES. Many, square-headed, with close and finely detailed tracery, and also intertwined branches, a green man, little naked men fighting dragons, a mermaid, etc. Also some Renaissance details. One end is dated 1534. – PLATE. Paten by *Joseph Clare* 1719; Flagon by *Joseph Steward* 1729; Chalice and

Dish by *Joseph Smith* 1734. – MONUMENTS. Thomas Carew
† 1766, by *Tyler* (R. Gunnis). Large Putti by an urn, against
an obelisk background. – Henry Lockett † 1778. By *Robins* of
Bath, with the usual female standing by an urn. – James
37a Bernard † 1805 (his wife died 1811). By *Westmacott*. Grecian
with the centre flanked by heavy Greek Doric columns split
vertically into two halves. Fine asymmetrically placed figure
of Charity. – CROSS SHAFT in the churchyard with damaged
figures against the shaft.

CHURCH HOUSE, SW of the church. Given to the parish in 1515.
With an Early Tudor doorway and Jacobean mullioned windows. Roof with arched braces and collar-beams.

CROWCOMBE COURT. Begun probably in 1725 (date on a
wind-vane in the stable court) and still under construction
when a contract was made in 1734 between Thomas Carew,
the owner, and *Nathaniel Ireson* of Wincanton, the mason-
sculptor. The architect before him was *Thomas Parker*. The
house is of brick and the finest of its date in Somerset S of the
54b Bath area. The façade faces S and is of seven bays and three
storeys. The centre three bays project a little and have giant
Corinthian pilasters of two storeys. Above them a Venetian
window in the middle of the third storey and a pediment, a
lively, though not a correct composition. The two central
windows and the doorway on the ground floor are arched –
probably a later alteration. The pediment of the doorway is of
the open scrolly kind and stands rather awkwardly on brackets.
The window above it has foliage volutes down its sides – all
motifs characteristic of the time of George I. Quoining of
even length along the angles of the façade – again an early
C18 motif. Round the corner to the E five-bay front with angle
pilasters. The capitals here have the inward-turned volutes of
the Bastards' work at Blandford, a motif taken over by
Ireson and used in other places as well. Doorway with Gibbs
surround. On the N side the centre is the Venetian window of
the staircase. Large Stable Court to the W. In the middle of
its N side the plain five-bay W side of the house, owing to the
fall of the site, is four storeys high. Its ground floor has open
banded-rusticated arcading. The next two floors are tied together by giant angle pilasters, again with the Blandford
capitals. Aprons to the second-floor windows. Plain third
storey. The arcading is continued to the l. and r. and bends
forward to link up with long two-storeyed wings with central
lanterns.

Sumptuous interiors of *c*. 1740. Entrance Hall with pedimented doorways to the l. and r., a fine fireplace and overmantel and a Venetian opening of *verde antico* columns towards the staircase. This is of the square open-well type. 55 Wooden handrail with delicately twisted balusters and very rich plasterwork on the walls as well as the ceiling. The Venetian window has already been mentioned. To the r. of the Hall the Drawing Room, to the l. the Dining Room. The Drawing Room was redecorated in a reticent manner by *Edward Barry c*. 1870, the Dining Room (as also the Hall) has a plaster ceiling. The floor of the Dining Room is painted to imitate tarsia or inlay.

In the grounds, up the combe behind the house, an c18 RUIN incorporating original Gothic fragments from the chapel of Halsway Manor, 2 m. from Stogumber.

(QUARKHILL FARM. The centre of the house seems to date from *c*. 1400. Inside a timber screen of heavy unmoulded members with a doorway with a two-centred arch. Also recently discovered remains of a small painting of the Trinity.)

(HALSWAY MANOR, 1 m. NW. The house looks interesting in Buckler's drawing in the Piggott Collection at Taunton. It has an embattled, pinnacled porch and an embattled, pinnacled front, and also a polygonal bay. I am told it still exists but is much altered. The l. half of the present façade is all after 1870, the r. half still essentially as drawn by Buckler, except for the gable, the entrance, and the window of the porch furthest to the r.)

CUCKLINGTON

7020

ST LAWRENCE. With good views to the w towards Wincanton. s porch tower, not large, but complete with two-light bell-openings with Somerset tracery, and battlements. A pretty cupola on top, no doubt of 1705, a date mentioned in an inscription on the tower. E.E. chancel entirely renewed. The E windows a group of three stepped lancets. To the E of the tower the Chapel of St Barbara, with its own (blocked) s doorway. Late Perp windows. Inside, the aisle arcade of two bays may be late c13. The pier has four chamfered projections, and the double-chamfered arches start without any interruption by capitals or abaci. The N chancel chapel opens into the chancel with a Perp arch. The opening into the chapel of St Barbara (s) has now a handsome tripartite form. This is an improvement of 1880, made by *G. R. Crickmay*. Originally there was only one arch. – FONT. Circular, Norman, with fluting at the foot of the bowl. – STAINED GLASS. Fragment of a small C15 figure of St Barbara in the E window of the chapel of St Barbara. – PLATE. Chalice 1572; Flagon and Salver 1754; Salver 1767.

SHANKS HOUSE, 1 m. S. A remarkable house of different periods. On the w side mullioned C17 windows; the N side, though georgianized, has in its general shape with two-storeyed porch also a C17 character. The E side on the other hand is Georgian, of five bays and two storeys. Behind this front rooms with good mid-C18 fireplaces. The main staircase spacious, with slim balusters and lavish wall decoration, also Early Georgian. (Some original plasterwork in the Georgian range.)

CUDWORTH

3000

ST MICHAEL. Norman N aisle doorway with one order of columns. Capitals with scrolly foliage. In the tympanum pieces of Norman carving with lozenge motifs. At the E end of the N aisle a round-headed recess inside with the tiniest Norman window. Above this a three-light window of the late C13 with plate tracery (a quatrefoil and two cusped spheric triangles). The chancel windows of the same date, or a little later. The E window has intersected tracery, the sides lancets and two-light Dec windows. The nave N side also lancets, and a cusped lancet, all with rere-arches. The S aisle has a low three-bay arcade with octagonal piers and double-chamfered arches, also of the same period. Only the S windows are Perp. No tower. – PLATE. Chalice 1656.

CULBONE

8040
inset

8   ST CULBONE. This church, whether with its total length of 35 ft it is indeed the smallest medieval church of England or not, is rightly famous. Its utter solitude is delightful, with the rushing stream, the screens of wooded hillside, and the distant corner of the sea. And equally delightful is its own shape and surface, with the little slate spire riding on the nave roof and the whitewash having come off in irregular patches to expose rubble underneath. Remains of Norman (?) masonry in the chancel. Also fragmentary evidence of an Anchorite's Cell on

the N side. If only the E window of the church had not been
renewed with such insensitive correctness. – REREDOS. By
Voysey 1928, neo-Gothic rather than in the earlier Voysey
style. For Lady Lovelace (*see* Porlock, p. 276). – ROOD
SCREEN. Assigned to a date earlier than 1400. One-light
sections. Heavy framework with quatrefoiled circles on stilted
cusped round arches. The mullions below unfortunately removed. – FAMILY PEW. Simple C17 work. – BENCHES.
Square-headed, completely plain, probably pre-Reformation.
– PLATE. Chalice and Cover 1573. – MEMORIAL to Lord
Lovelace † 1906 by *Voysey*. Stone inscription plates above a
plain seat, typical Voysey lettering.

GATEHOUSE, behind the church. Also very much *Voysey*
in its motifs, but apparently not designed by him. It is said
that *Lady Lovelace* was quite capable of doing her own designing. The house is picturesquely asymmetrical, with stone walls
in crazy-paving pattern, and brick dressings.

CURDON CAMP *see* STOGUMBER

CURLAND   *2010*
5 m. NW of Chard

ALL SAINTS. By *Ferrey* 1856 (GR). – PLATE. Chalice of 1574,
made at Exeter.

CURRY MALLET   *3020*

ST JAMES. Perp, except for the chancel masonry – *see* the S
doorway with a moulding typical of *c.* 1300. The W tower of
blue lias with Ham Hill dressings. On the buttresses bands of
blue and brown. Set-back buttresses and battlements without
pinnacles. Higher NE stair-turret. Very large W window of
four lights with transom. Two-light bell-openings with Somerset tracery. The S side of the same period. Lias ashlar-work.
S porch attached to the S chapel. The S doorway has a Perp
hood-mould on big curly stops. Inside, the tower arch and the
chancel arch are panelled. The N aisle arcade is of three bays
with piers of standard section with four hollows. There is,
however, one remarkable thing about them. Both the shafts
and the hollows are far more pronounced than usual and the
capitals are in style decidedly C14, and not too late at that.

The arches are four-centred. The N aisle is externally much less ornate than the other, but the panel tracery has sub-panels. S chapel with panelled four-centred arch, and between the two windows a handsome angel-bracket for an image. – FONT. The usual octagonal Perp type. – SCREEN. Under the tower arch, above the war memorial, is the top of a most elaborate C17 screen, perhaps of about the middle of the century. The workmanship is robust and illiterate. Tripartite. The lower tier has the Crucifixion and the Nativity flanking the Mallet arms. Four figures act as caryatids, carrying those flower baskets which were made popular by Floris in Antwerp. But the caryatids are not just decorative maidens, but important persons who should not have been degraded to such a function. The caryatids represent St Paul, the Magdalen, the Virgin, St Peter. On the upper tier Adam and Eve, and the Expulsion, and Moses supported by Aron and Hur. Semicircular tops, and ornament in openwork. – BENCHES. Jacobean, plain, with small shell-tops. – Jacobean PANELLING in the chancel. – STAINED GLASS. Bits of medieval glass (a kneeling figure) in the N aisle E window. – PLATE. Chalice and Cover, by *J. North* of Exeter 1574; Flagon 1620. – MONUMENTS. John Pyne † 1609 and his wife † 1628. Two kneeling figures facing each other, flanked by columns; open pediment. – Ralph Mighill † 1633. Fragmentary. All that remains is the somewhat ludicrous frontal demi-figure of the divine. – Kneeling female figure and two small semi-reclining daughters in front of her. No date, no inscription, early C17. Alabaster and of good quality (cf. Bishop's Hull, Wiveliscombe).

MANOR HOUSE, Higher Street. Much remodelled and added to. But some twisted stone chimneys seem original C16 work, and a few mullioned windows with arched lights are original (*see* Braikenridge's Collinson at Taunton Castle).

CURRY RIVEL

ST ANDREW. Although essentially a Perp church, and a very good one, the building contains some evidence of the late C13 which must first be examined. It is only visible inside and is confined to the N chancel chapel. Here – a most uncommon arrangement – along the N wall is a series of tomb recesses, six in all, of which three at least are treated as a group, a large one in the middle and two smaller ones l. and r. All three have trefoiled arches on short shafts, under gables, the gables flatly decorated with a kind of debased stiff-leaf. To the l. of the group is a yet smaller recess, to the r. a group of two of different stone and a little later – small, and smallish. – The MONUMENTS are all defaced. Under the largest arch lies a cross-legged Knight of *c.* 1280. The small effigies (3 ft to 3 ft 6 in.) to the l. and r., probably children, tally in date. In front of the two r. recesses lies yet another small effigy, and that again seems to be late C13. The Piscina of the chapel again tallies, and although the windows are Perp, they still show their original appearance inside, *see* the fine cusping of the N rere-arches and the shafts of the E window, with small nail-head decoration in the abaci. In the C13 there was a doorway in the W wall of the chapel. After that comes the Perp work. It is of lias and Ham Hill stone. The W tower must here be given priority, although it had to be rebuilt in 1860. It is a tall dominating piece with set-back buttresses and without pinnacles. Higher NE stair-turret. W doorway with traceried spandrels, five-light W windows, three two-light windows with Somerset tracery, and then the bell-openings. These are very tall with Somerset tracery, and transoms, and as there is normal tracery in the heads as well as below the transoms, the openings appear like two joined together vertically. Quatrefoil frieze at the foot of the bell-stage; panelled tower arch to the nave. After the tower the S façade ought to be examined. It has big richly cusped transomed four-light windows, a joy to the eye, and battlements. The S porch is two-storeyed and in the middle of the aisle, with two of the windows on each side. The porch has a quatrefoil frieze below its upper window, and in the frieze will be noticed the portcullis of the Lady Margaret and the feathers of the Prince of Wales, probably Prince Arthur. Fan-vault inside the porch. The S chancel chapel has the same type of window to the S, but to the E a four-light window with a quatrefoil frieze at its foot. The N side corresponds to the S side except that the N chapel is of two bays instead of one and more modest in its fenestration. The chancel E window is of five lights like the W window. Inside below the S window is a long seat, the Sedilia, and that has a quatrefoil frieze against its front. The aisle arcades are very tall and fragile. The piers are of standard type (four hollows). So are the W arches into the chapels, the N and S arches into the chapels, and the chancel arch. – PARCLOSE SCREENS. The screens into the N and S chapels are interesting, because uncommon, and probably rather earlier than most

Somerset screens. The four-light sections are separated by strong shafts placed in front of and detached from the posts and carrying the coving. Coving with ribs and bosses. A strong mullion in each section runs into the apex of the arch. The whole is in much higher relief than usual. – BENCHES. With poppy-heads and bold tracery. – STAINED GLASS. One C13 roundel which was found below the Crypt of Canterbury Cathedral and given to Dean Farrar. – W window, very gay colours and beefy Renaissance forms, in the Holbein fashion. Yet the window is dated 1865. It is probably Munich glass; in any case it cannot be English. – PLATE. Saucer 1634; Chalice and Cover 1637; Chalice and Cover 1692. – MONUMENTS. Robert Jennings † 1593. Plain, well detailed 'reredos' with effigy. Two flanking composite columns, and two inscription plates still in black letters. Crowning cornice. – Marmaduke and Robert Jennings † 1625 and 1630. Two recumbent effigies on a tomb-chest against which kneels the family. A thin coffered arch serves as a canopy, and on this lie two silly cherubs l. and r. of the achievement. A very rustic work. The original iron railings around.

⁹⁰³⁰
^{inset}

CUTCOMBE

ST JOHN. With a magnificent view towards the Brendon Hills. Plain two-storeyed C13 W tower with unmoulded tower arch towards the nave. Of the rest of the church C13 (or early C14) one short octagonal pier of red sandstone with base and capital and the octagonal shafts of others. Otherwise mostly of 1862. – PLATE. Chalice and Cover 1572; Flagon 1775.

CYNWIT'S CASTLE see CANNINGTON

DANESBOROUGH CAMP see NETHER STOWEY

DAW'S CASTLE see WATCHET

³⁰¹⁰

DILLINGTON HOUSE
1 m. NE of Ilminster

C16 house, considerably altered and regularized by *Sir James Pennethorne* in the later 1830s. The old work can still be seen on the N side. Preserved also parts of the original SCREEN with heavy muntins. In the kitchen a big blocked fireplace and a window to the S of which only the lights are preserved with four-centred heads. The date of all this seems to be c.1550 at the latest.

DINNINGTON
3 m. NW of Crewkerne

ST NICHOLAS. Mostly of 1863. Small. – PLATE. Chalice and Cover 1574.

DITCHEAT

ST MARY MAGDALENE. The best part of the church is its chancel, lofty outside, wide and light inside. This is due to the church being held by Glastonbury. The architecture of the chancel belongs to two periods, the very late C13 and then the late C15. The late C13 contributed the plan and the main windows. Those on the S and N are of two lights still with trefoils, but the E window of three lights has at its top a spheric triangle fitted with three unencircled trefoils. Inside, three windows have fine openwork cinquefoil cusping. In the E window, to the eye, this seems to cut quite dazzlingly into the tracery. The piscina has an ogee arch. Then under Dean Gunthorpe of Wells († 1498) who was rector of Ditcheat and under Bishop Stillington († 1491) and Abbot Selwood of Glastonbury († 1493) whose shields appear on the parapet, the chancel was heightened and given the usual feature of a clerestory. With the earlier of the two periods goes the crossing; for Ditcheat has a crossing tower instead of a W tower. The crossing arches stand on heavy piers and have continuous double-chamfered mouldings. Externally only the lower storey of the tower belongs to c. 1300, see the lancets. Above these there are two-light bell-openings, battlements, and pinnacles, and a higher stair-turret with a pinnacle spike. All this is Perp. On the W side there are two niches for statues, and the statues are still in position. To continue with the Perp work, the W front is embattled and has pinnacles. So have the aisles, the clerestory, the two-storeyed S porch, and the S transept. Internally the crossing was now given a fan-vault, and the arcades were built (four bays), with standard piers

(four hollows). Good Somerset roof in the nave and the transepts. – PULPIT and READER'S DESK, Jacobean, and evidently
originally belonging together. – PAINTING. A wall-painting
of a very large St Christopher was brought out from underneath the whitewash in 1931. It is work of c. 1500, and of
rustic quality. – SCULPTURE. Head of a Churchyard Cross
(Crucifixion) in the S transept piscina. – PLATE. Chalice and
Flagon 1635; Paten 1732. – MONUMENT. Effigy of a Priest
under a somewhat capriciously shaped ogee canopy; early c14. –
Day Monument signed by *Ford* of Bath. Weeping woman
seated on the floor by an urn. Bust on top.

THE ABBEY (formerly The Priory). Large house, now mostly
Victorian, but said to have been built by Dean Gunthorpe
about 1475. The Hall screen may be original.

MANOR HOUSE. Long, two-storeyed, symmetrically laid out
C17 N front with two big gables. A date 1603 is mentioned.
Two-storeyed porch and on each side of it four mullioned
windows on each floor. Inside a fine room of c. 1680 which
formerly contained the staircase.

MANOR HOUSE INN. Pretty three-bay Gothic Revival façade
of c. 1800. Red brick, pointed windows.

1040   DODINGTON

ALL SAINTS. Perp W tower; the upper parts seem c18. S porch
with two shields above the doorway. – STAINED GLASS. In
the E window heads of Christ and the Virgin, from a Crucifixion
window; c15.

MANOR HOUSE. Gabled Elizabethan house. Two-storeyed
porch. Mullioned and mullioned and transomed windows.
1581 over the fireplace in the Hall. Two stone sphinxes carry
Ionic capitals; smaller figures above. Screen of heavy planks
and muntins. Towards the front of the house at the dais end
a small room projects. It is reached by a big stone doorway
and has moulded beams. Beyond this the drawing room with
a plaster frieze and a good fireplace of c. 1760.

3010   DONYATT

ST MARY. Of moderate size, but designed with some ambition.
All Perp. W tower with set-back buttresses and battlements.
Four-light W window. Two-light bell-openings with transom

and Somerset tracery. On the s side on the stage below also a two-light window with Somerset tracery. Embattled s aisle and s porch. Embattled nave with three-light clerestory windows. The aisle windows are of three lights too. The chancel projects by one bay and has transomed windows, of three lights to N and s, four to the E. Arcade of four bays inside, of the standard four-hollow section. Tower arch panelled, chancel arch with leaves in the capitals. The same in the capitals of the N and s chapel arches. – PULPIT. Probably mid C17. Panels flanked by ill-understood Ionic colonnettes. – SCULPTURE. Head of a woman wearing a wimple, c. 1300. Chancel, window sill. Found at Donyatt. – PLATE. Chalice Cover 1574; Chalice 1639.

ALMSHOUSES. 1624. Range of six. Mullioned windows, four-centred door-heads.

SEA MILLS FARMHOUSE, 1 m. SE. C16 house of two storeys with three gables and three- and four-light windows with arched lights.*

DOWLISH WAKE

3010

ST ANDREW. Nave, tower, and chancel. No transepts. Much restored in 1860.‡ The lower parts of the crossing tower (double-chamfered arches on triple-chamfered piers) look c. 1300. An odd lancet, not in axis, looks into the anteroom of the N chapel. The tower has two-light bell-openings and a higher stair-turret. – In the N chapel BRASS to George Speke † 1528 'qui edificavit hanc partem ecclesie'. – PLATE. Chalice 1806; Chalice and Salver 1807. – MONUMENTS. A Lady in a recess with four-centred arch and open cusping, the cusps forming angel-heads. The effigy is of c. 1360. – John Speke † 1442 and wife, tomb-chest with weepers, two recumbent effigies, much restored. – John Henning Speke † 1864, the discoverer of the source of the Nile. With life-size bust above the tomb. Whom by? – Also in the N chapel STAINED GLASS of c. 1860, one signed by O'Connor and dated 1865.

MANOR HOUSE. By the church. C16 and later. Mullioned windows. On one side a blocked archway.

---

* Opposite the house the DAIRY, said to be a former chapel and still to possess its Piscina. The upper floor is tunnel-vaulted, without any transverse ribs. Not seen by me. N.P.

‡ Of that period clearly the Pulpit and Font.

4020

DRAYTON

ST CATHERINE. Lias and Ham Hill stone. Low embattled
Perp w tower with higher stair-turret. Two-light bell-openings.
Pretty openwork iron spirelet with weathercock. Externally
and internally the body of the church is also Perp.* Arcade
of four bays with standard piers (four hollows) and four-
centred arches. The chancel arch has in its imposts two
niches facing each other. – PLATE. Chalice and Cover by
Ions of Exeter, 1570s. – CROSS in the churchyard; C15,
clearly re-cut in the C17. *See* the drapery of St Michael, the
swags on the plinth of the figure, and the ball-finial on the
cross.

MIDELNEY MANOR. An Elizabethan house of moderate size,
built by the brothers Trevillian, one to use the l., the other
the r. half. Two storeys, originally with gabled dormers in
the roof. Two doorways, mullioned windows with hood-
moulds, and two gabled projecting wings. Nicely remodelled
interiors of the early C18 in the E half. Behind the house a rare
survival, a Falcons' Mews, also of the early C18. This is of
brick with stone dressings.

Remains of a ROMANO-BRITISH BUILDING of indeterminate
type were once unearthed on the vicarage lawn. There was also
a villa in the vicinity.

9020
inset

DULVERTON

ALL SAINTS. C13 w tower, plain, with buttresses only at the
foot, and battlements. w doorway with two-centred arch,
single-chamfered in a continuous moulding. The bell-openings are pairs of lancets. The church rebuilt in 1852–5 by
Edward Ashworth of Exeter. – PLATE. Chalice and Paten by
I.P. 1573; Set of 1831.

Dulverton is a pretty little town. Coming from the w and the
Barle Bridge one should first turn to the r. to have a look
at a former CREPE MILL, a fine, rational early C19 design
with plain broad stone uprights and recessed bays between
(reference to 1814 in a deed of 1844). The bays have six-light
windows and the wall plastered above and below. Past the
mill CONGREGATIONAL CHURCH of 1831 with lancet front.
The main street runs up to the LAMB HOTEL, a nice five-bay,

---

* But the N aisle w window has reticulated tracery under a depressed arch
and is said to be original – i.e. probably *c.* 1350 or a little later.

three-storey front with a well detailed Ionic porch, and then splits. To the l. up to the MARKET SQUARE with the former MARKET HOUSE of 1866, a seven-bay stone front with an arched ground floor and an arched later staircase leading in two arms from the l. and r. to a central upper porch like a veranda. The Market House replaces one of 1760 and was converted to its present use by *Sir A. E. Richardson* in 1930.

The church can be reached straight up from here or by a footpath from the main street. Along the path a terrace of white Georgian cottages all with straight hoods on brackets over their doorways.

PIXTON PARK. C18 house of five bays and three storeys, with angle pilasters and angle pilasters to the pedimented three-bay centre. In the former park above Louisa Gate a circular folly tower (1 m. NNE).

BURY BRIDGE, 2 m. E. Famous, picturesque bridge of three arches, not strictly a packhorse bridge.

BREWER'S CASTLE and MOUNSEY CASTLE are prehistoric fortifications that stand facing each other on opposite sides of the River Burle not far from Hawkridge. The banks of the encampments, which are small and not at all elaborate, are now difficult to trace. A third ruined camp on the banks of the Burle is OLDBERRY CASTLE, in Burridge Wood. Its original size and shape are now impossible to determine.

A much better preserved camp of this epoch in the Dulverton area is BURY CASTLE, sited on Bury Hill above the Minehead–Brampton road. The camp is circular, about 100 yards across, and possesses an extraordinary kind of platform with a mound on it at the s. The bank still stands 20 ft above its ditch.

Near Dulverton Station is a square enclosure, 60 yards by 50. It is a simple structure, and may have been a prehistoric or medieval CATTLE-POUND.

DUNDON BEACON *see* COMPTON DUNDON

DUNKERY BEACON

8040 inset

On the beacon an impressive cluster of Bronze Age ROUND BARROWS.

DUNSTER

St George. Built as the priory church of the Benedictine
priory of Dunster, which was a cell of Bath. The church was
conveyed to Bath by William de Mohun at the end of the C11.
Of the Norman church the following evidence survives: a
small part of the w portal with one column, now forming part
of the C19 neo-Norman w doorway, and parts of the crossing
piers, especially their w ends with, on either side, a big strong
attached column with capital, one scalloped, the other with a
volute and head decoration. Next in date comes the chancel
whose E windows, a group of three stepped lancets, shafted
inside, is a C19 reconstruction (the church was restored in
1875-7 by *G. E. Street*), but a correct one. C13 also the top of
the arch in the s transept E side (*see* below). The church otherwise is Perp. The date for the rebuilding of the crossing and
the erection of its tower is known exceptionally well. The
contract survives between the parishioners (not the monks)
and *John Marys* of Stogursey. It is dated 1443 and stipulates
that the tower up to its 'batylment and pynacles, with three
"french botras" (buttresses) and gargylles' should be put
up in three years. For some windows a 'patern (*i.e.* design)
made by the advyce of *Richard Pope*, Fre Mason' is mentioned.
The tower is plain but striking in its bulk and strength. It is,
like the whole church, of red sandstone. The buttresses are
diagonal, with pronounced off-sets. The stair-turret is oblong
and goes up higher than the tower top. The bell-openings are
of two lights with a transom. No exuberant ornament, as in
so many other Somerset towers. As for the rest of the church,
it is all mid C15 to mid C16. The w front has above the
Norman doorway the latest decorative features, a four-light
window with a transom and with that refined, crisp tracery
which was repeated at Cleeve Abbey, Selworthy, and in
other places. Perp s aisle with battlements and three-light
windows. The turret corresponds to the rood screen inside.
Embattled s porch. N aisle with three-light windows. Mid C15
N and s transepts. The s transept has a doorway, flanked by
two niches, an unusual feature. The priory buildings lay to the
N. The s arcade inside is of six bays, the N arcade, due to the
interference of monastic buildings, starts further E and has
only four bays. The piers have the standard section (four
hollows) and capitals only to the shafts. Only the E responds
have bands of carved foliage instead. Strong Perp crossing

piers with broad concave mouldings. An odd anomaly in the
s transept, where the arch towards the s chapel seems in its
mouldings c13, but stands on shafts like hoses bent out-
ward to allow for a wider arch. This is suggested as a Late
Perp adjustment. The chancel chapels are of two bays with
four-centred arches. The piers have in the diagonals two wave
mouldings instead of one. Original wagon-roofs with many
bosses. Only the s aisle has a flat panelled ceiling.

FURNISHINGS. FONT. Perp, octagonal, panelled stem,
bowl with quatrefoils containing shields, flowers, the wounds
of Christ, etc. – SCREEN, a splendid specimen, worthy of the
best in Devon. All across nave and aisles, by the fifth arch from
the w. There is a rood-loft door by the crossing as well. The
surviving screen was erected as the outcome of a quarrel
between monastery and town in 1498. Dado with slim thinly
canopied blank panels. Four-light sections with the main
arches subdivided into two of two lights. Ribbed and panelled
coving. Richly carved friezes. – SCREENS to N and S chapels
with uncommonly broad frieze of foliage in the cornice. –
CHANDELIER 1740; of brass, hanging from some big piece
of iron ornament. By *Francis Billot* of Bristol. – PAINTING.
The Brazen Serpent, attributed to *Thornhill*, former altar-
painting of the chapel in the Castle. – STAINED GLASS. Good
E window by *Clayton & Bell*.* – PLATE. Chalice and Cover
1573; Paten by *Gamble* 1711. – MONUMENTS. Effigy of a
Lady wearing a wimple. In the chancel, s side. Under a
canopy with an arch with open cusping, the cusps formed into
(re-cut) heads; *c.* 1300. – Coffin lid with foliated cross to
Adam de Cheddar, *c.* 1350, s transept. – Tomb-chest,
chancel, N side, with shields in quatrefoils, under a four-
centred arch with big leaves in the spandrels. Fine cresting.
On the tomb-chest two recumbent alabaster effigies, probably
Sir Hugh Luttrell † 1428 and his wife. The Luttrells came into
possession of Dunster Castle in 1376. – Lady Elizabeth
Luttrell † 1493, large incised alabaster slab,‡ s chapel. – John
Wyther † 1487, and wife. Brass, *c.* 20 in. figures, nave w end.
– Thomas Luttrell † 1571 and George Luttrell † 1629, s
chapel. Large Jacobean monument, set up by George Luttrell
after the death of his wife in 1613, for four persons, Thomas
and wife, and George and wife. George kneels, the others

* Miss J. J. Scott points out the similarity of this window to one at
St Mary Abbots, Kensington.
‡ The alabaster came from Watchet.

recumbent. The whole is treated as one composition, flanked by a column on the l. and the r. Not of special skill or elaboration. – Mrs Ann Luttrell † 1731, signed by *M. Sidnell* of Bristol, simple wall-monument with columns and pediment.

PRIORY BUILDINGS. Very little remains – no indication of cloister, chapter house, refectory, or dormitory. The house on the N side of the blank wall of the nave, partly beyond the line of the W end of the church, was the PRIOR'S HOUSE. It is L-shaped in plan. Former Hall in the range facing N with fireplace and timber roof. A little away the circular DOVE-COTE. To the E a C16 BARN. In Conduit Lane, on the way up Grabbist Hill, C16 WELL HOUSE of stone. The earlier supply for the priory came from here.

DUNSTER CASTLE. The castle was built by the Mohuns and bought from them by Elizabeth Luttrell in 1376. The price was 5000 marks. The castle has been in the possession of the Luttrell family ever since. It lies on a 'tor' the summit of which was crowned by a close group of structures known as the keep. These were in decay as early as Leland's time (1542) and finally levelled early in the C18. The oldest parts of the castle now are at its foot to the N, that is the town. Here is a later C13 Gateway. The arch is depressed-pointed, almost straight-sided, and double-chamfered. The Doors with iron bands are probably of the early C15. The gateway is flanked on the l. and r. by semicircular towers. One of them was interfered with when in 1420–2 a new Gatehouse was built at r. angles to it. The arch is tall and finely moulded; no break between jambs and arch. Tunnel-vault inside the passage. The windows are of two and three lights. About 1765 the C13 towers were given polygonal tops and battlements. At the same time an early C16 doorway from some other place in the Castle was inserted in the Gatehouse and given an oak door, also old and also transferred from another place.

The living quarters of the Castle are L-shaped. The range running SE from the gatehouse belongs to the extensive additions and alterations made from 1867 onwards by *Anthony Salvin*. The principal range follows at r. angles, running SW, with a NW entrance side and a SE front towards the precipitous fall of the tor. Of the C13 no more remains than two small pointed windows on the SE front. Between *c.* 1589 and *c.* 1620 (both dates occur inside) a thorough reconstruction was undertaken. The work was probably done by *William Arnold*, the architect of Wadham College, Oxford and Cranborne Manor, Dorset. George Luttrell made an agreement with him in 1617 to build a house at Dunster Castle. The entrance side was given as nearly as possible the E-shape favoured by Elizabethan designers. It can still be recognized now, although Salvin replaced the NE tower by a bigger tower, and the porch tower also by a bigger tower. Inside there remains the plaster ceiling of the Hall (with pendants), the coat of arms in the Hall (with the date 1589), an overmantel on the first floor with coarse caryatids, a central figure relief, much strapwork, and the date 1620,* the frieze in the Gallery, and a subsidiary staircase.

The claims of comfort led to further alterations later in the C17. The Dining Room was given panelling and one of the most gorgeous plaster ceilings in SW England. It is dated 1681. 52 The artistry of this detached leaf and flower work is miraculous.‡ Stucco of the same date and style in the Lobby next to the Dining Room and also on the ceiling of the new spacious Staircase. Stag-hunting and fox-hunting are represented with much zest. The staircase has in addition a handrail of oak with 53a scrolls and flowers of elm in the most elaborate openwork carving. The skill is without doubt a match of Grinling Gibbons's. This type of staircase – square with an open well – and this type of carving were developed in England about the middle of the C17 – see e.g. Forde Abbey and Eltham Lodge. At Eltham Lodge c. 1665 there are even the same vases with flowers on the newel posts.

The staircase projects from the SE front. Also as a projection a new chapel was built in 1722. This Salvin replaced by a mighty tower. There is no question that the highly picturesque appearance of Dunster from the town is due more to Salvin's than to any previous age. Inside the castle Salvin also made many changes, creating e.g. a Hall larger than that of the C17.

SUMMER HOUSE. 1727; on top of the tor. Octagonal but with one (re-used?) C15 window.

STABLES. NW of the Gatehouse. Early C17, with mullioned windows. The mullions are of wood. Inside the original boxes.

FOLLY TOWER on Conygar Hill, N of the town. This, though distant from the castle, is part of its C18 improvements. It was built c. 1760–70. It is circular, embattled, and has pointed windows. More than the Castle it is the beacon of Dunster for miles around.

* In the same room a well preserved *Pugin* wallpaper.
‡ The same hands seem to have been at work at Dunsland, North Devon.

THE TOWN

2a The little town nestling between the Castle hill and Grabbist Hill is unsurpassed in Somerset amongst towns of its size. As one enters the Market Square, a wide straight oblong space, from the N and E, one looks down towards the Castle, with the tower on Conygar Hill on its own bump behind one's back. In the market place the YARN MARKET, an octagonal market cross built by George Luttrell *c.* 1589 and repaired in 1647. Central stone core, lean-to roof on strong beams with dormers. The Shambles along by the Yarn Market has disappeared. Of the houses in the Market Place the LUTTRELL ARMS is by far the most important, the Dunster residence of the abbots of Cleeve, with an arched doorway of *c.* 1500 and an approximately contemporary N wing, timber-framed with handsome carving. Between 1622 and 1629 the house was much altered by George Luttrell. Inside an overmantel of that date, clearly by the same hand as that dated 1620 in the Castle. Three coarsely modelled figures. The house was an inn by 1651. The house opposite has two orders of angle pilasters and two gables. It may be of *c.* 1700, altered. There are no other houses of special note in the Market Place, but the white walls of the unbroken mostly two-storeyed terraces of cottages are very attractive. If, at the foot of the Market Place, one walks straight on the Castle is soon reached.

The main street turns and is now called CHURCH STREET. On the r. the NUNNERY, a fine partly C14 house of three storeys with ground floor of stone and two overhanging timber-framed storeys above. They are slate-hung. Then the churchyard. The church itself lies back and does not form part of the street sequence. The timber-framed lodge at the entry to the churchyard administers a regrettable jolt. Yet it is genuine. But *G. E. Street* restored it into a Home Counties appearance. His are the tiles on the roof and the chimneys. METHODIST CHURCH of 1878 on the r., with an odd rather Flemish-Baroque façade (by *S. Shewbrooks* of Taunton). After that more nice C18 houses (e.g. the Exmoor Guest House, with segment-headed windows), but none of special merit.

SCHOOL, St George's Street, W of the church. 1871 by *St Aubyn*.

BAT'S CASTLE. Iron Age camp in the Deer Park behind Dunster Castle. It is buried in the woods and is hard to locate. Its inaccessibility has ensured its superb preservation. It is circular in shape and 130 yards in diameter. The inner of the two banks is still 15 ft high in places – twice as high as the outer. An unusual feature is that there are not one, but two entrances, opposite each other on the E and W. There is a wonderful view from the camp over the Channel. Beneath Bat's Castle is another, smaller Iron Age camp, which no doubt served as an outpost to its larger companion. It is circular, 120 yards in diameter, with a single bank and a ditch. Its condition is excellent too.

DURLEIGH

2030

CHURCH. The masonry of the chancel and the proportion of its N and S windows indicate a Norman date. One C13 window remains in the S wall of the nave, E of the porch: two lights with quatrefoil over. Early C14 W tower, unbuttressed. The tower arch and the chancel arch are similar in their mouldings. – PLATE. Chalice and Cover 1573.

MANOR HOUSE (WEST BOWER). An impressive survival. 39b The house is small, and approaching it, one would not expect the front that now overlooks the new-made lake. Two polygonal towers flanking originally a gateway whose arch survives. Also three surviving doorways from the archway. On the upper floor between the towers a blocked window. In the towers on the upper floor delicious lantern-like rooms, quite small, with Dec two-light windows with one transom. The r. tower still has bits of the original glass in its windows.

DURSTON

2020

ST JOHN. 1853. – COMMUNION TABLE. Dated 1635. Sturdy baluster legs, not vertically symmetrical. Some sparing lozenge and leaf ornament. – PLATE. Chalice and Cover 1695; Paten later C17.

LODGE HOUSE. There are here pre-Reformation windows preserved, even if in a restored state. One is above the porch entrance which is an uncommonly broad Perp archway, the other is to the l. on the first floor. They are both of two lights with transom, but the simple tracery differs. The room above the porch has an original wagon-roof. Spiral staircase in the re-entrant angle between porch and house, i.e. between the two traceried windows.

EARNSHILL HOUSE *see* HAMBRIDGE

EAST BRENT

ST MARY. The church has one of the most elegant spires in Somerset. It stands on a tower with angle buttresses turning diagonal higher up. W doorway, W window of the same width, above this a niche with a seated statue with a framing course around it, again of the same width. Then on the S side two tiers of two-light windows, on the W side two more statue niches (but without statues) and then the disappointingly small two-light bell-openings, without any of the usual enrichments. Parapet pierced with trefoils in triangles, square pinnacles, and at last the spire. It has a collar with blank arcading, but this is attached so closely that it does not disturb the vigorous outline. Proud N aisle of five bays with tall three-light windows, buttresses and pinnacles, and a pierced parapet with quatrefoils in lozenges. The S side is plainer. The chancel was rebuilt in 1840–5, but the Sedilia with a low prettily crested back seem original. As for the interior, the first and lasting impression is the nave roof, a piece of early Gothic Revival due no doubt to the same workmen as, or at least the inspiration of, the Axbridge ceiling. Panels of lozenge, etc., shape, thin ribs to connect them, three pendants, but all these Elizabethan and Jacobean standard elements richly cusped so as to make them Gothic. The ceiling is dated 1637, and there is plenty more in the church of that date. But first the Perp ingredients of the interior must be described. The arcades have their piers with the four-waves moulding. On the S side there is only a two-bay chapel E of the porch. This has a pier of four-hollows type, rather broadly done and so probably earlier than the N aisle. – BENCHES. C15, with thin poppy-heads without vegetable forms. On one of the ends the initials of John Selwood, abbot of Glastonbury (1457–93) who built himself a house at East Brent. On other bench-ends a pelican, the signs of the evangelists, tracery, and plants. – EAGLE LECTERN. Wood, of the C15, one of twenty-one wooden medieval lecterns in England. The eagle seems to move forward aggressively. The stem is a big heavy baluster. – SOUTH DOOR, C15, with tracery. – PULPIT. 1634, with the usual short blank arches in two tiers. – WEST GALLERY, originally part of the rood screen, 1635. It is said that the vine columns on which it stands date from 1824, a date hard to believe. –

22a

PAINTINGS. Wall-paintings in the porch. By *Prebendary Henry Denison, c.* 1873, when he was curate to the Archdeacon of Taunton. The Virgin seated with angels, the Crucifixion, and the Pietà. In the mid C19 Italianate rather than a medievalizing style. – STAINED GLASS. N aisle E window. Nine scenes, much restored in 1852. They are early C15 in style and similar to e.g. Crudwell, Wiltshire. – N aisle NE window. Three large figures of Saints, C15, only yellow used as a colour. – This arrangement of three large figures in a three-light window was continued in the C19 in the other aisle windows. – Chancel E window, 1858 by *O'Connor* (TK). – W window Crucifixion, Virgin, St John, thin medievalizing figures; German *c.* 1845–50. – PLATE. Chalice and Cover 1632; Flagon 1735. – MONUMENTS. Two decayed effigies of Priests, mid-C14. – Reed Children, *c.* 1869, signed by *Casentini & Co.* of Lambeth, big Gothic tablet.

EAST CHINNOCK

4010

ST MARY. Perp W tower with diagonal buttresses, two-light bell-openings with Somerset tracery, gargoyles, and battlements. Plain C13 S porch and S doorway. The interior of the church probably completely altered in the C19 so that a former nave with aisles now forms one aisleless nave. Flat ceiling. – FONT. Good. C13 base with deep moulding. – PLATE. Chalice and Cover 1571; Chalice 1705; Salver 1725.

EAST COKER

5010

Church and house are of Ham Hill stone.

ST MICHAEL. Immediately NE of the house. N tower in a transeptal position. Probably earlier than Perp, but remodelled in the early C19, *see* the window tracery and the arcaded parapet. Nave and aisles, N and S transepts, and chancel. All Perp from outside. But inside the S arcade seems C13. Three bays, circular piers with moulded capitals, and double-chamfered arches. N arcade Perp with standard piers (four hollows). Access to the transepts from the aisles by panelled arches. The arches from the transepts to the 'crossing' space are clearly C18. – FONT. Circular, Norman, with one cable moulding. – NORTH DOOR. With tracery. – PLATE. Chalice and Cover 1627; Chalice and Cover 1722. – MONUMENTS. Two defaced figures, an early C14 Lady

6—S.S

(floor, s transept) and a mid c14 Civilian (w end N aisle).

COKER COURT. An uncommonly interesting and rewarding house. Chiefly four periods: the c15 Hall, the additions, alterations and furnishings attributed to Archdeacon Helyar who bought the house in 1616, the later c18 E front and s rooms, built, according to tradition, by *Sir William Chambers*, and the w and sw ranges round the central courtyard which date from the early c20, but may replace older buildings. It is quite possible that the Gothic house was a courtyard house. The Hall has large two-light transomed Perp windows on both sides. The entrance is from the N, and here the big bay-window projects. It is strengthened by diagonal buttresses. In the Hall heavy and soberly detailed Jacobean stone Screen with coupled Roman Doric columns. Frieze with lozenges in the metopes. The entrance arches are studded. Fireplace also with coupled Roman Doric columns. On the E side of the screens passage the three archways formerly to Pantry, Kitchen, and Buttery. The Hall roof has arched braces with a trefoil in the spandrel and wind-braces. The c18 range has a Venetian window facing N and one (belonging to the plain staircase) facing w into the courtyard. Excellent fireplaces. In two upper rooms Chinese c18 wallpapers, one with stories, the other with large flowers. The E façade is very plain, seven bays, with a three-bay pediment.

HELYAR ALMSHOUSES, founded *c.* 1640. Row with gabled dormers and mullioned windows. Just outside the grounds of house and church.

East Coker is a lovely village with plenty of attractive houses.

ROMAN VILLAS. An important group. One villa had a mosaic with a man shown in supplication before a woman. The pavement in another showed a dead stag being borne by hunters (Taunton Museum).

EAST HUNTSPILL

₃₀₄₀

ALL SAINTS. 1839 by *Manners* (GR). Neo-Norman, ashlar, of nave and chancel, with a Norman bell-cote and Norman box-pews.

EAST LAMBROOK

₄₀₁₀

ST JAMES. Nave, chancel, and bell-cote. Chancel arch of *c.* 1190, double-chamfered on Transitional capitals with trumpet-shaped scallops. These rest on shafts which stand on stiff-leaf corbels. E window *c*. 1300 with intersected tracery and cinque-foiled rere-arch. The other windows Perp and later. – PLATE. Chalice and Cover 1573; Paten 1637.

CONGREGATIONAL CHAPEL, Mid Lambrook. Front with two large arched windows with two mullions and one transom at the springing point of the arch. To the l. and r. of the windows, as usual, two smaller doors. These have segmental heads. These features go with the date of the chapel, which is 1729.

OLD MANOR. 1584, but with a two-light transomed Perp window in the E gable. The lights have cusped pointed arches. Elizabethan panelling in the Dining Room.

MID LAMBROOK FARM HOUSE. The house possesses a lavish porch of *c*. 1500 or a little later. It is of two storeys with diagonal buttresses, three-light windows, and a quatrefoil frieze along the parapet which rises slightly, following the pitch of the roof.

EAST LYDFORD

5030

ST MARY. 1866 by *B. Ferrey*. Nave and chancel and tower at the NE end of the nave. The tower starts square (with a memorial on its N wall) and then turns octagonal. Octagonal bell-stage and spire with big dormers at its foot. The embellishments of the church all late C13, Geometrical tracery (going in the E window beyond neo-1300) and naturalistic carving. The chancel arch stands on short thick-set coupled columns, their capitals with foliage enveloping the signs of the evangelists. – PULPIT. Jacobean, with much strap-like arabesque work. – SCULPTURE. C15 alabaster relief of St George. – STAINED GLASS. The E window a very early work of *Kempe*; 1879. His source clearly was the Dürer of *c*. 1510–25, and not the Pre-Raphaelites. – PLATE. Paten 1725; Chalice 1776; Chalice 1796.

EAST MYNE CAMP *see* MINEHEAD

EAST PENNARD

5030

ALL SAINTS. After the finery of so many Somerset towers and parapets East Pennard is refreshingly blunt. Plain parapets, a W tower with a parapet, not even battlements, let alone pinnacles. And the walls beautifully unscraped. The church is all

C15, except for the lower parts of the W side which were altered in the C18. Windows of two lights (chancel), three lights (specially nicely cusped, nave), and four lights (chancel E). Tall four-bay arcade with standard piers (four hollows) and a clerestory. Chancel arch of the same standard. Somerset roof on angel busts. – Above the easternmost tie-beam, i.e. above the chancel arch, PAINTING of angels. – FONT. Late C12, square, and remarkable. The bowl has shallow blank arches, but below it are boldly carved big monsters, such as a human-headed bird. – WEST GALLERY. As its front, parts of benches and perhaps the screen have been re-used, notably a BENCH END with a pelican above and the Crown of Thorns below. Some of the tracery panels have close Flamboyant patterns. – PULPIT. Early C18, with remarkably fine carving of leaves, flowers and fruit in the Gibbons tradition. – READING DESKS. Two with large putto heads and garlands from the former Reredos. – Some remaining BOX PEWS. – STALLS with re-used parts of Jacobean chests. – STAINED GLASS. In the E window panels with a patchwork of C15 glass. – PLATE. Chalice and Cover 1633; Chalice and Flagon 1727. – MONUMENTS. G. Marten † 1789 by *King* of Bath. The usual standing woman by an urn; against a large pink oval with drooping leaves draped over it at the top. – Prettier still E. Berkeley Napier † 1799, also by *King*. Urn and wreath against a grey background with thin clustered shafts l. and r., a Gothick arch, and again the drooping leaves.

The village is small and lies in a fold, with old trees and a winding street. The houses are dark grey, and well looked after, and the hedges are trim and dense.

PENNARD HOUSE. Jacobean, much altered in 1815. On the N side a one-storeyed colonnade.

EAST QUANTOXHEAD

1040

ST MARY. Grey in the shadow of the grey Court House. Two-storeyed W tower with diagonal buttresses and battlements. Higher stair-turret. Nave and chancel over-restored. The tower arch inside with its old double-chamfered arch on the plainest responds can hardly be later than the first half of the C14. – ROOD SCREEN. Perhaps before 1400. Two-light sections without mullion with two low ogee arches, cusped quatrefoils in the spandrels. Straight and plain top. – VESTRY SCREEN. A simple domestic screen, perhaps from the house, just with sturdy uprights. – PULPIT. Elizabethan, all the decoration is foliage. – BENCHES. A few original, in the usual type of the district with close tracery, foliage, and also a pattern of stars, and arms. – COMMUNION RAIL. Jacobean. – STAINED GLASS. E window by *Kempe*, 1891. – PLATE. Chalice and Cover 1573. – MONUMENT. Hugh Luttrell † 1522. Tomb-chest with shields under segmental cusped arches. Canopy on side-pieces pierced by two arches side by side in the W–E direction; four-centred arch, panelled inside; big cresting.

COURT HOUSE. A somewhat sombre, grey, plainly parapeted Jacobean house with older parts hidden or partly hidden. The house has been in the possession of the Luttrell family for about seven hundred years. The main front turns to the E. It is here of the E-type, but with the l. wing left out: porch, one four-light window with transom on either side and projecting r. wing with transomed four-light windows. Behind the porch the Hall. In the wing the Drawing Room – all in the Elizabethan and indeed earlier traditions. This whole range was placed, it is said, in front of the older house to which belong the SW angle, with battlements to the S, the S side, the tower rising above it, and the NW parts. Between these and the tower a small cock-pit. The early history of the house would need more study. Aesthetically the most interesting feature of the house is the fireplaces, Jacobean and a little later. The oldest is dated 1614, that in the (one-storeyed) Hall 1629. This has the Luttrell arms flanked by two soldiers and discreet, a little mechanical, strapwork friezes. An unusual feature of the Hall is the four-light window at the dais end behind the high table. Other fireplaces, on the ground floor and first floor, also of stucco, have as flanking figures women carrying baskets of fruit, and also (former Nursery) two termini caryatids representing Red Indians. There is plenty of coarse strap-work on the overmantels, and the centres are taken by scenes from the Gospels: Christ and the children, the Entry into Jerusalem, the Deposition, and 50b the Ascension. The staircase has square, fluted, vertically symmetrical, tapering banisters and fluted obelisks on the newel-posts.

EDINGTON

3040

ST GEORGE. 1879 by *Down & Son* (GR). – In the church a good Norman FONT. Bowl with two big scallops each side.

Cable-moulding below and cable-moulding on the base. Corner spurs. – PLATE. Chalice and Cover 1719–20; Plate 1799.

EDINGTON HOUSE. A nice house of 1780, the centre of three bays with the first and third projecting and pedimented. Older parts date from *c.* 1640. A wing was added in 1810 which contains a room with a coved ceiling.

0030

ELWORTHY

ST MARTIN. A small church. Low, unbuttressed W tower with battlements. Probably C13. One small lancet on the W side, unmoulded round tower arch. In the N side of the church also a small lancet. – PULPIT. Jacobean. – ROOD SCREEN. Dated by an inscription 1632. The two-light Perp tracery probably re-used. – COMMUNION RAIL. Jacobean or mid-C17. – PLATE. Chalice 1573.

WILLETT'S TOWER. *See* Brompton Ralph.

ELWORTHY BARROWS. Not barrows at all, but the remains of an Iron Age Camp. The camp was once circular and about 200 yards across, but it has been cut into sections by quarrying. The whole site is badly over-grown.

20 30

ENMORE

ST MICHAEL. S Doorway of *c.* 1185. The capitals of the colonnettes of the Late Norman trumpet type, the l. one actually with small stiff-leaves appearing in the openings of the trumpets. The arch has two zigzags meeting in the same way as at Stogursey, one parallel with the wall, the other at r. angles. The rest is Perp or of 1873 (*Ferrey*, GR). Of 1873 the N aisle and the renovation of the chancel. Panelled chancel arch between thin shafts. The E window of three stepped cusped lights with foils above reproduces the original (*see* Braikenridge's Collinson at Taunton Castle). Fine W tower. Diagonal buttresses ending in very tall pinnacles. Pinnacled battlements on the top of the tower as well. Two-light bell-openings with Somerset tracery. Four-light W window with nice cusping. Inside the tower a star-vault. The tower arch is moulded. – PULPIT. Jacobean, with two blank arches on top of each other, in each panel. – Two HELMS, *c.* 1620 (Malet family). – PLATE. Chalice and Cover 1618; Saucer 1727; Tankard 1751. – CROSS in the churchyard. Base decorated with shields.

ENMORE CASTLE. Built by John Perceval, Earl of Egmont,
before 1779. It was a large pseudo-baronial mansion with a
central courtyard, corner towers, curved intermediate towers,
and a turreted gatehouse. The stables and offices were all
below ground. Of this only about one quarter survives, under
an Early Victorian roof. Red sandstone, one round tower, one
angle tower, the windows arched and with broad frames.
The same windows characterize a house just s of the church
which has odd Baroque curved gables, and CASTLE HOUSE
on the main road, an older house with a porch to which five-
bay blank arcades were added, each with an archway in the
middle.

EVERCREECH   *6030*

ST PETER. The fame of the church is its w tower deemed by 16a
some one of the most perfect in Somerset. It belongs to the
Wells type in which an impression of extreme height is
obtained by continuing the tall transomed twin two-light
bell-openings below in yet larger twin two-light blank panels.
That is what happens on the upper stages. Otherwise the
composition of the tower is as follows. Set-back buttresses,
carrying very tall shafts with pinnacles. These reach up to
just above the cill of the bell-openings. But from between them
rises, set diagonally, another tall shaft, and this goes up far
enough to join in the intricate play of pinnacles at the top of
the tower. Battlements with pierced quatrefoils and at the
corners big crocketed pinnacles accompanied by junior pinnacles, and the one standing on the shaft from below becomes
one of them. There are also small intermediate pinnacles on
the middles of the sides, and these come out of shafts rising
between the blank panels and then between the bell-openings.
The church seems low behind this tower. It is, however,
treated ornately too : aisles and clerestory with pierced quatrefoil parapets and pinnacles (the s aisle dates from 1843), the
chancel with the same parapet on the s side and a plain parapet
on the N, but on both sides with pinnacles. The chancel is
the earliest part of the church. It has an E window with
reticulated tracery, and side windows only slightly later.
Internally the effect of the church is curiously cosy, thanks to
the N and s galleries of 1843 squeezed balcony-like into the
arcade arches. That is really the impression which remains
of the interior. The tower arch is uncommonly elaborately

panelled: four shafts and three sets of panels between. The arcade, as so often in Somerset, is disappointing. Standard piers with the familiar four hollows, rather short and insignificant. On two of the N piers angel brackets for images. Three-light clerestory. The roof is Somerset at its best, and the colouring, though of course renewed, helps to give something of what must have been the original effect. – CHANDELIERS. Two, of brass, one dated 1761. – PLATE. Chalice and Cover late C17; Flagon 1718; Dish 1744; several pieces 1844.

The church stands in the middle of a small square, with the VILLAGE CROSS (probably C15) in line with its W end, and a set of ALMSHOUSES at its E end. They date from 1825–7.

EVERCREECH HOUSE, a little to the NW. A plain Georgian house, but at its back provided oddly with three canted bays side by side, each with a simply treated Venetian window. Kitchen wing C19 Tudor. Entrance Hall said to be by *Sir T. G. Jackson*.

PECKING MILL, ½ m. SW. A Georgian mill treated with some dignity. Five-bay two-storeyed centre with a one-bay pediment which looks rather like a gable and has a finial. Venetian window in the pediment, plainly framed, as are also the other windows. Side-wings of one bay, a little lower.

SMALL DOWN CAMP. Prehistoric encampment on the top of the 800-ft-high hill N of Small Down Farm. It is oval in shape and covers 6 acres. It is double-banked, but in the E there are no less than three banks, the inner one being the tallest and reaching a height of 20 ft. Inside the enclosure is a piquant and original feature: a row of eleven Bronze Age barrows, which yielded funerary relics characteristic of their period.

8030
inset

EXFORD

ST MARY MAGDALEN (St Salvyn). Plain W tower with diagonal buttresses and higher square stair-turret. The tower arch has a continuous chamfer. Nave and chancel almost wholly rebuilt in the C19. The S aisle was added in connexion with the will of a blacksmith made in 1532. He left £3 towards 'the makyng of an yled'. Others in the same year left more money for the same purpose ('ad . . . ambulatorium'). Four-bay arcade. The piers of the standard four-wave section. The capitals are of the type with bands of foliage. The tracery of the straightheaded S aisle and the nave N side windows of the graceful design also to be found at Winsford, Exton, and Porlock. The three-light arched E window of the aisle is specially elegant. – FONT. Octagonal, Perp, with a stem with panels containing ogee arches addorsed and affronted; bowl with quatrefoils with leaves, etc. – ROOD SCREEN. From the medieval church of West Quantoxhead. With four-light sections in which each arch is subdivided into two two-light arches (cf. Devonshire). Ribbed and panelled coving. Four richly carved foliage friezes in the cornice. – PLATE. Chalice and Cover 1695.

STADDON HILL CAMP. Iron Age Encampment, high above the deep cut of the road, 2 miles out of Winsford. It is a small circular enclosure, 60 yards across, with a single bank and ditch. The bank is still 10 ft high in places.

EXTON

9030
inset

ST PETER. Herringbone masonry in the nave indicates a Norman date. The W tower has buttresses only at the foot and may be C13 work. Low and only slightly single-chamfered tower arch towards the nave. Chancel 1878. The S wall of the nave and the N aisle with straight-headed early C16 windows of the handsome tracery details common in this neighbourhood (cf. Exford, Porlock). The tracery of the pointed window at the E end of the aisle equally elegant. The aisle arcade is of three bays with piers of standard section. – FONT. Octagonal, Perp, with leaves, etc., in quatrefoils. – PLATE. Chalice and Cover 1574 (?); Paten 1635; Flagon 1771.

FAIRFIELD HOUSE
1 m. NE of Stringston

1040

Large symmetrical Elizabethan house. The date 1589 appears on the porch. This is three-storeyed, but had one more storey originally. Pinnacles and finials on the top. The porch is in the centre of the SE front. Wings project on the sides, on the familiar E plan. They end in canted bay-windows with mullions and transoms. Large mullioned and transomed windows in an orderly arrangement. On the NE side they are a conversion from C18 fenestration. The porch leads into the Hall, which has a vaulted Late Georgian plaster ceiling. Behind porch and hall a large Perp doorway. It tells of the earlier state of the house, whose building history is not sufficiently known. Good square open-well staircase in the NE wing.

2040

FIDDINGTON

St Martin. The w tower Perp, the rest all Victorian. – benches. Some are old, of the type usual in the district about 1500 and after. – pulpit. Jacobean. – plate. Chalice 1765. – cross-shaft in the churchyard, with traces of a figure under a canopy.

1020

FITZHEAD

St James. Red sandstone. Perp w tower with square stair-turret. The nave and chancel 1849, the n aisle 1881. In this some good original stained glass. – Original plain bench ends. – plate. Chalice and Cover 1573; Paten 1696.

In the churchyard the Tithe Barn, buttressed, but otherwise much remodelled.

Fitzhead Court. Georgian exterior, not of special interest. Contains a good late C17 plaster ceiling with shell and palm-leaf motifs, and cherubs.

3020

FIVEHEAD

St Martin. Late C13 chancel; see the two n lancets, cinque-foiled inside. The e window is probably contemporary but was altered, it seems after 1850 (Braikenridge's Collinson). Perp the w tower with diagonal buttresses, battlements, pinnacles, and higher stair-turret. Large five-light w window with a transom and panel tracery below it. Then follows a three-light window with Somerset tracery and then the two-light bell-openings. The interior details, arcade, tower arch and chancel arch all of standard type and much renewed. – The e window is not in its original state (cf. Buckler's drawing in the Pigott Collection). – font. Norman, circular, with a frieze of saltire crosses at the top and a cable-moulding at the bottom of the bowl. – plate. Chalice and Cover 1572. – brass. Jane, wife of Lord E. Seymour, son of the Duke of Somerset, † 1565, a 3 ft 6 in. figure.

Langford Manor House. Early Tudor house completely altered about a hundred years later. Of the early date just one roof-truss with arched braces. The general shape, a double E, the gables, the mullioned and mullioned and transomed windows, all appear late C16 or early C17. (Tudor staircase.)

Cathanger House. L-shaped, with mullioned windows; in-

scription and date 1559 on the porch; C18 front. The gatehouse is detached and gabled. It has a round archway and
arched niches to its l. and r.: C16.

FIVE HOUSES *see* WELLINGTON

GALHAMPTON *see* NORTH CADBURY

GERBESTONE MANOR   1010

The house is basically of before the Reformation (*see* one arched
brace left of the former hall roof and two wooden door-
heads on the first floor), but was much modernized in the
time of Queen Elizabeth I and again in 1925 by *H. Lidbetter*.
Most of the windows are Elizabethan; Mr Lidbetter's are
the main staircase and the pretty courtyard at the back. The
façade of the house is still of Early Tudor character with two
big cross gables at the ends and the gables of the two-storeyed
porch attached to one of them – just as e.g. at Cothay. The
porch leads into the screens passage. Hall screen and panelling
are preserved, as is the plain Hall fireplace. The outer wall of
this was of course originally also the outer wall of the house.
Next to it lies the original spiral staircase to the Solar. The
kitchen was at first in the s wing, but was moved to the N wing
during the Elizabethan alterations.

GLASTONBURY   5030

ABBEY

Glastonbury Abbey was founded on an eminence above the
meres by King Ine about the year 700. Legend tells that its
history goes back yet further, that Joseph of Arimathea landed at
Glastonbury bringing the Holy Grail with him, that he had been
sent out by St Philip, Christ's disciple, to evangelize Britain,
and that he built an oratory of wattle and sand, the venerable
vetusta ecclesia. Legend also identifies Glastonbury with Avalon
and makes it the burial place of King Arthur. With these traditions Glastonbury can in fairness be called the most famous of
Britain's monasteries. St Dunstan was a monk here, and then
abbot. He is said to have repaired the buildings which had been
damaged by the Danes. King Edgar made generous gifts towards
Dunstan's new works and was, when he died in 975, buried in

the abbey. After the Conquest a large scheme of rebuilding was set afoot, and probably completed by about 1120 or earlier. All this was burnt in the disastrous fire of 1184. Immediately after a new *vetusta ecclesia* and a new abbey church were begun in axis with each other and carried on simultaneously, the former, St Mary's Chapel, so rapidly that it could be consecrated in 1186, the latter more slowly. The style was at the outset a Late Norman Transitional but seems to have changed at once into a well understood Early Gothic – probably under the influence of the designs of the great architect who began Wells Cathedral about 1180. Work in the church went on into the middle of the C13 and beyond. Under Abbot Fromond (1303–22) the crossing tower was completed and the E part of the nave vaulted. Under Abbot de Sodbury (1323–34) the nave vault was completed, under Abbot Walter de Monington (1342–74) the choir leng-thened and re-faced and a retrochoir added, and finally under Abbots Richard Bere (1493–1524) and Richard Whiting (1524–39) an E chapel for the remains of King Edgar erected. The whole church from the Edgar Chapel to St Mary's Chapel was in the end c. 580 ft long (nave, chancel, and retrochoir c. 375).

The plan of the church will be described later, but a word must here be said of the church of King Ine and of St Dunstan, i.e. of c. 700 and c. 950, of which excavations of 1928, etc., have revealed much. The results have to be read; they were un-fortunately not left exposed. King Ine's church had an oblong nave c. 42 ft long with the usual *porticus* instead of aisles and with a chancel arch c. 14 ft wide. The form of the chancel is unknown. It was replaced by a square chancel in the C8 or C9, when also further *porticus* were built to the l. and r. of the w end and perhaps a narthex or atrium. St Dunstan extended the chancel yet further (21 by 17 ft) and added two more *porticus* to the l. and r. of his chancel. The chancel may have carried a tower. The building according to the excavations must have been a group of loosely connected square and oblong chambers and cannot have possessed much architectural unity.

The surviving buildings are described in the following order: St Mary's Chapel, Abbey Church, Monastic Buildings. They were all built of Doulting stone.

St Mary's Chapel. Begun in 1184 and dedicated in 1186. A plain oblong, four bays long, with pronounced angle turrets – an early forerunner of Late Medieval Royal chapels. With its decorative motifs and the relation of them to plain wall it is a

Norman building. On the ground floor outside tall intersecting arches, on the upper floor big round-arched windows, 9a
arranged at the w end in a generously spaced group of three.
The ornament on both levels is typically Latest Norman, that
is zigzags and similar motifs (crenellations with triangular
merlons, etc.), placed not parallel with the wall nor indeed at
r. angles to it, but at an angle of 45 degrees. The angle turrets
also have intersecting arches. Before beginning to watch for
certain details which tend to disturb the so far simple evidence,
a look at the roofless interior is to be recommended. Here also
are intersecting arches, but they are enriched by medallions or
paterae of foliage, and the foliage is of the Early Gothic stiff-
leaf variety. The zigzag, lozenges, etc., however, remain what
they are outside. But, and this is the essential point, the chapel
was vaulted, and the vaults are fully-understood Gothic. Not
only were they rib-vaults – there are after all plenty of Norman
rib-vaults including some in Somerset parish churches, and
including also the new building which was stylistically the
most important for Glastonbury, the w end of Worcester
Cathedral of *c.* 1175–80 – but they were consistently pointed
as shown by the surviving pointed wall-arches or dosserets.
The transverse arches again have rich zigzag motifs set transversely. Now to support these vaults the outside was given
buttresses up to the height of their springing, and they are
shafted in the angles with keeled shafts and have clearly
crocket-capitals, that is the capitals of the French Gothic style
of exactly that moment. Thus Norman tradition and Gothic
requisites of structure, and also Norman ornament and French
Gothic ornament, stand side by side – kept so neatly separate
that one is tempted to assume two masters, one who planned
the Late Norman chapel, and a second who replaced him
almost at once and rushed to apply the new Gothic methods
and idiom as far as could still be done. The gabled N and S
doorways would, in the opinion of most scholars, form part
of this story; for they exhibit the same odd combination. The
general disposition is entirely in the Anglo-Norman and more
specifically in West-Country traditions. Malmesbury of *c.* 1165
in particular ought to be compared. There also figures are
small and set in foliage trails and roundels, and no break by 9b
capitals or abaci is made between jambs and arches. The style
of sculpture at Glastonbury on the other hand is not entirely
Anglo-Norman. The wedge-stones or voussoirs show details
entirely Gothic, entirely French and hardly possible before

c. 1230, that is the beginning of the W front at Wells. What happened then? On the S side the medallions were never completed. Only two are recognizable, the creation of Eve, and the Fall. Could they not on the N side have been finished later than any of the other work? On the N side there are in the inner order of wedge-stones the Annunciation, Visitation, Nativity, and the Magi with Herod. In the next order the Magi (kneeling) can again be recognized, then the Magi asleep in their beds, and then the Massacre, with Herod on his throne and his soldiers in exact armour of the period. But there is also a woman milking a cow.

As antecedents for Glastonbury, Malmesbury and Worcester have been mentioned; and they seem indeed the immediate premisses, always subject of course to the possibility of others having been destroyed. Malmesbury in the sixties has pointed arches in a Norman setting, Worcester in the seventies a combination of pointed and round, and in addition keeled shafts and zigzag at r. angles to the wall, just like Glastonbury, and moreover at Worcester the aisles are rib-vaulted, and the decorative motif of *paterae* occurs consistently.*

The ABBEY CHURCH was begun in the same year as St Mary's Chapel, i.e. in 1184. How fast building proceeded, we do not know. There is no early dedication recorded, and not enough remains to arrive at safe conclusions. The plan of the whole church is laid out in the grass, easy to understand. St Mary's Chapel is continued to the E in a galilee of the same width, a width slightly less than that of the nave of the church. The nave is accompanied by aisles and has nine bays. On the S side was the cloister, on the N side a big porch of an internal depth equal to that of two bays of the nave. Crossing and transepts with E aisles and two E chapels to each transept. Aisled choir of five bays and straight-ended aisled retrochoir of two bays, and then the aisleless Edgar Chapel of 87 ft length. What survives, apart from the plan, is something of the outer walls of the C14 retrochoir and the late C12 chancel aisles, a large and tall fragment of the E crossing piers and adjoining transept walls, a three-bay stretch of outer wall of the S aisle, a substantial portion of the W front, and the outer walls of the galilee.

The late C12 CHANCEL has the same mixture of Norman and Gothic as St Mary's Chapel, though the proportion between the two is now reversed. There are still the old zigzags,

* For the Crypt underneath St Mary's Chapel, *see* below p. 176.

but the capitals are crocketed, and the arches are pointed with a purpose. The shafted windows also are pointed. The aisle vaults rested on triple wall-shafts as at the W end of Worcester (*c.* 1175–80), and the ribs had a similar profile too. The retrochoir was added by Abbot Monington (1342–74), but he seems to have preserved the same composition at least for the aisles – *see* the wall shafts, though their bases give away the later date. Abbot Monington also vaulted (or re-vaulted at a higher level?*) the chancel itself, and of the way in which he proceeded the blank panelling just E of the NE crossing pier is evidence. There remain five tiers of small blank-arched single-light panels. So one has to assume an arrangement based on that of the Gloucester choir, whereby the new style was put as a veneer on the late C12 or early C13 walls, and the new higher and probably wider clerestory windows were made part of that grid. As an early case of the Perp style in Somerset this choir must be remembered. The Edgar Chapel was an oblong, built by Abbot Bere and enriched by an apse (on the pattern of Henry VII's Chapel at Westminster?) by Abbot Whiting immediately after.

The TRANSEPT E side is most helpful in reconstructing the original appearance of the upper parts of the church of 1184, etc. The elevation consists of arcade, triforium, and wall passage in front of the clerestory windows. The piers of the arcade consist of a large number of shafts grouped towards the transept 'nave' so as to carry with a central triple shaft the transverse arch and the ribs of the high vaults, with further shafts for the moulded arcade arches, and with one shaft between these two groups to carry a wall-arch taller than the arcade and lower than the high vault. This wall-arch frames arcade and triforium together – a peculiarity of some earlier C12 churches in England and Scotland of which Jedburgh and Oxford are the most familiar examples, whereas Tewkesbury and Romsey are the examples nearest to Glastonbury. The arcade arches still have zigzag decoration. So have the arcade-cum-triforium arches. The small arches of the grouped triforium – three to each bay – are trefoiled and not pointed. In the spandrels above lozenge-shaped *paterae*. The clerestory windows are shafted (shafts with three shaft-rings) and flanked by smaller pointed arches with two orders of shafts (also with shaft-rings). Square *paterae* above these arches. The details of capitals, etc., here are clearly early C13.

* Height of the chancel *c.* 90 ft.

The NAVE continued this system, but from fragments found it is certain that, when the triforium stage was reached, the C13 was over (ball-flower decoration in the triforium arches). All that remains *in situ* is the outer s aisle wall, and here the C13 design was kept for five bays. Then there is clearly a break in the treatment of the vaulting springers, and it is assumed that it marks the period of Abbot de Sodbury, i.e. the second quarter of the C14. The outer wall as preserved has windows, round-headed inside but pointed outside. The W wall of the nave has, to the l. and r. of the W portal, trefoiled recesses of the same kind as in the transept triforium. The WEST PORTAL is not high. It is covered by a depressed pointed arch of English C13 type. Above this towards the W is a tympanum, and doorway and tympanum are framed by a stately, finely moulded arch on four orders of shafts. The tympanum is decorated by blank stepped arcading with foiled or cusped heads. The centre arch is trefoiled, those to the l. and r. have two rising foils or lobes each.

The W portal faces into the GALILEE. This has tall trefoiled blank arcading inside (shafts with shaft-rings), an elegant N doorway with segmental head inside and two orders of shafts outside, and upper windows re-made probably in the C15. At about the same time a CRYPT was built beneath the galilee and then also beneath St Mary's Chapel. The details of the latter are clearly Perp, but those of the former are equally clearly of the C13. To realize this it is only necessary to examine rib profiles and wall-shaft profiles. The explanation of re-used materials is not wholly convincing. The vault under the galilee consists of oblong bays with a longitudinal ridge-rib and a short transverse ridge-rib against the ends of which run the diagonal ribs which rise from the four corners.

MONASTIC BUILDINGS. The CLOISTER was about 135 by 135 ft. On its E side was the oblong CHAPTER HOUSE, on its S side the REFECTORY with an undercroft with a row of central supports. Of the W side little remains. S of the W end of the Refectory was the detached square MONKS' KITCHEN with two curved projections at the SW and SE angles and four central supports. The E range was continued to the S beyond the S wall of the Refectory by the DORMITORY range, also with an undercroft with middle supports. The undercroft was subdivided into three rooms. S of the Dormitory are the visible remains of the drains of the RERE-DORTER or lavatories.

But the most considerable remains of the monastic quarters

lie further w than the cloister ranges, sw of St Mary's Chapel. They are a fragment of the ALMONRY with part of a fine rib-vault and the complete ABBOT'S KITCHEN, one of the 44 best preserved medieval kitchens in Europe (for England cf. Durham and Chichester). The date of its erection is not known. The second half of the C14 seems most likely. The kitchen is square in plan but with fireplaces fitting the four corners so as to result in an octagonal interior. Octagonal truncated pyramid roof with tall lantern, crowned by a further truncated pyramid roof with a yet smaller lantern and a tiny octagonal pyramid top. The external square is heavily enforced by curved buttresses. The windows are Dec, of two lights, and simple in design. The fireplaces are arched, and the arches slightly chamfered. In the kitchen the Abbey MUSEUM, with many architectural fragments, a large number of TILES and a MONUMENT of the early C13 to an Abbot (William Vigor † 1223?). Above the head a cinquefoiled gablette.

GATEHOUSE. The Abbey Gatehouse faces Market Street. There are two entrances, one for vehicles and one for pedestrians. Depressed two-centred arches, double-chamfered without capitals. Above the pedestrians' entrance is a two-light window, and this is repeated symmetrically further l. where the Porter's House is attached to the Gatehouse. This is of two storeys and has a big canted central bay-window with battlements. The front is of six lights, the canted sides of two each.

BARN. Close to the SE corner of the walled Abbey area. It is of stone and has a length of three bays plus porch plus two bays. The arms of Abbot Bere date it as c. 1500 or a little later. The porch arch is four-centred and double-chamfered and has no capitals to rest on. On the short sides one window each in the gable which is in the shape of an arch head filled with three cusped spheric triangles. Interior with collar-beam roof.

St JOHN. A C15 church. With few hardly noticeable exceptions built after the collapse in 1403 of the Norman crossing tower. Its tall w tower with its lively crown announces the approaching town and has been alone in announcing it since the towers of the abbey have disappeared. The tower is the second tallest of any Somerset parish church (134½ ft high). It deserves close study from near to. It has set-back buttresses with a first set of shafts carrying pinnacles above the ground-stage, and a second at the bell-stage. The w doorway is uncommonly large, has tracery in the spandrels, big leaf sprays in one hollow of jambs and arch, and a niche to the l. and one to the r. There follows a six-light w window again with two niches, and then the display on the N and S sides starts also. Up the centres of the S and N sides and up from the apex of the w window rise triangular shafts ending in the intermediate pinnacles of the crown. The next stage and the bell-stage are one composition, both very tall. The lower stage of the two is covered with twin two-light panelling with two transoms, and the vertical lines of this are then taken up at the bell-stage by two four-light bell-openings with two transoms. On top of this stands the crown. Battlements pierced by arcading in two tiers. Big square angle pinnacles with crockets, accompanied by junior pinnacles and in addition by one which stands free of the corner corbelled out on a gargoyle. It is these projecting shafts and pinnacles which tend to make the crown look exuberantly top-heavy. The intermediate pinnacles on the middles of the sides whose source has been traced down to lower stages are also accompanied by junior pinnacles.

The S side of the church is all embattled, with pinnacles on the porch and the transept. The porch is two-storeyed with niches and a lierne-vault. The lower storey dates from 1428, the upper from shortly before 1498. The transept has a four-light window to the S, a five-light window to the E. The S chapel, to distinguish it specially, has five-light windows on S and E. Then follows the short chancel with its seven-light E window. The tracery below the transom is curious and capricious. It has no exact parallel anywhere. The chancel has some traces of the building preceding the present. They have been uncovered both outside and inside. But the chancel arch belongs in its date to the chapel arches and the aisle arcades, i.e. the C15. The nave appears tall with its clerestory – 'lightsome' is the word used by Leland for it. The arcade is of seven bays and piers of standard section, with four hollows, the four little round capitals of the shafts sparingly decorated with rosettes. Between the clerestory windows on angel-busts stand shafts which carry the Somerset roof of c. 1495–1500, a specimen not particularly ornate. The arches into the chancel chapels are lower and four-centred. The arches into the transepts with their plainer mouldings could be pre-1403. The transepts certainly existed then; for not only does the existence of a Norman crossing tower make the existence of Norman transepts at least very likely but the five-cusped rere-arch of one window of *c.* 1300 survives in the s transept.

FURNISHINGS. FONT. 1856–7 by *Sir G. G. Scott.* – PULPIT. 1877 by *Scott.* – SCREEN to the s transept, much restored. Two-light divisions with, in the spandrels at the top, Tudor roses, a Pelican, St George, etc. – CUPBOARD, domestic, in the s aisle. An extremely good piece of *c.* 1500. – WEST DOOR. Perp and with elaborate tracery. – CHEST. At w end of N aisle. With the arms of the Courtenay family. Bought in 1421. – ROYAL ARMS. Charles II; very good carving (above s door). – SCULPTURE. Small Italian C15 marble relief of the Nativity (s aisle). Bought in Sicily. – Small ivory Crucifixus, Italian?, Baroque. – PAINTING. On the altar of the s transept. Christ Crucified, with the Virgin, St John, and Ecclesia and Synagogue, German (?), late C15. Early in the C20 the picture was in the church of Pepinster near Liège. – STAINED GLASS. Chancel N, a good collection of C15 glass, put together so as to give the impression of a complete window. The kneeling figures at the foot specially handsome. – Chancel s, rather more a patchwork of original glass. – VESTMENTS. Pall of Abbot Whiting, with Assumpton and floral sprays. It must have been a fine piece of embroidery originally. – Gremial (Apron) of Abbot Whiting, with an extremely pretty spray of Tudor roses. – PLATE. Elizabethan Chalice by *Ions* of Exeter; Salver by *John Bignell* 1725; Salver and Flagon by *Gurney & Co.* 1744. – MONUMENTS. In the chancel N and s Richard Atwell † 1476 and Jane Atwell † 1485. He was a wealthy cloth merchant and no doubt helped to pay for the church. Two similar tomb-chests. The brass effigies are lost. Against both tomb-chests small figures between the usual panels with shields. – John Camell, *c.* 1470 (s transept). Alabaster effigy. Against the tomb-chest angels and camels. – Tomb-chest (N transept), large and with open lid. Quatrefoils with shields on the sides.

ST BENEDICT. The church was rebuilt by Abbot Bere *c.* 1520. His initials are over the N porch and on a roof-corbel in the N aisle. w tower with set-back buttresses, tall two-light bell-openings with transom and Somerset tracery, a shaft ending in a pinnacle between them, battlements and big square pinnacles accompanied by pinnacles which continue long shafts standing on the buttresses. The interior has the tower arch panelled between thin shafts. Arcade of four bays with the usual piers (four hollows) and four-centred arches. Three-light clerestory. The chancel is earlier, probably late C14, *see* the chancel arch. The S chapel dates from 1862. – In the N transept wall a big image bracket with foliage. – FONT. The usual Perp design. – PLATE. Chalice 1734; Flagon and Dish by *John Payne* 1753; Salver 1774.

ST MICHAEL (GLASTONBURY TOR). Only the tower remains, and this has lost its top storey. It dates from the late C13 and has angle buttresses, a doorway with a fine arch moulding, windows which are cusped lancets or of two lights with cusped Y-tracery, and a low E arch with characteristic moulding. S of the arch one large head-corbel of the arcade is preserved. Perp bell-openings and battlements. The W side is the most elaborate. To the l. and r. of the doorway are two relief panels, a woman milking a cow, and St Michael holding the scales. On the next stage two niches l. and r. of a window. On the tier above that three niches. In one of them a headless image is preserved. Even to the l. and r. of the bell-openings are image niches.

PUBLIC BUILDINGS. *See* Perambulation.

PERAMBULATION

The town stretches along the W and N sides of the abbey boundaries. Its centre lies at the meeting of these two axes. Here is the MARKET PLACE formerly with a big Market Cross, that is an octagonal structure like the ones at Shepton Mallet and Dunster. Now there is a kind of neo-Perp Eleanor Cross instead, 1846 by *Ferrey*. It looks right in the small square. Among houses in the Market Place only No. 8 needs notice, and this also less for its few surviving pre-Reformation details inside than for the fact that it probably was the Abbey school – the first instance which we are meeting of these exclaves of the Abbey in the town. In Benedict Street to the S nothing of note, in NORTHLOAD STREET only No. 56, a good early C18 brick house, three bays and two and a half storeys, quoins and plain parapet, the architrave of the doorway on giant carved brackets.

More in the HIGH STREET which runs E, and first of all the GEORGE HOTEL, originally the Pilgrims' Inn of the Abbey, with a façade remarkably sumptuous for its purpose. Stone-faced, embattled and incidentally three-storeyed, which in itself is something exceptional. The first floor is the *piano nobile*, taller than the others. The archway in it placed asymmetrically (Arms of the Abbey and Edward IV above). To the r. two windows, to the l. a canted bay flanked by one window on either side. The windows are of single lights, straightheaded with ogee arches and the spandrels filled by small quatrefoils in circles, a favourite Somerset motif in clerical and secular windows of the early C16. Only above the gateway the window arches have four-centred heads. All that has been described is set in a grid of vertical panelling and horizontal string courses and thus appears well-ordered, in spite of its lack of uniformity. Stone newel staircase and original panelling inside. The George Hotel is one of the most sumptuous of the small number of surviving English inns of before the Reformation.

Next to it LLOYDS BANK of 1885, by *G. M. Tilley*, quite unashamedly neo-Gothic, and with its two big gables very deliberately outdoing the real article. A few houses further on the TRIBUNAL, again a real Gothic stone-house, and again one built for the Abbey. It was the Court House in which justice was administered to those living under the abbot's jurisdiction. The building dates from the C15 with a front remodelled by Abbot Bere *c.* 1500. Two storeys, doorway with four-centred head on the l., eight-light window on the r. Above two two-light windows and a canted bay-window in the middle. All heads of the window lights are four-centred. The doorway leads into the screens passage, some linenfold panelling of which is now in the front room. The room has moulded beams. Behind it a passage with a small window and the spiral staircase. The back room has Elizabethan thin-ribbed plaster patterns between the beams and a fireplace with a high mantel-shelf. C15 back window with hood-mould on busts. On the upper floor was the lodging for the judges. The front room fills the whole front. The roof is rebuilt. The kitchen was added as a separate back wing in the Elizabethan age.

Further up in the High Street the parish church of St John and behind it the former MADRAS SCHOOL, built 1815, with Gothick windows with Y-tracery. No. 29, early C18, has a handsome door-pediment on carved brackets. Then the CONGREGATIONAL CHURCH, built in 1814 and altered in 1898. Stone front with bowed centre. The window tracery of a rounded debased Gothic kind, more usual in the C17 than the C19. Heavy porch on thick short columns.

From the end of the High Street straight up to No. 7 Bove Town, a former pilgrimage CHAPEL of the Abbey. One three-light window with four-centred arched lights. There were originally three of these 'slipper' chapels at Glastonbury. Back to the end of the High Street and to the s into LAMBROOK STREET. At the corner of Silver Street a pretty group, KYLMORE: a five-bay two-storeyed red brick house at r. angles to the street, and parallel with the street, but set back, a stone-fronted former Nonconformist chapel, early C19, with arched windows. Then within the Abbey precincts ABBEY HOUSE, symmetrical gabled Tudor Gothic of c. 1830–50. The gateway to the street is not older.

Finally from the Market Place to the s, down MAGDALENE STREET. The sequence on the E side is something so English that it must be seen to be believed. First, lying back, the ST PATRICK'S ALMSHOUSES, founded in 1517. Completely sheltered and away from the main street traffic. One enters under a gateway with the arms of Henry VIII. The much altered almshouses are on the l.; on the r. the small Perp chapel with bell-cote, three-light E window, and some original stained glass in the s window. After that the façade of the Abbey Gatehouse, see above, and incongruously side by side with it the TOWN HALL, a well-behaved stone-faced five-bay two-storey building, with arched rusticated ground floor and three-bay pediment. It was built in 1818* and now houses the Museum and the Cinema. The museum and the cinema – that is a good preparation for the nasty shock to come. From the r. of the Town Hall the Abbey appears for the first time, both St Mary's Chapel and the Abbot's kitchen, a sight to be cherished by any sensitive or indeed sensible community. What meets the eye instead? Between the street and the venerable remains is the chief car-park. A notice says 'To the Abbey Ruins 50 yards', another next to it 'Parking Fees, Cars 6d., Coaches 1s.' Neither is ever absent. At the back below the Norman and the Gothic is a line of fascia boards with notices reading 'Filling Station', 'Snack Bar', 'Gentlemen', 'Ladies', and more incongruously 'London and Manchester Assurance Company'.

Then, having disposed of the Abbey, the street continues quietly. It turns suburban now, with large detached Late Georgian houses, on the w side, first SOMERSET HOUSE (lying back; five bays with giant Doric pilasters and a Tuscan

* In it two silver-gilt MACES of 1705.

porch) then PRIORY HOUSE (five bays with Venetian doorway),* then the COPPER BEECH HOTEL. After that the
former PUMP ROOMS, opened in 1754. They were much
frequented when for a short time the chalybeate springs of
Glastonbury made the town a spa. Front of three bays with
gable and rusticated doorway, side with arched doorway. Next
to this finally ST MARY'S ALMSHOUSES. The MHLG dates
the chapel C13 and the houses C14. The chapel has a plain
single-chamfered doorhead and a twin bell-cote. Two ranges
of houses facing each other, with the chapel at the far end –
somewhat like a miniature edition of the Vicars' Close at
Wells. However, this appearance is deceptive. Originally the
whole was one building, like St Mary's Hospital at Chichester.
The space between the houses and the houses themselves were
under one roof, the centre serving as the Hall. The chapel was
the chancel of this building.

THE LAKE VILLAGE. All that remains of the famous and
flourishing lake-village that once existed a mile from Glastonbury Tor is a series of low, irregularly-shaped mounds in a
marshy valley. Here lived a prosperous agricultural and
industrial community in the last phase of the second or La
Tène period of the Iron Age. The village seems to have been
established about 50 B.C., and although it lasted until the
onset of the Roman legions it did not long survive the establishment of Roman rule. Its destruction was brought about by
warriors of the fierce Celtic tribe called the Belgae (see
Introduction). It was constructed in the middle of a substantial
sheet of water, which nowadays has shrunk to the dimensions
of a narrow watercourse known as the 'Old Rhyne'. This
sheet of water was originally the moat or natural defence of
the village. In shape the settlement was roughly triangular
and comprised between sixty and seventy-five circular huts.
The huts were between 20 and 30 ft in diameter, and a little
vestibule projected from the single doorway, which in some
cases may have contained an elaborate oaken double swing-
door. The roofs were conical, and a solid flooring of well-
shaped boards lay upon the wet clay of the artificial platform
which the villagers had erected on the floor of the mere. This
platform was an extraordinarily competent piece of work: a
good substructure of brushwood, faggots, stones, rushes, peat,

* Then the R.C. Church of ST MARY, 1939 by *J. H. H. Willman*. Lancet
windows and cross-gables, a concrete tunnel-vault over the nave, and a lower
pointed one over the chancel.

and clay, 3 to 4 acres in extent, strongly bound in by an outer casing of massive logs cunningly joined together. Around the margin of the artificial island ran a stout palisade of poles that ranged between 5 and 14 ft in height. Outside the palisade was a wooden causeway, and examples of the 20-ft dug-out canoes that once bobbed beside the causeway have been found.

It will have become evident from these architectural details that the villagers were surprisingly capable carpenters; and indeed their lathes, gouges, axes, saws, adzes, and other tools of advanced design have been unearthed. They were also adept at working iron, lead, bronze, copper, glass, and shale. In particular their brooches, bracelets, and intricate pieces of horse-harness are of magnificent workmanship. Perhaps the finest and most characteristic evidence of their skill is the celebrated Glastonbury pottery, first hand-made and then turned on the wheel, decorated with a multitude of designs derived from Celtic art. All manner of incised curvilinear patterns are represented, earlier Bronze Age motifs being skilfully developed according to the more freely-flowing designs of the La Tène epoch.

Although they were talented industrialists, the lake-villagers relied for subsistence on careful and methodical husbandry. Portions of their hurdles, farm-carts, and agricultural implements have survived, and their chief crops were barley, wheat, peas, and beans. They had also domesticated the horse, dog, pig, ox, goat, and sheep, and were skilled at trapping all manner of wild animals and wild birds.

Near the Glastonbury village is the site of Meare, an equally large lake-village, somewhat more diffuse in character. (*See* p. 235.)

Both Glastonbury and Meare were discovered, excavated, and described by Dr Bulleid, a local medical practitioner, and the famous Somerset antiquary Mr St George Gray. Their devoted researches have been carried on unremittingly over the span of half a century, and represent one of the most important series of excavations in the history of British archaeology.

PONTER'S BALL. An extraordinary antiquity, in the form of a gently curving earthen rampart 15 ft high, running continuously for ¾ m. It cuts the Glastonbury–Shepton Mallet road in the vicinity of the hamlet called HAVYATE. The bank is on the E, and it seems likely that it was erected to prevent incursions by sea-raiders in Iron Age or Saxon times. At that early period, the countryside to either side of Ponter's Ball (*Pontis Vallum?*) would have been a swamp and the earthwork would have provided a strong baulk across the tongue of solid land.

GOATHURST

ST EDWARD. Red sandstone. W tower with diagonal buttresses and battlements. Higher square stair-turret. Two-light bell-openings with Somerset tracery. The tower arch indicates a C14 date. The rest of the church entirely Perp. The S transept is the family pew and has a pretty neo-Elizabethan plaster ceiling, probably of *c.* 1830. – PULPIT. Jacobean, with big C18 tester. – HELM, GAUNTLETS, and SWORD in the family pew. – PLATE. Two Chalices 1729 by *James Wilkes*. – MONUMENTS. Sir Nicholas Halswell † 1633. Tomb-chest in a corner of the N chapel. Against the tomb-chest kneel the children, six sons on the long, three daughters on the short side. The recumbent effigies are well done. The canopy has two lowish arches and a top achievement. – Halswell Family *c.* 1650. Long inscription flanked by columns which carry an open segmental pediment. Two standing allegorical figures outside the columns. The ornament at the stage of transition from strapwork to the gristly form of the mid C17. – Sir John Tynte † 1742. By *J. M. Rysbrack*. Large wall-monument with a pretty Rococo cartouche at the foot and an excellent bust of Sir John, a clergyman, at the top. – Sir Charles Kemeys Tynte † 1785. By *Nollekens*. Standing wall-monument. A large female figure is extinguishing a torch. She leans on a pedestal with portrait medallion. – Isabella Anne Kemeys † 1835, aged three years and nine months. Sleeping child of marble – the type of Banks's Penelope Boothby. By *Raffaele Monti*. – In the churchyard: John Wilton † 1710, the C18 version of a churchyard cross. Fluted Corinthian pillar with a niche and flower decoration; an urn on the top.

RECTORY (former Manor House). The Dining Room has a tunnel-vault of plaster. Arms in the lunettes of the end walls.

ALMSHOUSES, founded in 1780, just S of the church. A plain straight seven-bay range of two storeys. Ogee-headed doorway; the windows with Y-tracery.

HALSWELL HOUSE, *see* p. 188.

GODMINSTER *see* PITCOMBE

GODNEY

HOLY TRINITY. 1839 by *G. P. Manners* (GR). Neo-Norman
with bell-cote. Remodelled from a building 'restored to its
ancient use' in 1737. The nave thoroughly Norman, especially
the w front, with broad flat intersecting arches on the ground
floor. The chancel 1902 by *E. Buckle* (Colvin).

GOLDEN FARM

Reached by a narrow avenue of very fine hazel-bushes. The
interest of the house is the Hall with its low extremely impressive plaster ceiling and fireplace. The principal motifs
are three big roundels with heavy garlands. In the centre of
the middle one a heavy pendant. In the others reliefs of King
David with his harp and the Angel of Judgement hovering
over the skeleton. Scrolls with biblical inscriptions in both
roundels and also in the fine broad frieze. Overmantel with
plenty of strapwork and crude figures. To the r. of the fireplace instead of the usual hall-bay a wooden screen screening
off a separate withdrawing room, known traditionally as the
Chapel. It all looks *c.* 1660, and the arms over the fireplace are
indeed those of the Turbervilles who owned Golden from
about 1660 onwards. Over the door between the Hall and the
so-called Chapel also are the initials I.T.

GOTHELNEY MANOR
1 m. E of Charlinch

A very impressive fragment of a manor house of *c.* 1500. The
evidence offered by the building has not been sufficiently
investigated. The front has a two-storeyed porch, to its l. an
original spiral staircase and to the l. of that a fine tall embattled
tower with a room on the top floor distinguished by a three-
light window with Perp tracery. Behind the porch lay the Hall,
but in it, facing towards the porch-side, is a large blank arch
and a smaller by its side. Corresponding with these two on
the outer back wall of the house is a very large arch. Was all
this at some time a gateway? And if so, was the surviving range
only the entrance range, and the Hall range lay at the back of
an inner court? Against this is the fact that the surviving
range has a roof obviously meant to be seen, with arched
braces on small angels, and with cusped wind-braces. The

wooden doorway from the staircase on the upper floor has the rare motif of fleurons in jambs and head. The Drawing Room has a thin-ribbed plaster ceiling, the motif being arranged centrally.

GREENHAM BARTON
1½ m. sw of Thorne St Margaret

0010

Greenham Barton is a manor house of about the size of Cothay, but less completely preserved. Like Cothay (and Holcombe Court in the adjoining part of North Devon) it belonged to the Bluet family. It consisted originally of three ranges enclosing a small courtyard with a gateway on the fourth side. The E range does not survive, the N range now contains the Kitchen. It was originally independent of the w range in which are the principal rooms of the house. The porch lies on the outer, i.e. w side of this range. It is two-storeyed and in its details (the arch moulding and the tracery of the two-light upper window) seems to belong to about 1400. The battlements are C20. The two large transomed five-light windows of the Hall on the other hand are clearly an early C16 insertion. At the back is the exit from the screens passage, the hall chimney, and between the two a spiral stair. The ornate Jacobean plaster ceilings are good C20 imitation by *Smallcorn* of Bath. The N range is probably older than the E range. In it remains a very large fireplace.

GREINTON
4030

ST MICHAEL. The church is assigned to the C15, but the evidence is confusing, with elements appearing of the C12 (s doorway), C13 (N doorway), and C14 (chancel N) – but the Victorians have done everything to make one suspicious (restoration *c.* 1850). – BENCH ENDS. On one of them the date 1621. – PLATE. Chalice and Paten 1573.

HADSPEN HOUSE *see* PITCOMBE

HALSE
1020

ST JAMES. Outside the village. Norman s doorway (*see* the arch inside). Plain w tower of the C13 to C14, *see* the slightly single-chamfered tower arch and the Dec bell-openings. The masonry of the chancel may also be C13. Otherwise mostly Perp. Three-bay N arcade with piers of four-hollows section, but leaf-band on capitals. In the spandrels between the arches two mysterious pieces, a plain blank quatrefoil and a roundel with a Green Man's face. The foliage is clearly of c. 1300. Did they belong to an arcade of that date? The use of such *paterae* comes from Glastonbury and Wells. – The S porch has three-light windows, probably re-set. – FONT. Circular, Norman, of a tapering shape, with arches originally interlaced. – ROOD SCREEN. Partly old, with four-light sections arranged in two two-light arches. Ribbed coving, and carved cornice. – SCULPTURE. In the porch two small stone panels with two small kneeling figures originally apparently flanked by buttresses or some such architectural motif. Could they belong to a cross-head? – PAINTINGS. Two large panels of the Annunciation, of good quality, Italian, late C16, typically Mannerist, probably Bolognese. – STAINED GLASS. In the E window six Flemish C16 roundels. – PLATE. Chalice, Paten, and Flagon of 1723.

HALSE HOUSE. Seven-bay two-storeyed house of the early C18, with quoins of even length at the angles and the angles of the middle bay which also has a pediment with a semicircular window. Staircase with slim turned balusters. The date 1759 on the weather-vane of the stables.

(STOFORD FARM. Oak archways probably of the late C13. Main doorway and plasterwork Elizabethan. Outbuilding of about the mid C14, *see* the floor beams and one small window. A. Vivian-Neal.)

HALSWAY MANOR *see* CROWCOMBE

HALSWELL HOUSE
½ m. S of Goathurst

Built in 1689 by Sir Halswell Tynte and the most important house of its date in the county. At the time of writing unoccupied and not as well looked after as it would deserve. The house took the place of an older one of which remains appear at the back. It is a three-storeyed massive block of buff stone seven bays by five bays, with a top balustrade, and, on the front, slightly projecting two-bay wings. In these projections the ground-floor and first-floor windows have segmental heads, in the recessed centre they are round-arched. The main accent is the doorway with the window above it. The two are connected and rather crowded in their motifs. Thus e.g. the doorway itself is set back in a curved niche à la France and Wren's St Mary-le-Bow. Trophies in the spandrels. This centre is flanked by groups of rusticated pillars stepping back twice towards the outside. The first of the steps is not represented by a pillar but by a quarter-column. In the case of the window above, it is even more difficult to describe what is happening. The window has a complex frame with ears, hanging garlands, pilasters with sunk panels carrying the broken pediment over the whole of the composition, and outer pilasters cut vertically in half and developing at the foot into volutes. Inside the house is an excellent large square open-well staircase with strong, twisted balusters. The ceiling here and in other rooms has good plaster-work, partly of the Jones–Wren type with wreathed circles or ovals, partly with the later, daintier motifs of intertwined branches and thin trails (Dining Room). Excellent contemporary wooden chimneypieces.

In the grounds several picturesque structures. Close to the house a Doric rotunda, and behind the house a STEPPED PYRAMID 'in honour of a pure nymph'. Another TEMPLE in the NW corner of the grounds has an Ionic portico and attached Ionic columns along the sides.* There is in addition a MONUMENT to a horse that died gallantly winning a wager for its owner. It is a pretty sarcophagus with garlands on a high base. Amongst the illustrations in the Tite Collection at Taunton Castle there is also a polygonal rusticated Hermitage. Recorded in addition a Grotto below the Rotunda, a Temple to Robin Hood, and a Druid's Temple. A design for a Temple of Pan was exhibited in 1778 by *John Johnson* (Colvin).

HAM *see* CREECH ST MICHAEL

HAMBRIDGE

ST JAMES. 1842 by *B. Ferrey*. Very dull. Dec details; the W tower too low for the nave roof. The best thing about the church is the two splendid cedar-trees by its side.

* This temple is being re-erected at Portmeirion, Mr Williams-Ellis's estate in Wales.

EARNSHILL HOUSE. Early C18 house of red brick. A cube with
raised principal floor. Front five bays, basement and one and
a half storeys, three-bay pediment, main doorway with
attached Tuscan columns. Far-projecting office and stable
ranges. (Good staircase.)

4010

HAM HILL

3b HAM HILL. A tremendous fortified settlement, though sometimes it is referred to as a hill-fort. It is a dominant landmark, visible for many miles around. It can be seen to particular advantage from the Yeovil–Ilminster road. Altogether
it covers an area of 200 acres, and the defensive rampart is
over 3 m. in circumference. The settlement was shown by
excavation to have been in continuous occupation from New
Stone Age times up to and beyond the Roman epoch. The
period of occupation cannot be less than twenty-five centuries,
and may well be longer. The range of finds extends from
Neolithic polished axe-heads, through a comprehensive series
of Bronze and Iron Age artefacts, to a large and varied agglo-
meration of Roman military and domestic utensils. The
discovery of the boss of a Saxon shield demonstrates that the
Hill was an important post in the succeeding Dark Ages, but
it is the Romans who appear to have occupied the site most
intensively. They evidently strengthened the prehistoric earthworks in a characteristically workmanlike fashion. The evidence of their centuries at Ham Hill includes a strange and
evocative rag-bag of articles: a chariot-wheel; metal plates
from the *lorica* or reinforced leather tunic of legionaries;
brooches; weaving implements; toilet articles; a steelyard.
There are also traces of Roman buildings within the confines
of the hill-top, including the remains of a villa that is believed
to have possessed at least twelve rooms. Most of the portable
relics from this classic archaeological site are now deposited
in the Taunton Museum.

5010

HARDINGTON MANDEVILLE

ST MARY THE VIRGIN. Low W tower, Perp in appearance,
but partly Norman in substance. The rest is all of 1863–4 including the sumptuous Neo-Norman chancel arch. This was
designed by the *Rev. John Hancock*. – FONT. Circular, Norman. Foot with one cable-moulding; at the top of the bowl a

band of lozenges. – PULPIT. Jacobean, with one tier of the familiar short blank arches and a row of panels with strap-work decoration. – PLATE. Chalice and Cover 1573.

HASELBURY PLUCKNETT

4010

ST MICHAEL. Perp w tower with diagonal buttresses and two-light bell-openings with Somerset tracery. Embattled aisles with C19 Perp windows. Inside, the aisles have been made into one with the nave. The arcades were taken out in 1920. Perp tower arch and chancel arch. But the N chancel chapel is E.E. The responds to the W and s with coupled shafts carrying capitals with upright leaves. Double-chamfered arches.* – PLATE. Chalice of *c.* 1700; Salver by *Robert Abercromby* 1742; Flagon 1760.

HASELBURY BRIDGE, to the w of the village, and N of the bridge carrying the A30 Road. C15, of two spans. Pointed, ribbed arches. 'The most perfect medieval bridge in this part of the country' (Jervoise).

HATCH BEAUCHAMP

3010

ST JOHN BAPTIST. In the grounds of Hatch Court, behind the house and close to the Home Farm. The manor house was originally no doubt nearer the church, and the C18 squire preferred to move away. Perp w tower, not high, of blue lias. Diagonal buttresses, four-light w window, three-light bell-openings with Somerset tracery. Pierced parapet with quatre-foils and arcades in the merlons. Angle pinnacles with de-tached corbelled-out shafts and also intermediate pinnacles. The s doorway to the church carries the date 1530. Inside, N and s aisles with low piers of four-waves section with capitals carved as leaf-bands. Four-centred arches. To the E of these a narrower arch, not of the same design on the two sides. The s aisle windows have panelled jambs and arches inside. The s chapel was added in 1834. In 1867 during a thorough renovation by *Sir G. G. Scott* nave and aisles were extended one bay to the E and a new N chapel was built (using the old panelled E window). s chapel s and N chapel N windows are both clearly C19. – FONT. Of the familiar octagonal Perp type. – BENCHES. Straight-headed, with many noteworthy motifs.

* Circular Norman arcade piers are preserved in a barn w of the church.

Apart from the usual large plants and close tracery the Resurrection of Christ with the Pelican beneath (cf. Bishop's Hull), a kneeling man, St George and the Dragon, St John Baptist, a cock-fight, and also Renaissance figures. – STAINED GLASS. Old glass in the heads of N windows. – S aisle W window 1854 by *A. Gibbs*. – PAINTING. Large Deposition of Christ, in the church already in 1791. In the Flemish C17 style; said to be by *Parriss*. – PLATE. Chalice 1572; Paten by *Thomas Port* 1713; Chalice and Cover 1793; Dish 1839. – OBELISK in the churchyard. Can it really be an C18 paganization of a cross-shaft?

HATCH COURT. Dated on a rainwater head 1755. By *Thomas Prowse*, of Axbridge, a friend of Sanderson Miller (Colvin). A fine square Bath stone mansion in the Palladian style, two-storeyed with the four square angle erections made popular by Colen Campbell and William Kent (cf. especially Hagley Hall). E and W fronts with canted bays, S front with an arcade of five arches. Balustrade on the upper floor. Some windows selected to be emphasized by pediments. Fine large staircase inside starting in one arm and continuing in two to a curved gallery on two columns.

HAVYATE *see* PONTER'S BALL, GLASTONBURY

8030
inset
HAWKRIDGE

ST GILES. Indeed on a ridge. The village lies about 950 ft up and is not at all easy to reach. Norman doorway with one order of colonnettes, the capitals with elementary upright volutes on stalks. Segmental lintel-stone. Bare tympanum. Zigzag ornament in the hood-mould. Plain two-stage W tower with square higher stair-turret. Battlements. The plainest straight-headed one-light bell-openings. Such a structure is hard to date. Is it ancient or simply primitive? W window with four round-headed lights and three plain circles above. The design looks C17. Three-light E window and part of the chancel masonry Dec. – FONT. Circular, Norman, defaced cable-moulding at the top of the bowl. – PLATE. Cup by *I.P.* 1573; Paten by *Philip Elson* of Exeter 1725. – MONUMENT. C13 coffin with foliated cross and inscription on the lid. Brought back in 1931 from St Nicholas' Priory, Exeter. Before that it had been at South Molton.

HAZLEGROVE HOUSE
½ m. from Sparkford

Plain seven-bay house of two and a half storeys, remodelled about 1732 by *John* and *William Bastard* of Blandford. The first-floor windows along the front are all pedimented. One room still has its Jacobean panelling and plaster ceiling. Entrance Hall with a good fireplace of *c.* 1735–40 (another on the first floor) and large open-well staircase with wrought-iron handrail and Venetian window at the back. – The GATEWAY from Sparkford with its segmental arch, its broad pilasters with rudimentary Ionic capitals, and its broad volutes is evidently earlier, *c.* 1690. It was indeed bought from Low Ham, where about 1685–90 Sir Ralph Stawell had begun to build a large mansion for himself.

HEATHFIELD

St JOHN BAPTIST. Red sandstone. Small and much renewed (1870). – PULPIT. Made up of old panels. – MONUMENT. The usual Elizabethan type with two kneeling figures facing each other across a prayer desk. The inscription is illegible. – CHURCHYARD CROSS. Base and shaft survive. On the shaft one figure in relief.

HENDFORD *see* YEOVIL

HENLEY MANOR
1 m. SW of Misterton

Elizabethan house with recessed centre and far-projecting gabled wing. The centre is probably of pre-Reformation date, *see* one small window at the back. The other windows mullioned with hood-moulds.

HENSTRIDGE

St NICHOLAS. Perp remains in the N aisle, the N arcade, and the tower arch. The rest 1873 with a W tower rebuilt in 1900. – PLATE. Chalice and Cover by *Orenge* 1574, specially good; Paten 1698. – MONUMENT. Between chancel and N chancel chapel William Carent † 1463 and wife (Margaret Stourton). Tomb-chest with eleven slim figures in elementary niches to

7—s.s.

the N, six figures and a plain oblong recess to the chancel. Recumbent defaced effigies. Canopy with depressed four-centred arch elaborately panelled inside. In the spandrels very elongated figures of angels. Cresting with shields. To the W of the monument small stone entrance into the former chantry chapel. On it towards the chancel an achievement, towards the N a fragment of a figure in long frock.

INWOOD HOUSE, 1 m. N. Large sham-Jacobean stone house of Victorian date. Irregular with shaped gables. By its side tall red brick water tower, dated 1881, exceedingly unattractive. Many small C18 lead figures in the garden and an C18 summer-house with a big fanciful lead pagoda-roof.

HESTERCOMBE
2020

HESTERCOMBE HOUSE. The house is now essentially what the Portmans made it about 1875, a large irregular mansion in a debased 'free Renaissance' with picturesquely placed and terribly detailed tower. Large porte-cochère, very large Entrance Hall with a staircase starting in one flight, splitting into two by 90 degrees and returning to the upper floor again by 90 degrees. Much lush acanthus stucco, marble columns, and marble pilasters. On the S side to the r. of this an older house.

56b   The fame of Hestercombe, however, is its gardens, laid out and, one can safely say, built by *Lutyens* in 1905, etc. Below the C19 terrace Lutyens laid out a large square parterre with a saltire-cross design. Along its S side runs a pergola 230 ft long. Along the W and E sides are the so-called Iris channels. Above the NE end of this composition and just SE of the house is the Rolunda Pool with a heavy retaining wall. From here, a long composition stretches to the ENE with the orangery in the middle. This is of three bays in a Lutyenized Late Wren or Vanbrugh style with a repeated Palladio motif. The use of levels is ingenious all the way through.

HIGHBRIDGE
3040

ST JOHN EVANGELIST. 1858–9 by *John Norton*, enlarged by the same 1882, restored by *F. Bligh Bond* 1914 (GR). Lancet church with the stump of a formerly higher NW tower. Interesting interior, wide, with short polished granite columns with crocket capitals set two-deep and carrying very tall arches.

HIGHER HADSPEN see PITCOMBE

HIGHER KINGSTON see YEOVIL

HILL FARRANCE

HOLY CROSS. The interest of the church is its W tower. The stair-turret in the middle of one side, as at Wellington, West Buckland, and in parts of Devon. The building of the tower then received financial help from John Peryn of Wellington (will of 1509), and the pierced parapet contains the initials I.P. Diagonal buttresses, two-light bell-openings with Somerset tracery. The body of the church over-restored (1857). Perp arch into the S transept. – BENCH ENDS. Straight-topped, with flowers, leaves, etc., and also such Renaissance elements as heads in profile.

HIGH HAM

ST ANDREW. The church faces broadside on a pretty village green, not a common thing in Somerset. The W tower is not up to much (early C14 below; see the tower arch with a continuous moulding of two broad waves; C15 above, with two-light bell-openings with Somerset tracery), but the rest has some grandeur. The rebuilding was due to Abbot John Selwood of Glastonbury, Sir Amias Poulett, and others. Tradition has it that it was all done in one year, 1476. Only the chancel may have come later. This was paid for by the rector John Dyer † 1499 (see below). The aisles are both embattled and have plenty of big gargoyles. Three-light windows and on the S side exactly centrally placed two-storeyed porch. Niche above the doorway triangular in plan. Porch roof on angels. Chancel embattled and provided with pinnacles. E window of five lights. Great care is taken with the chancel tracery. Interior with aisle arcades of five bays on long and thin piers of the standard four-hollows type. Fine nave roof of Somerset type. Tie-beams on slight arched braces starting from figures of angels. King-posts standing on bosses. Not much tracery above the tie-beams. The chancel is lower and the chancel arch panelled. Above the chancel arch a heavy beam with fleurons. The roof is similar to that of the nave. – ROOD SCREEN. Tall, of four-light sections. The middle mullion reaches up into the apex of the arch. Ribbed and panelled coving and carved cornice. – BENCHES. Some with poppy-heads. The end motifs tracery of not much interest. – LECTERN. Jacobean? Two turned balusters connected higher up by two battens. Between them a third turned baluster starts to carry the (renewed) lectern proper. – S DOOR with blank tracery. – STAINED GLASS. Some C15 figures in the chancel E and SW windows. – PLATE. Chalice and Cover 1570. – BRASS. Inscription only, to John Dyer † 1499, rector of High Ham from 1459, 'qui hoc cancellum de novo fieri fecit'.

WINDMILL, ½ m. E of the village on the Stembridge road. Still with its thatched cap.

ROMAN VILLA with two mosaic pavements.

4010   HINTON ST GEORGE

ST GEORGE. A good Perp church. Thomas Marsh, Rector, left £4 in 1494 towards the building of the tower. The tower has set-back buttresses continued in shafts set diagonally and ending in subsidiary pinnacles accompanying the main pinnacles on the top. There are also intermediate pinnacles corbelled out on the middles of the sides. The tower is embattled, and the battlements have shields in lozenges. On the S side on the second stage of the four-storeyed tower a statue niche. The bell-openings are long, of two lights with a transom, and reach down from the fourth into the third stage (cf. Crewkerne, Norton-sub-Hamdon). There is tracery in the heads and below the transoms, and Somerset tracery as well. So much for the tower. The church itself has a parapet, and on the N side only the Poulett chapel at the NE end is embattled. This chapel was rebuilt in 1814, when also the N transept was converted into a family pew. Embattled S porch with niche over the entrance, tunnel-vaulted with ribs and panelling inside. Embattled W corner of the S aisle. The tracery here is of the panel kind without sub-panels (cf. Yeovil). The other windows are mostly of four lights with two sub-arches. Inside, the S aisle arcade of three bays has standard piers (four hollows). The roof has no tie-beams or collar-beams or braces; just cusped principals. Chancel arch of the same section as the aisle arcade, N transept arch too. But the N and S chancel chapels open in panelled arches, as does the tower towards the nave.

FURNISHINGS. – FONT. Circular, Late Norman. – PLATE. Chalice 1815; Paten and Plate 1813. – MONUMENTS. An uncommonly large number, all in or near the Poulett Pew and

Chapel, and mostly of members of the Poulett family. Chronologically they follow each other thus: Knight in armour on tomb-chest (below the family pew), c. 1475. – Brasses of John Thudderle and his wife, late C15 (next to the previous). The figures are 18 in. long. The brass was originally in Hinton church, but found its way into some outbuildings at Grove Park, Warwickshire. It was restored to Hinton a few years ago. – Sir Amyas Poulett † 1537 and his son Sir Hugh † 1572. The two monuments are an identical pair, placed against the N wall of the Poulett chapel. The tomb-chests are re-used older pieces. The rest must date from c. 1540 and have been got ready by Sir Hugh after the death of his father. The date of his own death is indeed left blank in the inscription. Two couples, recumbent, their children kneeling below (and above the old tomb-chest fronts). The effigies are under two four-centred arches, panelled in the Perp style inside. But the back wall has exuberant Early Renaissance foliage and the coats of arms are supported by naked putti. The niches are flanked by candelabra balusters. Scrolls and shields in the spandrels. Foliate cresting. – Against the w wall of the chapel Sir Amyas II † 1588 (removed here from St Martin-in-the-Fields), reclining alabaster effigy, the head on a rolled-up mat. The inscription below is in French. Sir Amyas was for a time guardian of Mary Queen of Scots. Behind the tomb-chest coat of arms, and above this heavy entablature on two unfluted Ionic columns. – Sir Anthony † 1600 and his wife † 1601. Large monument between the Poulett Chapel and the chancel. Two recumbent effigies, their children kneeling against the long sides of the tomb-chest. Four-centred coffered arch, columns l. and r., obelisks and achievements above. – John Baron Poulett † 1649 (E wall of Poulett Chapel). This is in 36 many ways the most remarkable monument in the church. It is so unrestrainedly Baroque, it looks so much like the early C18 North of the Alps, that it can only be accounted for by being regarded as the work of an itinerant foreigner (Portuguese?). Even then 1665 (Kenneth Wickham's date) seems unlikely and the early C18 more acceptable. The monument is of plaster and not of stone, rich and coarse and naive. Sarcophagus on a sphinx and two lions. Two wild men (an un-Italian motif) to its l. and r. The top of the sarcophagus rises in the middle in thick, lush acanthus foliage. An angel stands here on skulls. Above the angel a thick garland hanging from the looped-up corners of a raised curtain. Outsize the

crazily over-sized tapering Ionic pillars. Entablature encrusted
with decoration and rising at the back in a curve to hold the
coat of arms. Two putti right at the top. – Bernard Hutchins
† 1733. Black sarcophagus between coupled pilasters and
below a pediment (w wall, above Sir Amyas II). – John, first
Earl Poulett, 1745 (Poulett Pew, E wall). By *Rysbrack*. Plain
large classical inscription base and free-standing bust of
telling features. – Rebecca Poulett † 1765 (nave). Obelisk
background. A flying putto holds the portrait medallion. –
Bridgett Poulett † 1747. Bust against obelisk background
(Poulett Pew, w wall). – Anne Poulett † 1765 (nave). Obelisk
with two elegant small standing figures by an urn. Portrait
medallion above. – Vere Earl Poulett † 1819 (Poulett Pew,
E wall). Tablet with two flanking female figures. By *Sir R.
Westmacott*. – John Vere M. Amyas Poulett † 1857 (Poulett
Pew, w wall). Large standing female figure mourning. By
E. J. Physick of London.

HINTON HOUSE.* Large irregular house of various periods.
Leland mentions Sir Hugh Poulett's 'goodly Manor Place'
with an inner court and two high towers. But of this nothing
seems to remain. The earliest surviving part is said to be of
c. 1630–40. It is probably the s w corner. In a room a plaster
ceiling is mentioned in the style of Forde Abbey Dorset and
dated 1636. The s front appears to be of *c.* 1700; regular
composition, nine bays, two storeys, with steep triangular
window pediments. Early C18 State Rooms inside. For the mid
C18 work by *Matthew Brettingham* is recorded (Colvin). More
enlargements were made late in the C18 (*see* rainwater heads of
1796) by *James Wyatt*. They are castellated. The w front (one
plus seven plus one bays) forms part of this work. It is cobbled.
The heavy Gothic porch on the N side is by *Wyatville* 1814.
In addition the gatehouse and clock tower was bought from
Clifton Maybank (cf. Montacute) in the late C18 and re-
erected. It is separated from the entrance hall by an archway.

HOLBROOK HOUSE *see* WINCANTON

HOLFORD

ST MARY. Short w tower with saddleback roof. The rest
mostly rebuilt *c.* 1850. E and w windows Perp. – CROSS-SHAFT
in the churchyard, with a mutilated figure.

* An adequate appreciation of Hinton House is impossible, as Earl
Poulett would not allow me to see the inside.

ALFOXTON PARK. Early C18, the N side Late Georgian. Seven bays, two storeys, with three-bay pediment. Tuscan porch. Wordsworth lived in the house in 1797.

HOLNICOTE HOUSE
½ m. SW of Selworthy

9040
inset

Of the manor house no more remains than a gateway (now in the garage yard) with a two-light cusped straight-headed window above to the outside and the inside. Nor does the *cottage orné* of Sir T. Dyke Acland remain, which had verandas and was thatched.

HOLTON

6020

ST NICHOLAS. Several original features point to the C14: the elaborately moulded S porch doorway, the chancel arch, and perhaps also the double-chamfered tower arch, dying into the imposts. N aisle added 1888. – PULPIT. Perp, polygonal, of stone, with panel tracery. – PLATE. Chalice Cover 1570; Chalice 1573.

HORNBLOTTON

5030

ST PETER. 1872–4 by *Sir T. G. Jackson*, and a really important little church to learn what a disciple of Norman Shaw wished an interior to be like. The church is small and with its tile-hung belfry, its square little timber bell-openings, and its tiled broach-spire looks SE England rather than SW – in spite of the deep yellowy brown of the local stone. The window details are Geometrical to Early Dec. The walls inside are treated with strawberry red and white plaster in ornaments and figures. The ornaments here as also in the reredos are those which Eastlake and Edis and Mrs Haweis recommended for artistic interiors, branches of leaves, sunflowers and so on. To the l. and r. of the altar the four Evangelists on blue and white tiles. Above the altar Stained Glass of the Crucifixion and Angels. This as well as other stained glass and the chancel pavement were designed by Jackson and made by *Powell & Sons*. – PLATE. Chalice and Cover 1637.

MANOR HOUSE. Built as the Rectory in 1867 by *Penrose*, and consecutively enlarged. The big upper window in the recessed part between the two gabled wings looks as if Jackson at a later date may have had something to do with the house as well.

8040
inset

HORNER

PACKHORSE BRIDGE. On Hacketty Way; single arch. Another, ½ m. N, at West Luccombe.

7020

HORSINGTON

ST JOHN BAPTIST. Perp W tower with C18 bell-openings. The rest 1885 by *Willcocks* of Bath. Big two-bay opening into the chancel S chapel with ogee cinquefoil above the spandrels. – FONT. Perp, octagonal, with crudely carved angels supporting the bowl. – TOWER SCREEN. 1903, with florid Arts-and-Crafts-Perp decoration carved by a local class at North Curry. – STAINED GLASS. E (1885) and a S window (1887) by *Kempe*. – PLATE. Standing Cup and Cover 1614 (cf. Bath Abbey); two early C18 Chalices; Paten 1723; Chalice and Cover 1734.

HORSINGTON HOUSE. Big five-bay three-storey house, High Victorian Italianate. Outside the gates the base and shaft of the VILLAGE CROSS.

MANOR HOUSE. Plain five- by five-bay three-storeyed Georgian block with parapet. Built some time between 1753 and 1770.

OLD RECTORY. Five-bay two-storey front with projecting doorway. Pediment on brackets. The window above is enriched by ears. This part has been dated both 1686 and c. 1730. Additions of 1856.

3010

HORTON
1 m. W of Ilminster

Close to the cross-roads several houses worth a glance: Horton House of the C18, and Horton Farm House probably of the C17, then to the E an octagonal early C19 lodge with Gothic windows, and SOUTHFIELDS with a pretty brick gazebo of the C18, and a little more distant to the N JORDANS. Fine stone-faced Late Georgian block of five by four bays with a lower wing (perhaps older) at the back. Top balustrade. Two porches of coupled columns. Groin-vaulted Entrance Hall and elegant carved staircase with iron railing at its back.

Thatched summer-house with coloured glass dome and sea-shell, starfish, and fossil decoration.

ROWLAND'S FARM, ½ m. NE Jordans. An impressive mid-C16 house. Buttressed porch leading into the Hall which still has its screen, the three doors (one blocked) to Kitchen, Buttery and Pantry, original windows including a four-light window with transom and arched lights, and the fireplace. Ceiling and roof are well preserved.

HORWOOD
1 m. SE of Wincanton
7020

(Mineral springs were found in 1810. The buildings then put up remain and are now a farmhouse and offices).

HUISH BARTON
½ m. N of Nettlecombe
0030

The front and a hall in the back wing are of *c.* 1700. The hall has tall cross-windows and original leading. Over the fire-place a handsome cypher and the date 1698.

HUISH CHAMPFLOWER
0020

ST PETER. W tower with diagonal buttresses. On the stage below the bell-openings on each side two statue niches, one stage further down one. The rest of the church over-renewed in 1875–80. The most interesting feature of the church is the N arcade. The piers obviously do not fit their present position. Also they have the unusual section of a core with eight attached shafts, a C14 not a Perp design. But the capitals are the Devon leaf band, uncommonly thin. Double-chamfered arches. The N chapel E window is of six lights, again a surprise. Mr Eeles has suggested that piers and windows were taken over from Barlinch Priory. – LECTERN. Of oak, the body C15, the wings C19. – COMMUNION RAIL. Pretty Early Georgian work, with thin balusters of three different designs. – PLATE. Chalice and Cover 1573; Teapot Stand (?) 1795.

HUISH EPISCOPI
4020

ST MARY. Built of blue lias with Ham Hill stone dressings. Big Late Norman S doorway, Ham Hill, reddened by fire. Two orders of shafts, the inner decorated, outer jambs with zigzag at right angles to the wall. The same position in the two zigzag friezes in the arch. Hood-mould with decorated nail-head. Aisleless nave, transepts and chancel; a C14 arrangement. The best surviving piece of the C14 is the N transept N window, evidently early, say *c.* 1310–20. The wilful way in which two trefoils in circles are deprived of the steadying quality they possess in the Geometrical style must be seen to be believed. The circle is left open on one side for a mouchette to push up into it. Hamilton Thompson attributed the chancel arch to the same century. It has straight shanks and no capitals. These straight-sided arches are repeated at the entry to the N and S transepts and also to the W addition of the S transept (which is of different stone and later). The responds of these lateral rooms are of the Perp four-hollow section, the pier between the two S bays is very thin. Small polygonal capitals to the shafts only. Externally the S chapel is embattled and looks quite stately. But the fame of the church is its W tower, 100 ft tall, a companion-piece to that at Kingsbury Episcopi. Set-back buttresses with three tiers of attached pinnacles all on tall shafts. The angles themselves are given set-offs and small pinnacles high up. W doorway flanked by shafts with pinnacles. Leaves in the spandrels. Quatrefoil frieze above. Four-light W window. Quatrefoil frieze at the foot of the next stage, big three-light transomed window with Somerset tracery, flanked by niches on shafts. Quatrefoil frieze at the foot of the following stage. Two-light bell-openings with transoms flanked by shafts with pinnacles. Quatrefoil frieze below the battlements. These are of pierced pointed quatre-foils on lozenges, and pierced arcaded in the merlons. Angle pinnacles with projecting detached shafts carrying subsidiary pinnacles. Also intermediate pinnacles. The N and S sides differ below. They have statue niches on the W window stage. – FONT. Octagonal, Perp, with quatrefoil frieze. – PULPIT. Dated 1625 (the date not old), with tall blank arches and arabesque decoration. – STAINED GLASS. S chapel E window, 1899 by *Morris & Co.*, designed by *Burne-Jones.* Adoration of the Magi, with many angels. A very complete statement of Burne-Jones's later style. – PLATE. Chalice Cover 1571; Chalice inscribed 1689; Paten 1700.

16b

HUNTSPILL

ST PETER. W tower of the late C14 or *c.* 1400. Sturdy, with set-back buttresses, a tower arch with responds of four-hollows section, but treated broadly, a big w door meant to start one composition with the w window. Strong shafts l. and r. of the door, and niches outside these. However, the shafts are not continued, as no doubt intended, to flank a four-light w window. A five-light window was put in instead (before 1843; *see* the Buckler drawing at Taunton Castle). Two-light bell-openings with Somerset tracery, and battlements. Prettily varied N side, parapet and two-light windows for the aisle, battlements for the three-bay N chapel, and then a two-storeyed N vestry with a smaller parapet (altered inside). S aisle and two-storeyed S porch again with plain parapet. The chancel E window is of five lights. The interior is roomy and dark, getting impressively lighter towards the E end. Five bays plus two narrower bays for the chapel. Piers of standard section (four hollows). – PULPIT. Very broad example of the typical Jacobean pulpit. One tier of the usual blank arches. Small busts support the top edge. Panels and long inscriptions in black letter below. The pulpit comes from Stogursey church. – STAINED GLASS. E window of five lights by *Clayton & Bell*, *c.* 1880. – PLATE. Chalice and Paten 1672; Flagon by *Mason* 1729; Salver 1825. – MONUMENTS. Effigies of Knight and Lady under a low-arched recess in the S wall. The cusping of the arch is all renewed. The effigies date from the middle and the late C14. – CHURCHYARD GATES AND RAILINGS. Early C19, Gothic, and made at Coalbrookdale.

HURCOTT *see* CHARLTON MACKRELL *and* ILMINSTER

HURST *see* MARTOCK

HYMERFORD HOUSE *see* NORTH COKER

ILCHESTER

Ilchester was the Roman Lendiniae (not Ischalis as has often been assumed). In the Middle Ages it was a town of some importance. It had four parish churches says Leland (1542), ten says Gerard (1632), sixteen says Stukely (1724).* In addition there was a small Dominican friary founded before 1261, an Augustinian nunnery founded before 1281 and known later as

---

* Mr J. Stevens Cox has proved the existence of eight.

White Hall, and a leper hospital. Famous also was Ilchester Gaol.

ST MARY MAJOR. Massive C13 tower, square below, octagonal above. Angle buttresses to the square part. Lancet bell-openings. Plain parapet. Low tower arch inside, double-chamfered on moulded corbels. Nave and chancel. Large S aisle of 1880. The former S aisle was smaller. Witness of it is one short circular pier in the churchyard W of the church. The chancel is also C13 work, probably a generation earlier than the tower. The E window is of three lights renewed. It has above the lights plate tracery of two quatrefoils and an octofoil. Inside, this window has a deep double-roll-moulded rere-arch and shafts with big shaft-rings and stiff-leaf capitals. Perp nave and chancel windows; Perp S transept. The N windows of unusual, late shape, of three or five lights, straight-headed with a depressed four-centred arch and leaves in the spandrels. In the S transept two thickly canopied niches. – PULPIT. Jacobean. The usual arches are here treated in per-spective. – PAINTING. Remains of C13 wall paintings on the N wall of the nave. – PLATE. Chalice and Cover 1573; Paten 1628.

To the N of the church triangular village 'green' with C18 CROSS, a Tuscan column on a high base, with big entablature and bell finial. Several Georgian houses face into the square, of three and five bays. One of these is the Town Hall.

37b TOWN HALL. This possesses a MACE which is a rare treasure not only from the county point of view, but also from that of all England or indeed Europe. It is the oldest staff of office in England and clearly dates from the C13. The head is $7\frac{1}{2}$ in. long and of brass. On it, separated by twisted shafts, four figures, three kings and an angel. Three of the figures are in purple. The inscription is cryptic. It runs: Ie su de drverie. Ne me dunet mie.

(MANOR FARM. Early C17.)

(BRIDGE. Partly of c. 1200.)

(PILL BRIDGE, 2 m. W. A C17 packhorse bridge.)

ROMAN VILLA, $\frac{1}{2}$ m. S. In course of excavation.

3020

ILE ABBOTS

ST MARY. Ile Abbots is outstanding among Somerset churches, both internally and externally. This is meant architecturally, but historically also the church is of interest. As for the exterior, the W tower has certain points all its own, and they

give it its singular classicity. To start describing it, the w
doorway has the usual big leaves in the spandrels. Above it
is an extremely large transomed four-light window. Above
this follows a transomed two-light window with Somerset
tracery, and above that the bell-openings, a pair of two lights
each, again with transoms and Somerset tracery. They are
flanked by thin pinnacled shafts. But niches are placed to the
l. and r. of the doorway, the big w window (at the springing
of its arch), and the upper window, and they are all in line
with the outer shafts of the bell-openings. So there is here a
firmness of positions established which is so often lacking in
parish church design, including that of Somerset. The tower
follows on the whole the same scheme as St James's Taunton,
though it is much less high (81 ft). Set-back buttresses, with
two tiers of applied pinnacles. The angles of the tower have
in addition set-offs and higher up pinnacles. The buttresses
end on the bell-level in diagonally set shafts again crowned by
pinnacles, and behind these shafts, covering the angle of the
tower diagonally, is yet another pinnacle of the tower, the
pinnacle on the corner of the battlements. There are intermediate pinnacles on the middles of the sides too. The battlements have pierced quatrefoils and above them pierced
arcading. Higher NE stair-turret with octagonal pyramid roof.
Some points of detail must be added. On the s side instead of
the w window there is one sculpture niche, on the N side the
arrangement is altogether a little disturbed by the stair-turret.
The windows below the bell-openings have one curious motif:
in addition to hood-moulds on square stops, there are at their
foot moulds of the same kind (functionally useless) and they
have diagonally-set square stops. Finally another distinguishing feature of the tower of Ile Abbots is that most of the
niches are still filled with the original images. They are not
defaced and alas only serve to prove that the strictly sculptural
value of such Late Perp sculpture in England was a rule low.
The tower belongs to one group with Bishop's Lydeard,
Kingston, and Staple Fitzpaine. They are all similar to
Huish and Kingsbury but a little less exuberant.

The other piece of external display at Ile Abbots is the N
aisle, short and compact, of four bays, with four-light windows under four-centred arches and with a pierced pinnacled
parapet of quatrefoils and saltire crosses with pointed trefoils
above. The s side is less splendid, except for the s porch which
has pierced battlements of two tiers of quatrefoils. All this is

of course late medieval. But a further study of details reveals, even before one enters the church, that it is by no means all of one date. The chancel clearly is of *c.* 1300, *see* the five-light E window, a group of five stepped lancet lights under a low two-centred arch, and *see* also the lovely N and S windows, which are groups of three stepped and cusped lancet lights with three quatrefoiled circles above. The tracery is of the bar, no longer the plate, variety. There is also a small doorway on the N side, with a continuous double-chamfer. Now the same type of doorway is used on the S of the nave and also as the outer entry into the S porch. There is, moreover, in the porch a stoup whose details point to *c.* 1300. So the porch was only made more splendid later. It is indeed quite easy to see inside that the fine fan-vault with its pendant is an addition. Then the nave S windows. One of them is a group of three cusped and stepped lancet lights under a big Perp hood-mould, the other is a two-light Dec window. It looks then as if the church was complete by *c.* 1300. The C14 made only small alterations. Major work was left to *c.* 1500.

On entering through the S doorway one is at once transported into an atmosphere of great purity and lucidity. Perhaps that is due more to the fine harmony of honey-coloured stone and recent whitewash than to architecture, but surely the chancel at least has something peculiarly perfect in its proportions too. The designer certainly intended to do something special here, or else he would not have produced his unique Piscina and Sedilia. The PISCINA is framed by two panels on each side, and the group is surmounted by five more. There is then an oblong panel of Ham Hill stone divided up by relatively broad buttresses and decorated by blank arches with crocketed gables. Then the SEDILIA. The three seats are low and have backs and arms developed as one curve (as in tub-chairs, only very low). They are decorated by very shallow blank cusped arches. The arms end in the front in circles (in plan), and on these no doubt originally there stood shafts. Now there is a back panel of different stone instead, though apparently of the same date and stylistically in keeping.

The nave is separated from the aisle by an arcade of familiar type. The piers have four shafts and four wave mouldings in the diagonals, and the capitals are bands of foliage. The arches are depressed pointed. Thin wall-shafts between the aisle windows. Good panelled aisle roof of low pitch. Panelled chancel arch, moulded tower arch.

FURNISHINGS. – FONT. Square, Norman, re-worked Gothic. The Norman carvings survive on one side, an animal carved in the primeval way of, say, the Luppitt font in Devon. Then the bowl was, it seems, turned upside down, the animal carving was placed out of sight, and the other side received small pointed arches, quatrefoil fleurs de lis, and other motifs. – ROOD SCREEN. Remarkably humble for such a church and surely not made for this position. Two-light sections and heavy straight top. No coving. – BENCHES. Straight-headed with simple tracery, not the intricate type of further West in Somerset and of Devon. – TOWER SCREEN. Made up of the parts of a Jacobean communion rail. Balusters of vertically symmetrical shape.

BETHESDA CHAPEL, 1805, small oblong building with arched windows.

ILE BREWERS   3020

ALL SAINTS. 1861, by *C. E. Giles* (GR). Blue lias, Ham Hill stone, and red tiles. s porch tower with octagonal upper part (à la Bishop's Hull, Ilchester, etc.), and tiled spire. The detail all late C13. It looks as if the style was suggested by one original piece, the outer doorway of the tower porch. However, this does not appear in W. W. Wheatley's drawing (Mells Manor House). So it must be re-used and re-set. Complex arch moulding on two orders of quite strong shafts. An original later C13 window was drawn in 1850 for Braikenridge's Collinson (Taunton Castle). – PLATE. Chalice 1570; Cover 1760.

ILMINSTER   3010

ST MARY. An impressive, large, and consistently designed church, all Perp, and culminating in its crossing tower, the design of which is inspired by that of Wells Cathedral. Set-back buttresses with two sets of pinnacles. Three two-light bell-openings on each side, with transoms, normal tracery, and Somerset tracery. The bell-openings are continued blank with descending mullions right through the stage below the bell-stage. Battlements and pinnacles. The pinnacles cluster in threes at the corners, and there are in addition two intermediate pinnacles on each side, in keeping with the piers between the bell-openings. It is a firm and clear composition, rich yet sober. W front with a five-light window, a gable, and embattled aisle fronts. Embattled aisle sides, except for the gabled S transept front and the parapeted N chapel. Long three-light aisle windows. S porch with ogee gable over the doorway and blank panelling above this. Chancel with three-light windows, and, to its E, a low projection, also embattled, containing the Vestry. The S chapel has a five-light S window and otherwise again three-light windows. The N chapel is the most splendid part of the church. It was probably built by a bequest of Sir William Wadham who died in 1452. It is a glass-house. Only the panelled buttresses seem to remain of solid wall. The windows are transomed. Decorated parapet and pinnacles. The N window rises above the parapet to be topped by a crocketed gable and pinnacles. The window tracery on the other hand looks puzzlingly like a fanciful design of *c.* 1300. Could it be re-used?

Inside, the arrangement of the nave arcade in three widely-set arches is an alteration of 1825. It destroys the axiality of the aisle windows and the clerestory windows. But the piers of the usual section (four hollows) are original. Tall impressive crossing with fan-vault. The arches are panelled on all sides. Entry into the N and S chapels by arches of the same moulding as the nave arcade. Huge squints into the chancel. Here the roof principals rest on wall-shafts. The nave roof with the moderate pitch usual in Somerset churches and with tie-beams, king-posts, and tracery above the tie-beams. – FONT. Octagonal, Perp, with panelled stem and pointed quatrefoils on the bowl. – SCREEN to N chapel. Jacobean, re-set. – STAINED GLASS. E window by *Burlison & Grylls.* – Crucifixion and Magi in the nave by *Heaton, Butler & Bayne.* – PLATE. Chalice and Cover 1592; Standing Cup 1611 (cf. Bath Abbey); Paten 1633. – MONUMENTS. Sir William Wadham † 1452 and wife, N chapel. Large tomb-chest with niches thickly adorned with nodding ogee arches. On the short side two small figures kneeling to the l. and r. below a seated figure of Christ. Thick leaf-frieze below the lid. On the lid brass figures surrounded by a gable on thin shafts. The figures are 3 ft 6 in. long. – Nicholas Wadham † 1618 and wife, also N chapel, 4 ft brass figures on a tomb-chest with a back wall behind, flanked by black columns. Restored 1899 by *Sir T. G. Jackson.* – Humphrey Walrond † 1580, S chapel. Plain standing wall monument with columns and pediment but without effigy.

THE TOWN. Not much of interest. The centre is the
MARKET SQUARE with the MARKET HALL, one-storeyed
and open on all sides. Depressed arches with attached Tuscan
columns. Called newly built in 1813, but must be older, at
least in its elements. To the E in East Street the UNITARIAN
CHAPEL. The date is 1719, and to this date the structure and
the main elements of the façade may belong. Two large
windows in the middle with pediment over, and two small side
doorways. The details are altered. To the S in DITTON
STREET No. 1 is a somewhat ambitious and urban Georgian
house. To the N in North Street the GEORGE HOTEL, a long
C18 front of nine bays and two and a half storeys. From the
top of North Street HIGH STREET turns W running along
above the lower town and the church. Here the BELL INN
with mullioned windows. To the S COURT BARTON leads
down to the W side of the churchyard. Along the NW corner
of this the most rewarding houses: the CHANTRY, five-bay,
two-storeyed Georgian but with to the N two-light windows
of the C15 and also a C15 doorway, CROSSE HOUSE with a
Tuscan porch on its side and Georgian windows towards the
churchyard, and the former BOYS' SCHOOL, now Girls'
Grammar School, founded by Humphrey Walrond in 1549.
The house was built in 1586, but the very symmetrical façade
with slightly projecting gabled sides and four-light transomed
windows in the centre is too much restored.

HURCOTT, 2½ m. ENE. A ROMAN VILLA with mosaics was
excavated here.

ILTON

ST PETER. Much renewed, but it seems that the tower, S transept, and chancel go back to the early C14. The tower stands
on the S side of the church. It has on its W side a cusped lancet
with rere-arch and also an ogee-headed niche. The chancel E
and S transept S windows represent more ambitious ideas of
c. 1300: three lights with in the one three encircled spheric
triangles, in the other three circles with quatrefoil and trefoil
cusping. The S transept windows have inside elaborately
cusped rere-arches. Rere-arches also in the chancel. The
piscina here has an ogee arch and rests on a head corbel. The
arcade and the tower top are standard unambitious Perp. –
PULPIT. Plain, probably mid C17. – PLATE. Chalice and Cover
1610. – MONUMENTS. Alabaster effigy of a Lady, defaced,

c. 1475. – Nicholas Wadham † 1508, small brass figure in a shroud.

WHETSTONE'S ALMSHOUSES, on the Stocklinch road. Founded 1634. Plain range with two projecting wings. Three-light mullioned windows.

WADHAM'S ALMSHOUSES, SW of the church. One-storeyed, with dormers in the thatch. Four projecting chimney–breasts. Mullioned windows, four-centred doorheads.

INWOOD HOUSE *see* HENSTRIDGE

IVY THORN MANOR
1½ m. S of Street

A country house of Abbot Selwood of Glastonbury (1456–93) whose arms appear above the porch. Much altering in the Elizabethan age. A date-stone 1578 has been found. The house then had an E plan of which one arm has since been pulled down. In the other arm a room remains with moulded beams. But the most interesting thing is the windows in this arm, of five lights and two lights, and though they now have Elizabethan mullions, their hood-moulds on angel busts may well be of the last years of Abbot Selwood. Large kitchen at the back. The house deserves study. Dovecote, rectangular, perhaps of 1578. Gatehouse built in 1904.

JORDANS *see* HORTON

KEINTON MANDEVILLE

ST MARY MAGDALENE. E.E. chancel with two N lancets, with trefoiled rere-arches inside. At the E end also just one lancet. The nave rebuilt, it is said, in 1800. Typical pointed windows with Y-tracery. The W tower probably of the same time. No internal features of interest. – PLATE. Chalice and Cover 1575; Paten 1819.

KENTSFORD BRIDGE *and* KENTSFORD FARM
see WATCHET

KILTON

ST NICHOLAS. 1862 by *J. Norton* (GR), incorporating Perp bits. – FONT. Perp, octagonal. Panelled and decorated stem, bowl with pointed quatrefoils. Demi-figures of angels on the underside. – PLATE. Chalice and Cover from Lilstock 1574.

LILSTOCK CHAPEL. A medieval chancel (see the hood-mould of the E window) made into a miniature church in the C19 by adding a porch and a bell-cote.

KILVE

1040

ST MARY. The church reaches out from the village towards the sea. Grey stone, not red. Short W tower, perhaps partly C13. The church was much restored in 1861, and some old parts seem to have been re-set. The fenestration especially appears confused now. However, the odd window for the pulpit is original. – FONT. Circular, Norman, with a cable-moulding at the foot. – SCREEN. One four-light section preserved. Leaves in the spandrels. The tracery not what is usual in this part of Somerset. – PLATE. Chalice and Cover 1573.

CHANTRY. A group of C15 buildings in ruins, including a chapel with a large E window, shafted inside. Also remains of a staircase. The buildings deserve closer study (cf. the Buckler drawing in the Pigott Collection at Taunton and the Wheatley drawing at Mells Manor House.)

KINGSBURY EPISCOPI

4020

ST MARTIN. The church is of blue lias with Ham Hill stone, the proud W tower, 99 ft high, is all of Ham Hill. The tower, a companion-piece to that of Huish Episcopi, is very ornate; perhaps ornateness is indeed a little overdone. Set-back buttresses with three sets of attached pinnacles, all on long shafts. Higher NE stair-turret. The decoration of the tower starts at the foot with a frieze of pointed quatrefoils in lozenges. A second one of these friezes is placed above the W doorway with figures in the S W angle of the buttresses. Niches l. and r. of the doorway, one niche on the ground floor S, none N. Then follows the five-light W window. On the S two niches l. and r. on shafts with four heraldic shields. One niche on the N. Normal quatrefoil frieze at the foot of the next stage. Here a four-light window (an unusual size at that stage) with tracery in the head and below the transom and Somerset tracery as well. Niches on shafts l. and r. Quatrefoil frieze at the foot of the bell-stage. Twin two-light bell-openings with transoms and Somerset tracery, flanked by shafts with pinnacles. Quatrefoil frieze below the battlements, pierced battlements with quatrefoils in lozenges and arcading in the merlons. Angle pinnacles with outer shafts standing free of the corners (cf. Taunton). Also intermediate pinnacles. The niches of the upper tiers still have their original statues; nothing outstanding. Splendid s façade, embattled except for the plain clerestory and the chancel which is given a pierced quatrefoil parapet. s aisle with three-light windows, s porch of two storeys, s chapel with five-light s window. A recessed seat outside the aisle. Chancel gloriously lit. Five-light windows with transoms and finely detailed tracery to the s and N, E window also of five lights, but not as high, because below it, as at South Petherton, Ilminster, and Crewkerne, an original (embattled) E vestry projects. The chancel is gabled and has a quatrefoil frieze below the gable. The N side is like the other, but has an embattled rood-stair-turret.

The interior is a little bald. Its memorable features are at the E and W ends, at the E end the gloriously lit chancel and chapels, veritable glass-houses. One ought to see this on a fine morning. The surprise at the W end is that the tower besides its usual tall panelled arch and its fan-vault high up has its E buttresses right inside the nave. That must have been decided on for reasons of structural security, and then a virtue was made of a necessity. Two tiers of niches are placed on the buttresses and a second panelled arch is struck from one to the other. The nave is less interesting. It is older than the rest, no doubt of before 1400, and not yet infected with the later exuberance. Octagonal piers with moulded capitals, rather short for the distance they are from each other across a notably wide nave. Double-chamfered arches. The last arch is wider than the others, evidence of a transept which the church must have possessed when this aisle was built. The chancel is of fine erect proportions. The chancel arch (capitals with bands of foliage) and the two-bay chapel arcade (also with foliage bands in the capitals) are Late Perp. The chapels differ in their fenestration. – ROOD SCREEN. With tall four-light sections, the middle mullion reaching up into the apex. Each four-light arch has two sub-arches. The coving has disappeared. Two of the leaf friezes in the cornice survive. – PLATE. Chalice and Cover 1573; Dish by *Thomas Tearle* 1730; Flagon 1749.

Plenty of old houses in the village, and several worth looking at. The WYNDHAM ARMS stands at the main crossing. N of it the LOCK-UP, octagonal, with ball finial. Between the Wyndham Arms and the church the WESLEYAN CHURCH (1810 and 1852, front with Y-tracery windows) and closer to the church a C16 (?) cottage with an absurdly leaning chimney-breast and chimney-stack.

KING'S CASTLE see WIVELISCOMBE

KINGSDON 5020

ALL SAINTS. Perp in appearance except for the s transept with a window with intersected tracery and the E window which has genuine reticulated tracery. Aisleless nave, transepts and chancel. That plan also looks earlier than Perp. The w tower has set-back buttresses banded with Ham Hill stone. The twin bell-openings of two lights (with Somerset tracery) are widely spaced. Shafts start from corbels, run up l. and r. and between them and finish at the string course below the battlements (cf. Long Sutton). Higher NE stair-turret. Panelled tower arch. – PULPIT. Jacobean, with blank arches. – PLATE. Two Chalices and Paten 1831. – MONUMENT. Cross-legged Knight, late C13, not too badly preserved.

ROMAN VILLAS. Two Roman villas are recorded at Kingsdon.

KINGSTON 2020

ST MARY. The church is not big, but its w tower stands out so beautifully against the hill-side, especially from the w and NW, that it remains in one's mind as one of the most memorable of a district rich in towers. The style is that of Bishop's Lydeard, Ile Abbots, and Staple Fitzpaine. Red sandstone. Set-back buttresses with applied pinnacles. Pinnacles up the angles of the tower between the buttresses. Very tall detached diagonally set pinnacles to crown the buttresses. Battlements pierced, a lower tier of quatrefoils, an upper of arcading (cf. Bishop's Lydeard). Angle pinnacles surrounded each by four detached shafts. Also intermediate pinnacles. Bell-openings flanked by pinnacled shafts. However, to make it clear that we are in a village here and not a town, the bell-openings are twice two lights, not twice three (transoms, and Somerset tracery), and the stage below has only one two-light window on each side (transoms and Somerset tracery) with niches l. and r. w doorway with big leaves in the spandrels and niches l. and r. s aisle and s porch with pierced quatrefoil pinnacles, two-light windows. N aisle without parapet but with two-light windows. The s porch has niches above the big four-centred archway, and inside a fan-vault. The interior after this is a surprise. It displays the arcade of an aisled church of the C13. Four bays with circular piers and double-chamfered arches, light grey stone. N and s chapels Perp with the standard four-hollows section of the responds and small rosettes or narrow leaf-bands in the capitals. – FONT. Octagonal, the Perp standard. – BENCHES. A large set, one dated 1522, in another initials I.S. of Abbot Selwood of Glastonbury (1456–93). The type of the district, square-headed, with motifs of close tracery, leaves, and flowers. In one end a long hanging rosary. Yet other benches are High Victorian. – PLATE. Chalice late C17; Flagon 1716; Paten by *Clare* 1721; Plate 1739. – MONUMENTS. Very large tomb-chest. Shields in ogee-arched panels, with ogee at the foot as well as the head. No effigy. Said to be late C14. – Coplestone Warre Bampfylde † 1791 (cf. Market House Taunton), tablet signed by *Greenway* of Bristol.

MANOR HOUSE. Early Elizabethan with much remodelling *c.* 1702 (the date on the porch). E-plan minus the r. arm. Porch; the frame of the doorway typical of 1702. At the end of the former Hall facing the front the two-light windows (arched lights) of the former spiral staircase. The l. arm of the E with cross windows and some oval windows, typical of *c.* 1700. Fine William and Mary panelling, staircase with slender but still strong turned balusters and carved tread-ends.

KINGSTONE

St MARY. Short embattled nave with large three-light Perp windows. w front with doorway decorated with fleurons up the jambs and the arch and with leaves in the spandrels. Large three-light w window. Central tower between nave and chancel with higher stair-turret. Two-light bell-openings. On the s side Somerset tracery in the bell-opening and the window below. Inside, the tower arches are moulded, not panelled. – STAINED GLASS. Bits of C15 glass in the heads of the N windows. – PLATE. Chalice and Cover 1573.

KINGWESTON

ALL SAINTS, 1855 by *C. E. Giles*. With a thin s porch tower, very bare below but blossoming out above in an octagonal spire over an octagonal bell-stage with big gabled bell-openings. All the tracery of the church late C13 in style. In the chancel much sumptuous foliage carving in the Southwell style, especially above the two angels by the Sedilia. Of the old church the Norman s doorway remains with one order of colonnettes with decorated scalloped capitals. In the arch two zigzags. But the inner moulding of jambs and arch is a continuous trellis of four zigzags. – PLATE. Flagon of 1812.

KINGWESTON HOUSE. Plain Late Georgian house. Large open-well staircase with glazed centre. About 1825 *William Wilkins* added on the side a heavy Greek Doric porch with two columns between two pillars.

ROMAN REMAINS. A villa is recorded at Kingweston. Remains of another are recorded at COPLEY to the w. Yet a little further w at LITTLETON remains are scattered over 30 acres, probably belonging to a Roman village.

KITTISFORD

ST NICHOLAS. The w tower is pink-washed except for the set-back buttresses – an odd, not unpleasing effect. Inside a two-bay s arcade of the four-hollows section. But piers as well as arches are of oak (cf. Nymet Rowland, Devon). N chapel added in 1659. It still has a cambered door-head and essentially Perp windows, though they have the unusual feature of lights with trefoiled heads. The windows are straight-headed, and one has an architrave on brackets instead of a hood-mould. – FONT. Octagonal, Perp, panelled stem, bowl carved only on five sides, with quatrefoils of different kinds. – PULPIT. 1610, decorated without the familiar short blank arches. – PLATE. Chalice and Cover 1574; Flagon 1705; Plate 1814. – BRASS. Richard Bluett † 1524 and wife. 2 ft figures.

KNOWLE ST GILES

ST GILES. 1837–40 by *Lewis Vulliamy*. In the lancet style with bell-cote. Much original STAINED GLASS. Dates 1843, 1850, 1860. – PLATE. Several pieces of the 1840s. – MONUMENT. In the churchyard s of the church former ALTAR or TOMB-CHEST with Perp blank arches along the sides.

LAMYAT

ST MARY AND ST JOHN. Late C13 W tower with, on its W front, above a new (renewed?) lancet window, two faces set in, typical of the late C13 in their style. They may however be re-used and originally have been corbels somewhere inside. Low tower arch of two chamfers dying into the imposts. Perp nave and lower chancel. Panelled chancel arch. Nave-roof of the Somerset type with tie-beams and kingposts. – FONT. Norman, circular, with a cable-moulding at the foot of the bowl. – FONT COVER. Of the C15. – PLATE. Chalice and Cover by *Orenge* 1572; Flagon by *Bowles Nash* 1725; Dish 1739. – MONUMENT. One († 1807) by *Reeves* of Bath.

LANGFORD *see* FIVEHEAD

LANGFORD BUDVILLE

ST PETER. Red sandstone. In 1509 John Peryn of Wellington left money to the building of the W tower (and that at West Buckland). The W tower has a big SE stair-turret, set-back buttresses, and battlements. S aisle and S porch with pierced quatrefoil parapet. The aisle has pinnacles in addition. Three-light Perp windows. The N aisle dates from 1866. The S aisle has piers of the standard section with four hollows, but capitals with the leaf bands which usually belong to the four-wave type. On one S capital a needle and thread are carved. The arches are finely moulded. The same features in the S chancel chapel. Wagon roof ceiled, with a *ceilure* over the former rood screen. – FONT. Perp, octagonal. Stem with panels and angle buttresses. Bowl with panelled underside. The form and carving of the bowl itself look very late, perhaps Marian. The same date has been suggested by Bligh Bond for the arcade, on account of its debased pier details. – PLATE. Chalice and Cover 1573; Dish mid C17. – MONUMENT. W. Barry Wade † 1806, by *Thomas King* of Bath. Large hanging oval of grey marble and on it inscription and two draped standing figures by an urn. A replica of the monument at Bishop's Lydeard.

LANGPORT

ALL SAINTS. The church lies on a hill with open views to Muchelney Abbey on the S side. The little town spreads along at its feet to the w. There is nothing visible that could be earlier than the c15, except for one remarkable piece of carving not so far sufficiently noticed. It is a Late Norman lintel-stone, [7] dating probably from about 1190–1200, and is now placed above the s doorway. In all probability it has always belonged to the s doorway. It has a slightly pitched top and contains in the centre a circle with the lamb holding the cross. That circle is supported by two angels in the Romanesque tradition. Their inner wings rise to follow the line of the circle, the outer are in normal position. Further outside on each side a standing figure. The figures are quite small, and their style could perhaps, if they were better preserved, be compared to that of the Glastonbury portal. The Perp parts of the church are more ordinary. The w tower is a companion piece to that at Long Sutton. It has set-back buttresses connected diagonally across the angle of the tower, battlements, and small pinnacles. Higher stair-turret. Five-light w window. The n and s sides at that stage are quite bare. Two-light transomed windows at the next stage with Somerset tracery and niches to the l. and r. Two-light bell-openings of the same type flanked by untransomed blank two-light openings. Three shafts with pinnacles. Inside a tall panelled tower arch and fan-vault high up. Embattled aisles and chapels. Embattled chancel with pinnacles, embattled low e vestry (cf. North Petherton, Crewkerne, Ilminster, Kingsbury). The chancel windows are uncommonly tall and sumptuous: four lights with transom (and tracery below it) to the n and s, five lights without transom to the e. The tracery is richly and crisply cusped. Four-light windows also in the two-bay s chapel. The aisle arcades are not high, and there is no clerestory. Slim piers of standard four-hollows type, small round capitals to the shafts only. Chancel arch of the same type. The n and s chapel arches are four-centred, the aisle arches two-centred. In the e respond of the s aisle two niches for images. The chancel gives an effect of great luminosity after the lowish nave. A c17 source says that most of the church was built with the money of John Heron, a portreeve and supporter of Henry VII. – FONT. Octagonal, Perp, of the usual elements. – PULPIT. Simple and nice, probably of the later c17. – S DOOR. Uncommonly fully carved, with tracery and a band of big leaves round the head. – STAINED GLASS. The e window contains more original stained glass than is found in most places in Somerset. Ten whole figures in two tiers in the five lights and small figures in the tracery. The colours are rich, but the surfaces too small to give richness to the whole. The large figures are surrounded by white quarries with small yellow ornament. So the total effect remains pale. – In the s chapel much mid-c 19 glass. – PAINTING. Mourning over the dead Christ. In the Venetian High Renaissance taste. Signed *Reuben Sayer*, London, 1863. – PLATE. Chalice and Cover by *Orenge* of Sherborne 1574; Set of 1839.

THE TOWN. E of the church is the HANGING CHAPEL. It was the gild chapel or corporation chapel of the town. It is a plain Perp building over a gateway with a pointed tunnel-vault. Through the archway to the E appears Huish Episcopi tower, less than half a mile away. To reach the town from the church one walks down The Hill. At its foot the junction with North Street and the high street of the town called first CHEAPSIDE, that is Market Street, and then Bow Street. At the junction by the SE corner a nice five-bay Late Georgian brick house with graceful doorway. Opposite, at the NE corner, the Post Office with a Tuscan porch. The NW corner is rounded and of brick. Opposite to the s Lloyds Bank, a three-bay stone building with a pedimented doorway with attached Tuscan columns and segment-headed windows. Then follows, in Cheapside, on the s, the Langport Arms Hotel, also with a Tuscan porch, a two-and-a-half-storeyed house with segment-headed windows opposite, another with the same windows, of two storeys, to the W of the hotel, next to this the Westminster Bank, a handsome ashlar-faced three-bay house in a classical Palladian style, said to be as late as *c.* 1875, and so to the GUILDHALL on the N side. This is dated 1733 (wind-vane). It has three round arches on the ground floor, faced with Ham Hill stone. The upper floor is of brick, with stone quoins and other stone trim. Pyramid roof with lantern. Opposite the Guildhall the continuity of the street is thoroughly ruined by the car park and public conveniences. In BOW STREET the Market House Inn again has segment-headed windows. To its W Ensor House, a more ornate two-and-a-half-storey house of brick with Gibbs surrounds to all its windows and extremely elongated angle pilasters. These are clearly Early Georgian, and as segment-headed windows also usually are Early Georgian, and the Guildhall is datable *c.* 1733, it looks as if much rebuilding became suddenly possible or necessary at about that time.

EARTHWORK. To the N and E of the town is a great pro-

tective rampart 300 yards long. It may have been built to
protect the river-crossing in ancient times, for there are
remains of ROMAN VILLAS N and S of the town to prove that
Langport was an important ford early in our history. On the
other hand, some authorities believe that the rampart was
erected as late as the Civil War.

LEIGH HOUSE
1 m. W of Winsham

3000

Sizeable Jacobean mansion on the E-plan. Dated 1617 on a
rainwater head. Pink sandstone, two storeys and dormers,
mullioned windows in the wings, mullioned and transomed
in the centre. Round-headed porch doorway. Plain gables
with obelisk finials. Inside panelled rooms and a plaster ceiling
with thin ribbing.

LEIGHLAND
4 m. S of Old Cleeve

0030

ST GILES. 1862. – PLATE. Chalice of 1671.

LILSTOCK *see* KILTON

LILYCOMBE *see* PORLOCK

LIMINGTON

5029

ST MARY. The earliest datable feature of the church is one N
window in the nave. This is of three lights with plate tracery
consisting of two quatrefoils and one octofoil in circles. At
the back a pointed cinquefoiled rere-arch. This must be late
C13. But by far the most interesting element of the church is
its N transept founded as a chantry chapel in 1329 by Sir
Richard Gyvernay. It has flowing tracery of simple forms in
the windows and a heavily ribbed tunnel-vault (single-
chamfered ribs). The transept is entered by a doorway, and
next to this is a double-chamfered arch dying into the imposts.
Here the tomb of the founder must be expected. Similar the
arch over the S doorway to the nave and also the tower arch.
This rests on bust corbels, both grotesque. The W tower is of
three stages with diagonal buttresses, two-light bell-openings

with Somerset tracery, and a parapet. To the l. and r. of the
chancel arch two large recesses of uneven size. They were
probably for side altars. – STALLS. The ends with fleur-de-lis
poppy heads. The fronts and backs with linenfold panelling. –
PLATE. Chalice and Cover 1573; Paten 1787. – MONUMENTS.
Remains of coffin lids with foliated crosses, against the back
of the l. altar recess. – Below the arch between chantry chapel
and chancel two recumbent Effigies, he cross-legged in
prayer, she wearing a wimple. They are probably the founders.
The date then would be c. 1330. They are carved from one
block of stone. – In a recess in the N wall of the chapel (arch
with open cusping on shafts) Effigy of Knight in armour, also
cross-legged and of about the same date as that of the other
Knight. – Below on the floor Effigy of a Lady, a little earlier
than the others.

LITTLETON see KINGWESTON

LONG LOAD

4020

CHRIST CHURCH. 1854 by *C. E. Giles*. A somewhat silly turret
with spirelet at the NE end of the nave. Geometrical detail.
Nothing of interest inside.

(LOAD BRIDGE. C15 bridge of four pointed arches with
triple ribs in two orders. Down-stream face rebuilt. Railings
1814. Jervoise.)

LONG SUTTON

4020

HOLY TRINITY. A big Perp church, all of c. 1490 (so stated in
Bishop Fox's licence to consecrate). Tall W tower very
similar to Langport. Set-back buttresses connected diagonally
across the angles of the tower. The buttresses end in short
pinnacles at the foot of the bell-openings. Battlements, higher
stair-turret. W doorway with large leaf in the spandrels. Niches
l. and r. W window of five lights. Instead of a transom the
meeting in each light of an arch and a reversed arch. Next
stage with two-light window flanked by niches. Then the bell-
openings. They are of two lights with Somerset tracery and
flanked by blank two-light windows. Shafts flanking the
windows and between them. The outer shafts end in pinnacles,
the inner ones run from the string below the bell-openings to

the string below the battlements, thus establishing a firmer system of co-ordinates. On these two shafts pinnacles are placed above the battlements. Similarly the main pinnacles at the angles of the battlements are the continuation of the diagonals across the angles of the tower between the buttresses. So there is plenty of ingenuity in the design. The interior of the tower has a lierne star vault. The tower arch is panelled. The s side which has the stair-turret is bare of any decoration (except for one niche), until the bell-stage is reached. N and S aisles embattled, clerestory embattled, chancel chapels embattled, chancel without battlements. Windows of three lights in the aisles, of four in the chapels, of five at the W and E ends. Clerestory windows two lights only. – The arcades are of four bays plus one E of the chancel arch. Piers of four-hollows section, but panelled W arches to the chancel chapels. Fine Somerset roof in the nave with tie-beams and angel figures supporting the kingposts. Little tracery above the tie-beams. Angels support the sub-principals. In the chancel a ceiled wagon-roof. – FONTS. Two. One in the churchyard, defaced. It resembles that at Ruishton, octagonal with bold buttress-like pieces in the diagonals and sculpture on the four uncovered faces. The other in the church, Perp, octagonal, big, with a flat bowl. Two quatrefoils on each side.* – ROOD SCREEN. Not of a usual design. Four-light sections with the main mullion reaching up into the apex of the arch. No sub-arches, i.e. all three mullions run into the arch. Very thin tracery. The upper parts are modern. – PULPIT. Perp with twelve small niches (statuettes of 1868) under nodding ogee canopies, cf. Devon. – PLATE. Chalice and Cover 1781.

MANOR HOUSE. s of the church. Probably of the C17. Mullioned windows, partly altered early in the C18 into segment-headed sash-windows. E-plan, porch with round arch.

FRIENDS MEETING HOUSE, N of the village, on the A road. 1717. Plain parallelogram, each of the long sides with one doorway and two windows. Original glazing bars. Plain scrubbed benches inside in the original arrangement – an atmosphere of peace and neatness.

COURT HOUSE, to the W of the Meeting House. Early Tudor, altered in 1658. The present porch with its round arch belongs probably to the latter date. The original porch (with diagonal buttresses) is at the back, filled in. Hall now horizontally subdivided, but the roof survives with arched braces up to the

---

* This is suggested to have been the base of the village cross.

collar-beams and kingpost, and also the big brackets which once supported the minstrels' gallery. Remains of the stone spiral staircase to the S of the present porch, i.e. the original back door.

LOPEN

4010

ALL SAINTS. Mostly of 1834. The W window with intersecting tracery apparently even later. Other windows Perp and perhaps representing genuine evidence. – PLATE. Chalice and Cover by *Robert Brown* 1738.

LOTTISHAM

5030

ST MARY. By *Sir T. G. Jackson*, 1876. As pretty externally as Hornblotton which he had built a few years before, but internally not as telling. Built of the same dark yellowy-brown local stone as Hornblotton. Nave and chancel and a bell-cote over the E end of the nave, shingled, with pyramid roof. The detail Dec and Perp. The best thing about the interior is the chancel arch formed of heavy rough timbers: two tie-beams close behind each other, on heavy ogee-arched braces. – Nice BENCHES of original shape.

LOVINGTON

5030

ST THOMAS A BECKET. C13 W tower, *see* the big diagonal buttresses and the S lancet. N aisle and much else, 1861. – BENCHES. With poppy-heads and plain tracery motifs. – AUMBREY in a most curious stone surround, with three blank circles and a kind of cresting of big leaf motifs something like fleurs-de-lis. What can its date be?* And was it an aumbrey originally and not a low-side squint? – PLATE. Chalice and Cover C18.

LOVINGTON MILL. An extremely pretty group of Georgian stone buildings with two depressed rounded arches at two different levels to let the water through. The Miller's House has three storeys of three bays with a pedimented doorway.

(CHURCH FARM. Mural paintings of the C17. Two-storeyed summer-house.)

(CHARITY FARM. Here also are some C17 mural paintings.)

* The surround is old in any case; for it was drawn by W. W. Wheatley *c.* 1845–50 (Mells Manor House).

LOWER MARSH FARM
½ m. N of Dunster

A C15 manor house with two-storeyed porch and hall on its
r. The doorway is of oak with a two-centred arch. The upper
storey of the porch is the Chapel with a tall two-light window
and a handsome little wagon-roof with carved wall-plate and
bosses. There is also a statue niche and a piscina. Of the Hall
the arched braces remain, though it has been divided into two
storeys. The original kitchen, etc., to the l. of the porch was,
probably still in the C15, converted into a larger Hall, of which
also the roof construction with arched braces survives.

LOW HAM

CHURCH. As one approaches and examines Low Ham church,
a queer feeling gradually grows that there is something incongruous about the building, which however makes it all the
more fascinating. First of all it stands not in a churchyard,
but pat in a field, with no paved path leading to it nor any
flagging separating it from the green. Secondly it is remarkably
compact in its proportions, the tower not high, the nave not
long, and the clerestory tall (three-bay aisles, two-bay chancel).
The tower is Somerset Perp standard. So are the arcades
inside. But the tracery of all the windows, while clearly
Gothic and in its motifs nearest the playful forms of the early
C14, will not fit in precisely with anything of any Gothic date.
The answer to all this is that the church was begun shortly
before 1623 and consecrated in 1669. It is one of the most
instructive cases of early Gothicism in England. The dates
come from an inscription in the E window quoted by Collinson
but now hardly legible. – MONUMENTS. Sir Edward Hext
† 1623, who began the church, and his wife † 1633. Two
well-carved recumbent effigies. Original iron railing. – Sir
Ralph Stawell † 1689. Standing wall-monument of white and
black marble. Two putti at the foot; no other figures. Below
the inscription plate a fine military trophy in relief. Also with
the original iron railing. – ROOD SCREEN. Four-light sections
in the Perp tradition with the centre mullion touching the
apex. Much tracery in very small busy forms. No coving, but
carved cornice and cresting. Only the busts of angels and the
inscription show the C17 date. – TOWER SCREEN. Stone,
early C19, from the Lord Mayor's Chapel at Bristol, with
very rich doorway and cusped ogee gable. The interstices

all filled in with GLASS. Four figures by *David Evans* (TK).
– STAINED GLASS. The E window with the Cross with
allegorical inscription and the Virgin and St John l. and
r., c. 1690. Not really stained glass, but a transparency. –
PULPIT. Honestly Jacobean, with arabesque decoration.
– BENCHES. Honestly Jacobean, with tall blank arches
on the ends. – PLATE. Chalice, Paten and Flagon 1664; Dish
1669.

Nothing survives of Sir Ralph Stawell's ambitious mansion
begun c. 1685 and left unfinished at his death. It was to be
400 ft long and 100 ft deep (cf. for a part of the former gateway Hazlegrove House).

MANOR FARM HOUSE. The front C18, the back gabled. Oak
doorway, and in the Hall moulded beams and C17 panelling.

ROMAN VILLA. An important Romano-British villa was unearthed here in the Second World War, and excavations were
begun in 1945. The villa can be dated to the C2 A.D. and was
probably of courtyard type. Its most notable feature was
a luxurious bath block (cold room, hot room, sweat room,
plunge bath, dressing room). The furnace and hypocaust of
the bath block were well-preserved. The villa was built of
local stone and roofed with local slate, and finer work was
carried out in stone from Ham Hill. The most striking feature
was a fine large mosaic in the cold room, portraying individual
scenes from the Aeneid and in particular the story of Dido
and Aeneas. The mosaic is fluid in feeling and executed with a
lively primitive grace.

9040
inset

LUCCOMBE

ST MARY. E.E. chancel, the rest Perp with the S aisle coming
last. The E.E. work is recognizable by the N and S lancets and
the three (reconstructed) stepped lancets at the E end. Perp W
tower, quite tall, with diagonal buttresses, battlements, and
square higher stair-turret. Moulded tower arch. S aisle arcade
of four bays with piers of four-waves standard. The capitals
are finely carved bands of foliage. The roof is treated similarly
though not quite so richly as that of the S aisle at Selworthy.
Carved wall-plate, beams and purlins, very big bosses. The
(renewed) E window of the aisle also has the same type of
elegant tracery as at Selworthy, four lights and transom. –
FONT. Octagonal, Perp, with panelled stem and pointed
quatrefoils on the bowl. – ROOD SCREEN. This incorporates

bits of tracery and parts of the old frieze. – PULPIT. Of C17 and C18 parts. – STALLS. The fronts make use of Jacobean panels. – TILES. Some C13 tiles E of the tomb chest (*see* below). – STAINED GLASS. Old fragment in the S aisle E window. – The pale flowers in the S windows, very much in the Arts and Crafts taste, are like those in Porlock church. (Restoration 1896.) – PLATE. Cover 1816; Chalice and two Patens 1843. – MONUMENTS. Tomb-chest with two tiers of square panels with big leaves. Probably first half of the C16. – Brass to William Harrison † 1615, a 2 ft figure in front of the chancel.

LUFTON

5010

ST PETER AND ST PAUL. 1866 by *Benjamin Ferrey* (GR). Small; nave and chancel, and W bell-cote corbelled out on very Victorian heads and flowers. – FONT. Circular, Norman, with one cable-moulding and crosses in circles. – PLATE. Chalice by *John Fawdery* 1713; Paten by *Bowles Nash* 1721; Paten C18.

MANOR FARM. By the church. With mullioned and transomed windows.

ROMAN VILLA. A late Romano-British corridor house was discovered in 1945 and excavated between 1946 and 1952. Like the villa at Low Ham it appears to have been built after A.D. 200 and to have lasted until the departure of the Legions. Again like Low Ham, its main feature was an elaborate bath suite, consisting principally of an octagonal room with a pyramid roof that contained the plunge bath. Round the bath was a beautifully designed and perfectly carried out mosaic depicting fish disporting themselves. The bath suite was surrounded by modest but soundly-built dwelling-quarters.

LUXBOROUGH

9030

ST MARY. The W tower probably early C14. Dec two-light W window. Unmoulded tower arch towards the nave. Unmoulded S door arch. The top of the tower C19 with a steep saddleback roof. The chancel has lancet windows, but they are all renewed. – STAINED GLASS. Lethbridge window at the E end, † 1899. By *Kempe*, it is said. – PLATE. Chalice 1702.

8—s.s.

1030

LYDEARD ST LAWRENCE

St Laurence. Red sandstone. The chancel is Dec, with reticulated tracery in the E window, flowing tracery in the S window, and cusped Y-tracery in the N window. The N window has a rere-arch. The Piscina with an ogee arch in a normal pointed arch. The spandrels are pierced, and the arch rests on two head-corbels, at different heights because of the proximity of the Sedilia. These are shafted and have ogee arches. The rest of the church is Perp. W tower with diagonal buttresses, higher stair-turret, and battlements with pinnacles. Three-light bell-openings with Somerset tracery. On the S and W sides two-light windows below, also with Somerset tracery. The S side of the church itself has three-light windows and one of four lights and a porch, with pierced quatrefoils in the battlements and gable. N side with the same battlements and pinnacles. Gable at the E end; rood-stair turret. N porch decorated like the S porch. The N aisle arcade has piers of standard four-hollow section and capitals with leaf bands. Also angels and animals. The arch between chancel and N chapel has angel-busts with long scrolls. – ROOD SCREEN. In the dado some parts with original carving. – PULPIT. Broad, ambitious Jacobean piece, with the usual short blank arches doubled in each panel and in addition in two tiers. – BENCHES. Of the accepted type of the district, with close tracery and intertwined branches. – PLATE. Chalice by *Ions c.* 1574; Paten 1633; Chalice 1767; Chalice and Salver 1817.

LYDFORD BRIDGE *see* WEST LYDFORD

3050

LYMPSHAM

St Christopher. Perp church, restored and in parts remodelled in the 1820s to 1840s by A. J. Stephenson, rector, and his son Prebendary J. H. Stephenson. A. J. Stephenson bought the manor in 1809. His son succeeded him as rector and lord of the manor in 1845 and died only about 1900. Four-staged W tower with set-back buttresses ending in tall shafts with pinnacles. W doorway, W window, then on the S side two tiers of two-light windows, on the W side two tiers of niches. Then the twin two-light bell-openings with Somerset tracery. A shaft goes up between them and ends in an intermediate pinnacle above the tower parapet which is pierced and arcaded.

The main angle pinnacles have accompanying junior pinnacles. N aisle with parapet with pierced cusped lozenges, S side with pierced trefoils. On the S side the vestry projects S, and this has a pierced parapet of trefoils in triangles. Inside the church the N arcade of four bays has piers of the four-waves section, not usual in this part of Somerset, and capitals to the shafts only. Their comparatively bold mouldings indicate a date about 1400. Wall-shafts in the aisle on leaf-corbels. The aisle was much restored in 1840. It is recorded in a pretty niche inside it, that at that time the church was *renovata* and *ornata*. Wagon-roof in the nave, fine panelled roof in the aisle. The chancel roof has a typical early C19 ogee-panelled pointed tunnel-vault of plaster. – STAINED GLASS. E window by *O'Connor*, 1863. The theme is Suffer little Children. The representation is without any medievalizing, and the figures present are clearly to a large extent portraits of the Stephenson family. – PLATE. Chalice 1577; Dish inscribed 1742.

THE MANOR (former Rectory). An exceedingly prettily pinnacled and castellated little manor house in the fanciful Gothic taste of the early C19. Built probably *c.* 1820; illustrated by Rutter in 1829. Two polygonal towers at the back, good imitation Early Tudor bay-window in the front. Divers inscriptions in black letter such as *Pax intrantibus*. Also a pinnacle to the S in the garden, again with an inscription.

In the village a CROSS of the same time, with an inscription too, and also several Gothic cottages and outbuildings.

LYNCH

9040 inset

CHAPEL. The early C16 chapel of a former manor house of the Sydenhams. Hence its unusually ambitious E window (renewed 1885); three lights with a transom, the details similar to what appears at Doverhay Manor House and the church at Porlock and also at Selworthy. N and S windows of two lights. Wagon-roof. Panelled dado, W gallery with plain C17 balusters.

The villages of Lynch and Bossington have plenty of pretty cottages whitewashed and otherwise.

LYNG

3020

ST BARTHOLOMEW. Simple two-light Dec windows with rere-arches in nave as well as chancel. The broad Sedilia in the

chancel with ogee arch also Dec. The rest is all Perp, and the
tower, as usual, is what counts most. Blue lias and Ham Hill
stone. Set-back buttresses connected diagonally across the
angles of the tower. On the buttresses pinnacles on shafts set
diagonally. W doorway with tracery in the spandrels. W
window of four lights (with two two-light sub-arches), above
this two-light window with Somerset tracery, and then a pair
of two-light bell-openings with Somerset tracery, flanked by
attached shafts and pinnacles. Top battlements with quatrefoils and angle pinnacles. The tower arch is panelled. –
PULPIT and Reader's DESK made up of bench-ends, etc. –
BENCHES. Square-headed with such motifs as flowers in a
vase, a couple in Renaissance clothes, a stag, birds, an eagle,
a winged ox (the signs of St John and St Luke), and also a
carpenter with an adze. – PLATE. Chalice and Cover 1691.

MONUMENT, ¾ m. ENE, in the so-called Isle of Athelney.
It was erected in 1801 to commemorate King Alfred's wait in
879. It is a short plain truncated obelisk of no architectural
merit.

5020

LYTES CARY

Lytes Cary is a mixed building, with parts of the C14, C15,
C16, C18, and C20. Yet all parts blend to perfection with one
another and with the gentle sunny landscape that surrounds

38a   them. As one approaches the house from the E, the main front
has the C18 part on the r., higher and straighter than the rest,
the mid C15 with a C16 addition in the centre, and the C14 on
the l. The C14 part is the lower far-projecting and originally
probably free-standing CHAPEL. This was built, it seems,
about 1343. It has a three-light window with reticulated
tracery, two-light N and S windows which are straight-headed
but also have reticulated tracery, a N doorway to the outside
with two-centred head, and a squint on the W side towards the
house. The roof has thin arched braces leading up to collar-
beams. – SCREEN and COMMUNION RAIL date from 1631.
The screen is not a work of any ambition. Its balusters like those
of the communion rail are vertically symmetrical. – STAINED
GLASS. In the E window eight roundels with scenes from the
Life of Christ, c. 1830 in the style of the C13. In the W window
Virgin and Child; the heads here are original.

The HALL is ascribed to the mid C15, but windows, porch,
and bay belong to about 1515–20. The porch is two-storeyed

with a handsome oriel on the upper floor. The bay has just such an oriel on its upper storey, and the windows of the oriels, the bay, and the Hall both towards the E and the W are all upright and mullioned with four-centred heads to the individual lights. The Hall windows are large and of three lights. Inside, the Hall has an impressive roof with a finely quatrefoiled wall-plate, arched braces supporting collar-beams, and three tiers of cusped wind-braces. The Screen is not original. At the dais end of the hall panelled arches open to the back as well on the front. At the back is the spiral stair-case to the solar, in a square projection, at the front the one-storeyed hall-bay. This was, however, divided from the hall by a screen and served as a separate small withdrawing room or cabinet – an unusual arrangement (but cf. Golden Manor).

The s wing with the GREAT PARLOUR on the ground floor is an eminently interesting addition. It is dated 1533 and in some ways remarkably advanced for its date. The s windows are, it is true, still of the same type as those of the Hall, but the bay-window is set symmetrically in relation to the windows on either side. The bay is crowned by a parapet with the typical Somerset motif of a pierced frieze of quatrefoils and has above this crenellations. Inside, the arch of the bay is again panelled. Above the Parlour lies the GREAT CHAMBER and this has a plaster ceiling with thin ribs forming stars and diapers – the type of pattern which one does not expect to find before the time of Queen Elizabeth I, but which did indeed begin already under Henry VIII whose arms appear in the Lytes Cary plasterwork (Screen King's College Chapel, Cambridge, Great Watching Chamber, Hampton Court). Even so, it remains a surprisingly early case. In the Parlour is Jacobean panelling and a timber lobby of Jacobean detail, in the Great Chamber the lobby has its original linenfold panelling.

Circular DOVECOTE E of the house, in line with the porch. ROMAN VILLA recorded at Lytes Cary.

MAPERTON

ST PETER AND ST PAUL. Fine group of the church above and the house below. Perp w tower, the rest 1869 by *Henry Hall*. The chancel with much naturalistic foliage. In the porch a panel of C12 interlace, of curious outline and asymmetrical design, much as in the initials of manuscripts. Also some

corbel-heads. – STAINED GLASS. E and W windows by *Powell*
1869. – PLATE. Chalice and Cover 1573.

MAPERTON HOUSE. S front of seven bays, tripartite with giant
pilasters flanking all three parts. Built *c.* 1805, the back
perhaps older.

3040

MARK

ST MARK. Entirely Perp but with an instructive difference
between the earlier S aisle (of two bays) and the later and
longer N aisle. The S piers have four shafts with fillets and four
pronounced hollows in the diagonals, the N piers are slimmer
and have piers of four-wave section. The S capitals and abaci
are of three-eighths shape on each side, in the N arcade there
are the standard small capitals to the shafts only, and they are
decorated with small fleurons. The N aisle externally makes a
fine picture, one composition with the N porch of equal height
and also with the W tower. All three have parapets pierced
with quatrefoils in lozenges and pinnacles. The S side is
treated much less conspicuously. The W tower is tall for its
three stages. It is banded in grey and buff stone. The buttresses
are in the set-back arrangement and end in diagonally-placed
shafts with pinnacles. The angles of the tower themselves
also develop pinnacles but a little less high up. Above W doorway and W window a two-light window (on the N side between
two niches) and then the bell-openings. They are of two lights
and flanked by identical blank two-light windows. Shafts
with pinnacles to their l. and r. and between them. Now back
into the church. Moulded tower arch, panelled chancel arch,
panelled arch from the chancel to the N chapel. The W arch
of the chapel, however, corresponds to the aisle pattern. –
Unceiled wagon-roof in the nave, the principals on heads.
Among them King Edward VII and Queen Alexandra. Good
panelled aisle-roof. – FONT. Octagonal, Perp. Stem with
shafts separating blank tracery panels. Angel-busts against
the underside. Small quatrefoils at the top, two in each panel
(cf. Axbridge). – ROOD SCREEN. Perp, with three-light sections, the nave part repaired Jacobean. – PULPIT. With two
tiers of the familiar short blank arches. – SOUTH DOOR. With
tracery, probably early C16. It has the unusual motif of many
small quatrefoils in circles. – BENCHES. Kenneth Wickham
suggests a C13 date for them. – PLATE. Chalice and Cover
1573; Salver 1624; two Chalices 1820 and 1821. – STAINED

GLASS. In the N aisle W window, eight C15 figures. – CHAN-
DELIER. Brass. Dated 1758. – SCULPTURE. Good figures of
the four Evangelists with their Signs. About 2 ft 6 in. high.
Wood-carved, said to be of c. 1524. From Bruges Cathedral and
bought by a former Vicar. – The same vicar bought in Belgium
the two LIONS of terracotta which lie incongruously in the
sunshine outside the porch. – CHURCHYARD RAILINGS.
Gothic, made locally in 1848.

MARSTON MAGNA   5020

ST MARY. Norman chancel with broad clasping buttresses.
Herringbone masonry on the N side, one window and traces
inside of a second. The E side has a group of three small
stepped C13 lancets. The chancel arch has a profile which
seems C14 rather than C13. – Plain Perp W tower, with
double-chamfered tower arch. Perp nave and S porch and
Perp N chapel.
   In the chapel a canopied niche to the l. of the E window.
The position of the N doorway and S doorway close to the W
end makes it likely that the nave originally extended further
W and that its W bay was replaced by the tower. There is,
however, no evidence of a change of style between nave and
tower. – FONT. Circular, Norman, with decorated flutes or
scallops. – PULPIT. Nice plain C18 piece with tester (ogee
outline). – SCREEN to the N chapel, made up of Perp
and later bits. – STAINED GLASS. Old bits in a nave S and a
chancel N window. – PLATE. Chalice 1573.
MANOR HOUSE. SW of the church. Long low C17 house with
mullioned windows grouped together in twos and threes with
hood-moulds. Doorway with cambered head.

MARTOCK   4010

ALL SAINTS. A large church lying at the bend of the wide
main street of the little town. The churchyard is entered
by two plain C17 GATEWAYS with round arches. The
earliest surviving element of the church is the E wall of the
chancel with five separate stepped lancets, each outside under
its own hood-mould, but the group together under one rere-
arch inside. Small lancet in the gable. The rest is Perp. Big W
tower with set-back buttresses. W door with triangular shafts
l. and r., renewed five-light W window. Much bare wall on all

sides. On the third stage two-light window with Somerset
tracery, on the fourth two two-light bell-openings with transoms and Somerset tracery. Embattled aisles and chancel
chapels with large Perp windows. On the N side the C19 porch
and a rood-stair turret, on the S side a two-storeyed embattled porch, with a star vault inside resting on head-corbels
and enriched by bosses. The chancel projects two bays beyond
the chapels. The nave was heightened early in the C16 by a
four-light clerestory and this has a pierced parapet with
quatrefoils and battlements. The heightening was the occasion
for providing a new roof inside. It bears the date 1513 and is
the most lavish of the best type of roof developed in Somerset, the type with moderate pitch, embattled tie-beams, and
angels on the E and W sides of the middle of each tie-beam
carrying the kingposts. Tracery, and heavily panelled roof
above. The late Kenneth Wickham worked out that there
are 768 panels in all, with six different patterns repeated. The
interior is remarkably airy and spacious. Six-bay arcades, not
too high, the piers of standard section (four hollows). Spandrels with blank tracery – an East Anglian motif, unique in
Somerset. Shafts up their middles end in angels, and above
these niches for statues are inserted (now empty, but painted
in the C17 or C18 with figures of the Apostles). The elaborately panelled tower arch comes forward into the nave. Its
sides have two tiers of statue niches.* At the E end of the nave
the chancel arch also has statue niches (in the spandrels).
The chancel chapels are of two bays, their arcade a little
lower than that of the nave, but of the same detail. – PLATE.
Flagon and Paten by *R. Cox* 1758. – MONUMENTS. Defaced
early C14 Effigy of a Lady (S wall recess). – Tablet of 1830 by
G. Lewis of Cheltenham.

The best buildings of the little town lie close to the church,
and by far the most important of them is the TREASURER'S
HOUSE, so called because the rector of Martock was Treasurer
of Wells Cathedral. This is a house mainly of the C13 and C14
and still inhabited. It lies back from the street and is reached
by a two-centred archway to the l. of which the original
carriage entrance has disappeared. The house consists of a
later C13 wing, recognizable by the two-light Solar window
with cusped lights and plate tracery – a quatrefoil – and, at
r. angles to this wing, the Hall range which is of *c.* 1330. The
Hall has two-light transomed windows with simple tracery

* The W wall of the nave pierced by the tower arch is assigned to the C13.

and cinquefoiled rere-arches. The roof is open and has arched braces up to a collar-beam and four tiers of wind-braces of alternating design. An exceptional feature is a doorway out of the Hall next to that at the back of the Screens Passage. This must have led direct into the garden. The C15 Kitchen with its big fireplace lies back behind the C13 wing, in line with it.

In the corner to the W of the churchyard a house with two transomed two-light windows. This is what remains of the original MANOR HOUSE of Martock. It is surrounded by a moat.

To the N of the church the street bends past the present MANOR HOUSE, 1679, with mullioned windows, largely rebuilt in the C19, towards the TOWN HALL, a small Georgian building on an arcaded ground floor (segmental arches) and with a Venetian window below the S gable. S of it the MARKET CROSS, a Roman Doric column. Opposite to the E lying back behind a former building the somewhat incongruous sight of a large Villa of c. 1840, ASHFIELDS, with a Greek Doric entrance *in antis*. Opposite it N of the Town Hall some Georgian houses, e.g. one facing the C18 stables of Ashfields, and then a block three by three bays of c. 1830 with Greek Doric columns for the entrance, set oddly in a plain semicircular niche.

Back to the church, where, on the S side at the entry to a side lane, THE CEDARS, a five-bay early C18 house and at the end of the lane MOAT HOUSE, the gabled fragment of a larger house standing inside a moat. It is dated 1659. S of The Cedars in the main street the old GRAMMAR SCHOOL, with mullioned windows, dated 1661. Yet the windows still have four-centred arched lights.

At BOWER HINTON, THE HOLLIES, late C17, and other good houses. More in the surrounding hamlets, HURST, STAPLETON, and MILTON (MHLG).

MAUNSEL *see* ST MICHAEL CHURCH

MEARE   4040

Meare owes its name to the fact that it lay by the side of a lake the circumference of which is given as five miles. It was drained only late in the C18. There was a summer house of the abbots of Glastonbury here, and the church was in their keeping.

St Mary. Dedicated in 1323. That date may well refer to the present chancel and w tower. The chancel especially is interesting with its three-light E window the tracery of which has decidedly no longer the poise of the Geometrical, but does not yet introduce flowing or ogee forms either. Three lancet lights of which the middle is lower, and above them a spheric quadrangle cusped into three trefoils. The other chancel windows are renewed, but look convincing (spheric triangle in plate tracery above two lights). The w tower is unbuttressed, and the moulding of its arch towards the nave looks early C14. Battlements and higher stair-turret. The next building period was that of Abbot Selwood (1456–93), whose initials appear on the parapet of the E end of the S aisle. This is indeed the only ornamental piece of parapet of the church (pierced pointed quatrefoils in lozenges), the rest is plain. Finely cusped three-light aisle windows, three-light clerestory, three-bay arcades of usual details. Simple nave roof with angel-busts, chancel arch supported by two angels instead of capitals, chancel roof of a lively design. The principals have tie-beams and two queenposts, the sub-principals arched braces up to a collar-beam. Cusped wind-braces, as in a domestic roof. – FONT. Octagonal, Perp, with no other decoration than a series of deep very heavy mouldings on the stem and the bowl. An unusual design (cf. Weston Zoyland). – PULPIT. Perp, of stone, each side with two narrow panels with small leaf in the spandrels, rather like in the dados of screens. – SOUTH DOOR. With the most florid ironwork in the county, issuing, large and flowing, out of a kind of cuffs. It may well be early C14 work, and the C14 was indeed proposed by Hamilton Thompson. – CHANDELIER. Brass; given in 1777.

MANOR HOUSE. A summer palace of the Abbots of Glastonbury, built, according to the surviving details, as early as 1340 at the latest. L-shaped. The Hall was to the E of the entrance and on the upper floor, with at least three (now blocked) big pointed windows. In the back wing a yet larger upper room, 60 ft long, with its original fireplace (projecting hood with canted front) and tall two-light windows. That to the N has a transom, the two to the E have not. The simple tracery is of the most familiar Dec pattern. On the N, below, a smaller two-light ground-floor window with the ogee-heads of the lights shouldered.

FISH HOUSE. Across a field to the E of the Manor House lay a fisherman's house which at the same time served to salt and store fish caught in the mere. It also belongs to the early C14. Plain oblong, three rooms on the ground floor, two on the first floor. The latter were no doubt the living quarters. They were reached by an outer staircase and had within living memory a fine open timber roof. In the gable ends two-light Dec windows.

LAKE VILLAGE. Meare Village was constructed in a swamp rather than in an actual expanse of water, and appears to have been established earlier – in the first or Hallstatt phase of the Iron Age – and to have persisted later than Glastonbury. Like Glastonbury, the moisture and the peaty soil helped to preserve its huts and artefacts in the most astonishing way, so that even delicate basket-work has survived and can be examined by twentieth-century eyes.

MERRIOTT

4010

ALL SAINTS. A church intended to be stately, but left incomplete. The W tower is only a stump, embattled a little above the church roof to finish it off.* The nave has a good and quite tall four-bay arcade. The piers are standard (four hollows). The aisles have spacious three-light Perp windows and are embattled. Embattled S porch, very similar to that at Norton-sub-Hamdon. Statue niches outside and inside. Above the latter a circular stone closely covered with blank tracery. E end of nave, chancel and chapels added 1862 by *Ferrey*, very much in the High Victorian taste. They have STAINED GLASS of the same period.

In LOWER STREET three dated houses deserve attention. *See* p.73 First Manor Farm of 1663, entirely Tudor in its motifs. Then No. 69 of 1729, also still entirely in that tradition, but now at least on the ground floor with a continuous string course from which the windows seem to hang. It rises to embrace the door-head. But on the first floor still separate hood-moulds. Finally The Girdlers opposite. This is of 1766. It also still has mullioned horizontal windows, but now they are framed in an C18 manner. The classical conventions came late to the villages.

(LOCKUP. Small and gabled, with a door reinforced with iron, and a small barred opening in the gable. Probably C18. MHLG.)

(TITHE BARN. In the Vicarage orchard, recently restored.)

---

* This is the tower supposed to have influenced *C. R. Mackintosh* in his Queen's Cross church at Glasgow.

MIDDLE CHINNOCK

St Margaret. Low Perp w tower. The w door has a hood-mould on two angel figures. The tower arch has a continuous moulding of three thin ribs. Plain Perp s porch. s Doorway Norman. Jambs with vertical zigzag bands. Lintel with vertical beaded zigzag. Tympanum with outer band and fish-scale inside it. – Most of the rest of the church is C19, the nave of 1837, the chancel of 1874, the transepts of 1887. – FONT. Tub-shaped, Norman, with a band of beaded foliage. – BENCH ENDS. A few, Jacobean, in the s transept. – PLATE. Chalice and Cover 1574. – MONUMENT. Upper half of a C14 figure of a priest; now below one of the porch seats.

Opposite the church the RECTORY, C17, with mullioned windows. To the N MANOR FARM HOUSE, C17, gabled, with mullioned windows and a spiral staircase.

MIDDLEZOY

Holy Cross. In the s aisle a three-light E window with reticulated tracery, that is of c. 1330. The s windows all seem renewed. The original features include a small, internally shafted lancet window, an ogee-headed Piscina, and early C14 corbel-heads for the roof. The s doorway is small, double-chamfered, and has a plainly trefoiled niche above. Then the chancel. This has (renewed) N and s windows with typical tracery of c. 1300 (two lancet lights with trefoils above them and a quatrefoil under the main arch) and an E window of the same type, but of three lights and thus culminating in a large seven-foiled shape. This is excellently preserved. Inside, these windows have rere-arches, and there is also a cusped Piscina with the top cusp slightly ogee-shaped. The rest is Perp. The w tower has set-back buttresses connected by a diagonal across the angle of the tower. They end in tall diagonally-set shafts with pinnacles. Battlements with pierced quatrefoils and pinnacles set diagonally at the angles. Higher stair-turret. w window of four lights, then a two-light window with Somerset tracery flanked by two niches, and then twin two-light bell-openings with Somerset tracery, flanked by thin shafts with pinnacles. Inside, the tower arch is tall and panelled. Small angel-busts at the springing of the arch. A fan-vault was begun but not continued. The outer buttresses are caught up inside by two larger angel-busts. Arcade of five bays with standard piers (four hollows). N chapel of the same design.

Ceiled wagon roof in the nave, the 'ceilure' above the former
rood emphasized by pendants, instead of bosses. – FONT. Of
the octagonal Perp standard type. – ROOD SCREEN. Tall, of
four-light sections with middle mullion up to the apex of the
arch. The coving is not preserved. – TOWER SCREEN. Planks
and muntins below, vertically symmetrical balusters above,
perhaps half Jacobean and half older and originally domestic.
– PULPIT. With the usual blank arches in two tiers. Dated
1606. – BENCHES. Not many survive; some have original
poppy-heads. – STAINED GLASS. Small early C16 figure of
St Dorothy; S aisle; in the small window. – PLATE. Chalice
and Cover 1573.

MIDELNEY see DRAYTON

MID LAMBROOK see EAST LAMBROOK

MILBORNE PORT   6010

ST JOHN THE EVANGELIST. The church is historically remarkable for its Saxo-Norman 'overlap'. It contains unmistakable Norman work in immediate conjunction with
characteristic Saxon features. These Saxon features are now
clearest in the chancel S wall. Such pilaster-strips or lesenes,
such plain horizontal bands, such a tier of pilastered arcading
above are familiar from churches like Bradford-on-Avon. In
addition the chancel has the tall and narrow proportions of
Saxon work, and the original W front had triangular 'arches',
an even more revealing Saxon motif. Yet in the chancel there
are also windows, visible from inside, which, with their roll-
mouldings and their sturdy shafts with foliage capitals, cannot
possibly be pre-Norman. The distinguishing character of
the best work inside Milborne Port church is indeed Early
Norman. The church has a crossing tower, and this must
be Norman in its lower parts, see the remains of external
arcading on the N side and especially the powerful piers and
arches inside. Three orders of strong columns. The capitals
are of plaster and rather a band than proper capitals. They   4
have elaborate foliage. The arches are strongly roll-moulded
on the N and S sides, Perp on the E and W. The S transept is   5a
also Norman, but was refaced in 1843. Its most interesting
feature is the stair-turret in the re-entrant angle, which is
faced with small square slabs set diamond-wise (cf. the Early
Norman work at Westminster). The transept has a thickly

shafted Norman window on the w side.* The big s doorway
is Norman too and very much like the crossing arches, but it
is mostly reconstruction. However, its tympanum with two
affronted ferocious animals is original. The whole nave was
rebuilt and much lengthened in 1867. At the same time the
N aisle and N transept were rebuilt. The nave w front was
copied, and the original canopied niches are now built into
the mortuary chapel N of the church. Of the late C13 some
chancel windows, especially one s lancet, internally with
cinquefoiled rere-arch and, more to the w, two lancets reaching down much lower. The upper parts of the crossing tower
See
p.73 are Perp and comparatively plain. Two-light bell-openings
with Somerset tracery, battlements, and tiny pinnacles. –
FONT. Norman, octagonal, but was square originally, of the
Purbeck type with five shallow blank arches. – ROOD SCREEN.
Perp. The four-light sections are straight-topped. The usual
arches and panel tracery are set into these bold mullions in
much finer timber work. – STAINED GLASS. E window by
Bainbridge Reynolds, 1908. – PLATE. Chalice and Cover
c. 1642; Paten 1688; Flagon 1733. – MONUMENTS. Lady, s
transept, *c.* 1290. – Sir W. Medlycott † 1835; large Gothic
tablet by *H. Hopper*.

To the E of the church in the centre of the village the TOWN
HALL, three bays by one, C18, with originally arcaded
ground floor and with giant Tuscan pilasters. Between the
Town Hall and the Church on the s side the so-called GUILD-
HALL which has a Norman arch of unknown provenance.
The jambs have zigzag on intrados and extrados, the arch has
a crenellation motif in deep relief.

VEN HOUSE, *see* p. 327.

BOWLING GREEN, on the Sherborne road just outside Milborne
Port, with a fine view to the s. 1925 by *Sir Guy Dawber*.
Symmetrical two-storeyed stone house, in a neo-C17 style.
H-plan with projecting kitchen wing on the r. of the entrance
side. Gables and pedimented doorways.

MILTON *see* MARTOCK

MILVERTON

1020

ST MICHAEL. Red sandstone. Late C14 and C15 except for the
base of the w tower which seems *c.* 1200. Otherwise the tower

* One small Norman window and one lancet are in the E wall of the Vestry.

is Perp and not too elaborately decorated. Diagonal buttresses, battlements, and pinnacles. Square higher stair-turret. Bell-openings of two lights with Somerset tracery. All the window tracery with ogee forms. s aisle with c14 w doorway and w window. The other s and the n windows and the windows of the projecting chancel may be later. Wide and plain interior. The octagonal arcade piers do not give it enough weight or character. The n arcade is original c14 work, the s arcade c19. Double-chamfered arches. The w end is curious with the aisles half-embracing the tower. Tower arch double-chamfered on head-corbels. – FONT. Circular, Norman, with a frieze of saltire crosses in rectangles at the top and a cable-moulding at the bottom of the bowl. – PULPIT. 1928, but with arched and decorated c16 panels. – ROOD SCREEN. Incorporating some c15 or early c16 pieces and a date 1540. – STALLS. c15 or early c16 with poppy-heads, and on the fronts the twelve apostles, re-cut probably in the c17. – BENCHES. Uncommonly many, ends as well as fronts and backs. Square-headed. The date c. 1540 (see the panel re-used in the Screen). The motifs include the Arms of Henry VIII, many kneeling figures (some re-cut in the c17), faces in roundels or lozenges, frontal or in profile, saints, two men carrying a bunch of grapes, a stoup and sprinkler, flower vases, much foliage, etc. – PLATE. Two Chalices 1785. – MONUMENT. Catherine Spurway † 1845, signed by *P. Macdowell*. With a seated female figure in profile.

PARSONAGE, E of the church. An extremely interesting house of the late c15. Two-storeyed porch with diagonal buttresses. Inner doorway wooden with four-centred head. Hall windows and other windows of four lights or less with four-centred heads to the lights. Large hall fireplace and, leading into added parts, the tall panelled arch of the former bay-window. Original moulded hall beams. Original square stair at the back of the Hall. Excavations have proved that there was a separate wing at the back, probably for the kitchen.

THE TOWN lies around the eminence on which the church stands, with Fore Street below to its s and North Street to its n. NORTH STREET has the best houses. It is indeed in its modest way an uncommonly pleasant Georgian street. Description in detail is not needed. Above FORE STREET and between it and the church stands a house called THE FORT, basically gabled c17, but much altered. In Fore Street the humble CONGREGATIONAL CHAPEL of 1821 and a house on the s side which has five bays, Nos 1, 3, 5 with pointed windows, Nos 2 and 4 straight-headed. From the w end of Fore Street SAND STREET turns s. Here CHORLEYS, a late c17 house with a broad doorway with Doric pilasters and pediment and cross-windows with their original leading. Further s THE NOOK, a small but swagger Georgian three-bay house with Venetian windows on the ground floor.

9040

MINEHEAD

Defoe calls Minehead the best port and safest harbour in Somerset. Its trade was chiefly with Ireland but also with Virginia and the West Indies.

ST MICHAEL. A dedication usual internationally for churches on rocks or hills (Mont-Saint-Michel, Monte Gargano, etc.). Minehead church lies against the side of a steep hill. Superb views towards Dunster and over the bay. A large church looking externally a little too fresh. Light grey stone. Big w tower with set-back buttresses and battlements, higher SE stair-turret. Little square pinnacles. w window of four lights with one transom. Three-light bell-openings with one transom. On the s side a niche with the representation of the Trinity, God holding Christ crucified, on the E side a relief with the interesting combination of St Michael and the Virgin of the Misericord (sheltering little human beings under her mantle). Embattled s side with quatrefoils in the battlements, s porch, rood turret, unembattled chancel. Large four-light window E of the porch. Otherwise nicely detailed two-light windows, with and without transom. The pierced quatrefoils l. and r. of ogee arches are characteristic of the district. The same motif in the E window. The chancel chapels come forward as far as the chancel, and a group of three windows under three gables results, typical of Devon and Cornwall. Much of the detail is renewed. – N arcade inside of eight bays, i.e. no division between nave and chancel. Slim octagonal piers, as in Devon. The capitals indicate a c15 date. Double-chamfered arches. Heavily moulded tower arch very much like the crossing arches of Dunster. So perhaps Minehead tower is also the work of *John Marys*. That would give a mid-c15 date. The arch to the N into the Vestry, a former chantry chapel, is of oak, broad and rustic. Inside the vestry wagon-roof. Wagon-roofs also in nave and chancel.

FURNISHINGS. – FONT. Octagonal, Perp, with richly panelled stem and, seated on the ledge at the foot of the bowl, figures, their legs hanging over the underside. It is a great pity that they are not better preserved. – ROOD SCREEN. A fine example of the current Devon type, current also in this part of Somerset. Across nave and aisle. The dado with the same quatrefoils l. and r. of ogee arches as described for the windows of the church. Four-light sections with the arches subdivided into two of two lights. Ribbed and panelled coving and sharply carved foliage friezes. – PULPIT. A mid-C17 type with the frieze still Jacobean, but the panels no longer. – COMMUNION TABLE, N chapel. Elizabethan, with bulbous legs and in addition two angels supporting the top. – CHANDELIER. Brass, dated 1727. – SCULPTURE. A clock-jack, that is a rustically painted C18 figure of a man formerly with a hammer to strike the hours. On the top of the aisle screen. – STAINED GLASS. Several windows (c. 1901–5) by *Holiday*. – PLATE. Chalice 1624; Paten 1674; Flagon 1705; Chalice and Paten presented 1731. – MONUMENTS. Brass to a Lady with high head-gear, c. 1440, the figure 28 in. long. Most of the shafts and canopy which belonged to the composition have disappeared. – Tomb-chest with eight empty niches. – Effigy of a Priest holding a chalice, two angels by his head, early C15. The canopy is later C15, with fine gables. Originally six angel figures at their springing. Panelled vault inside. Straight cresting. A fine, quiet design.*

ST ANDREW, Wellington Square. 1880 by *G. E. Street*. Red sandstone. The tower, planned at the SW (ritual E) end, not built. Tracery in the style of c. 1300 and the early C14. A buttress goes up in the middle of the (ritual) W front. Simple interior. The arcade piers octagonal without capitals, the arches dying into them. Heavy hood-moulds on unmodelled corbels. Small clerestory. Roof with plain hammer-beams and arched braces. The chancel arch is marked by plain wooden boarding. – STAINED GLASS. E window by *Kempe*, 1889.

PERAMBULATION. Minehead is four things in one, the village with its big church on the steep hill-side, the picturesque harbour with its white cottages, the little town below the village by the church and half a mile inland from the harbour, with Wellington Square as its centre, and the

* BURGUNDY CHAPEL, ½ m W along the coast from Greenaleigh Farm. Ruins now very much overgrown.

extension to the sea front, when Minehead became a sea-bathing resort. The pier was built in 1610, at a time when Minehead was quite an important harbour. It was enlarged in 1901 to a length of 700 ft. Minehead as a seaside resort began in a small way before 1800* but visually little takes one back further than to the late C19. Seaside Minehead belongs mainly to the C20, as the hotels on the front, the houses, and the dreary semi-detached gabled houses along THE AVENUE show. Concurrently, attracted by the mild climate and the sheltered position of Minehead, villas began to sprout out between the older development and all up the hills. Of the larger ones two characteristic examples may be singled out, CLEVELANDS W of the church, brick and much half-timbering, an asymmetrical, quite big, yet cosy front, 1877 by *Foster & Wood* of Bristol, and PERITON MEAD, in Periton Road, almost facing the top of Park House Road. This is cultured neo-Tudor, *c.* 1922 by *Morley Horder*.‡

A systematic perambulation of the little town should start from WELLINGTON SQUARE. Here a STATUE of Queen Anne under a Late Victorian canopy. An uncommonly fine piece with great skill in the rendering of the details of the clothes. It was made in 1719 for Sir Jacob Bancks, a Swede who married into the Luttrell family. The statue is made of alabaster and attributed to *Francis Bird*. It would not do discredit to him. It stood originally at the E end of the N aisle of St Michael's church. A little down THE PARADE is the MARKET HOUSE of 1902 (by *W. J. Tamlyn*), neo-Baroque with a diagonally placed cupola, and then at the beginning of THE AVENUE the PRIORY CAFÉ, a former manor house, used also as court-house and manor offices. In the gable a two-light window of Early Tudor date. Round the corner an oaken doorway with leaves in the spandrels.

Back to Wellington Square and up to the old town. The way up is by Holloway Street and HOLLOWAY, rightly so called, as it cuts its way through the red sandstone. At its top with Nos 1 and 3 the whitewashed cottages of the old hill-village begin. They are continued in Middle Street and Moor Road, but remain intermixed with houses of the C20. More closely built CHURCH STREET and then CHURCH STEPS. The first cottage on the l. here with its wooden

---

* A Directory of 1794 says: 'A number of persons of fashion have been induced to visit it as a bathing place'.

‡ (KILDARE LODGE, Townsend Road, is by *Barry Parker*, 1903.)

mullioned windows and projecting chimney-breast is a good example of the C17. To the E of the church (THE CROSS) also cottages; this small area was the whole village.

Back to Wellington Square and to the W, where THE PARKS has the nicest Late Georgian and Early Victorian groups of houses, nothing special (except perhaps for Nos 12–16), but an indication of prosperity in the small lower town before the amenities of the seaside were appreciated. At the beginning on the r. the BAPTIST CHAPEL, enlarged 1901, but the front with its Tuscan porch and the attractive lettering still of the former building of *c.* 1821.

EAST MYNE CAMP. A small prehistoric encampment, magnificently sited on the headland, near the ruins of Burgundy Chapel. It is circular, about 80 yards across, and the rampart is now about 8 ft high.

MINNINGTON PARK CAMP *see* WIVELISCOMBE

MISTERTON

ST LEONARD, 1840, by *Kempthorne* (GR). In the lancet style.
OLD COURT. Mostly with mullioned and mullioned and transomed windows, but one small two-light window with Dec tracery. This came out of the old church. – PLATE. Exetermade Chalice and Cover, dated 1635.
MANOR HOUSE. To a C17 house a new part was added early in the C18. Five-bay, two-storey front, with giant angle pilasters, a doorway with Ionic columns, and an eared window above it.

MONKSILVER

ALL SAINTS. Red sandstone. On the N side of the chancel a small Norman window. W tower with top-heavy battlements. Unmoulded tower arch to the nave. The W window is of two lights, Dec. Small one-light bell-openings. Fine S aisle with attached S porch, embattled with quatrefoiled merlons and pinnacles. Rood-stair turret. Nicely detailed Perp three-light windows, one of them made straight-headed by opening the spandrels l. and r. of the two-centred arch. Porch doorway panelled. Three-light window from the porch into the aisle. Ceiling of the porch heavily panelled. Wagon-roofs otherwise. The S aisle arcade has piers of standard section (four hollows)

with polygonal capitals. N of the aisle E window a broad
bracket for a statue. It has the bust of an angel with out-
stretched arms holding a scroll. – ROOD SCREEN. Sadly
mutilated, but originally a simpler version of the type of
Dunster and Minehead. Probably brought in from another
church. Parts of the original screen perhaps the coved
panelling along the S ends of the benches as the nave S side.
– BENCHES. Straight-headed, with close tracery, flowers,
leaves, and a stag. They may be C17 work. – PULPIT.
Contemporary with the screen and benches, with panels of
close tracery. – LECTERN. Large wooden eagle. Only the body
is original. – PLATE. Chalice and Paten by *Nathaniel Lock* of
London 1716. – MONUMENT. Chancel N wall. Tomb-chest
with seven panelled niches of two lights with tall crocketed
gables. Thin buttresses between them. No effigy.

MONTACUTE

4010

ST CATHERINE. The oldest part is the chancel arch. This is
Norman of three orders. The arches are plain, but in the
nave N wall is a re-set decorated Norman arch (lozenges
overlaid with beaded circles). The N and S transepts and the
two-storeyed N porch (with a later star-vault inside) are of
c. 1300. In the transepts the arches clearly belong to that date.
They are double-chamfered on triple shafts with fillets. The
windows of the transepts are all renewed, but point to the
same date. The chancel windows also correspond. In spite of
the transept there is no evidence of a crossing tower. The nave
is aisleless and has Perp windows. The pride of Montacute
church is its W tower. It has set-back buttresses, a higher NW
stair-turret, four quatrefoil friezes to mark main divisions,
battlements, and no pinnacles. The bell-openings are of two
lights with transom and Somerset tracery. The W door is
flanked by triangular shafts crowned by pinnacles. Large W
window of four lights with a transom. The tower arch
panelled. Of about the same date as the tower is the curious
extra porch or lobby inserted between the N porch and the N
transept which was the family chapel of the Phelipses. Panelled arches to W and E. The rood-loft stair starts from here. –
FONT. Octagonal, Perp, with quatrefoiled panels. – PLATE.
Chalice and Cover 1573; Candlesticks 1691; two Patens by
Francis Garthorne 1713; Salver 1724; Ewer early C18. –
MONUMENTS. In the N transept. Knight, probably David

Phelips † 1484, defaced. – Husband and Wife, defaced, late C15. – Lady, c. 1600. – Sir Thomas Phelips † 1588 and wife, recumbent effigies under depressed arch with columns l. and r., panelled ceiling inside. – Edward Phelips † 1690. Standing wall-monument with coupled Ionic pilasters and pediment; no effigy. Inscription from the Gospels in black letter.

CHURCHYARD GATE, C17, with four-centred arch.

The village extends mainly along the main road to the S and E of the church. It is a village of beautifully honey-coloured cottages of Ham Hill stone. The quarries are only a few miles away. Bishopton, the street to the S, leads straight to the church tower. Its continuation past the W end of the church ends to the SW of the church by the PRIORY GATEHOUSE. The Cluniac priory was founded c. 1102. No remains of the C12. The gatehouse range has a tall gateway with typical Perp responds and stair-turrets on the inner side, one higher than the other. Above the gateway are on both sides handsome oriel windows with quatrefoil friezes and battlements. The oriels have mullions and depressed-arched lights. The whole range is buttressed and embattled. Big chimney-breast on the l. Nothing but this one range remains of the Priory.

Further along through the village to the E. The main square, really square, is called THE BOROUGH. Nice, even, two-storeyed houses, C17 and C18. The Post Office has a bay-window with a relief which bears the initials RS and must be Early Renaissance, no later than 1550. From here to the S lies the entrance to the House.

MONTACUTE HOUSE. There are those to whom Montacute remains the most lovable of Elizabethan houses. The reasons deserve consideration. The house is built of Ham Hill stone, whose warmth of colour, varying from a soft biscuit to a tanned tone, is unmatched. It is large yet not overpowering, it is neither as bleakly direct as Hardwick nor as flamboyant as Wollaton. And it still has in front of its garden façade an area of closed-in garden more complete than most, with balustrade (vertically symmetrical balusters) crowned by numerous obelisks and punctuated on the l. and r. sides by a transparent rotunda with a transparent boldly top-heavy ogee cupola and finial, and two summer houses or plaisances in the corners. These have ogee roofs and also finials. Finials also on the gate piers. It is through these gate-piers and through the garden that the house should be approached.

It exhibits to that side, its E side, its principal façade, a 49

characteristic Late Elizabethan façade. The house was built
for Edward Phelips, later Sir Edward, Speaker in the House
of Commons and Master of the Rolls. It is not known when
it was begun; but *c.* 1590 seems a reasonable assumption.
1599 appears on a chimney-piece inside. The architect may
have been *W. Arnold (see* Dunster Castle. Suggestion of
Mr A. Oswald). The E façade is designed on the familiar
E-pattern. It is of three storeys with large windows of three
to five lights with two transoms on the ground floor and first
floor, and one transom on the second floor (as at Longleat in
the 1560s). Either wing has one two-storeyed bay-window to
the E, one four-light window to the forecourt, and a large
shaped gable with curves and double curves, embellished by
small obelisks. The porch has a semicircular gable and also
obelisks. Between the wings and the porch on each side are
four windows and in the middle another two-storeyed bay-
window. Top balustrade like that of the garden and again
obelisks. In addition the round-headed rusticated doorway of
the porch must be mentioned, the oddly paired shell-headed
niches in the plinth of the house, the equally odd circular
niches in the cill-zone of the first floor (again just like Longleat), and between the windows of the second floor the niches
with statues of soldiers. This is the main front of the house.

However, Montacute is now mostly approached from the
W; and there the character is different, owing above all to the
purchase in 1786 of the porch and surrounding buttresses
and balustrade of Clifton Maybank house in Dorset. These
parts belong to an earlier period and their re-use and re-
erection is a sign of the doting medievalism or Gothicism of
the late C18. For Gothic the elements are, though the date
must be *c.* 1535 and certain characteristic motifs of the Italian
Renaissance do appear. The porch has a four-centred hood
to its doorway, thin fluted polygonal angle buttresses with
twisted finials, and a balustrade with pointed quatrefoils in
lozenges. This as well as the thin buttresses is continued on
the recessed parts to the l. and r. of the porch. On the porch
itself there is more decoration, quatrefoils in niches, shields
and shafts of triangular section on brackets. These shafts
are not treated in the Gothic tradition but with Renaissance
candelabra, and on them stand putti – not Gothic angels. The
main element between the shafts is a large coat of arms in a
lozenge, and around this again Renaissance foliage scrolls
abound. There are also two large beautifully carved angels.

The windows of the w side of the house, however, belong to the Elizabethan work, as do the gables which are plainly triangular, not curved or shaped as on the E side.

The N and S sides of Montacute are simpler, and have only one motif which is at first surprising: a semicircular oriel with three transoms, high up in the middle of the second floor. The justification lies in the plan of the house. For here, on the second floor, a Long Gallery runs all the way from N to S and along the E front. It is 189 ft long.

The arrangement of the principal rooms on the ground floor is as follows. In the accepted medieval way the porch leads into the Screens Passage and to the r. of this lies the Hall, to the l. a smaller Dining Room and then the kitchen and offices. The Hall is only one storey in height. The Screen is of stone with columns carrying fancy capitals and some heavy, broad strapwork cresting above. The fireplace is also of stone. It has coupled Tuscan columns and a metope frieze. At the far end of the room is a plaster frieze, surprisingly informal for such a mansion. It shows the story of a hen-pecked husband, just trying to get at some beer secretly, then beaten with a shoe by his wife, and then paraded round the village on a pole. What can have made Edward Phelips choose this representation for his house? There is often more naivety in Elizabethan and Jacobean sculpture and decoration than one might expect. Beyond the Hall are Parlour and Large Dining Room. The latter is panelled and has another stone fireplace. This time there are two orders of columns, Tuscan below and Roman Doric, i.e. fluted, above. Another such fireplace is in the Small Dining Room the other side of the screens passage. In the overmantel here is the date 1599, a shield, and a surround of strapwork. Behind the Hall, the Small Dining Room, etc., runs a corridor which was added in 1786, to facilitate communication between these parts of the house. In the original Elizabethan state it had been only one room deep. In the re-entrant angles of the w side are two large oblong staircases. They are of the square newel type and run between solid walls of stone. On the first floor above the Large Dining Room is the Library with a Victorian plaster ceiling. Stone 50a fireplace with coupled columns and bold strapwork in the overmantel. Another plaster frieze in an adjoining room.

To the S of the house a GARDEN PAVILION of three bays with open arches and a curved top.

The COURTYARD S of the house with mullioned windows

and four-centred door-heads was originally two-storeyed. The STABLES on the W side of the drive now used by visitors seem to be of c. 1790. Of the same date perhaps the LODGES. The dates and history of these outbuildings seem unrecorded.

ST MICHAEL'S HILL. The original 'mons acutus'. Originally Montacute Castle stood on top of the hill. Now it is crowned by a FOLLY TOWER, circular with tapering top, built in 1760.

MOORHAYES FARM see WINCANTON

MOORLYNCH

3030

ST MARY. The view to the S over Sedgemoor is not easily forgotten. The exterior of the church is much cleaned up, but the church is by no means lacking in interest. The broad, low, unbuttressed W tower belongs to the late C13, see the S lancet window and the W window of three stepped lancet lights, cinquefoiled inside. The chancel is Dec, see its two-light N and S windows. But what can be the date of the S porch with its odd outer doorway? Is this a case of re-used materials?* – PULPIT with Perp panels. – READER'S DESK. The Perp bits here seem to come from the rood screen. – BENCHES. With tracery, leaves, etc. – SOUTH DOOR heavily traceried. – STAINED GLASS. In the chancel, mostly of c. 1840–50. – PLATE. Chalice and Cover 1635. – EFFIGY of a lady with square, carefully detailed head-dress, c. 1375.

MOUNSEY CASTLE see DULVERTON

MUCHELNEY

4020

MUCHELNEY ABBEY. The abbey was founded for Benedictines, it is said, by Æthelstan in 939, and re-founded. The site takes advantage of a height slightly above that of the surrounding moor and marsh. Mucheln-ey means the big island. The church which is being excavated was 260 ft long after the Lady Chapel had been added at the E end. The Norman church, probably of c. 1100 or a little later, consisted of a chancel with an ambulatory and three radiating chapels, placed so that one faces E, and the other two not, as would

* It was in its present shape when the drawings were made from Braiken-ridge's Collinson.

have been done in France NE and SE, but N and S; a crossing, no doubt with a tower; transepts each with an apsed E chapel; and a nave of six bays. There were no W towers, it seems. Across the nave, cutting off its E bay, ran the pulpitum. No Norman fragments found during the excavations were yet exhibited at the time of writing this account.

The plan of the cloister and the ranges on its four sides is exposed. In the E range the chapter-house deserves notice, with a Norman apse, and later also lengthened, and the Day Room further S with a central pillar. Above that range, as usual, lay the Dormitory or Dorter, continued to the S by the projecting lavatories or Rere-dorter. This still stands, with slit-windows to the E, and at the foot of the W wall the five arched discharging openings. The Refectory, again as usual, was on the S side. Its inner N wall forms part of the most interesting group of buildings at Muchelney. This group, containing chiefly a portion of the Abbot's Lodgings, must have been rebuilt early in the C16, when so much was also done at Forde in Dorset and Cleeve in Somerset. The refectory wall has very tall blank five-light panelling. The heads of the panelling are missing. It reflects no doubt the shape of the S windows. Adjoining this to the N is the the S wall of the cloister rebuilt at the same time with fan-vaults (cf. Gloucester Cathedral) and tall four-light openings. To the W of the refectory is a much lower anteroom with moulded beams. From here a stone staircase of quite comfortable width ascends to the abbot's quarters. These extended above this anteroom, above the S walk of the cloister and also to the W round the corner into the W range. Above the cloister three relatively small rooms. One of them has remains of ornamental wall-painting, another a wagon-roof. But the finest remaining room is above the anteroom. This possesses one of the most sumptuous pre-Reformation fireplaces in the country. The overmantel is decorated with a frieze of four large quatrefoils enriched in every way and with two foliage friezes. Shafts rise from the angles and end in excellently carved large lions couchant. They are no doubt not in their right context now, and others are built into the external walls. The S windows of this chamber are two, again large, of two lights, straight-headed and with transoms. The tracery details are similar to Cleeve and the Dunster–Minehead neighbourhood. The most interesting thing about this chamber is however the un-Gothic way in which its S side forms itself into an orderly façade. Here the

45

coming of Renaissance ideals (not Renaissance forms) can be watched. The buttresses establish vertical co-ordination, and the ground-floor and upper-floor windows are exactly in line. In front of the s gable runs a band of crenellations to give horizontal finish. The gable of this range which faces w has a two-light window with two-centred head. To the l. of this gable another, the w termination of the Abbot's bedroom. This has a straight-headed plain four-light window with hood-mould.*

St Peter and St Paul. The parish church immediately adjoins the abbey, as was so often the case in the Middle Ages (cf. e.g. Westminster Abbey). There is no more at Muchelney than 3 ft between the transept of the abbey and the s chapel of the parish church. It was of course approached from the N, and the s side is treated more plainly. w tower with set-back buttresses connected diagonally; battlements, higher SE stair-turret, and pinnacles. For these *see* below. w door with a hooded outer stoup on the r., five-light w window, then on the w side a two-light window flanked by niches. On the 'N side this motif is repeated below in place of the w window. The bell-openings are on each side two of two lights, set rather far apart. They are placed between shafts, and the shafts have pinnacles. The outer shafts in fact continue the buttresses below and their pinnacles become juniors to the main angle pinnacles on the tower top. The shaft between the bell-openings becomes the not unusual intermediate pinnacle. – The N side of the church is embattled (quatrefoils in the merlons) and has a two-storeyed porch with a star-vault. The chancel projects one bay with three-light N and s windows and a five-light E window. Of internal features the following must be noted. Panelled tower arch and fine fan-vault with big bosses in the tower. Three-bay arcades, not high, with piers of standard type (four hollows). Chancel arch of the same type. Chapel w, N, and s arches panelled. At the E end of the s chapel a stone Reredos of five niches. In the chancel SEDILIA with damaged canopies. – The wagon roof of the nave has lovable very incompetent PAINTINGS of angels in clouds, probably of the C17. – FONT. Octagonal bowl, the diagonals strengthened by short stone posts, originally no doubt connected with the stem. In the four main panels the Crucifixion and three quatrefoils with kneeling figures. –

---

* A lesser cloister has recently been uncovered E of the day room with an aisleless Infirmary running N–S on its E side.

TILES of various dates from Norman to Perp. – ORGAN. An early C19 barrel-organ is preserved. – PLATE. Chalice and Cover 1633.

In the square or rather triangle N of the church the CROSS of which base and shaft are original. On the N side stood the abbey ALMONRY pulled down within living memory. All that remains of it is a small piece of SCULPTURE over the door of a cottage.

E of the Almonry the PRIEST'S HOUSE, a rare and delightful survival – a small house of the C14 to C15, with the internal arrangement just as in a large mansion. Two-storeyed thatched cottage. The doorway is two-centred. To the r. lies the Hall which went up into the roof. It has a four-light transomed early C16 window of the same type as those in the Abbot's Parlour, only smaller. To the r. of this was the study and a small room over, to the l. the kitchen, etc. The hall fireplace curiously enough stands against the screens passage (cf. Yorkshire).

Muchelney is a pleasant village to walk through. In many of the cottages and houses fragments of windows, etc., of the abbey have found a home, notably so in COURT HOUSE. Plenty of houses with mullioned windows with hood-moulds, mostly C17 but also C18. Even brick houses (e.g. School Farm House) carried on with them.

MUDFORD

fore

ST MARY. Nave, chancel, and W tower. Chancel E window Dec with reticulated tracery. The rest is Perp. Nave and S porch embattled with big gargoyles. The nave has three-light windows. Chancel N and S sides also of three lights. Low N transept with straight-headed windows. Chancel arch and arch to the transept C18; classical. The W tower has set-back buttresses, a higher NE stair-turret, battlements, and pinnacles. Additional pinnacles corbelled out in the middle of each side. W door, W window of three lights, two-light bell-openings and a quatrefoil frieze running just above the sill-level of the bell-openings. On the W side a panel of Christ Crucified with three figures at the upper ends of the cross. The tower arch is panelled inside. – PULPIT. Jacobean. – PEWS. Jacobean, with shell-tops on the ends. – PLATE. Paten 1718; Chalice and Paten 1772. – BRASS. William Whitby † 1617, and wife. Small whole figures (c. 6 in.) to the l. and r. of an inscription.

MANOR HOUSE, at Up Mudford. Early C17, with mullioned windows and gables and a gable above a two-storeyed canted bay-window.

NASH PRIORY

½ m. N of North Coker

1010

One range of a Perp mansion. On the N side doorway with richly decorated and traceried door of *c.* 1400. Above it an oriel window on a coving of two fan-vaults. The oriel is crowned with pinnacles. Corresponding to the doorway on the S side of the range a panelled arch of another doorway. In the E gable end a large two-light Perp window with transom. Smaller windows on the N. The w end has diagonal buttresses.

NEROCHE CASTLE

1010

NEROCHE CASTLE, or Castle Neroche, is an enormous Norman defensive work. It may have been adapted from a prehistoric earthwork. There are three huge banks, the inner 25 ft above its ditch, the middle 20 ft, the outer 15 ft. The mound where the keep once stood is to the N. A prodigious structure.

NETHER STOWEY

1030

ST MARY. At the E end of the village next to Stowey Court. Much renewed. Inside in the chancel on two brackets opposite each other two bishops' mitres, to commemorate two vicars who became bishops. Probably late C18 work. – Excellently carved ROYAL ARMS above the chancel arch; *c.* 1710. – PLATE. Salver 1709; Paten early C18; Flagon by *Clare* 1724. (VICARAGE. The old part of the house dates from 1681.)

STOWEY COURT. (The house is said to be partly C15 and partly of after 1588.) – In the garden a pretty C18 GAZEBO with a Venetian window and an ogee roof.

From here into the village one goes past a cottage with curved projecting front and Gothic windows. Then a few Late Georgian and Early Victorian houses, and so the centre is reached with the CLOCK TOWER of 1897. Its crowning display of timber is a pity. Along the Minehead Road the CONGREGATIONAL CHURCH with windows of Y and intersected tracery (1802) stands opposite Coleridge's cottage. The third street starting from the Clock Tower leads on to Over Stowey. On the r. POOLE HOUSE, Tom Poole's House, a seven-bay Georgian house.

DANESBOROUGH CAMP. An Iron Age camp on Danesborough or Dowsborough Hill, rising over 1000 ft above the Holford–Stowey road. The camp, which is oval in shape, crowns the hill. It is 370 yards long and 170 yards wide, and the inner of its two banks rises to a height of 12–14 ft.

STOWEY CASTLE, between Butcher's Lane and Castle Hill, is the circular mount and base-court of the ruined castle. Only the ruined foundations of the square keep are now visible on the platform.

NETTLECOMBE

0030

ST MARY. The church stands immediately to the SE of the house, so close to it that not even a hedge, only a fence separates the two. Red sandstone. W tower of the C15, with diagonal buttresses and battlements. Two-light bell-openings. Tower arch towards the nave of an unusual section (one wave, one hollow). The rest of the church much renewed in 1869. The chancel E end and the clerestory seem to belong to that time. Arcades of three bays. Piers of standard section (four hollows) with leaf-band capitals. The N chapel, with straight-headed windows and a humble two-bay arcade, was the Trevelyan chapel, founded by Sir John Trevelyan who died in 1522. The S chapel was the Raleigh chapel. In the S wall the most remarkable feature of the church, a pair of TOMB RECESSES which are so deep that they project beyond the outer wall. They have vaults with single-chamfered ribs, starting on big head-corbels or plain corbels. They differ in date, though not by a long time. The earlier is that further E with shafts carrying the outer arch and heads clearly of *c.* 1300. At the apex of the outer arch a fine small King's head. The younger arch has no head in that position and no shafts. The arch runs through in one continuous moulding. Also the big head-corbels inside are later C14 in costume and in style. – The MONUMENTS are indeed a cross-legged Knight of the late C13 and a Knight and Lady of *c.* 1350–60. – Other monuments: John Oatway † 1798, a minor work by *King* of Bath. – Joan Wolseley *née* Trevelyan † 1904, with a fine small bronze Madonna of *c.* 1945; by *Ernest Gillick*. – FONT. Octagonal, Perp, and quite uncommonly ambitious in its sculptural decoration. The scenes represent the Seven Sacraments and Christ in Glory. Such fonts are usual in East Anglia but do not exist in the s w except in this one example. The date seems to be c. 1460–70, the figures are too badly preserved to judge their quality or style. – PULPIT. Handsomely carved c18 piece (cf. Carhampton). – BENCHES. Straight-headed; early c16; mostly with ornament, but one head in profile. – STAINED GLASS. Interesting mid c19 windows on which no information could be obtained. – Also original stained glass in the Trevelyan Chapel. – PLATE. Chalice and Paten 1479. The date letter is B. Lettermarks were introduced by the Goldsmiths Company in 1478; hence B is 1479. Six-cornered concave foot. Christ's head on the paten. The piece is the oldest piece of goldsmith's work in England which carries a date.

NETTLECOMBE COURT. Many-gabled red sandstone mansion dated on the porch 1599. The initials are those of John Trevelyan. Symmetrical s front with five gables. The three-storeyed porch is matched by the Hall bay. The Hall lies back between the two. It has tall windows with two transoms, three lights in the hall itself, five lights in the bay. The other windows are simpler. All windows have hood-moulds. The porch doorway incidentally does not have a round arch, as one would expect, but still a four-centred one. The gables are quite plain, except for small obelisk pinnacles. The s front has buttresses, and that would point to the masonry being that of a house earlier than 1599, and to 1599 as only the date of a re-modelling. The w front was georgianized before 1768. It is now of nine bays and two storeys with a pedimented Ionic porch. The Hall has one of the most sumptuous plaster ceilings in Somerset, no longer with thin ribs but with broad bands and heavy pendants. The bands form interlocked cross and lozenge patterns. Fireplace with large strapwork overmantel. In the middle coat of arms flanked by two badly carved figures.

Another overmantel, still with strapwork, is dated 1641. This is in the former Servants' Hall, and the ceiling there has modest motifs between the beams in the new Inigo Jones or Forde Abbey style (cf. Poundisford). There are more plaster ceilings in that style, especially one with, as its centre, an oval field with the Leaping Horse, the device of the Trevelyans. The Staircase is of 1733. It has charming, light, and delicate Rococo motifs, very thin with much space left bare. The staircase itself is of the square open-well type and has slim

turned balusters and carved tread-ends. The rooms of the w
front later. In one a nice Adamish ceiling and a contemporary
fireplace.

NEWTON SURMAVILLE
1 m. SE of Yeovil

Built of the fine buff local stone between 1602 and 1612.
Symmetrical N front with three gables. The porch, which is
two-storeyed and ends in a balustrade with corner obelisks,
lies to the r. of the middle gable and is matched by an identical
bay-window to the l. All windows are mullioned and transomed. The other fronts are only a little less formal, but that
to the E, that is the gardens running down to the river Yeo,
has identical chimney-breast projections (of which one is
false). The w (towards the hill) is given two gables and a one-
storeyed porch between. The Hall is one-storeyed and has
original panelling and pretty Queen Anne cupboards at the w
end. At the E end a Queen Anne niche. Behind the hall newel
staircase with square solid stone core (cf. Montacute). Dining
Room and Drawing Room lie to the E of the Hall. They have
their original plaster ceilings preserved, still of the Elizabethan thin-ribbed type. In the Dining Room a fireplace with
Tuscan stone columns, in the Drawing Room fireplace with
wooden overmantel. The caryatid figures are rustic in style as
usual at the time and in the county. Another thin-ribbed
ceiling in the Tapestry Room, i.e. the room above the Hall.
Victorian additions at the back.

On the hill to the w a pretty octagonal SUMMER HOUSE of
c. 1750 with a pyramid roof and lower one-bay attachments on
two sides. Good C18 gatepiers to the N of the N front.

NORTH BARROW

ST NICHOLAS. Perp w tower. The rest 1860 (by *H. Perry* of
Blandford). – PLATE. Chalice and Cover 1572.

NORTH CADBURY

Church and house form an uncommonly fine picture.

ST MICHAEL. The church is called 'de novo edificata et con-
structa', when Lady Elizabeth de Botreaux in 1423 applied for
a licence to make it collegiate. This apparently never happened,

but the chancel is clearly built with a view to the members of a college of priests. North Cadbury is a large church. It has a w tower with higher stair-turret crowned by a polygonal pyramid roof. Diagonal buttresses with many set-offs. w door, three-light w window, plain second stage, plain bell-stage, battlements, no pinnacles. All this is not spectacular. The body of the church is. Two-storeyed N and S porches panelled above the doorways and vaulted inside with lierne-vaults of different design. Large three-light aisle windows with panel tracery, three-light clerestory windows. Chancel with tall three-light windows of the same design as the aisle windows. Five-light E window. Plain, unenriched parapets all the way through. Inside the church a tall arcade of five bays. The pier section is the usual (four-wave) standard, but – a sign of relatively early date – the capitals and abaci are not confined to the shafts but taken round the waves as well. Contemporary roof of moderate pitch with tie-beams and short kingposts, i.e. Somerset type. The responds of the tower arch are very simple, just attached demi-shafts. The capitals are decorated with plain leaves. The chancel arch is like the arcade piers, but has two tiers of responds on top of each other. Behind it extends the splendid chancel. The large windows start high up, evidently with a view to chancel stalls. Sedilia on the S side all renewed.

FURNISHINGS. FONT. Octagonal, Perp, with quatrefoils, etc. – BENCH ENDS with plain poppy-heads. Dated 1538. The panels below have figures, frontal and profile, the women in modish dresses, also a crane (?), a man with a donkey, a church exterior with a crossing tower. The technique is inadequate or caricaturing. – ALPHABETS. Two in black letter in the Vestry, apparently for the vicar to teach children. – STAINED GLASS. Good original small figures set in the panes of the W window. – PLATE. Chalice and Cover 1631; Chalice and Cover by *Thomas Mann* 1742. – MONUMENTS. William Lord Botreaux † 1391 and Lady Botreaux † 1431. Defaced recumbent effigies under daintily ribbed canopies. He wears a bascinet, she a horned head-dress. Against the tomb-chest standing angels with shields and at the foot a standing Virgin with two kneeling figures apparently of good quality. – Two Jacobean tomb-chests without their effigies. The one probably Sir Francis Hastings † 1610. The date of the other is 1611. – Brass to a Lady who died in 1596, with 96 lines of English verse (A. C. Bouquet).

NORTH CADBURY COURT. Immediately E of the churchyard. The house was built by Sir Francis Hastings, the Puritan writer and pamphleteer who died in 1610. Large Elizabethan mansion* with an irregular earlier C16 W wing. The roof of the Hall in this wing still exists. The N front is symmetrical and wholly Elizabethan, seven bays under four gables, arranged in the first-floor windows as follows: eight-light, four-light with porch under, four-light, four-light, six-light bay-window of the Hall, eight-light. The Hall is entered by the porch. The Screen is renewed, as is most of the interior. Original one first-floor ceiling with fine ribbed plasterwork with many ogee shapes and small foliage motifs attached to them. The S front consisted originally of two broad projecting wings and a rather narrow courtyard between them. This had an asymmetrical spiral stair tower in the NW angle. One two-light window of this vanished tower still faces into the Hall. The courtyard was filled in c. 1790 with a large bow-fronted room (altered inside), and the whole front was sashed. In the eight-light window of the (new) W staircase a number of fine pieces of heraldic STAINED GLASS of c. 1580–90.

STABLES of 1715 with two-light mullioned and cross windows.

Many good houses in and around the village, especially N of church and house. Farther afield e.g. GALHAMPTON MANOR HOUSE, C18 (five bays, two storeys.)

NORTH CHERITON

6020

ST JOHN BAPTIST. Small Perp W tower. The body of the church remodelled and enlarged 1878. – FONT COVER with ogee ribs; Jacobean. – ROOD SCREEN, bought from Pilton in the 1870s. Much restored. The sections of four lights with the middle mullion reaching up into the apex of the arch and with panel tracery. Is this the screen of 1498–1508 (see Pilton)? – PULPIT. Dated 1633. The panels each have two of the familiar squat blank arches above each other. The top frieze with vine foliage. – PLATE. Chalice and Paten 1623.

NORTH COKER

5010

HYMERFORD HOUSE (also called Manor House, Bridge Farm, Grove Farm). Tudor Hall with two-light transomed windows and a two-storeyed porch.

* Collinson in 1791 mentions the date 1581 in the Hall.

9—S.S.

NORTH CURRY

The approach to the church at the very N end of the village is something one will remember, with the Old Vicarage, still gabled, and a three-bay Georgian house on the r., and GWYON HOUSE of c. 1850 on the l., an incongruously townish Italianate façade.

ST PETER AND ST PAUL. The church is large and stately, and somehow strikes one as very complete, both externally and internally. Externally the dominating accent is the broad octagonal crossing tower of grey ashlar. Its lower stage is clearly of c. 1300, with its cusped Y-tracery in the windows. The roof-line of the original S transept appears outside too, and that of the original nave inside, with a small window that gave on to the roof. There is also one long lancet in the stair-turret outside. The upper parts of the tower are Perp, the parapet must be Victorian. Internally the crossing arches go well with the date of the windows outside, but the piers must in some way have been tampered with. The W piers are simply large plain masses cut diagonally, those on the E side have an undulating contour with shafts and a continuous capital and abacus line of decidedly Perp character. Perhaps some strengthening and recutting had taken place. There are now stone seats along these piers; not a usual arrangement in the Middle Ages. The W arches of the transepts are plain double-chamfered and again belong to c. 1300, and the S transept windows have rere-arches in the same style. The E window is of five cusped and stepped lancet lights. That completes the evidence referring to the period when the church received its essential features. Whether its Norman predecessor had a crossing already, we cannot say, but that a Norman church existed is evident from the plain and modest N doorway of c. 1180, with a segmental arch decorated by zigzag at r. angles to the wall. Now the Perp contributions: the S side is the show side. Embattled S aisle and S chapel, embattled S porch. Clerestory with pierced quatrefoiled parapet, solid arcading in the S transept parapet. The aisle has three-light, the chancel four-light windows, the transept a five-light S window. The S porch is given three niches over its doorway, one over the inner doorway, and a fan-vault. The W front has a five-light nave window with battlements over, and parapets for the aisles. The N side is plainer, though also embattled and also provided with windows as large as on the S. The chancel is

two bays long and ends in a five-light window. As one enters
the nave, the width and breadth of the whole interior is
striking. Then, at once, a problem poses itself. Two former
windows have been exposed on the N side of the nave. They
are both Dec, i.e. c. 1325–50. They must belong to the
clerestory of a former aisle the height of which can be seen at
the E end of the present aisle. This and the other aisle must,
however, have been built very soon after; for their piers and
arches are of a decidedly C14 design and certainly pre-Perp.
The arches are two-centred and their profile is in one continuous moulding with the piers; no capitals, no abaci. The
moulding is of two quarter-circles divided by steps. The
clerestory again came later, and is not in line with the arches.
The best roof is that of the N aisle. In ancient furnishings
the church is poor. – ORGAN CASE. By *J. Oldrid Scott*;
good. – CHEST. Found c. 1930. According to F. Roe of
before 1200. – ALTAR CLOTH. Dated 1633. – PLATE. Set
of 1831. – MONUMENTS Defaced Effigy in the chancel;
c. 1360. – Tomb-chest with a cadaver. Against the chest
blank arches with shields divided by panels with four small
figures.

NORTH NEWTON
1¾ m. SE of North Petherton

2030

ST PETER. The church was rebuilt – rockfaced! – in 1884 (GR).
The tower must be older, but how old is it? Kelly says
'supposed Saxon', the *Little Guide* 'very ancient'. But its
windows look Jacobean, and as its Pulpit and Screen are dated
1637 and the Plate is too (cf. below), the same date can perhaps
be assumed for the whole tower. That a Saxon church existed
at North Newton is however certain; for the ALFRED JEWEL
was found here in 1693. It is now at the Ashmolean Museum
in Oxford. – The SCREEN has depressed rounded arches l. and
r. of the round-headed doorway and quite large figures
attached to the uprights. – The DOOR of the church is of the
same date and style. It has panels with figures under round
arches, but also (re-used?) panels with Perp tracery. Of
Jacobean style again the shell-top of the doorway. – The
PULPIT has none of the usual short blank arches. – PLATE.
Chalice and Cover and two Flagons 1636.

MAUNSEL: *see* St Michael Church, p. 283.

NORTHOVER
½ m. N of Ilchester

St Andrew. Plain Perp w tower with diagonal buttresses at the foot. Tower arch double-chamfered and dying into the imposts. Parapet on top of the tower. Nave and chancel Perp. Shallow transepts. – No furnishings of interest. – PLATE. Salver 1722 by *Thomas Morse*.

Barn. Substantial remains of a large medieval barn (*see* the Buckler drawing in the Pigott Collection at Taunton).

NORTH PERROTT

St Martin. Cruciform with tower over the crossing; yet in spite of this early type of plan apparently all Perp. Crossing tower with two-light bell-openings filled with Somerset tracery. Four-light windows at the N and S ends of the transepts, low five-light w window above a w porch. Four-light nave N and S windows. Nave roof on head corbels. Crossing arches panelled. Capitals with bits of decoration. – REREDOS. The sides are Spanish C17 carving, the centre is by the younger *Westmacott*. – PLATE. Chalice and Cover 1571; Paten 1694; two Salvers 1752; Flagon 1768; Chalice 1817. – MONUMENT. W. Hoskins † 1813 by *Sir R. Westmacott*; very plain.

Manor House. 1878, Jacobean, by *T. H. Wyatt*.

NORTH PETHERTON

St Mary. The church lies back from the main street and faces it with its N side across an uninteresting square of grass. It is all embattled, and has two porches, nave with clerestory, aisles, chancel, chancel chapels a little higher than the aisles, and w tower. The tower, even amongst Somerset towers, is a special *tour de force*. It is 109 ft high, of light grey stone with set-back buttresses decorated by three tiers of excessively long pinnacles. On the lowest stage is the w doorway flanked by niches. In one is still a fragmentary seated figure. Quatrefoil frieze above the door and four-light window above this with transom (tracery also below the transom). On the N and S sides there are statuettes in niches on this stage. They also survive but can never have been of high sculptural quality. The second stage starts with a quatrefoil frieze corbelled out triangularly in the middle of each side. On it three-light transomed windows with Somerset tracery. Third stage again with the same

quatrefoil frieze and triangular projections. The bell-openings
are lavishly arranged, two of three lights on each side, with
transoms and Somerset tracery. The wall above the bell-
openings is panelled and, to do yet more, Somerset tracery
fills the panelling. The stair-turret is low, lies on the s side,
and causes some irregularity in the arrangements. The windows of the church are all large and Perp, of three or four
lights. In the clerestory they are of three lights. The most
striking feature of the interior is the tower arch, as high as
nave and clerestory, and panelled. Inside the tower there is a
fan-vault. Otherwise the architecture of the church has little
to attract. Five-bay arcades, rather thin, with standard (four
hollows) piers. Circular capitals to the shafts only, studded
with small rosettes. Chancel arch and w arches to the chancel
chapels of the same type. The arches between chapels and
chancel have as their E responds busts of angels. Panelled
roofs of low pitch on busts of angels. No interesting furnishing to make up for the architectural dullness of the interior. –
PULPIT. Perp, with fine traceried panels. – BALCONY GAL-
LERY, opening to the aisle from the upper floor of the s porch.
Dated 1623. A strong piece on deep corbels, with a small
figure of Father Time. – BENCH ENDS. Two carved ones in
the nave dated 1596 and 1629. – DOOR. Good carved door into
the sacristy. – SCULPTURE. Crouching figure known as Samson. Originally he carried the Pulpit. Now over the tower
clock. – STAINED GLASS. N chapel E end, by *Kempe* (1837–
1907), dated 1896, and one of his best pieces. There is much
poetry in the verdure behind the Nativity and the choir of
angels above. – w window by *Sir Henry Holiday* 1911–13,
chancel N by the same 1917–18. – PLATE. Chalice and Cover
1573; Paten 1630; Flagon 1631. – BRASS. Indent of Alianora
Poulet † 1413, 3 ft long, below a gable with concave sides,
s aisle floor. – Priest (not Alexander Sydenham † 1523). 15 in.
figure, kneeling. It fits into an indent in the sacristy E wall. –
Katherine Morley † 1652. Kneeling figure, nave floor. – CROSS
in the churchyard, with decoration on base and shaft. The
head is missing.

The village, although big, is lacking in special visual attractions.

NORTH WOOTTON

ST PETER. Small Perp building. – FONT. Very elementary
Norman, with cable-moulding at the bottom of the bowl. –

PROCESSIONAL CROSS. Oak, overlaid with brass, recently made in the village, good and without the self-consciousness of so much Sacred Art. – PAINTING. Copy of a Botticelli Madonna by *Thomas Matthew Rooke*, who was a pupil and assistant of Burne-Jones. – PLATE. Chalice and Cover by *John Robinson* 1750.

PROVIDENCE CHAPEL. 1830 with the typical Gothic windows of that date, i.e. of two lights with Y-tracery.

CHAPEL FARM HOUSE, next to the chapel. C17 with symmetrically placed mullioned windows carrying hood-moulds.

NORTON FITZWARREN

1020

ALL SAINTS. Mostly rebuilt in the C19. Original the w tower and the N arcade. The base of the tower c. 1300 – *see* the w doorway. The rest Perp. Set-back buttresses. At the exposed angles three tiers of big gargoyles to mark the principal stages. Battlements, higher NE stair-turret. Two-light bell-openings with transom. On the s side a niche for a statue. The N arcade has octagonal piers with plain capitals and double-chamfered arches, late C13 or early C14. Good N aisle roof. – ROOD SCREEN originally right across nave and aisle, entirely in the Devon style. Now divided, and one part between chancel and N chapel. Four-light sections with the central mullion running up into the apex, ribbed coving, perfect on the w side. Rich display of foliage in the cornices. The lowest frieze illustrates the story of the Dragon of Norton Camp and in addition contains the name of Raphe Harris, a churchwarden who died in 1509. – BENCH ENDS. Square-topped with rich tracery. – PLATE. Flagon and Paten by *Robert Cooper* 1712; Chalice and Cover 1740; Salver 1810; domestic Cup 1827.

CONGREGATIONAL CHAPEL. 1821. Built as one with the adjoining Manse.

NORTON COURT. The house has a balustraded porch of *c.* 1600.

Immediately N of the Church, upon the hill, is an IRON AGE ENCAMPMENT. It is circular and is about 150 yards across. Its bank now reaches in places a height of 15 ft above the bottom of the ditch. Excavations have shown that it was utilized by the Romans.

NORTON-SUB-HAMDON

4010

ST MARY. An uncommonly perfect church, perfect in its setting on an eminence with an exquisite view to the E over some houses of the village towards Ham Hill, and perfect also in its display of Perp pride. The only objection that could be made is that nave and chancel are a little too short to be a match for the proud 98 ft high tower. The tower has set-back buttresses, and these go right up to the top where they end in pinnacles. That gives one pair of pinnacles close to each corner. There are in addition another eight in the middles of the sides,·two-deep, with the outer on a shaft which rises from the string course below the battlements. Big gargoyles. The bell-openings are so tall that they run through two stages of the tower (cf. Crewkerne, Hinton St George). They are of two lights, divided by a transom and with tracery in the head as well as below the transom. Somerset tracery in addition. The transom does not run in line with the string course between the two stages of the tower. – Polygonal NE stair-turret, higher than the rest and also pinnacled. Low W door with a quatrefoil frieze above, and large transomed four-light W window (the tracery divided into twice two arches). Much spare space between it and the bell-openings. The nave has N and S aisles of five bays, and the chancel projects only slightly beyond them. The aisle windows are of four lights designed like the W window. Buttresses between the windows; battlements, gargoyles, and pinnacles. E window also of four bays, flanked inside by statue niches.

The interior is wonderfully lofty, 50 ft high, with tall slim arcades and no clerestory. The piers are standard (four hollows). The fifth arch is separated from the others by a broader pier, marking the beginning of the chancel, which is not otherwise emphasized. The fifth aisle bays are in fact chancel chapels and thus separated from the aisles by arches. The aisles have wall-shafts between the windows. Tall panelled tower arch. Ceiled wagon-roof in the nave. The church is ascribed to *c.* 1500–10. The S porch has been attributed to the C14. It has a ribbed barrel-vault.

FURNISHINGS. FONT. Alabaster, *c.* 1904, by *Henry Wilson*, Sedding's principal pupil. Circular. Boldly spiral-fluted with some flower-decoration and four fishes at the base. Pretty wooden Cover. – TOWER SCREEN. Also by *Wilson*, typical of Arts and Crafts woodwork at its best. – PULPIT and ROOD SCREEN. Iron, 1890 and 1880. – STAINED GLASS. Much glass of *c.* 1500 in the heads of windows. – E window by *Wailes c.* 1861; chancel S by *Heaton, Butler & Bayne c.* 1875; S chapel

E by *Wilson*, 1904; sentimental. – PLATE. Chalice and Cover 1601; Chalice 1796.

DOVECOTE. Just s of the church. Circular.

Pretty village street. Amongst houses, at the w end, MANOR HOUSE (C17 with early C18 addition) with an C18 Summer House and C18 Stables opposite. Near the E end, off to the N, THE CLOSE, C17, with mullioned windows and gabled dormers.

ROMAN VILLA. A Roman villa with mosaic pavement was found at Norton.

5030   NORWOOD FARM
                    1½ m. ENE of Glastonbury

Much enlarged, partly in 1910. The original fragment has diagonal buttresses in the front, a canted bay-window with battlements and the initials of John Selwood, Abbot of Glastonbury († 1493), and several pre-Reformation windows.

1020   NYNEHEAD

ALL SAINTS. Red sandstone. Simple church, mostly Perp. Of the C13 perhaps the tower arch and certainly the Piscina in the chancel. Perp most of the w tower, the s aisle, s porch, s chapel, and N transept. The N transept was enlarged on the N side about 1830, and its large Perp N window had to be converted into an arched opening. The three-bay s arcade has standard piers (four hollows; capitals only on the shafts). Money towards the building of the aisle was left in 1410. The s chapel has the same type of pier. The church was much pulled about by the Rev. John Sanford, who also gave it valuable pieces of Italian sculpture. – SCULPTURE. Small marble tabernacle attributed to *Mino da Fiesole*. In the centre small painted figure of Christ perhaps by *Granacci*. – Virgin and Child, perhaps by *Andrea della Robbia*. – Virgin kneeling and worshipping the child, probably by *Luca della Robbia* himself. – FONT. Octagonal, Perp, panelled stem and underside of the bowl. – ROOD SCREEN. Of four-light section, arranged in two two-light arches. Ribbed coving, ornamental cornices. – REREDOS. Centre carving by *Seymour* of Taunton, the enamel side parts by *Powell's*, c. 1880–5. – STAINED GLASS. Much mid-C19 work. A C15 panel of St Margaret, s chapel E window. Also heraldic glass of 1638, the late C17, and the mid C19 in the N chapel. – PLATE. Chalice and Cover by *Ions* of Exeter 1574; Flagon 1681; Salver by *Thomas England* 1731; Paten 1734. – MONUMENTS. Bust of John Sanford by *A. Castoli*, 1835. – Henrietta Sanford † 1837. Large free-standing figure of a kneeling angel. Also by *Castoli*. – Edward Clarke † 1679 and wife † 1667, erected during his life-time. The usual Elizabethan composition of kneeling figures facing each other across a prayer desk, reactionary even for *c.* 1670. The monument is said to have been made at Milverton for £25.

NYNEHEAD COURT. The main part of the house belongs to 1675, a date appearing on a stone doorway with broad seg-mental pediment inside. This was probably the original outer doorway. The house is of two storeys with projecting wings and quoins, broad upright windows with original glazing bars, and a hipped roof. It is a remarkably early example of the classical style in Somerset. The walls are no doubt earlier, or else the doorway would be in the middle and not in the traditional position of the Hall porch. At the back remaining Tudor doorways correspond with that entry. The back of the house is of brick exposed. In the drawing room a good fire-place of *c.* 1760.

AQUEDUCT. The canal crosses the drive (1838) and the railway (1844).*

OAKE

1020

ST BARTHOLOMEW. Red sandstone. Perp and of little interest except for the six-light N window, with Perp tracery arranged in two three-light arches. This is said to have come from Taunton Priory and to have been bought for Oake after the priory church had been dissolved in 1535. In this window C15 STAINED GLASS. The arcade is of two bays with octagonal piers and double-chamfered arches. The S porch of the church has a quatrefoil frieze, a surprising piece of enrichment for so modest a church. – PLATE. Chalice 1782; Salver 1805.

OAKHAMPTON HOUSE *see* WIVELISCOMBE

OARE

8040
inset

ST MARY. In a green valley just behind a wall of hills. Behind this, only two miles away, is the sea. The W tower was rebuilt

* Information received from R. J. Sellick.

in the mid C19, and the chancel lengthened. Domestic-looking
s windows. Oaken N doorway with two-centred single-
chamfered arch. – BOX PEWS with PULPIT and READER'S
DESK all late C18 or early C19. – Nice slate and painted
MEMORIALS. – PAINTING. Moses, 1718, as rustic as can be.
– PLATE. Chalice 1573; Flagon and Paten 1802; Almsdish
1813.

ODCOMBE

ST PETER AND ST PAUL. The church has a central tower.
Inside the evidence of the crossing arches is confused. It
indicates a date earlier than Perp. But most of the church was
rebuilt in 1874. The upper part of the tower seems original
and Perp, though the two-light bell-openings filled with
Somerset tracery, and the battlements and pinnacles may also
be of 1874 (cf. W. W. Wheatley's drawing at Mells Manor
House). Original also the s porch. This has pinnacles and
inside a fine panelled ribbed tunnel-vault and a quatrefoil
frieze below it. – FONT. Square, of the Purbeck type, with
five shallow arches on each side. The lid has Perp tracery and
may be C15 or early C16. – PLATE. Standing Cup and Cover
1614 (cf. Bath Abbey); Dish 1806.

OLDBERRY CASTLE *see* DULVERTON

OLD CLEEVE

ST ANDREW. A fine four-square Perp w tower rising at the end
of the village. Built of buff limestone. Money for the building
of it was left in a Will of 1533 by John Tucker, who also left
'to the byldynge of the tower' his 'tokers shers'. Set-back
buttresses, battlements, and tiny pinnacles. w doorway, then
a quatrefoil frieze below the four-light w window, a quatrefoil
frieze below the next, three-light, blank window, and on the
next stage the three-light bell-openings with Somerset tracery.
On the s side one statue-niche. The body of the church is C15,
except for some herringbone, i.e. Norman, masonry in the N
wall of the nave, a blocked C13 doorway, and the remains of a
lancet window in the chancel on the s side, and the early C16
w end of the s aisle which contains very fine w and sw windows, work no doubt of the Cleeve Abbey masons. The tracery
with the little shouldered arches is unmistakable. Arcade of

four bays with piers of standard four-waves section and poor capitals to the four shafts only. Four-centred arches. Original wagon-roof in the nave and lean-to roof in the s aisle. – FONT. Octagonal, Perp, panelled stem, pointed quatrefoils on the bowl. Pretty cover of ogee outline, also with blank panelling. – LECTERN. Brass, with an eagle, 1911. Handsome, in the Arts and Crafts taste. – BENCH ENDS. Two in the panelling behind the high altar. – CHANDELIER. Brass, 1770, by *Thomas Bayley* of Bridgwater. – TILES. Quite a number, similar to those at Cleeve Abbey. – STAINED GLASS. In the s aisle w window, c. 1905, by *Sir Henry Holiday*. – s aisle E by *Morris & Co.*, c. 1897. – Chancel s, 1898, by *Kempe*. – Chancel E, 1953, by *Comper*. – PLATE. Cup and Cover by *Ions* of Exeter 1573; Paten 1639. – MONUMENT. Civilian of c. 1425, in a recess under a coarsely made ogee-gabled recess. At his feet a cat holding a mouse in her paws. The porch floor is cobbled with the date 1614 and a big heart in lighter cobbles. In the churchyard the SCHOOL ROOM of 1811 with a lancet front.

CHAPEL CLEEVE, a grange of Cleeve Abbey with a chapel. What remains of medieval parts is an archway with a four-centred arch, several ground-floor windows of which one has two ogee-headed lights with the typical spandrels of Cleeve Abbey, etc. Further to the r. under a gable a larger upper window, with two lights and a transom. Behind this a room with an original roof and an original fireplace. The rest of the house dates from 1913. Good imitation Elizabethan plaster ceilings by *Bankart*.

ORCHARD PORTMAN

ST MICHAEL. Norman N doorway. Arch with zigzag and zigzag at r. angles to the wall, also pellets. Perp nave and chancel. Modest late Perp w tower for which money was bequeathed in 1521 and 1532. An original s transept was replaced by a C19 porch. Family Pew built in 1910. The Norman s transept arch was then restored to its original position. Jacobean PANELLING in it. – Three HELMS. – PULPIT with Jacobean material. – PLATE. Chalice and Cover 1646; Flagon and Saucer late C17.

Orchard Portman house, the mansion of the Portman family, seems to have been built about the middle of the C16. It was demolished during the second third of the C19.

0030

ORCHARD WYNDHAM

A house with a complicated plan and a complicated history.
The two main fronts very different from each other, that to
the W of *c.* 1600, two-storeyed, on an E-plan, with four- and
five-light transomed windows with the individual lights all
still arched, that to the S completely informal, long, rambling,
and like a country parsonage, with barge-boarded gables of
several heights and sizes. The oldest part of the house is said
to be at the NE end, though the windows are also of *c.* 1600. It
has a timber roof with arched braces. The windows of the W
front conceal evidence of the Hall range of *c.* 1500, *see* a partly
uncovered window jamb with the characteristic encircled
quatrefoil in the spandrel to the l. of an ogee-headed light.
Indeed the Hall itself survives to a spectacular height inside
(recently exposed). Open timber-roof without wind-braces.
Large Perp doorway at the back of the Hall in line with what
must have been the original front door and porch. Smaller
Perp doorway to the N of the large one. Queen Anne fireplace,
panelling, and doorway. Queen Anne staircase, square with
an open well, behind the Perp doorway. Plaster ceilings of
c. 1600 on the first floor in the NE and SW corners. A chapel
originally projected to the W from the SW corner.

3030

OTHERY

ST MICHAEL. The church extends round a crossing tower. This
stands inside on C14 piers but outside appears all Perp. The
piers have the standard section of the Perp style in Somerset,
but the mouldings are so broad and the capitals so simple that
a date not too late in the C14 must be assumed. Above there
are slim diagonal buttresses, battlements and pinnacles, a
higher stair-turret with spirelet, and two-light bell-openings
set in blank panels which make them appear to be of four lights
with a transom. Tracery in the heads as well as below the
transom. On the stage below the bell-openings are niches
with statues happily preserved but unhappily not of a very
good quality. Aisleless nave, N and S doorways simple and
indicative of an earlier date than the windows, perhaps that
of the crossing. Perp W window of four lights. Chancel and
transepts much restored (1850). Broad big arches act as
squints from the transepts into the chancel. – BENCHES.
Some are original, with poppy-heads and representations of a
saint, a pelican, etc. One has R.B., the initials of Abbot Bere

of Glastonbury. The benches in the s transept look *c.* 1665.
Many more are Victorian. These were carved by *William
Halliday*, a self-taught craftsman. The Screen and Misericords
are also Victorian, but not by him. – SOUTH DOOR. Original
and traceried. – COPE. Velvet with delicate C15 embroidery.
Assumption of the Virgin in the middle, angels round her.
The cope has been considered foreign. – PLATE. Chalice and
Paten 1639.

OTTERFORD
1¾ m. WNW of Buckland St Mary

(ST LEONARD. Mostly of 1861. – PLATE. Chalice and Cover
with the date 1599.)
LONG BARROWS. Two, of some importance, on Brown Down.
They are of Neolithic age.

OTTERHAMPTON

ALL SAINTS. Restored to such an extent as to reduce its architectural interest to nil. – FONT. Norman, circular. At the foot
two friezes of saltire crosses. – SCREEN. Small, with four-light
section. The arches depressed-pointed, with nearly straight
sides. – PLATE. Chalice and Cover late C17; Salver 1811.
HILL HOUSE. Late Georgian. Five bays and two storeys. One-
bay pediment. In one of the main rooms an Adamish plaster
ceiling.

OVER STOWEY

ST PETER AND ST PAUL. Perp w tower; the body of the church
enlarged (*Carver* 1840) and too much restored to be of
interest. Plain three-bay arcade with standard four-hollows
piers and capitals blocked as if intended for carved leaf
bands. – BENCHES. Some of the usual type of the district. –
STAINED GLASS. The E window by *Hardman* 1857 (TK).
In contrast some other windows which were provided by
Morris & Co. Two are early and very good: N aisle E: Mary
Magdalene and the angel at the tomb (1870); N aisle W: four
angel figures († 1874). The s and N windows were made by
the firm after the death of both Morris and Burne-Jones.
They record people who died 1905, 1907, 1920. – CANDELA-
BRA. Brass, in two tiers, made by *Street & Pyke* of Bridg-
water, 1775. – PLATE. Chalice and Cover by *Ions* 1574; Paten

early C18. – MONUMENT. Thomas and James Rich † 1813 and 1815, by *H. Wood* of Bristol. A sarcophagus above, and at the foot a very engaging 'trophy' of plough, harrows, and other tools of the field.

MONKS' CHAPEL, Adscombe. Ruins, with plenty of ivy. The w doorway and the window above can still be distinguished.

CHEST HOSPITAL. Built as Quantock Lodge by *Clutton*, 1857. A large, rather dull Tudor house, asymmetrical with a tower, crowned by an ogee roof. Gothic stables, a specially crazy Gothic Dovecote, and a big Gothic Lodge on the Aisholt road.

PARK PLANTATION. Iron Age Encampment, now almost obliterated, but with portions of bank and ditch still visible.

3040

PAWLETT

ST JOHN BAPTIST. Norman s doorway. No columns, but the inner responds have flat patterns. The arch has an inner moulding of lozenges, a second of zigzag at r. angles to the wall, and an outer of beak-heads or biting beasts, a great rarity in Somerset. – The rest of the church externally nothing special. Embattled w tower; transepts. The interior has plenty of C17 interest, but the individual pieces do not blend together into one composition. – PULPIT and READER'S DESK, rather plain. – FONT COVER, STALLS, BOX-PEWS; sturdy COMMUNION RAILS. – The ROOD SCREEN is Perp, simple, with ogee-arched one-light sections and only one frieze in the cornice. – The chancel ROOF was plastered in 1779, in three parts, nicely bordered in a style which makes one suspect self-conscious Jacobeanism. – PLATE. Chalice and Cover 1637; Paten 1707.

PECKING MILL *see* EVERCREECH

5010

PENDOMER

CHURCH. Small Perp church with a w tower, probably older. Interior without division of nave and chancel. In the N wall big cusped early C14 RECESS coarsely carved. The cusps originally carried angels. Above the recess a cresting borne by two male figures standing with one foot a little higher than the other. One carries with both hands, the other with only one. Under the recess but not belonging to it EFFIGY of a cross-legged Knight, *c.* 1320. Body, hauberk of mail, surcoat and coif of mail, quite well preserved. – STAINED GLASS. Remains of the C15 in some windows. – PLATE. Chalice Laudian; Paten 1693.

MANOR HOUSE. Its back faces the churchyard on the E and an attached cottage on the SE. Doorway with two-centred arch. Most of the mullioned windows with arched lights are new or renewed.

PETHERTON BRIDGE *see* SOUTH PETHERTON

PILL BRIDGE *see* ILMINSTER

PILTON

5040

ST JOHN BAPTIST. Beautifully placed in a village down in a dip with all the main roads above it. The best view is obtained from the Tithe Barn (*see* below). The church is curious and a little abrupt in its appearance, because it has a clerestory but no S aisle, and also a clerestory in the chancel which is again without chancel chapels (cf. Ditcheat). The architectural history of the church begins with the S doorway, which is Norman. One order of strong columns with scalloped capitals and arch with two orders of zigzag. The doorway could be contemporary with the N arcade, though it would be reactionary work then. The date of the arcade must be *c.* 1180–90. Five bays with octagonal piers and trumpet-scalloped capitals. The fifth bay is separated from the others by a short stretch of wall. C13 W tower with strong angle buttresses and lancet windows. The upper part of the tower is Perp. The buttresses turn diagonal, and the top has two-light bell-openings with Somerset tracery, battlements, pinnacles, and a spirelet on the higher stair-turret. The tower arch, though low, must have been remodelled in the C15. The N doorway seems to belong to the tower rather than the arcade. In the N aisle wall tomb-chest in a Dec recess. Ball-flower in one arch moulding. No effigy, but a foliated cross carved on the lid of the tomb-chest. The head inside the cross-head is much later rustic work. Perp chancel with large five-light E windows, two N and two S windows, and three on each side in the clerestory. Parapet with pierced quatrefoils. Chancel arch four-centred, low and panelled. The arch starts with three angel-busts on either side. N aisle with parapet with blank arcading, S side with

battlements and pinnacles, s porch with gable and pinnacles.
Original collar-beam roof in the porch, carried on angel-busts
and heads. Original nave roof of Somerset type. The tie-beams
start from busts of angels, the sub-principals from whole
figures of angels. Angels also support the kingposts. Original
aisle roof of the same type. – EASTER SEPULCHRE. With head
of Christ inset in a pastoral crook. – PARCLOSE SCREENS of
the N chapel. The W Screen has robust Renaissance motifs in
the dado and the spandrels of the doorway. The sections are
of one light, the foliage frieze is in good order. The s screen
has four-light tracery but no mullions. Neither screen seems
to be in its original state. Churchwardens' Accounts refer to a
screen made between 1498 and 1508. – COPE. Fragments, not
in a good condition, as it has been used as a frontal. The
motifs are familiar, the Assumption of the Virgin twice and
Cherubim. – Another fragment of embroidery was given to
the church by Richard Pomeroy, *custos* of Wells Cathedral
c. 1490. – STAINED GLASS. Chancel. A kneeling figure,
probably Thomas Overay, precentor of Wells, 1471–92. –
Nave SE window, Ascension of Christ, Victorian, signed
'Designed and painted by *James Bell*'. – CANDELABRA. In
the chancel. Made in 1749 by *R. Rice* of Bristol. – PLATE.
Paten of *c*. 1490; Chalice and Cover 1570; Chalice 1684;
Flagon 1786. – MONUMENTS. Two defaced late C13 effigies
in the churchyard, Knight and Lady.

MANOR HOUSE. sw of the church. The front is plain five-bay
Georgian with a central Venetian window. But it is castellated
and has corner pinnacles. The tradition is indeed that this was
a summer house of the abbots of Glastonbury. There is little
to suggest a medieval past of the building, except for the
polygonal turret on the s side and some cusped one-light
windows which may be medieval and restored or re-set or
copied. Next to it the façade was vigorously gothicized about
1800, with three tripartite Gothic windows, stepped lancets
with broad frames – in no detail justifiable on archaeological
grounds. At the back of the house some two-light mullioned
C17 windows. The building history needs some study. There
exists a vaulted cellar, 18 by 13 ft, and remains of the wall
arches of a cloister. Square Dovecote.

TITHE BARN of Glastonbury Abbey, higher up to the s of the
manor house. A fine stone barn with good roof. Medallions
of the four Evangelists on the gables. Collar-beams, heavy
arched braces, and wind-braces.

PITCOMBE

ST LEONARD. Simple Perp w tower with thin diagonal buttresses. Panelled tower arch. The rest by *G. E. Street* 1858 (GR). – STAINED GLASS. Fragments of C15 Crucifixion window at w end, also a window of 1859 by *O'Connor* (TK). – MONUMENTS. Tablets by a local man (*Rawlings* of Burton) and also by *Reeves* of Bath.

Several good houses at COLE to the N (Cole Mill House with mullioned windows, and Cole Farm House dated 1766) and at HIGHER HADSPEN to the w. A house of 1688 here still has mullioned windows.

HADSPEN HOUSE, 1 m. S (1¼ m. SW of Pitcombe) is of *c.* 1750–70, with a five-bay front with three-bay pediment and pedimented ground-floor windows. Pedimented doorway. Recessed wings.

GODMINSTER MANOR, ¾ m. E. Seven-bay Georgian front with pedimented doorway and ground-floor windows. Older at the back.

THE TOWERS, ¼ m. S. Large gateway formerly at Redlynch House (*see* p. 281). Gothic of the late C18, with the typical quatrefoils and Y-tracery.

PITMINSTER

ST ANDREW AND ST MARY. Much renewed, but enough evidence to imagine a church of *c.* 1300 with a square unbuttressed w tower and a nave arcade of piers consisting of a circular core with attached shafts on three sides, and a cluster of three thin shafts towards the nave. The original work can still be seen in the two S responds. The rest is new. New chancel arch, new clerestory, and no doubt alteration also at the w end which has two chapels embracing the tower. The upper stage of the tower is C14 and octagonal (cf. South Petherton, Ilchester, Podimore, Stoke St Gregory). Leaded spire. Perp chancel with chapels. Wagon-roof. – STAINED GLASS. The N aisle E window by *Kempe* 1894. In the head are some C15 figures. The w window is also by *Kempe*. – BENCH ENDS. A few are original. – PLATE. Chalice 1640; Paten by *Clare* 1725; Flagon by *Bayley* 1728; Dish by *Jacob Marsh* 1767. – MONUMENTS. Humphry Coles † 1570. Recumbent effigy, newly painted. – John Coles † 1607, and wife. Recumbent effigies, he lying behind her and a little higher up. The children kneel against the tomb-chest. Newly painted.

– John Coles † 1627 and wife † 1634. The same composition, but larger kneeling children, and the effigies treated less stiffly. A baby lies at the feet.

PITNEY

St John Baptist. w tower c14 below (*see* the tower arch inside, the w doorway, and the three-light w window with flowing tracery), c15 above (two-light bell-openings with Somerset tracery). The s doorway to the nave also seems c14. Much restoration in 1853 (chancel) and 1875. The most interesting features inside are the carved roof bosses which look c14 and the squint which has a pointed tunnel-vault with three single-chamfered ribs. – FONT. The plinth is original, with lamb's heads at the corners. – PULPIT. Jacobean. – PLATE. Chalice 1572; Paten 1736.

Two ROMAN VILLAS are recorded here. One was a large court-yard-type building with numerous elaborate mosaics.

In 1898 a beautiful late Saxon openwork BROOCH was found here.

PIXTON PARK *see* DULVERTON

PODIMORE

St Peter. An early c14 church of nave and chancel, and a w tower which turns octagonal above the lowest stage. Dec windows in nave and chancel, narrow single-chamfered chancel arch (which could be older still, if it is original), tower arch double-chamfered on moulded brackets. Double-chamfered squinches lead over from the square to the octagon (cf. Pitminster). – COMMUNION RAIL. c17, probably after 1660, slim vertically symmetrical turned balusters. – PLATE. Chalice c. 1575; Paten by *Bayley* 1729.

POLDEN HILLS

Prehistoric Remains. A magnificent hoard of bronze ornaments dating from the latter part of the Early Iron Age was unearthed here in 1800. The bulk of them is in the British Museum, though some went to Bristol and Taunton. The products of the La Tène Celts, they were over seventy in number, and largely consisted of horse-trappings. The casting, engraving, decoration and, above all, the application of the red *champlevé* enamel (characteristic of the La Tène Celts) are unsurpassed.

PONTER'S BALL *see* GLASTONBURY

PORLOCK

8040 inset

St Dubricius. A Celtic, Welsh Saint of *c*. 600. Low heavy C13 W tower with shingled spire. One W lancet renewed and probably altered. Tower arch towards the nave with one slight chamfer. Nave, chancel with an original E vestry, and S aisle. Two-storeyed N porch C15. Additions of *c*. 1890. Inside late C14 S arcade of five bays with octagonal piers, very elementarily shaped capitals, and double-chamfered arches. Under the fifth arch of the arcade is the HARINGTON MONUMENT, not in its original position. Tomb-chest with many small niches and tall canopy with fleurons up the jambs and along the four-centred arch. Cusped arch, tracery in the spandrels. On the tomb-chest the recumbent alabaster effigies of John Harington † 1418 and his wife, of good quality, and dating from *c*. 1460. – Other MONUMENTS. Tomb-chest with quatrefoils and without effigies in the chancel, and another in the S porch. – In the S wall two recesses with segmental arches. In one of them effigy of a cross-legged Knight, late C13, badly defaced. – FONT. Octagonal, Perp, much decorated, with the usual motifs. – REREDOS. By *W. H. R. Blacking*, not without a touch of the Voysey style. – SCULPTURE. Two small fragments of a Saxon Cross-shaft with interlace decoration (W wall). – STAINED GLASS. The church has mostly plain glass in its windows, but quite large panels are set in with pale-coloured flowers, their outlines formed by the leading of the glass, in the Arts and Crafts manner. The date is 1890. – PLATE. Chalice perhaps partly Elizabethan; Dish 1727.

The nicest groups of cottages are W of the church by the Ship Inn, where also is *Voysey's* VILLAGE HALL, quite a plain uninteresting building. On Voysey's work in this neighbourhood, *see* below. At the E end of the village DOVER- HAY MANOR HOUSE, a fragment of a C15 manor house, and now the COUNTY LIBRARY READING ROOM, much re- stored and remodelled in 1883. The Hall window is sur- prisingly grand, a four-light window with transom and

tracery characterized by the small circles in the spandrels of
ogee arches which are typical of churches in this neighbourhood. Big fireplaces inside and original ceiling.

2b PORLOCK WEIR is famous for its whitewashed cottages by the
little harbour. They make pretty pictures indeed, without any
of the close completeness of Clovelly or Mevagissey.

Charles F. Annesley Voysey, one of the best domestic
architects of England about 1900, did much work on the
estate of Lord Lovelace. WORTHY MANOR, to the W of
Porlock Weir, must have been altered by him, as his characteristic chimneystacks and metalwork details prove, especially in
the stables and coach-house. Yet, it is said that *Lady Lovelace*
herself was quite capable of designs in Voysey's style and spirit
(cf. Culbone). ANSTEY COMBE, the Italianate Lovelace
mansion of 1866, also received a group of estate cottages by
Voysey. They are one of his last works, of 1936.

LILYCOMBE, $3\frac{1}{2}$ m. W of Porlock, on Porlock Hill, facing S, was
built by *Voysey* in 1912. It is not one of his best domestic
compositions, although his pebbledash, his buttresses with
their marked batter, and the handsome S veranda on stone
pillars are unmistakable.

BERRY CASTLE. Destroyed IRON AGE CAMP in Berry Castle
Combe.

There is also a Bronze Age STONE CIRCLE just S of the
Church on a path to Dunkery Beacon, at a height of almost
1500 ft. It consists of ten medium-sized megalithic stones or
part-stones still erect and eleven fallen ones. The diameter of
the circle is 80 ft.

2020
POUNDISFORD

POUNDISFORD PARK. The great importance of Poundisford
Park in architectural history lies in the fact that it was built
shortly after 1546 and thus represents the years just before the
creation of the Elizabethan style. It is indeed in plan as well
as details closer to Henry VIII than to Elizabeth I. The
building is designed on an H-plan, but on the N or entrance
side the court between the two projecting wings is narrowed
on the l. by the porch and on the r. by the bay corresponding
to the dais end of the hall. What remains is a recess rather than
a court. All main divisions are marked by buttresses. Wings,
porch, bay, and recessed courts are gabled. The walls are
roughcast. The mullioned windows still have their Late Perp

four-centred arched heads to each light and their hood-moulds. On the s side the court is larger. The recessed centre here shows the back exit of the screens passage, the hall fire-place with a spiral-stair tucked in between the two and not projecting, and a bay corresponding to the dais and the N bay.

Inside the house the most impressive room is the Hall. This was altered *c.* 1570, still by William Hill who had built the house over twenty years before. He was the son of Roger Hill of Poundisford Lodge (*see below*). The hall has a plaster ceiling with thin ribs forming star patterns and with pendants. On these the initials of William Hill and his wife. Also *c.* 1570 the screen was remodelled, with the use however of the heavy circular muntins of *c.* 1550, and the front of the gallery above the screen was closed and plastered except for a picturesque little oriel window opening into the hall. The screens passage as well as the gallery has ribbed plaster ceilings, and there are more in first-floor rooms. Two more rooms require attention, one converted about 1670, the other added shortly after 1737. The first, now the Library, lies to the NW of the Hall and was originally the Justice Room – *see* the small blocked N door necessary to allow direct access to those attending the court. The Library has a plaster ceiling of a style very different from that of the other rooms. The principal motif is an oval with a dove of peace surrounded by a band of scrolls and a broad wreath. Foliage panels also in the four corners. This style is a reflection of the innovations of Inigo Jones and John Webb and appears for the first time in the SW of England at Forde Abbey Dorset, not far away from Poundisford, about 1650. It is handled with more freedom and artistry there, and Poundisford may represent a job done locally on the pattern of Forde or by a minor member of the team working at Forde (cf. also Golden Farm). The room of *c.* 1738 lies to the NE of the Hall. It has a screen formed by two Ionic columns at the entrance and very sparing decoration. The fireplace was, it appears, bought in London from *Samuel Norman*. On the upper floor a small Ladies' Room above the porch and small Muniment Room above the back (s) bay of the Hall.

Near the house a separate oblong building which may have been the original kitchen, and a very pretty brick-built SUMMER HOUSE of the late C17, with pyramid roof and open pediment to the doorway.

POUNDISFORD LODGE owes its name to the fact that it represents the site of a lodge of Poundisford Park, the hunting estate of the Bishops of Winchester who held Taunton Castle. In 1534 the chase was divided and a lease granted for the part now the lodge to Roger Hill. The other half came into the hands of Roger Hill's son William Hill, as has been mentioned before. Poundisford Lodge is about contemporary with Poundisford Park, and built on the same type of plan. The windows also are of the same pattern. Inside three rooms with Elizabethan plaster ceilings, one on the ground floor (in this room a fireplace of *c.* 1760 bought in London) and two on the upper floor. These are coved and more sumptuous. Both these ceilings have the same thin ribs as Poundisford Park, but as in one room there is a date 1590, they were done much later. Both rooms have original fireplaces. One of them has its overmantel flanked by two wild men.

PRESTON PLUCKNETT

5010

ST JAMES. Of the first half of the C14 the transepts and chancel; *see* the typical two-light windows and the reticulated E window, and also the transept arches (that on the S side on good head-corbels). W tower plain Perp. Much restored. The shallow porch and the lectern and pulpit of a heavy High Victorian. – PLATE. Chalice and Cover 1574; Chalice and Paten by *Tearle* 1728.

ABBEY FARM. A remarkable C15 grange, probably of the Abbey of Bermondsey. At the r. end of the front the Hall, partly damaged in the Second World War and rebuilt. The tall r. window is renewed. So is the hall roof with arched braces, kingposts, and wind-braces. A two-storeyed gabled porch leads to the screens passage. The doorway is two-centred, the window above is of two lights with a transom. Inside the porch a vault with ridge-ribs and diagonal ribs. To the l. of the porch
42b   were the offices. The kitchen chimney ends in a picturesque octagonal turret-stack. The roof-height of the range is not the same all the way. At r. angles to the house the splendid stone
43   BARN, 114 ft long. It is of ten bays, with buttresses and long cross-shaped slits. Bays six and seven are filled by the porch. The archway has a two-centred arch, double-chamfered, no capitals or abaci. Original roof.

Opposite Abbey Farm is KNAPP HOUSE, with grange and cottage, a pretty C17 group.

PUCKINGTON

St Andrew. c13 chancel. One N window of two lights with bar tracery. Renewed E window of three stepped lights with three cinquefoiled circles. Inside stepped group of Piscina and Sedilia with continuous mouldings (cf. Shepton Beauchamp). Perp nave, Perp W tower. The tower has set-back buttresses ending in pairs of pinnacles on the corners of the battlements. W doorway flanked by triangular shafts, W window of four lights with transom, two-light bell-openings. – FONT. Norman, circular, renewed. With one cable-moulding. – PLATE. Chalice 1637; Paten 1724.

PURITON

St Michael. Early c13 W tower without buttresses and of thrice receding girth. Battlements; pyramid roof. Low rectangular staircase projection. On the W side two lancet windows one on top of the other. Low double-chamfered tower arch on moulded brackets typical of their date. Nave, N aisle (arcade of four bays, standard piers of four-hollows type), and chancel – all Perp. – SCREEN. Not well preserved; three-light sections with some panel tracery. No frieze, embattled top. – PLATE. Domestic Tankard 1713 by *John Eastt*; Almsdish 1722; Saucer 1730; Chalice by *Fuller White* 1752.

PYLLE

St Thomas a Becket. W tower with diagonal buttresses, battlements, and pinnacles. Higher stair-turret with spirelet. Two-light upper windows with Somerset tracery and above them two-light bell-openings also with Somerset tracery. The rest all 1868. – PLATE. Set of 1737.

Manor House. The lower wing on the r. of the present front is part of a large house which stood here and to which a preserved date-plate 1621 may belong. The present three-bay two-storeyed façade with quoins of even width and cross windows must be of *c.* 1700 and will be contemporary with the former Stables and a handsome outbuilding that has two pedimented doorways and circular apart from upright mullioned windows of two lights.

PYRLAND HALL

1¼ m. N of Taunton

(1758, and not much altered since. Now belongs to King's College Taunton.)

QUANTOCK LODGE *see* OVER STOWEY

QUEEN CAMEL

St Barnabas. Most of the architectural evidence points to a later C14 date, and the church is important as evidence of that period. High, but relatively severe W tower, completely sheer on the N and S sides up to the bell-openings. Set-back buttresses carrying shafts with pinnacles. Higher NW stair-turret. W doorway, three-light W window with niche for an image over, two-light bell-openings, battlements, pinnacles. These are, of course, doubled at each corner as they continue the buttresses. Tower arch moulded, not panelled, and not high. Aisle windows Early Perp; parapets, no battlements. Chancel later Perp. Window tracery of the panel type, but, as against the aisles, with sub-panels. Fleuron frieze below the eaves. Very tall E window of three lights with transom and tracery below this. Niche with figure above the apex. Panelled chancel arch inside. The N chancel chapel has a three-light window with transom. Earlier than the rest the aisle arcades. They are hardly later than *c.* 1360, with their relatively low octagonal piers (four bays) and moulded arches. Niches for images in two piers. Some capitals are decorated with leaves. Of the same date as the arcade must be the outer wall of the S aisle; for it has a recess with pierced cusping originally enriched by heads which is Dec in style. In the N aisle wall an ogee-headed recess higher up. The chancel N doorway is 1886. Of *c.* 1400 apparently the Piscina and Sedilia, placed under thickly decorated canopies, ribbed inside. – The latest part of the church is, as usual, the clerestory (of three-light windows) and the roof. This is of Somerset type with embattled tie-beams, kingposts, and tracery above the tie-beams. The tie-beams rest on short braces, and these start from decorated stone corbels. The sub-principals begin with angel figures. Earlier wagon-roof in the chancel, on angels and with many bosses. On some of these animals from the Bestiary (phoenix, amphisbaena, syren, griffin, hyena, basilisk, aspido-chelone, unicorn, elephant, etc.). – FONT. Octagonal, Perp, but of unusual design. Four angle supports reaching up to the rim. On them four defaced figures in style evidently rather early C15 than later. – ROOD SCREEN. Of Devon type, *c.* 1500, with broad, luxuriantly decorated cornice. Ribbed coving below. The sections are arched, of six lights with transom.

The middle mullion runs up into the apex of the arch. – PULPIT. Of the same period, with narrow niches for statues, and nodding canopies. – MONUMENT. Mrs Mildmay † 1772, elegant, with an urn; unsigned.

The village is specially carefully looked after. Plenty of pleasant houses. Many of those in the main street have front gardens.

EYEWELL HOUSE. Pleasant neo-Georgian, only five bays wide, with big hipped roof and two tall chimney-stacks. By *Sir Guy Dawber*, c. 1926.

PACKHORSE BRIDGE, Black Well Road, about ¼ m. from the church.

RADDINGTON 0020

ST MICHAEL. All on its own in the hills, with no lane to approach it. Perp small unbuttressed W tower, plastered. Small embattled nave with straight-headed windows. Squarely projecting rood-turret. The S doorway has a wooden frame with two-centred arch. – Inside, between nave and chancel, the old plastered TYMPANUM survives. Below it the ROOD SCREEN, damaged but unrestored. Three-light sections with ogee-headed lights and panel tracery, dated by experts rather before than after 1400. – FONT. Octagonal, c13, of the Purbeck type, with shallow blank arches. They are trefoil-pointed. – DOOR. S Door with long heavy decorated iron hinges. – READER'S DESK. The decoration is of the incised Jacobean type; yet there is a date 1713. – PLATE. Chalice and Cover of 1574.

REDLYNCH 7030

ST PETER. 1750, with arched windows (none in the E or W ends) and a bell-cote. Five bays long. Nice pedimented plaster reredos. – PLATE. Chalice and Cover, Paten, Flagon, all of c. 1672; Almsdish 1757.

REDLYNCH HOUSE. Built 1672, burnt and rebuilt after 1912. Two storeys, stone, simple with parapet and pedimented doorway. Projecting wings at the back. Office wing to the l. with cupola.*

DISCOVE HOUSE. Opposite St Peter. Long, irregular thatched house of the C17 with mullioned windows and a three-storeyed porch. C18 and other alterations.

* GATEWAY *see* Pitcombe, p. 273.

ROUNDHILL GRANGE, 1¼ m. SW of Redlynch House. Handsome two-storeyed brick house of five bays with quoins and cross windows. Phelps gives the date as 1701.

RIMPTON

6020

ST MARY. Chancel of the late C13 with a group of three renewed lancets at the E end and cusped lancets. Rere-arches inside. Nave Perp, embattled (but an earlier S doorway). Transept Perp and embattled. Chancel arch and transept arches Perp. W tower Perp with low tower arch to the E, no W doorway. – FONT. Octagonal, Perp, with Jacobean cover. – PULPIT. Jacobean. – BENCH ENDS with poppy-heads. Panels below with flowers, and at the foot blank cusped panels. – PLATE. Chalice and Cover 1637; Paten by *Mason* 1731.

ROAD CASTLE *see* WINSFORD

ROCKWELL GREEN
1 m. SW of Wellington

1010

ALL SAINTS. 1888 by *J. Spencer*. The S porch tower with spire 1908 (GR). In the E.E. style inside, with exposed brick work. The exterior red sandstone. – STAINED GLASS. Most of the windows by *Mayer & Co.*, of Munich, c. 1900. The one English design (N aisle W) in comparison looks very English indeed.

ROUNDHILL GRANGE *see* REDLYNCH

ROWLAND'S FARM *see* HORTON

RUBOROUGH CAMP *see* BROOMFIELD

RUISHTON

2020

ST GEORGE. Remains of a late Norman S doorway. One shaft with trumpet capital, the other with beaded flutes. The arch is altered. The building history is not clear. The tower is certainly Late Perp. Perp also the S chapel with a two-bay arcade. Pier of four-waves moulding, four small polygonal capitals. But the chancel is not in line with the nave, *see* the stone-screen-like cusped double-squint. The w tower was meant to be as ambitious as any in the villages around. It is a variant of those of Huish Episcopi and Kingsbury Episcopi. Moneys were left for it between 1530 and 1535. But it was given up and finished even without battlements. Lias with Ham Hill dressings. Set-back buttresses, with diagonal pinnacles on the bell-stage. w doorway with a hood-mould on busts of angels. Quatrefoil frieze and four-light w window, another quatrefoil frieze, two two-light bell-openings with Somerset tracery. Shafts with pinnacles l. and r. of them. The tower arch has panelling between thin shafts. The s porch is attached to the s chapel (cf. Curry Mallet). – FONT. Big octagonal bowl with big square crocketed pinnacles covering the diagonals. Perp, and of an unusual design. – PAINTING. Adoration of the Magi, Flemish, C16. – PLATE. Chalice and Cover 1574; Salver 1795. – MONUMENTS. John Arundell † 1784 by *Jones, Dunn & Drewett* of Bristol. – C. Proctor Anderton † 1824 by *King* of Bath, both with mourning women, the earlier over the indispensable urn, the later over a broken column. – CROSS. In the churchyard, with four defaced figures against the shaft.

RUNNINGTON
1½ m. NW of Wellington

ST PETER. Red sandstone. Small, with small w tower. The only feature worth noting is that even so small a church possessed a rood-loft, *see* the preserved staircase. – PLATE. Chalice and Cover 1573.

ST AUDRIES *see* WEST QUANTOXHEAD

ST MICHAEL CHURCH

ST MICHAEL. Very small, with unbuttressed N tower crowned by a low pyramid roof. Anything old restored away outside and inside. – PLATE. Chalice and Cover c. 1574.

MAUNSEL. The oldest part of the house is the s side with a large two-light window to the E. N of this range the (later) porch and in the roof arched timbers. The N side is probably of c. 1791, the date at which Collinson calls the house newly built. The w side is C19.

SAMPFORD ARUNDEL

HOLY CROSS. Slender unbuttressed W tower with unmoulded tower arch and other details that point to a C13 date. Completed Perp. The rest now almost entirely C19. – RECESS in the N aisle. In it a curious fragment, a small ogee gable and under it two hands holding a heart (?). Does this mark a heart burial? – PLATE. Chalice and Cover by *Thomas Parr* 1706; Paten 1723. – MONUMENT. Tablet to Christopher Baker † 1729, the long inscription on a draped cloth.

SAMPFORD BRETT

ST GEORGE. Unbuttressed C14 S tower with small bell-openings and battlements. Large S doorway, with a double-chamfered arch dying into the imposts. In the N transept N front a two-light window with trefoiled pointed lights and a plate tracery quatrefoil, i.e. late C13. The rest mostly remodelled 1835 and very pretty in parts. No-one could call the W front pretty. The imitation Gothic tracery here is monstrously ignorant and aesthetically of no value. But the colour-washed interior and especially the chancel with its foliage trails around the arches is sweetly romantic. The original wagon-roof rests on white putto-heads. – WOODWORK. A queer mixture. Some benches clearly Late Perp of the square-headed type with close tracery and leaf and branch motifs current in this neighbourhood. Other woodwork probably skilful C19 imitation. In addition the first (taller) bench end at the W end to the N with a formal figure and two small piping cherubs. That seems to be a piece of Jacobean carving, *Volkskunst*, but impressive. The story is supposed to be that of Florence Wyndham who came back to life just when the vault was closed over her. – PLATE. Chalice and Cover 1573; Paten by *Clare* 1720; Flagon 1776. – MONUMENT. Badly defaced Effigy of a cross-legged Knight (Vestry) late C13.

SANDHILL PARK
½ m. NE of Ash Priors

Built in 1720 and altered and enlarged in 1815. Seven by five bays with quoins of even length. Two and a half storeys, the half storey being above the main cornice. The original doorway with attached Tuscan columns and a metope frieze

now inside the Tuscan eight-column porch of 1815. Also a
large canted bay added on the r. Fine entrance hall of *c*. 1750.
Doorways with pediments. Panels with large and free Rococo
stucco. Niche in the middle of the back wall opposite the
entrance. The large room to the l. has also lively plasterwork
on the ceiling.

SEA MILLS FARMHOUSE *see* DONYATT

SEAVINGTON ST MARY   *4010*

ST MARY. The lower part of the tower, the s doorway, and the
chancel are supposed to be C13 work. Chancel arch with
continuous moulding – anyway earlier than Perp. Contemporary recess to its l. probably for a side altar. – PLATE.
Chalice 1715.

SEAVINGTON ST MICHAEL   *4010*

ST MICHAEL. Small; nave and chancel only. Panelled chancel
arch. Two heads in the nave walls w of it, perhaps brackets
for the lenten veil. The man puts his tongue out. The head-
dress of the woman dates the pair as *c*. 1350–75. – EFFIGY.
Civilian, late C13, badly preserved. This is to be placed on
a chancel wall.

ROMAN VILLA, with mosaic floors, recorded here.

SELWORTHY   *9040 inset*

The village with its many pretty whitewashed cottages is
reached from the w along an avenue almost closed overhead
by ivy and holly. Before reaching the church one passes on
the s the TITHE BARN, stone with a curious window arch.
The moulding seems early C14. Hood-mould with a pig, a
sheep, and a sheaf of corn.

ALL SAINTS. Save for the lower parts of the short unbuttressed w tower which seem to be C14, this is a Perp church,
and one remarkably lavish for its present hidden-away position. Its great glory is its s aisle, unsurpassed in the county.
It has the date 1538 on the capital of the w respond. The
embattled s front has a three-light and a four-light window
separated by a two-storeyed s porch with a doorway finely
panelled up the jambs and along the arch. The tracery of the

large, transomed windows is of that exquisite, elegant, yet by no means exuberant design worked out probably at Dunster or Watchet and used at Cleeve Abbey, Luccombe, etc. The N aisle is plainer, but its E window is of the same type. The chancel E window is probably a little earlier. Note the knobs on the cusps. The interior is remarkably airy with its tall slim piers and large windows. Four-bay arcades. Piers with four-waves section. The capitals have partly very crisply modelled leaf bands, partly just small polygons for the four shafts only. Wagon-roofs original, though much repaired. That of the S aisle is one of the finest in the county. It has richly decorated wall-plates with angels holding shields, braces, and purlins, and large bosses with the face of Christ, the Symbols of the Passion, etc. – WEST GALLERY. Dated 1750, a big, heavy, classical piece, on Doric pilasters carrying a metope frieze. – SQUIRE'S PEW, a delicious little Gothic pavilion in the parvise chamber of the porch. Thin clustered shafts to the l. and r.; early C19. – PULPIT. With early C16 panels; restored. – COMMUNION RAIL. Of c. 1700, with quite slim turned balusters. – SOUTH DOOR. Original, with linenfold panels. – STAINED GLASS. Some old fragments in the N aisle E window. – CANDLESTICKS. C16, very good, probably Flemish. – PLATE. Chalice early C17; Paten, perhaps Dutch and domestic C17; Flagon 1760. – MONUMENTS. Tomb-chest in the chancel, of the usual Perp type; no effigies. – C. B. Dyke Acland † 1837 and C. R. Dyke Acland † 1828, by *Chantrey*. A pair of identical monuments, each with an altar in relief, draped, and with a portrait medallion in profile. Grecian detail. – William Blackford † 1730, handsome wall-monument with cherubs' heads at the foot and a curly open pediment at the top. Attributed to *W. Palmer* by Mrs Esdaile.

BURY CASTLE. IRON AGE CAMP, on Selworthy Hill. The camp, though very dilapidated, is still impressive. It is roughly square with rounded corners, measuring c. 70 yards by 50. The ditch rises in places to a height of 12 ft.

SHANKS HOUSE see CUCKLINGTON

403)

SHAPWICK

ST MARY. Application to build 1329; consecration 1331. Unbuttressed central tower of that time, internally on characteristic low double-chamfered arches continued in the piers without break. Battlements, higher stair-turret. Five-light Perp w window. The other windows renewed in the style of 1300. – Much mid-C19 STAINED GLASS. – PLATE. Set of 1746 by *Gurney & Co.* – MONUMENTS. Two quite sizeable wall monuments: Jane Bull † 1657, Henry Bull † 1691.

MANOR HOUSE. Asymmetrical, with gables and a two-storeyed porch. In front of the house a former garden enclosed by a handsome wall with vertically symmetrical balusters and obelisks. Round-headed gateway.

SHAPWICK HOUSE. Longish C17 house on an E-plan, said to have been built by Sir Henry Rolle, the judge, who died at Shapwick in 1656. Much altered in the late C18, but the round-headed porch doorway is original.

SHAPWICK HEATH. Sporadic prehistoric finds have been made here. The principal discovery was that of a hoard in 1936, which consisted of a late La Tène tankard in Romanized style and two Iron Age bowls, one of bronze and one of pewter.

SHENTON COURT *see* STOGURSEY

SHEPTON BEAUCHAMP   4010

ST MICHAEL. Fine Perp w tower with set-back buttresses, battlements, and no pinnacles. But pinnacles were projected if not carried out; that is proved by the corbelling for inter-mediate ones in the middles of the sides. Higher polygonal stair-turret. w door with triangular shafts with pinnacles l. and r. Quatrefoil frieze over. Tall four-light w window with one transom, the tracery in two sub-arches. Quatrefoil frieze at the foot of the second stage and to the w contemporary statue of a bishop; not good. The bell-openings of two lights reach down from the third into this second stage. The lower part is blank. The openings are traceried, but not with the patterns of Somerset tracery. Tall panelled arch to the nave. Fine fan-vault with big bosses and large circular opening for the bell-ropes. The w tower was not the original tower of the church. It had at an earlier stage a N tower as is proved by the double-chamfered arches at the E end of the N arcade, one to the nave, one to the aisle. The N and S arcades have octagonal piers and double-chamfered arches. All this is probably early C14. Compare also the S doorway. Clerestory Victorian. The chancel is Dec (much renewed). The N and S windows have ogee-sided triangles in the tracery, the E window of three lights has a circle with a wheel of four mouchettes. Inside the chancel a good (over-restored) stepped group of Piscina, Sedilia, and a doorway. Continuous mouldings. In the Sedilia the walls between the seats are prettily pierced by an ogee-sided triangle and a cinquefoiled circle. High embattled Perp N chapel with three-light windows. Panelled. – PLATE. Chalice and Cover 1573; Chalice designed by *Street* 1874.

SHEPTON MONTAGUE

6030

ST PETER. In the chancel one long lancet window, the cusping perhaps later. S porch tower Perp. All much renewed. Inside an extremely pretty C18 W gallery painted white, with nine small paintings of angels, evangelists, Moses, David, and Aaron. – PLATE. Chalice and Cover 1573; Paten on foot of 1684.

SHERFORD

2020

1 m. S of Taunton

ST JOHN. 1860.

SHERFORD HOUSE. Inside an overmantel of remarkable conservatism. It is dated 1679 and yet still has two of the typically Elizabethan blank arches on short stubby balusters, and also three little figures and two flowers in vases which look no later.

SIGWELL'S CAMP *see* COMPTON PAUNCEFOOT

SIMONSBATH

7030
inset

ST LUKE. Nave, chancel, and bell-cote. The W wall completely slate-hung. The style is E.E. with lancets. The simplicity of the composition and the lack of mouldings look C20, but the church was built in 1856. The architect seems unrecorded. Disappointing interior.

COW CASTLE. Enclosure on top of a steep hill at a narrow point between White Water and the River Barle. It must have served some defensive purpose in antiquity, though the rampart is low and amateurishly constructed.

SKILGATE

9020

5 m. E of Dulverton

ST JOHN. 1872. – PLATE. Chalice and Cover of 1573.

SLOUGH FARM *see* STOKE ST GREGORY

SMALL DOWN CAMP *see* EVERCREECH

SOMERTON
4020

St Michael. A large church which is not predominantly Perp
– quite a rarity in Somerset. Dark grey stone with brown Ham
Hill dressings. Nave and aisles, chancel, transeptal, octagonal
s tower, and embattled clerestory. The building history is
interesting and begins with the tower, the arch of which into
the nave seems to be early C13. The rest is C14, notably the
nave and the aisle arcades (four bays). Octagonal piers with
plain moulded capitals, double-chamfered arches. Very wide
proportions, which make the piers appear too short. The
discrepancy must have been worse before the clerestory was
built. The tower has inside a trefoiled piscina, a tomb recess
with single-chamfered arch, a single-chamfered doorway on
the w side, and to the nave a triple-chamfered arch dying into
the imposts. Small E lancet and similar, but enlarged lancet
(blocked) to the w. Outside, the transition from square to
octagon is made by the most primitive, plain, large broaches.
Lancet window in the s gable. Traces of a double-chamfered
opening below the battlements. Perp bell-openings of two
lights with Somerset tracery; battlements. So far all this is C13.
After the nave and tower follows the N transept. Its N window
has Y-tracery, i.e. dates from *c.* 1300. Again a generation later
the s aisle wall was rebuilt, no doubt further to the s. The
windows are of three lights and have reticulated and other
contemporary tracery. At the same time the w window of the
nave must have been enlarged to five lights and given its
flowing tracery. The w window is so high that it presupposes
the erection of the clerestory. This has three-light windows
with four-centred arches. In the N aisle one reticulated window; the rest Perp. The moulding of the chancel arch could
be *c.* 1300 or *c.* 1350. Splendid Late Perp roof of the best
Somerset qualities: moderate pitch, tie-beams decorated with
foliage and castellated. At the w and E ends of the nave shallow
arched braces instead. Kingposts on angel figures. Plenty of
tracery to the l. and r. of the kingposts. The wall-plates are
decorated too. The roof itself is panelled with quatrefoil
panels. They are all identical – repeated, Kenneth Wickham
says, 640 times. – Communion Table. 1626. With bulbous

legs. – REREDOS, or panelling behind the altar. Also Jacobean, five bays of coupled arches. Six smallish figures. – PULPIT. 1615, with the usual blank arches. – CANDELABRA. Brass; C18. – PLATE. Chalice and Cover 1573; Set of 1692; Paten late C17. – MONUMENT. J. T. Hall † 1812, by *Physick* of London. The monument to John Pinney † 1818 is better, but unsigned.

PERAMBULATION. The market-place of Somerton is one of the most happily grouped urban pictures in Somerset. The church lies back from its N side. The W side is indifferent; but look E or look S, and the irregular little square has plenty that is attractive. The MARKET CROSS was rebuilt in 1673, a broad, low, open octagonal structure with segmental arches and battlements. To its S the TOWN HALL which, with its gable and mullioned windows, at first also appears C17. The large window at the back however has mullions, a transom, and an arch, and that must indicate a date *c.* 1700 or perhaps even later. The front windows in fact are in their elongated proportions also different from the Tudor and Stuart tradition. On the S side of the square houses which infringe on the site of the former CASTLE of Somerton of which some masonry and vaults are supposed to remain inside the White Hart Hotel. On the N side of the market-place is a specially good C16 house with two symmetrical oriels and dormers above them, individually the best house at Somerton. At the NE corner Lloyds Bank with a rounded corner and a Tuscan porch. To its S another C16 house with an oriel.

At the corner of Lloyds Bank BROAD STREET starts, a broad street indeed, and short, with two rows of trees. The RED LION stands at its SE end, the most ambitious of the inns of the town. A long symmetrical five-bay front, two storeys with parapet. The windows are tripartite, and the centre is a depressed rounded archway with a Venetian window and a broken pediment over. This bay is flanked by rudimentary giant pilasters. In Broad Street likewise the WESTMINSTER BANK deserves notice (five bays, two storeys, quoins, and rusticated window jambs) and CRAIGMORE which must date from *c.* 1700, *see* its upright elongated mullioned windows and the odd smaller arched two-light window in the middle. At the N end of Broad Street, that is the end of Somerton, in its own grounds lies LYNCH, a nice Adamish three-bay villa with tripartite arched windows on the ground floor. To the W of the Market Place there is less to notice, the UNI-

CORN HOTEL perhaps, a Tudor house, with an asymmetrically placed two-storeyed porch with round-headed outer doorway and cambered doorway inside, and then the HEXT ALMS-HOUSES, dated 1626. They are one-storeyed, each dwelling provided with a cambered doorway, a two-light window, and a second small window curiously set in a deep round-arched niche. This gives the whole row an unusual rhythm.

Outside the town to the SE two worth-while houses, the OLD PARSONAGE, a regular C17 façade of two storeys with mullioned windows, and a two-storeyed porch, the upper floor of which has a canted oriel. Yet further SE, on the main Yeovil road, is SOMERTON COURT, a larger house with mullioned windows and a centre porch, dated 1641. Early in the C19 it was made more baronial by battlements and quite successful turrets to the porch. Originally there were gables and gabled dormers. SOMERTON ENDLEIGH, NE of Somerton Court, is a large, plain, ashlar-faced C18 house with ample outbuildings, partly Early, partly Late Georgian. (Some late C18 fireplaces and ceilings.)

SOUTH BARROW 6020

ST PETER. The doorway is reached by a short avenue of yew-trees, trained fan-wise. The exterior of the church all over-restored (1850), except for the W tower. Diagonal buttresses with many set-offs, two-light bell-openings with Somerset tracery. Battlements. – FONT. The stem C13, the bowl completely plain, octagonal, with initials and the date 1584. – PULPIT. Jacobean. – BENCHES. Two with poppy-heads, the rest straight-headed. Plain tracery patterns. – COMMUNION RAIL. Jacobean, with vertically symmetrical balusters and arabesque-work on the rail. – PLATE. Chalice and Cover 1576. – BRASS. Richard Morris, 1584 (nave, N wall), plate 24 by 14 in.

SOUTH BRENT see BRENT KNOLL

SOUTH CADBURY 6020

ST THOMAS A BECKET. Nice W tower with higher NE stair-turret. Diagonal buttresses, two-light bell-openings, battlements and pinnacles. The rest much renewed. The S aisle externally rebuilt 1835. In 1876 a splay of an original s aisle window and a piscina were discovered. In the splay C15 PAINTING of a Bishop. The s aisle arcade seems to be of the early C14: two quatrefoil piers with moulded capitals; the w and E responds single demi-shafts with two tiers of odd shaft-rings. Double-chamfered arches. The chancel arch is Perp and panelled. Cambered panelled roof with angel brackets and carved bosses. – PLATE. Chalice and Paten 1774.

Opposite the church the RECTORY, C18, and CASTLE FARM HOUSE, dated 1687 and still with four-light mullioned windows.

CADBURY CASTLE. A tremendous IRON AGE CAMP, covering 18 acres. It is the mightiest prehistoric camp in Somerset, and one of the mightiest in Britain. In ancient times it was certainly the focal point of many trackways and encampments. It is easy to understand why its construction should have been attributed in folklore to King Arthur, and why it became identified with the legendary Camelot. The fortress is three-sided, guarded by no less than four huge banks and ditches. In places the height of the bank is over 40 ft above the bottom of the ditch.

SOUTH CHARD see CHARD

SOUTHFIELDS see HORTON

SOUTH PETHERTON

4010

ST PETER AND ST PAUL. The church lies at the highest point of the little town, a large spreading building crowned by a tall and prominent crossing tower. Historically the chancel and the lower parts of the tower come first. They are later C13. The chancel has several windows with bar tracery (quatre-foiled circles). They are shafted inside, and the shafts carry capitals with stiff-leaf (and one with three charming heads). The E window must once have been a bold Geometrical com-position. Its C13 shafts show that the present four-light Perp window is not longer than it originally was (one transom, panel tracery). The crossing arches differ. To the N and s they are triple-chamfered and die into the piers. To the w and E they have three orders of columns with shafts with moulded capitals. The abaci between the capitals are carried on tiny

pointed-trefoiled arches which slope forward, like the gables
above the heads of C13 effigies – forerunners of the nodding
ogee. One would date them c. 1300, if it were not for the fine
crossing vault which rests on corbels with the Signs of the four
Evangelists. The head of St John's angel is of a type more like
c. 1250 than much later. Mid-C14 the N transept with reticulated N and straight-headed reticulated E window. This is the
only embattled part of the church (save for the tower). The
rest has parapets. Perp the nave with standard piers (four
hollows). Aisle walls with wall shafts. No clerestory. Perp also
the octagonal upper parts of the crossing tower. Two-light
bell-openings with Somerset tracery, gargoyles, battlements,
and a later spike. And Perp finally the S transept (five-light S
window). – PLATE. Chalice and Cover 1573; Flagon and
Paten 1716; Dish by *Bayley* 1724; Paten 1776. – MONU-
MENTS. In the S transept cross-legged Knight in a recess,
early C14. The effigy must have been of fine quality. – In the
floor of the S transept Brass to Mary Daubeney † 1442, c. 2 ft
6 in. long. – On a tomb-chest with quatrefoils and shields,
also in the S transept, brass to Sir Giles Daubeney † 1445 and
his wife. The figures are c. 3 ft 9 in. long and lie under concave gables. The date of the monuments seems c. 1430. –
Henry Compton † 1603 and wife, thin long bad kneeling
figures facing each other (S transept). – Finally in the Vestry
W of the N aisle monument to William Ashe, with three kneeling figures. Two frontal children in niches behind. Open pediment. Bad workmanship; 1677. – Underneath, a copper plate
of 1679 to William Ashe's brother-in-law William Sandys, on
which it says of him:

> . . . 'His gracious King and laws he did obey;
> And out of conscience justly taxes pay.
> Rebellion he did openly abhor,
> Though gilded with the name of Civil War.
> Rome's impositions and Scotch Covenant
> He did dislike, and therefore was no Saint.
> But prayers of our Church he more admir'd
> Than theirs that madly think themselves inspir'd.'

The church lies a little way from the Market place. S of it
the town ends. NE of the church the Gothic SCHOOL, dated
1828. The WILLIAM BLAKE MEMORIAL HALL dates partly
from the C18, and partly from 1911. It has an arched ground
floor. Quite a number of noteworthy houses, but none which

can be singled out here, except for the MANOR HOUSE (formerly known as King Ine's Palace), a C15 house (on the road to East Lambrook), which was much rebuilt in the C19, but preserves on the s side its splendid two-storeyed decor-
41 ated bay-window under a gable. The two-light hall window from the N side has been removed to an outbuilding. It has pretty decoration of the typical Somerset kind below the transom.

PETHERTON BRIDGE, halfway between Ilminster and Ilderton. C15, of three spans, with pointed arches. Built in are the upper halves of two EFFIGIES, Civilian and Lady.

ROMAN VILLAS. Remains of three villas have been found at or near South Petherton.

6020   SPARKFORD

ST MARY MAGDALENE. Perp w tower. The body of the church 1824 by *Thomas Ellis*, with windows with the characteristic Y-tracery. Chancel arch apparently Perp. Also Perp the s chapel. – PLATE. Chalice and Paten 1736.

HAZLEGROVE HOUSE, *see* p. 193.

2030   SPAXTON

ST MARGARET. Evidence of *c.* 1300 in the shape of two cusped two-light windows with a pointed quatrefoil in plate tracery above. One is in the nave N wall, the other at the E end. The rest is Perp. A fine display in the s aisle, with a pierced quatre-foil parapet, and two-storeyed porch with the same parapet. The aisle arcade of standard type, the two-bay arcade between chancel and chapel has bands of leaves as capitals. In the nave below the the present roof a stucco cornice is a sign of an C18 conversion otherwise gone. – BENCHES. The usual square-
27 headed type of w Somerset. Amongst the motifs birds, a fuller and his tools, Renaissance heads in medallions, but mostly large plants. Two dates appear, 1536 and 1561. – PLATE. Chalice and Cover 1662; Almsdish 1662 probably Dutch; Flagon by *Simon Paulin* 1708. – MONUMENT. Knight in armour; *c.* 1460, and Lady. Between chancel and vestry. Tomb-chest with panels arched at head and foot and con-taining shields, cusped and sub-cusped four-centred arch, panelled inside, high attic with panels containing shields. Much foliage decoration. – CROSS in the churchyard. The

head is preserved, with a defaced Crucifixion on both sides.

COURT FARM. N of the church. Large L-shaped building with a remarkable number of two-light windows of c. 1500. The lights are arched and cusped. The original plan has not yet been investigated.

STADDON HILL CAMP see EXFORD

STAPLE FITZPAINE

2010

ST PETER. Norman s doorway without columns. Decorated abaci and arch, zigzag, small heads, rosettes, and diaper. The rest Perp, with a surprisingly ornate w tower, almost identical with Bishop's Lydeard, Ile Abbots, and Kingston. Blue lias and Ham Hill stone. Set-back buttresses decorated with two tiers of attached pinnacles and ending in pinnacles set diagonally. Meanwhile the actual angles have also developed into pinnacles. Moreover the pierced battlements carry big and heavy angle and finer corbelled-out intermediate pinnacles. w doorway flanked by niches, w window of four lights. Next stage with a two-light transomed window with niches l. and r. on busts of angels. The next stage is the bell-stage. Two two-light openings on each side with triangular shafts carrying pinnacles. The N side simpler than the others. The church itself after this display seems modest. Three-bay arcade of standard elements (piers of four-hollows type) plus a very narrow fourth. – ROOD SCREEN. Of four-light sections with depressed pointed arches. From Bickenhall Church. – SCREEN to the Vestry. Fragment of a larger screen. Also four-light sections. The arches less depressed. Big leaves in the spandrels. – PLATE. Paten 1726.

CASTLE NEROCHE, see p. 252.

STAPLEGROVE

2020

ST JOHN. s porch tower two-staged and corbelled. Doorway with continuous double-chamfer. The rest largish and essentially of 1857. Inside, the imposts of the chancel arch are clearly early. Their simple profile seems to belong to c. 1200. – STAINED GLASS. w window by *Kempe*, 1897. – PLATE. Chalice and Cover 1573; Paten by *Clare* 1723; Flagon and Paten 1729.

STAPLETON *see* MARTOCK

STAWELL

CHAPELRY. The W tower was started with diagonal buttresses and a three-light W window. Then work stopped for good and a plain gable was put on. The church is over-restored (1874). In the chancel N and S walls are one lancet window each; the E window is a group of three stepped lancet lights. But is that acceptable evidence of a C13 date? The nave is aisleless. – PLATE. Chalice Cover 1573; Chalice 1661.

(In the village a house of pre-Reformation date with a big chimneybreast at the gable-end and two- and three-light windows.)

STAWLEY

ST MICHAEL. On the N side of the nave herringbone masonry, i.e. a Norman wall. C13 chancel, the windows renewed. In the nave on the S side a doorway and one cusped lancet window: C14. Perp W tower, modest. Above the W doorway a quatrefoil frieze and in the centre an inscription on scrolls. It refers to Henry Howe and his wife and has the date 1523. The words 'Pray for the soule' are carved in reverse. The interior gratifyingly unaltered and unrestored. Ceiled wagon roofs. – COMMUNION RAIL and PULPIT (with ogee tester) late C18. – BOX PEWS and panelled dadoes probably early C19. – SOUTH DOOR C13 with iron hinges.

STEART *see* TRULL

STEDDON GRANGE *see* WINCANTON

STEYNING MANOR
Cockwood nr Stogursey

Irregular, gabled, with mullioned and transomed windows. Said to incorporate parts of *c.* 1500 or earlier. Good plaster-work inside, partly thin-ribbed, but also (Hall) a thickly scrolled overmantel with cartouche and cherubs and a ceiling with thick garlands on the heavy frames of the panels. This must be of *c.* 1660 or a little later.

STOCKLAND BRISTOL

2040

St Mary Magdalene. 1865–7 by *Arthur* of Plymouth (?).
Of silvery lias with Bath dressings. w tower, all details Dec. –
font. Octagonal, Perp, with frieze of pointed quatrefoils. –
rood screen. Incorporating original parts. – stained
glass. e window 1867 by *Clayton & Bell*. Their typical
scenes of many small figures, with much red and brown. –
plate. Chalice 1574; Salver 1750; Flagon by *Cox* 1754.

STOCKLINCH

3010

St Mary Magdalene, Stocklinch. Chancel with one late c13
window with plate tracery. s transept Dec with a remarkable
s window. Nave windows Perp. s porch with stone roof.
Modest Perp w tower with battlements. – plate. Exeter-made
Chalice and Cover; Paten by *John Wisdom* 1705. – monument. Effigy of a Lady of *c.* 1280–90 originally in an arched
recess in the s wall with cusps.
St Mary, Stocklinch Ottersey. Chancel Dec. The three-light
e window has simple flowing tracery. No tower, but a bell-cote
for three bells. – pulpit c18, with tester and reading lectern
below. – box pew. e of it, made up from a chancel stall. –
tympanum with painted Royal Arms in the (Perp) chancel
arch. – Handsome c18 west gallery. – plate. Chalice
and Cover 1573.

STOFORD

5010

½ m. se of Barwick

Nice village green. On its n side the Guild House, c16,
two-centred doorway with big hood-mould, mullioned and
hood-moulded windows. Other good houses on the s side.
Bridge, across the river Yeo. Of two arches, mentioned as a
stone bridge already by Leland.

STOGUMBER

1030

Stogumber church lies on the top of a village which climbs up
a hill with plenty of picturesque cottages. c17 almshouses
on the main street to the sw of the church.
St Mary. A large and ambitious church, and at the same time
one which is equally interesting in its architectural history and

its furnishings. The tower comes first, of red sandstone and in relation to the present church in a SW position. It has to the nave a big arch with a continuous triple-chamfer and to the aisle a double-chamfer. Diagonal buttresses, two-light transomed bell-openings and battlements. Higher stair-turret. The S porch is attached, also red, and also embattled. All this seems to have gone up in the first half of the C14. Contemporary the S aisle arcade, to go with a nave which exists no longer. Of this the W respond and one pier survive, octagonal with the plainest capitals. Then in the C15 the aisle was continued, in different stone with the standard four-hollows piers and small circular capitals to the shafts only. Of that there are two bays. Again a little later in the C15, on the other side of the chancel arch, three more bays were added. They form an important family chapel and are from outside taller than the rest of the aisle, and have battlements and pinnacles. Two of the big three-light windows are blocked by later monuments. The S aisle windows are straight-headed, and one has the pretty tracery characteristic of Dunster, Watchet, Old Cleeve, etc. The chancel was renewed in 1878. The W front has two gables, for nave and N aisle. The N aisle is the last part of the church. It must be of *c.* 1500 or later. It faces the village square and is therefore given special prominence. Grey stone. Tall gabled porch and to its r. two, to its l. two tall three-light windows. Then the rood-stair turret and two more windows – a fine display with battlements with quatrefoils and pinnacles.

18b   Now we must go back to the interior. The N aisle arcade has five bays, piers with the standard four-wave section and capitals with well-carved bands of leaves. Past the chancel arch follow two bays, where the piers are stretched so much in depth that they could be opened in W–E arches across. There was here no doubt the Easter Sepulchre and probably the tomb of the founder of the chapel. The capitals are yet broader and bolder bands. – Good original wagon-roofs. The chancel is nicely tiled and stencilled, and its roof nicely painted too – all the work of an intelligent follower of William Morris, the *Rev. Edward Henry Jones.* – FONT. Octagonal, Perp, with quatrefoils. – PULPIT. Of stone and no doubt the work of the N aisle carvers. – BENCHES. Many, straight-headed, the ends mostly with close tracery. – DOOR to rood stair, an original door, small, but closely traceried and also with foliage decoration. Original ironwork too, especially an excellent door-

handle. – CHANDELIER. Brass, very large and signed by its
maker, *Thomas Bayley* of Bridgwater. – PLATE. Chalice 1615;
Paten 1733 by *Bayley*; Flagon 1733. – MONUMENTS. Low
recess in the N aisle. In it, but not belonging to it, brass to
Elizabeth Windham † 1585. – Sir George Sydenham † 1597
with his two wives rather uncomfortably tucked in by his
sides. At his feet the small figures of three babes with their
nurse. A monumental canopy, finely detailed, rises above the
tomb-chest, with three pairs of half-fluted Corinthian columns
to the chancel and three to the chapel. Each pair is connected
by an arch, and the vaults thus formed are coffered. – William
and George Musgrave † 1723 and 1724, large, with pilasters
and broken segmental pediment. Skull and palm branches at
the foot (E wall of the s chapel). – Thomas Rich † 1731 (nave),
with an oddly shaped pediment on which two putti. By the
sides volutes go down embellished by finely carved oak and
acanthus. – George Musgrove † 1742 (s chapel), large and
pretty, with Rococo ornament. Attributed to *Rysbrack*.

CHANTRY CHAPEL, 1 m. N. Now part of a cottage. Original
cambered doorhead, small two-light window, and ceiled
wagon-roof.

CURDON CAMP. Obliterated and inaccessible IRON AGE CAMP,
in Curdon Copse.

STOGURSEY

2040

ST ANDREW. Stogursey, although now a parish church, was the
church of a Benedictine Priory, founded by William of Falaise
c. 1100 as a cell of Lonlay in Normandy. Stogursey is the
englished form of Stoke Courcy. Of the first church, which
was quite ambitious in size, the crossing remains in fine
completeness: four broad and strong arches on sturdy
attached columns. Three of the arches are single-stepped, the
fourth, the chancel arch, has a complex moulding, probably
refined into its present shape when the chancel aisles were
built. Above it remains a Norman window looking now into
the chancel. The capitals of the eight columns ought to be
studied one by one. They are of many different types, and all
decidedly Early Norman in character. They all have stunted
volutes; otherwise there are upright leaves of various kinds,
one, two, or three rows, animals, addossed animals, and one
human head. The floor-level of the present church is higher
than the Early Norman had been, and only recently the old level

has been restored, much to the advantage of the architectural effect. At the same time the apses have been laid bare which went off to the E of the transepts. The Early Norman choir had an apse as well. This plan of three staggered apses, two attached to the transepts and one at the E end, is not frequent in Norman England (Melbourne, Old Shoreham), but familiar from the Continent. It occurs in Normandy as well as in other parts of France and especially in C11 Germany.

Late in the C12 the chancel of Stogursey was lengthened, and the chancel aisles as they now appear belong to that time. Their level is higher than that of the old crossing. So there must have been a broad flight of steps here, again something more often found on the Continent than in England. The piers are circular, the capitals many-scalloped, and the arches display all the exuberance of the latest stage of Norman: zigzag, zigzag at right angles to the wall, at an angle of 45 degrees to the wall, a kind of crenellated zigzag, and also dog-tooth. That makes 1180 or 1185 the most likely date; for work started at Glastonbury in 1184 and at Wells a little earlier, and that is decidedly one step in advance of Stogursey. The E end is neo-Norman of 1865.

Neo-Norman also the W portal. The nave otherwise is Perp, with a plainly traceried five-light window above. The detail looks early C15. The remodelling of the nave, which was parochial, was probably done after the suppression of alien monastic dependencies in 1414. Large three-light Perp windows on the N and S sides of the nave. On the N side inside the building next to the usual small rood-stair a larger panelled arch, no doubt a tomb recess. Behind it lies the broad square Norman stair-turret. The crossing tower is, according to its recently exposed herringbone masonry, original Early Norman work. Traces of a lower N transept roof against it. In the tower W face a curious splayed doorway. In the transept W wall a small Norman doorway. In the S transept a Perp doorway, also small, which must have communicated with the monastic buildings. The chancel aisles are externally Perp and also have inside Perp access arches from the W. The crossing tower has a slated recessed spire behind a C19 parapet. The bell-openings also were enlarged in the C19.

FURNISHINGS. FONT. Norman, with four masks, very elementary in the carving. – PULPIT. Made up of Jacobean parts. – BENCHES. Many of the usual Quantock type of c. 1530–

40. Amongst the motifs, apart from the familiar close-knit tracery and large plants, also the pelican, a double-eagle, and certain Renaissance arabesques. – PLATE. Set of 1722. – MONUMENTS. In the S chapel. Effigy of a man, holding his heart, said to be William de Verney † 1333. – C15 tomb-chest with small relatively well-preserved figures of mourners. The effigy is supposed to represent John de Verney † 1472. – Peregrine Palmer † 1684, good tablet with cherubs' heads and flowers, in the style and of a favourite type of the Gibbons period. – Nathaniel Palmer † 1717. Standing wall-monument. Two mourning putti l. and r. of an obelisk garnished with flowers. – Sir Thomas Wroth † 1721 and Thomas Palmer and wife, † 1734 and 1737. Excellent standing wall-monument with a large white marble putto holding a Rococo shield. Two brown marble urns l. and r. Reredos background. Certainly by an uncommonly good sculptor.

PRIORY BUILDINGS. Nothing has yet been ascertained or excavated. Only the circular DOVECOTE (cf. Dunster Priory) remains above ground.

CASTLE. All that remains of the castle of the de Courcys is some outer walls, the moat, the lower parts of the two rounded gatehouse towers, and ivy-clad walls of the inner ward. The castle seems to have belonged principally to the late C13 or early C14.

SCHOOL. At the W entrance. Given by Peregrine Palmer Fuller Palmer Acland. Red sandstone, Gothic and elaborately picturesque. By *John Norton*, 1865.

SHENTON COURT, ½ m. N. Five-bay two-and-a-half-storey Georgian house with central Venetian window and doorway on attached columns.

STEYNING MANOR, *see* p. 296.

WICK. Large round barrow called the PIXIE'S MOUND. It was actually explored by amateur archaeologists in Roman times, and they whimsically planted in the barrow to puzzle later generations a coin and a mortarium. Later digging showed that the barrow contained a covered stone of the Early Bronze Age.

STOKE PERO

8040
inset

CHURCH. Save for one whitewashed farmhouse all alone in its fold of Exmoor. It must be one of the most solitary churches in Somerset. Only a farm-track leads to it. W tower of only

one stage and a bit. Probably meant to go up higher. Covered
with a saddleback roof. Nave and chancel in one. Straight-
headed windows. Doorway of wood, a two-centred arch.
Tower arch round on the simplest imposts. Is that a sign of
Norman workmanship or of enormously retarded local workmanship? – PLATE. Chalice of 1573.

STOKE ST GREGORY

3020

ST GREGORY. The church, although much of its finest work is
Perp, belongs to an earlier type, that with transepts and
crossing, and its crossing and crossing tower are indeed (as at
neighbouring North Curry) its earliest parts. The tower
externally is octagonal. The lower stage has shafts at the angles
and double-chamfered cusped one-light windows with hood-
moulds running into the shafts. The bell-stage is Perp (two-
light bell-openings with transom) embattled and crowned by
a pretty little recessed stone spire. Of the same date as the
lower tower windows or only a little later are the two small
ogee-headed windows in the S transept. Inside, these are
flanked and connected by altered recesses. Inside the crossing
the arrangement is sturdy and impressive. Triple-chamfered
and even quadruple-chamfered arches and then again triple-
chamfered squinches (an unusual sight in England) to lead
from the square to the octagon. The piers are just solid pieces
of walling set diagonally. All this looks c. 1300 and hardly later.
The Perp contribution is as follows. S aisle and S porch with
quatrefoiled pierced parapet. Clerestory with windows of three
and (chapel) four lights. S transept with a four-light S window,
the latest in style in the church. The N side is similar. The
clerestory windows are of two lights. The W front has a fine
five-light window, very large, with transom and tracery below
the transom and aisles with sloping pierced parapets. The
chancel is lower, has simple windows, and is altogether very
modest. The arcades in the nave inside are tall and slim, and
there is plenty of light everywhere. Four bays with piers of
standard section and four small capitals to the shafts. Perp
arches also into the transepts. That on the S stands on little
angel corbels. – PULPIT. With Jacobean figures of Faith,
Hope, Charity, Father Time, and the Virgin, in a naive fruity
style. – BENCHES. Square-headed, Perp, mostly with broad
tracery motifs. – CUPBOARD. Tall, of three parts. Jacobean or
later, with small figures and linenfold panelling. At the top

angel-busts and two dates: 1595 and 1628. – PLATE. Chalice 1573; Salver 1734.

SLOUGH FARM. A very remarkable survival of the Early Tudor decades. Small manor house of banded lias and Ham Hill stone, also with lozenge patterns. Buttressed round archway in front of the building with I.M. and a coat of arms. The archway must have led into a small front court. Two-storeyed broad, gabled porch. Windows with mullions and four-centred arches to the individual lights. But the most impressive thing is the Hall. The original screen of planks and muntins remains and, in spite of the smallness of the Hall, two bay-windows at the dais end, one fairly complete, the other fragmentary. They have panelled arches between thin shafts. The Hall has heavy moulded beams. Traces of the spiral stair-case also remain.

STOKE ST MARY

2020

ST MARY. Good two-staged C13 W tower. One W lancet and an uncommonly vigorously moulded tower arch. The chancel arch also has shafts and capitals of the C13.

STOKE COURT. One part with a two-storeyed porch and mullioned windows seems early C17, another has rusticated frames to the windows and appears to be of c. 1700.

STOKE-SUB-HAMDON

4010

The local name is Stoke-under-Ham, and the village lies indeed immediately below Hamdon Hill or Ham Hill, the source of the famous biscuit-coloured stone. The village consists of two separate parts, East Stoke, where the church stands, and West Stoke, the more closely built village with the more interesting houses.

ST MARY. An uncommonly varied assortment of parts and motifs, divers styles all overlapping each other, in pleasant disorder. Well restored in 1862 by *Ferrey*. Norman nave and chancel, *see* the corbel-frieze outside the chancel, the chancel arch inside, two small nave windows, and the S and N doorways to the nave. The S doorway has one order of colonnettes. One shaft with spiral fluting, the other with a scale motif. Fluted capitals. The rest has disappeared. But the N doorway is complete. The colonnettes here have a polygonal shaft with

lozenge decoration and a shaft with scales. The capitals have
volutes. The tympanum is a most curious and seemingly
haphazard assembly of parts: the tree of life in the middle,
with three big birds, to the left a figure whose surprising
presence is attested by the inscription

SA

GI

TAR

IUS

To the r. the lamb and the cross and below it a larger animal,
labelled LEO. Why this choice of just two signs of the zodiac?
Leo represents August, Sagittarius December. So perhaps
they were meant to stand for Summer and Winter. At the
same time the carver may well have applied to them his more
rustic conceptions, the lion as strength and the archer as the
forces of evil.* The chancel arch is of three orders and largely
renewed. The columns have scale and zigzag motifs, the
capitals volutes, the arches zigzag, lozenges, etc. One of the
nave windows on the N side, close to the W end, has an arch
carved into one block of stone. The stone is decorated with
interlace and a man and a dragon. It looks more Saxon than
Norman.

The next building period is represented by the tower, which
stands on the N side. This has a rib-vault on the ground floor
which from the Transitional details of the capital-shaped
corbels in the four corners can hardly be later than 1190.
Trumpet-shaped flutes and leaves. A rib-vault of that date is a
rarity in a parish church in Somerset. The upper parts of the
tower are C13, *see* the lancets and the bell-openings which are
coupled lancets with a roll-moulding all round. On the E side
a stair projection like a chimney-breast. The tower top is Perp
and has gargoyles and battlements. Perp also the N tower window (three lights). Much more was done *c.* 1300. To this
period belong the cusped lancets of one and two lights, of
different length and arrangement, which occur everywhere.
The chancel has them of one light, one light but much longer
(near the W end), and of two lights. They have rere-arches
here. The chancel E window is Perp (four lights, the tracery
in two sub-arches). In the S transept the cusped lancets of
c. 1300 are in an even row of four, both on the E and W side,
and have rere-arches on shafts. In the nave they also exist,
and in the N porch too. During the first half of the C14 the w

* The latter suggestion was made to me by Miss Marjorie Daunt.

front received a new large window with reticulated tracery, and the same motif is to be found in the three-light window on the upper storey of the two-storeyed porch. Inside the porch a heavy quadripartite rib-vault on head-corbels. Inside the church itself various furnishing elements contemporary with the architecture. Of *c.* 1300 the Double Piscina with a large cusped arch placed curiously across the SE corner of the chancel, the similar, also cusped but shafted Piscina in the S transept (which has a shelf), and a tomb recess in the S transept. – Heavily panelled Perp nave roof.

FURNISHINGS. FONT. Norman, circular, with two cable-mouldings and a lozenge frieze. – SCREEN. To the N transept. Not in original position. Stone, the side parts of four lights with a depressed four-centred main arch. – PULPIT. Jacobean. – COMMUNION RAIL. C17, with turned balusters. – BENCH ENDS. With Perp panelling and quatrefoils. – SCULPTURE. Reclining figure (N transept), fragmentary, seems C14. – PLATE. Chalice and Cover 1635. – MONUMENTS. Priest, early C14, S transept, very defaced. – Tomb-chest with quatrefoil panels, now the N transept altar. – Thomas Strode † 1595. Recumbent effigies under a depressed arch on pilasters. Open at the back towards a chancel N window. – In the churchyard a C17 GATEWAY and C15 CROSS, complete with head on which a Crucifixion and a Madonna.

At West Stoke in the main street several good houses, e.g. TAN-Y-BRYN, C18 with porch, THE COTTAGE dated 1696, still with mullioned windows, and the house opposite it.* At r. angles to the main street a street leads down towards the hideous CONGREGATIONAL CHURCH of 1865–6 with its SW spirelet and its curly flying buttresses reaching down to the ground. On the way the PRIORY FARM HOUSE, a remarkable C15 house. It has its wing to the street, its front to the yard. Here the two-storeyed porch, the Screens Passage, and the Hall (now two-storeyed). The Hall has a five-light window with depressed-arched lights. The archway into the yard has its pedestrian entrance blocked. Barn and Dovecote.

HAM HILL, *see* p. 190.

VENN BRIDGE. In the river the base was found of a statue, 4 ft high, with the Latin inscription: 'To the Emperor Flavius Valerius Severus'. A.D. 306–9.

---

* (No. 47 High Street has a two-storeyed bay and gable and is dated 1674. MHLG.)

7020

STOKE TRISTER

St Andrew. 1841. The windows with the typical Y-tracery of the early C19. The chancel arch could be pre-Reformation. – PLATE. Paten 1718; Chalice 1774; Almsdish 1839.

Stoke Farm House. Essentially Pre-Reformation; *see* the angle buttress, the large chimney-breast next to it, and the one original (blocked) two-light window with pointed heads to the lights.

6020

STOWELL

St Mary Magdalene. 1913 by *F. Bligh Bond* (GR). Not a touch of the C20 in the design. Simple Perp w tower. The bell-openings of 1748. The tower arch with responds of a typical Perp section. – PLATE. Chalice and Cover 1574.

Stowell Farm House. L-shaped. A small two-light window with pointed-arched lights at the back. Big chimney-breast at the gable-end; probably C15 or early C16.

Stowell Court, ½ m. NNE. Symmetrical, two-storeyed, neo-Georgian stone façade. By *Sir Guy Dawber*, *c.* 1925.

STOWEY CASTLE *see* NETHER STOWEY

4030

STREET

Holy Trinity. Chancel of *c.* 1330, *see* the tracery of the E window which is derived from the Lady Chapel at Wells, the ogee-headed Sedilia and Piscina, and also the s and N windows which one would rather date *c.* 1300. The unbuttressed w tower also looks *c.* 1300. One lancet window on the N side. Top post-medieval. Plain parapet. Much alteration in 1826 and 1843, e.g. the N aisle and the chancel roof. – PLATE. Chalice and Cover 1720; two Patens 1724; Flagon 1841. – MONU-MENT. A monument with an urn († 1808) by *Reeves*.

Friends Meeting House. Uncommonly stately. Built in 1850 by *J. Frank Cotterell*. Towards the street three-bay two-storeyed house. But this is only part of a rectangular block including the meeting house proper with tall arched windows and a Tuscan porch.

The Grange, Grange Street. Late Georgian front with a ten-column Tuscan colonnade on the ground floor. At the back evidence of *c.* 1600. Over the archway sundial with the date 1811.

Much of the architecture of Street is due to Messrs C. & J. Clark. Their FACTORY borders on the High Street. The centre-piece is the clock tower of 1897. The main block is of 1857, and on its r. is an addition of 1933, but on the l. there is still the first factory building, erected in 1829.

CRISPIN HALL (Institute), 1894–5 by *G. T. Skipper*.

BEAR INN, 1894, also by *Skipper*.

THE TANNERY (now Co-operative Society), Portway. Built in the early C19.

STRINGSTON 1040

CHURCH. Much rebuilt and restored (1878). w tower with tiled broach spire. The chancel arch seems original and Perp. In the chancel roof one original carved wall-plate. – FONT. Octagonal, Perp, with a frieze of pointed quatrefoils. – BENCHES. Plain, of the Perp shape of the district. One with the date 1602. Many with initials. – PLATE. Chalice and Cover 1573. – MONUMENT. John St Albyn † 1766. By *Ford* of Bath. Nice relief of a seated weeping woman by an urn; the indispensable obelisk above. – CROSS-HEAD on the churchyard cross, Crucifixion in small free-standing figures; badly defaced.

PRIOR'S FARM. In one room on the upper floor a tablet with the date 1641, in a room on the ground floor plaster ceiling, the panels framed by heavy beams. The style of the plasterwork is still entirely Elizabethan; yet the date modelled on the wall is 1658.

FAIRFIELD HOUSE. *See* p. 169.

SUTTON BINGHAM 5010

ALL SAINTS. A tiny church. Nave and lower chancel, without tower, or turret, or even bell-cote. In the nave Norman windows, otherwise lancets, cusped lancets, a two-light window with bar tracery (an encircled quatrefoil) – that is later C13. These windows have rere-arches. In the chancel the rere-arches are pointed-trefoiled. At the w end the main window seems a little later, say *c.* 1300. Above it in the gable two arched niches for the bells. Plain Norman N doorway; sumptuous Late Norman chancel arch: three orders of sturdy columns.

The capitals are fluted or otherwise geometrically decorated. Only one has a bit of leaf. In the arch one order with zigzag on the intrados. Hood-mould with intermittent nail-head. The same motif occurs in the doorway. – The most important thing about this small church is however its WALL PAINTINGS. They are probably of *c.* 1300. In the nave a fine large Death of the Virgin. In the chancel, crudely retraced, a large Coronation of the Virgin, and otherwise single figures, Bishops and Saints, both on the wall and in the window splays. Also one smaller kneeling figure holding up a cushion (?). – FONT. Norman, circular, with one cable-moulding. – PLATE. Chalice by *Thomas Coke* and *Richard Gurney* 1735.

MANOR HOUSE. Immediately SW of the church. It forms a good picture with it. How the Reservoir will affect it which (at the time of writing) is being built just to the N, cannot yet be said. The Manor House is probably of the early C17. Quite large, on an informal plan, gabled and with mullioned windows.

SUTTON MALLET

CHAPELRY. 1829 by *R. Carver* (GR), except for the low unbuttressed W tower, which however was hollowed out on the W side to place the W window further E – a curious arrangement. The church is aisleless, and has a flattish S porch and a chancel with a flattish polygonal E end. – High BOX PEWS. – Three-decker PULPIT. – PLATE. Chalice and Cover 1572.

SUTTON MONTIS

HOLY TRINITY. C13 W tower, *see* the coupled lancets which serve as bell-openings and the unmoulded tower arch inside rising on the plainest imposts. Norman chancel arch. The responds with abaci identical with those of the C13 in the tower arch. One colonnette on each side towards W, zigzag decoration on the arch. The chancel windows seem to be of the late C13, but are renewed. Rere-arches with shafts carrying moulded capitals. The nave was rebuilt in 1805. The N windows have Y-tracery, and instead of the usual church porch there is an entirely domestic-looking porch with Tuscan columns. – PULPIT. Jacobean, panelled, with back, and early C18 tester. – PLATE. Chalice and Paten 1839.

ABBEY HOUSE, W of the church. Gable-end with one diagonal buttress and on the upper floor a large two-light Perp window. Several small two-light windows with arched lights. Big chimney-breast, i.e. essentially Early Tudor.

PARSONAGE FARM, E of the church, with mullioned windows; C17. Large C18 (?) barn.

SWELL

3020

ST CATHERINE. Like a chapel belonging to the house. Nave and chancel, and no tower or turret. Norman S doorway with two orders of colonnettes and in the arch a trellis of four zig-zag friezes. Panelled chancel arch. Perp windows. – PULPIT. Jacobean in style; dated 1634. – BENCHES. Original completely plain, very bleached benches. Also some tall BOX PEWS. – STAINED GLASS. Several original bits, especially the angel in the E window.

SWELL COURT. Much remains of an Early Tudor manor house, the two-centred doorway with big leaves in the spandrels, the traceried door, the screen and back doorway, parts of the hall roof (hidden), the three tall hall windows with four-centred-arched lights and one or two transoms, the six-light drawing-room window to the l., in the front of one of the two symmetrical projecting wings with diagonal buttresses (cf. Barrington), and more original windows, also in the wing projecting at the E end to the back, that is the N.

SYDENHAM MANOR
1 m. NE of Bridgwater

3030

Now the Canteen, etc., of British Cellophane Ltd. Picturesque many-gabled house. An early C17 range set in front of a C16 house. The older parts have windows with arched lights and hood-moulds on big square stops set diagonally, the later windows are mullioned. The interior is all altered to adapt it for its new purpose.

TARR STEPS

8030
inset

(On the track from Winsford to Hawkridge. Clapper bridge of seventeen spans, 180 ft long. One of the finest clapper bridges in the country. Jervoise.)

TATWORTH

St John the Evangelist. 1851, by *C. Pinch* (GR).

Parrock's Lodge. Late C18 house of five bays and two
storeys with Tuscan four-column porch.

Lace Factory. The oldest part looks as if it might have been
built as a Nonconformist chapel (five by three bays) with three-
bay pediment.

TAUNTON

St Mary Magdalene. Here more than anywhere one is
puzzled by the contrast of scale and care between tower and
body of the church. The church is big, and its double aisles are
certainly an effort to do the exceptional. Yet much more would
have been needed for an interior to stand up to the pomp and
17   circumstance of this 163 ft high tower. It was rebuilt from the
ground in 1862 by *Ferrey* and *Sir G. G. Scott*. But the job was
apparently done extremely carefully and no visual damage has
come of it. The design of the tower is brought out to perfection
by the Hammet Street approach, an C18 idea of course and
quite alien to medieval conceptions. But it is only from a
greater distance that one realizes to the full how capricious the
contour of the tower is, with the pinnacles standing distant
from the wall below the battlements, and with the whole
crown projecting so that it would be top-heavy if air were not
let through all its parts, the filigree battlements and the filigree
top pinnacles. It is like looking through lace, an effect which
one often experiences inside churches in looking at Late
Gothic chantry chapels, but rarely outside. Yet with all its
fancies it is still very much English Perp in that all major lines
are kept straight, and nothing of the flowing and swelling
occurs which France or Germany or Spain would have in-
dulged in at the time. The time incidentally can be deter-
mined by wills offering money for the building of the tower.
They date from 1488 to 1514.

Now in detail. The tower has set-back buttresses with
attached pinnacles on three tiers and then the already mentioned very big and tall detached pinnacles set diagonally.
They reach up to the bell-openings. The w front has a w
doorway with big spandrels filled by defaced scenes of the
legend of the Magdalen. Above is a transomed five-light
window. Doorway and window are flanked by niches for
images. Then follows what is unique at Taunton: three tiers

of twin three-light windows with transoms and Somerset tracery. So instead of a contrast between bare wall and a blossoming out into open and ornamented forms at the bell-stage, Taunton prefers an even display of its riches. The first tiers of these window stages are of about the same size, the bell-stage is a good deal taller. All the windows are transomed and have Somerset tracery, below all of them run quatrefoil friezes, and all are flanked by shafts and pinnacles. In addition the transoms of the bell-openings and the windows immediately below are enriched by demi-figures of angels. Furthermore, the lower two tiers of windows carry crocketed ogee gables, above the bell-openings the whole wall is blank panelling, and then yet another quatrefoil frieze prepares for the crown. This consists of very large battlements pierced in two-storeyed arcading. At the angles stand uncommonly tall pinnacles. They have four little storeys and then a crocketed spirelet. Once again, all this is pierced. Finally to accompany battlements and pinnacles there are, corbelled out from the corners and the middle of the sides, yet thinner wholly detached shafts with pinnacles.

On the S side there are three niches at the level of the W window niches, on the N side only two, because here the stairturret rises – but not, as is the Somerset custom, higher than the crown.

The rest of the exterior of the church is easily described. The aisles have five-light W windows, the clerestory four-light windows. The N side is less important than the S side, the former has only a plain parapet and is of red sandstone, the latter is of Ham Hill ashlar and has a parapet with pierced quatrefoils. This is continued over the chancel and the S porch, whereas the nave parapet is pierced in a frieze of trefoils in triangles. The S porch is of two storeys and made the subsidiary centre of display. It carries the date 1508. Three niches above the doorway, the middle one carried on a candelabra-like support. Star-vault inside.

The peculiarity of the interior is its double aisles of six bays, the inner narrower than the outer. They differ in date. The arcade between the two N aisles is indeed the only conspicuous survival of the church before the present one. It dates from the later C13. The piers are circular with four attached shafts, the capitals are of simple moulded form, and the arches double-chamfered. The E arch ending the inner aisle also belongs to this period, and more, perhaps even earlier work survives, less articulate, round the chancel arch. The rest is Perp, and there the surprise is that no more is done to distinguish this large parish church from others in the county. The piers have the standard four-hollows section. In one of them is a large niche filled by a C19 statue. The capitals of the piers are a handsome set of angel-busts. Angel-busts also high up in the capitals of the panelled tower arch. Higher up still a fine fan-vault. On head-stops in the spandrels of the arcade rise thin shafts which carry niches and lead on to the roof (cf. Martock). The roof has the moderate Somerset pitch with cusped tie-beams, king-posts, and angels against the kingposts. Little tracery.

FURNISHINGS. FONT. Of the familiar octagonal Perp type but all the details just a little more elaborate than usual. –REREDOS. By *G. E. Street*, 1869–72, when the E end was renewed. – STAINED GLASS. s chapel, s window. Some C17 and C18 bits. – PLATE. Two Chalices and Covers and three Flagons 1639; Almsdish 1699; two Salvers 1773. – MONU-MENTS. Elizabethan Plate with six panels containing shields, achievement above the central one on the upper tier. It com-memorates Thomas More † 1576. – Robert Graye † 1635. Life-size standing figure flanked by columns which carry a segmental pediment without base. – Many later minor tablets, e.g. by *King* of Bath 1808. – In the churchyard, SE of the church, a tomb-chest apparently of the Early Tudor decades. On a quatrefoil frieze, segment-headed cusped arches.

ST JAMES. Also a parish church. Originally standing close to the priory. The church is quite big, though smaller than the Magdalene, and its tower is proud, though also smaller than that of the Magdalene (120 ft high). In many ways it heralds the themes of that prodigy tower. Both have set-back buttres-ses, both have three tiers of applied pinnacles on them, and both have large and tall diagonally placed pinnacles on the but-tresses. What is above is not as it was when the tower was built. It had to be rebuilt (in 1870–5), and the crown was not accu-rately reproduced. Tall pinnacles, parapet with quatrefoils and, in the merlons, arcading. Higher stair-turret with pyra-mid roof. This and the intermediate pinnacles on the parapet were due to the restorer. Where St James is much less lavish than the Magdalene is in fenestration. The two window stages have only one two-light window on each side, and only the bell-stage has the twin three-light windows of the other church. Somerset tracery throughout. w doorway with a niche on either side. No niches by the six-light w window. One pair of niches however on the s side (third stage). Attached pinnacles in the actual angles between the buttresses (different from the Magdalene but as at Bishop's Lydeard). The body of the church is in its details over-restored. Inside there is a lowish five-bay arcade. The fifth arch is much wider than the others, pre-supposing transepts. Piers of standard section (four hollows) with the usual thin round capitals. The tower has a fan-vault inside and a tall moulded arch. – FONT. One of the most adorned of C15 fonts in the county. Stem C19, on the octagonal bowl three figures on each side, except one where there is the Crucifixus and the Virgin and the Magdalen. The sculptural style is naive. – PULPIT. 1633. Panels of various sizes, chiefly with arabesque and leaf decoration; no arches, no strapwork. – STAINED GLASS. s chapel s window, C18 shields. – PLATE. Chalice and Cover by *Ions* of Exeter 1574; Chalice probably Flemish, 1617; Chalice and Cover 1639; Plate by *Heath* 1721; Plate by *Robert Brown* 1737. – CHURCH- YARD GATES. Cast iron, *c.* 1820, Gothic.

ST GEORGE (R.C.), Billet Street.* 1861 by *B. Bucknell*. At the end of the street in the *point de vue* just like the Magdalene at the end of Hammet Street. The street was made in 1847. A competent imitation of a Somerset exterior, but the details of flowing rather than Perp style. – Good STAINED GLASS of the building period, especially the E window with six more than life-size figures, and the s aisle E window.

ST JOHN BAPTIST, Park Street. 1863 by *Sir George Gilbert Scott*. E.E. with a big SE tower with a spire. At the foot of the spire four large spirelets and four large dormers. Another tier of dormers higher up – not at all in any local tradition.

HOLY TRINITY, Trinity Street. 1842 by *Carver*. In a starved lancet style. w tower with big pinnacles, broad nave with three galleries, narrower chancel, lancet windows with minimum Perp tracery, open timber-roof with tie-beams and much thin tracery. Quite original and decidedly pre-archaeological. – STAINED GLASS in the E window.

BAPTIST CHURCH, Silver Street, 1814, but with a horrid five-bay façade of 1870 by *J. H. Smith*, stuccoed, in a debased round-arched Italian Trecento.

METHODIST CHURCH, Upper High Street, 1868 by *J. Wilson*. Yellow brick, and, with the church school, quite a happy humble group.

* For the former R.C. church see Masonic Hall, The Crescent, p. 317.

OCTAGON (Plymouth Brethren, formerly Methodist), Middle
Street. Built in 1776–8 under the direction of Wesley, who
preached at its opening. Red brick with two tiers of windows,
arched and circular. Inside cream and brown paint, flat ceiling,
galleries on four sides, lower preaching end.

UNITARIAN CHAPEL (formerly Baptist), Mary Street. The
interior survives of the original building of 1721. Square
pillars with Corinthian capitals, wooden galleries between
them. Contemporary PULPIT. – Brass CHANDELIER, given
in 1728. – PLATE. A set given in 1745; Bread Plate 1688. –
The five-bay front made Italianate about 1850. In 1886 to
the r. a new school was built, in the fashionable Norman Shaw
style, with asymmetrical turret.

PUBLIC BUILDINGS

Taunton has so clearly an area of public buildings, not to say
a Civic Centre, that they must be taken as a group instead of
the usual classified arrangement. Starting from the same centre
as the Perambulations below, i.e. the Market House, this must
come first. Then into Corporation Street and on into Park
Street. The Castle, now the Museum of the Somerset Archaeological and Natural History Society, will be treated together
with the other Perambulations, on p. 319.

MARKET HOUSE. 1770–2 by *Coplestone Warre Bampfylde* of
Hestercombe, an amateur of wealth and influence. Red brick.
In the very hub of the town. Two-and-a-half-storey, five-bay
front with five-bay pediment. The doorway rusticated and
connected with the window above. The two-storey attachments on the l. and r. were formerly open market arcades, and
the centre contained an assembly room, a reading room, and a
billiard room. The C20 conversion done by *H. S. W. Stone*.

MUNICIPAL BUILDINGS, Corporation Street. They incorporate in their r. half the former GRAMMAR SCHOOL, built
c. 1480 and improved by Roger Hill, a merchant of Taunton,
who died in 1544. Symmetrical with small doorway and large
mullioned and transomed windows with all lights depressed-
arched, two on each side. Large room inside with big roof.
Collar-beams on arched braces, three tiers of wind-braces.
The l. half of the building is in two storeys. It was altered
picturesquely in the Tudor style in 1905.

Opposite the PUBLIC LIBRARY, 1904 by *Colbourne, Little
& Goodson*, red sandstone, in a much freer and more imagina-

tive neo-Tudor. This is followed by the SOMERSET COLLEGE OF ART, 1907 by *C. Samson* and *A. B. Cottam*, five bays, neo-Classical, with giant columns and pilasters.*

Park Street starts on the r. with ST PAUL'S HOUSE (Corporation Offices), partly a house of *c.* 1800, partly the steep and tall neo-Gothic or neo-Tudor buildings of the former Convent of Perpetual Adoration. Attributed, says the MHLG, to *J. F. Bentley* and the year 1867. In fact the Order settled down in 1868. Opposite the COUNTY HALL, a large formal composition by *Vincent Harris*, 1936. Two wings set at right angles and connected by a concave centre. Light brick. Hipped roofs. The chief accents are two of the familiar and meaningless aedicules with columns and pediments. Also, which is worse, the building turns away (in its neo-Georgian superiority) from the Shire Hall instead of taking it into a large 'campus' composition.

SHIRE HALL, 1855–8 by *W. B. Moffatt*, Scott's former partner. Large irregular Early Tudor group with its entrance in Shuttern. Here a broad central porch with large glazed bay-window above and an asymmetrically placed turret to its r.

Now other Public Buildings in the usual order:

RURAL DISTRICT OFFICES, Mary Street. A pleasant five-bay house of two and a half storeys. Brick with a porch of four thin Tuscan columns. Late Georgian.

GAOL. Built originally in 1754, enlarged in 1815 and in 1843, when it was made the county gaol. Centre with three wings, T-shaped.

GRAMMAR SCHOOL, *see* Municipal Buildings, above.

KING'S COLLEGE, South Road. In the Gothic style. The main buildings by *C. E. Giles* 1867–9: tower, main dormitories, assembly hall, dining hall, and headmaster's house. New Chapel 1898–1908 by *W. E. Tower*. Of 1906 the wing connecting it with the old buildings. Of 1926–7 new headmaster's house. These are also by *W. E. Tower*.

QUEEN'S COLLEGE, Trull Road. Founded in 1843 as the Wesleyan Collegiate Institution and Proprietary Grammar School. Symmetrical Early Tudor with tower in the middle and projecting wings. By *Giles & Gane*, illustrated in 1874.

TAUNTON SCHOOL, Staplegrove Road. Founded in 1847 as the West of England and Dissenters' Proprietary School. By the entrance a Late Georgian house. Then the main building,

---

* Opposite this the GAUMONT CINEMA, *see* p. 319.

Gothic of 1867–70, symmetrical, with tower and two projecting wings. By *Joseph James* of London. Chapel 1906 by *Sir
Frank Wills*.

PRIORSWOOD SECONDARY MODERN SCHOOL, Priorswood
Road. A good recent school by the County Architect, *R.
Oliver Harris*.

TAUNTON AND SOMERSET HOSPITAL, East Reach. Begun in
1809–12. The façade of this building survives at the E end of
the present one, behind a Victorian portico. The centre of the
present building was erected in 1839, cf. e.g. the characteristic
sans-serif lettering. Many later additions (1842, 1843, 1873,
1888).

VIVARY PARK. Ornate Victorian cast-iron gates of *c.* 1876.

PERAMBULATIONS

The hub of the town is the junction of High Street, North
Street, and East Street. The triangle whose centre is the
Market House is called FORE STREET. Traffic on the
A roads represented by these is so thick and noisy that one
can only in the evenings or on Sundays get an impression
of the spot as it was some 120 years ago or earlier. For there
is first of all on the S side the only surviving group of
at least partly pre-Georgian town houses. No. 18 has the
best plaster ceiling in Taunton, probably of *c.* 1600. No. 15,
the Tudor Café, is the centre. It was the town house of the
Portmans. It has a Perp stone doorway on one side, but is
otherwise timber-framed. The date of the timber-work, so far
as it is not renewed, is inscribed: 1578. Three overhangs, two
oriels, one of nine lights. Richly carved bressumers. The
adjoining Nos 14 and 16 are also gabled, and with overhangs
and oriels, and any amount of irregularity, a convincing evoca-
tion of C17 Taunton. That the extension of the old White Hart
Inn at the corner of High Street has so completely disappeared,
in spite of its historical associations, is a disgrace. Inside a
good early C18 staircase. The Late Georgian and Early
Victorian houses of Fore Street are more numerous but not
individually conspicuous. Note the Early Victorian lettering
on No. 8, and the total mess which remodelling has made of
the former Victoria Rooms, built by *W. H. Burgess* of Exeter,
in 1821, as the New Market.

Now the Perambulation must fan out. First to the S, along
HIGH STREET. No. 63 has angle pilasters and sunk panels
and a niche with a figure in the centre. This is early C19. No. 62

is probably Early Georgian. No. 61, again early C19, has angle pilasters and the windows of the two upper floors vertically tied together by blank arches with fan-heads. Nos 35–36 further out are in a pretty Gothic taste. Doorways with clustered shafts. No. 34, Powlett House, has a projecting wing marking a narrowing of the very wide street. It is good solid Georgian brick with a doorway with attached Tuscan columns and a pediment. At the s end the urban area stops and we reach houses in gardens and cottages. This applies to Upper High Street as well as Mary Street (*see* Rural District Offices, above). To the N of Upper High Street, THE CRESCENT, an introduction of urban conventions into this outer district. It was built (by Sir Benjamin Hammet; *see* below) in 1807 in the style of, say, the Exeter terraces and crescents. Red-brick, two-bay houses, the crescent so shallow that it is hardly noticeable. Arched doorways, no further decoration. The TELEPHONE OFFICE of 1941 breaks this modesty by its thick-set Tuscan porch. At the s end of The Crescent the MASONIC HALL, former Roman Catholic Church. Built in 1821 and a remarkable example of monumentality on a small scale. One-bay front, very large doorway with Ionic columns and pediment, set in a bare wall with Ionic angle pilasters and no pediment. Side-elevation also with Ionic pilasters.

Next from the centre to the E. Here on the s side is the pleasant group of CHEAPSIDE and the COUNTY HOTEL, stuccoed four- and three-storeyed with some Grecian details. The style of Cheapside is that of the West Strand Improvements in London, and the date probably the same, *c.* 1835. The County Hotel (originally London Hotel) has a big Tuscan porch and was also built *c.* 1835. Further on in EAST STREET the PHOENIX HOTEL, again of about the same date. Incised Soanian ornament. Then GRAY'S ALMSHOUSES, inscribed 1635. Two-storeyed, of brick (a very early case in this part of Somerset) with, rising above the roof, nine chimney stacks, each with two diagonally placed chimneys. Off in SILVER STREET No. 23 is the stateliest Georgian house in the town – brick, three-bay, three-storeyed centre with projecting three-bay, two-storeyed wings. Silver Street is continued in SOUTH ROAD. At its beginning on the r. the CONVENT, begun in 1772 as a hospital for Taunton (by *P. Stowey*), and completed as a convent in 1840.

In East Reach, the Taunton and Somerset Hospital, *see* p. 316, and then in HAMILTON ROAD the building known as

ST MARGARET'S. This was a leper hospital, rebuilt in the early C16 and converted into almshouses in 1612. Of that date the oak doorways. Nothing else is of architectural interest. The building with its thatched roof stands rather alone and precious in a semicircle of neo-Georgian council housing, an example of too self-conscious a preservation of the individual monument out of its context.

We must now retrace our steps to the Market House and turn N. In North Street, nothing of special interest, nor in Bridge Street. In STATION ROAD, that is quite a way outside the old town, FLOOK HOUSE, a C17 manor house with porch and mullioned windows. In a room on the first floor an over-mantel dated 1652 and yet still entirely in the Jacobean strap-work fashion. If one wants to see more of interest one must turn away from the N axis almost at once to the E into Hammet Street and to the W to the Castle. HAMMET STREET was laid out in 1788 by Sir Benjamin Hammet (1737–1800), son-in-law of E. J. Esdaile, the banker, Alderman of Portsoken Ward in the City of London, M.P. for Taunton, and Keeper of the Castle. The houses are in plain brick: terraces with doorways flanked by attached Tuscan columns and carrying broken pediments. The purpose of the street was to obtain a vista of the tower of St Mary Magdalene which until then had been separated from the centre by small irregular streets. The effect obtained is splendid and, as has already been said, wholly of the Age of Enlightenment. The architecture of the street continues on the N side of CHURCH SQUARE. The S side and Magdalen Street have no shape. On the N side, to the NE of the church the OLD VICARAGE, brick with not much of Tudor or early C17 features left. Along to the E into CANNON STREET. Here towards its N end the scanty remains of TAUNTON PRIORY.

The Priory was Augustinian. It had been founded about 1220. It was a large and important house, with twenty-six canons in 1339, fifteen in 1377. Nothing at all remains of the church, though fragments seem to have found their way into village churches (cf. Oake).

In Cannon Street there is no more than old walling, made demonstratively Gothic probably about 1800 when the stepped gables and pointed windows were introduced, to create two lodges to The Priory, a stuccoed house with Tuscan four-column porch. In the garden wall some original tracery. More suggestive the PRIORY BARN in Priory Avenue, although here also the two windows with plate tracery of the late C13 and the small cusped arch above, all in the SW gable, are either re-set or the building was not a barn. They are of Ham Hill stone, whereas the original dressings of the barn are red sand-stone.

Back to North Street by St James Street and off to the castle by CASTLE BOW. The bow or curve means the archway which led into the Outer Bailey. Taunton belonged to the Bishops of Winchester. The CASTLE was built of stone in Norman times perhaps by Bishop Henry of Blois. The C13, the C17, the C18, and the C20 added and altered. The castle was one of the most important in the county, if not the most important. The Keep and the Inner Bailey can still be traced and understood. The Outer Bailey looks confusing and, at least on its S side, scrappy. One enters it through the GATE-WAY already mentioned. This has plain double-chamfered arches and may date from the C13. The upper storey has two typical pointed Gothic windows of shortly after 1814. On entering the former Outer Bailey the visitor sees in front an accumulation of parked motor cars, and on the l., that is the s, the back of the Grammar School of *c.* 1520 (*see* above), the back of the Municipal Buildings, and the back of the GAUMONT CINEMA, the latter of light brick, in square modern forms (1932 by *Benslyn*). The W and E sides both have pretty castellated late C18 houses, the WINCHESTER HOTEL, built (according to the deeds) probably about 1820, and the CASTLE HOTEL (originally Clarke's Hotel), the latter with a round bow at the N end.

To the N of these lay the Inner Moat and the KEEP. This dates from the C12, was excavated in the 1920s, and is now in the garden of the Castle Hotel. Also of the C12 are important parts of the solid N and W ranges of the castle, which now belong to the MUSEUM of the Somerset Archaeological and Natural History Society. Both ranges have original buttresses outside. The N range was the HALL. It was shorter than the present hall. The C12 part had an undercroft of two parallel tunnel-vaults. The hall itself was on the first floor and must have been 30 ft wide. So there must have been aisles. The hall of today is in its W half essentially C13, in its E half *c.* 1700. The C13 roof-line can still be seen at the W end. The N win-dows with their mullions and transoms are a replacement made necessary after damage in the Civil War. The lengthen-ing to the E is datable *c.* 1700 by the characteristic horizontal

oval windows which belong to a heightening of the hall.
The N windows in this part were copied from those further W.

At the NW corner of the hall is a (restored) stair-turret. The
W range contained the CAMERA or Parlour. The ground floor
is C12. It was given its tunnel-vault in the C13, when the walls
were also considerably thickened (*see* a W loop which stops in
the thickness of the wall). Remains of small lancet windows to
the E, i.e. the court. There were originally four of them. Also
two lancets to the N, one in a remarkably good state, even
externally.

The SW tower is ascribed to the early C13. It was in ruins
in the C18 and restored in connexion with the repairs carried
out *c.* 1785 by Sir Benjamin Hammet. They have given the
castle its present character on the S side towards the Outer
Bailey. The S range consists of the range of the former chapel
and the Inner Gatehouse. Of the GATEHOUSE the S side
with its plain chamfered segmental-pointed arch is early C13,
the N side and the upper part with its shields and inscriptions
is of *c.* 1495. To the r. of the gateway inside the inner ward
a pleasant late C17 front, with cross-windows. The doorway
is surmounted by a big shell-hood. In the chapel range one C13
lancet towards the courtyard on the ground floor. The upper
windows are of *c.* 1500. Inside the LIBRARY (of the Somerset
Archaeological and Natural History Society). It has a pretty
plaster vault with some Adam-style detail. The SW round
tower was matched by one at the SE end of the Inner Bailey
which is only partly recognizable now.

PYRLAND HALL, *see* p. 279.
SHERFORD HOUSE, *see* p. 288.

7020 TEMPLECOMBE

The railway main line divides Abbas Combe, where the church
is, from Temple Combe, so called after a Preceptory of the
Knights Templar.

ST MARY. The nave S doorway seems older than the Perp W
doorway and W window and the S porch tower. E of the tower
a S chapel added to the nave. The two are connected by a Perp
arch. The nave and chancel much renewed. C19 N aisle. –
FONT. Square, of the Purbeck type, with four shallow blank
arches on each side, C12 or early C13. The bowl stands on
five supports. – PLATE. Chalice and Cover 1628; two square
Salvers by *Anthony Nelson* 1725.

MANOR FARM. It contains the scanty remains of the Templars' Preceptory. On the road small C17 house with mullioned windows and a middle porch at the back. E of this the long range formerly supposed to have contained the Refectory and Kitchen (large fireplace). The windows and other details are not older than those of the house. Further E ruins of the Templars' CHAPEL. N doorway, two N windows and the E window. No significant details left. The E window is known to have had plate tracery; so the chapel belongs to the C13.

TETTON HOUSE

2030

1½ m. NW of Kingston

Partly 1800 but largely by *G. S. Goodhart-Rendel* 1924–6. Originally a brick house of two and a half storeys with pediment. The main front, the courtyard, and the large main staircase by Mr Goodhart-Rendel. Open well, glazed top, and Adam-style stucco.

THEALE

4040

CHRIST CHURCH. Lovely views towards the Mendips. 1820 by *Richard Carver*. No tower, projecting corner pieces at the W as well as the E end. Shallow, thin W porch with four-centred arches. Slightly projecting chancel, glazed completely above the altar, as if it were the bow-window of a house, a surprising and attractive effect.

GREAT HOUSE. Dated on the iron roof finials 1670. The façade is of five bays width, with wooden cross-windows on two storeys. The staircase is the finest of its date in the county. It runs in a square open well through two storeys and has newel posts with openwork finials and openwork panels below the handrail. They are of scrolls (not yet of the acanthus kind contemporarily reached at Forde in Dorset) and symmetrically placed snake-bodied beasts. On the staircase wall two wall-paintings, a head of a Roman emperor, and an architectural fantasy, an interior with many columns in perspective. The latter is in the Dutch rather than the Italian taste. Excellent woodwork also in the hall passage and the hall doorway. The front door itself is of the same time too, though it still looks Jacobean.

THORNE

St Andrew. Nave with bell-cote, and chancel. The w and e
windows (renewed) suggest a Dec date. – PULPIT, 1624. –
PLATE. Chalice and Paten 1573.

Thorne House. Neo-Elizabethan by *Sir T. G. Jackson*,
c. 1882.

THORNE ST MARGARET

St Margaret. Perp w tower. The s bell-opening small with
very curious tracery. The rest of the church rebuilt 1865. –
PLATE. Chalice and Cover by *Ions* 1574; Chalice 1676. –
BRASS. John Worth, *c.* 1600, an 18 in. figure.

THORN FALCON

Holy Cross. Nave windows Early Perp. Thin rere-arches on
small angels or well-carved and well-preserved heads. w
tower later. w doorway with a hood-mould accentuated by
five animals' heads. Set-back buttresses, battlements, higher
stair-turret. – PULPIT. Georgian, with Ionic pilasters folded
round the angles. – BENCHES. Almost entirely with close
tracery. The date 1542 occurs twice. – STAINED GLASS. e
window of 1853, very naive. – PLATE. Chalice and Cover 1573.

THURLBEAR

St Thomas. The church from outside, apart from its beautiful
position, promises little. Chancel renewed *c.* 1864. The rest
Perp, modest in scale and details and also altered *c.* 1864
(windows). But inside two complete if much restored Norman
arcades. That is a Norman church was here with aisles, which
is in itself a rarity, and moreover the width of the aisles was
never enlarged to satisfy later medieval taste. Circular piers
with flat bases with angle-spurs. Scalloped capitals of three
scallops. Unmoulded arches. The date, if one can trust the
details, hardly later than *c.* 1110. In the present chancel
scanty evidence of transepts (abaci of the arches) and outside
the chancel of a wide chancel arch (semicircular respond).

THURLOXTON

St Giles. Plain little building of red sandstone. n aisle with
three cross-gables added in 1868. – What is interesting in the

church is its woodwork which dates from *c.* 1634 (the date is on the pulpit). – ROOD SCREEN. A very pretty piece of three arches, the middle containing the doorway. The usual short blank arches on the dado. – PULPIT. With the same arches and four rustically carved figures above. The back-panelling survives, but not alas the tester. – BOX PEWS. Also part of the work of the 1630s. – The FONT COVER probably contemporary too. – PLATE. Chalice and Cover by *Ions c.* 1574; Salver 1749.

MANOR HOUSE. In spite of two big buttresses in the front the house was apparently built *c.* 1885.

TIMBERSCOMBE

9040
inset

ST PETROCK. W tower of 1708 with C19 top (pyramid roof). Perp details of nave, and S aisle. To be noted especially the aisle E window of the Dunster–Cleeve–Selworthy type and the pretty N and S windows like the lower halves of the transomed windows of that type. Arcade of four bays, not high. Piers of the standard section (four hollows). Small polygonal capitals to the four shafts only. Nave and aisle with wagon-roofs. – FONT. Octagonal, Perp, with quatrefoil frieze. – ROOD SCREEN. Of four-light sections, with the four lights divided by sub-arches into twice two. Ribbed, panelled coving. Cornice with four carved strips. The dado has the same pretty motifs of ogee arches flanked by circles as the Dunster windows, and the motif is quite usual for screen dados, especially in Devon. – PULPIT. Probably about mid C17. – DOOR. Perp, with the original metal-work. – PLATE. Chalice and Paten 1571.

BICKHAM. Of the medieval manor house nothing is now visible from outside and nothing of interest inside. The chapel wing disappeared within living memory. Pretty staircase balustrade with Chippendale fretwork.

TINTINHULL

4010

ST MARGARET, V.M. C13 church. Nave, chancel, and slightly later N tower. The tower rather bare, with higher stair-turret and parapet. Angle buttresses at the foot. On the third stage two lancets, on the fourth three cusped lancets (with inserted Somerset tracery). C13 chancel (*see* the buttresses). E window C19. The other windows preserve their C13 outline but are filled with Perp tracery. Inside there is a typical roll-moulding all along the walls at window-sill level and rising round doorways. The chancel windows are shafted. The tower when it was built blocked a shafted nave N window. Double Piscina with two pointed-trefoiled arches, reconstructed. The chancel arch stands on short shafts which rest on head corbels. It looks early C14. – Perp S porch, inside with a ribbed tunnelvault. The middle rib stands on wall-shafts. – PULPIT. Jacobean, complete with back panelling and tester. – BENCH ENDS with Perp panels and flowers.* – ROOD SCREEN. Part of the stone base preserved. – PLATE. Chalice and Cover 1635. – MONUMENT. Brass to John Heth, priest, † 1464, demi-figure 18 in. long. – Outside the porch the so-called STONYING DOOR erected in 1515 by Prior Chard of Montacute who was also vicar of Tintinhull. With Latin inscriptions.

(CHURCHYARD CROSS. By *Sir Ninian Comper, c.* 1920. MHLG.)

TINTINHULL COURT. The house overlooks the churchyard with its back windows. Mostly Jacobean, but C15 parts, notably an embattled piece close to the Hall chimney-breast.

More good houses close by: DOWN HOUSE, late C17, symmetrical seven-bay front, mullioned windows, over the doorway an oval window, to the r. archway into the yard, with depressed arch and pediment on pilasters. – Further E TINTINHULL HOUSE, early C17 (mullioned windows) with an added façade of *c.* 1700. This is of seven bays with evenly rusticated quoins and giant pilasters and pediment to stress the three middle bays. Circular window in the pediment. The surround still in a C17 tradition. Large cross-windows. Good rooms behind the façade of 1700. One has a mid-C18 fireplace. One staircase is partly early C17, partly of *c.* 1700. The other is of the C18, with carved tread-ends and three slim turned balusters to each tread.

TIVINGTON

9040
inset

CHAPEL OF ST LEONARD. The chapel now forms the W part of a cottage, whitewashed, with a thatched roof and (added) chimney-breasts. The chapel has two straight-headed twolight windows, a Reader's Desk made of parts of an C18 pew, and plain straight-headed Benches, still entirely in the

* The Rev. W. V. Ruston kindly informs me that the benches, according to the church books, were made in 1511.

medieval tradition though made (for Milverton church) as
late as *c.* 1850.

TOLLAND

1030

ST JOHN BAPTIST. Very short C13 W tower, with one small
lancet window in the S wall. Tower arch double-chamfered,
dying into the imposts. S side of the church with rood-stair
turret. All else renewed. Small arcade inside with octagonal
piers, very plain capitals (one is original), and double-chamfered arches. This could be contemporary with the tower. –
PLATE. Chalice and Cover 1573; Patens 1635 and 1636.
GOLDEN FARM. *See* p. 186.

TONEDALE *see* WELLINGTON

TREBOROUGH

0030

ST PETER. With pebbledash plastering. S porch tower with C19
pyramid-roof. The Pillar Piscina with ogee niche is a good
minor piece of the Perp style. – PLATE. Chalice 1614.

TRISCOMBE HOUSE *see* WEST BAGBOROUGH

TRULL

2020

ALL SAINTS. Late C13 W tower, *see* the W window of three
stepped lancet lights, the absence of a W doorway, and the
triple-chamfered arch dying into the imposts. The rest Perp,
the S arcade earlier than the N, the difference being noticeable
in the abaci. The piers have the standard four-hollow section
and capitals only to the shafts. They are convex, rather tall,
and funnel-shaped. The abaci on the S side form a continuous
strip, on the N side they are also interrupted to let the hollows
run continuously from the piers into the arches. The S side
is given preference outside by battlements over aisle and porch.
Original nave and tower roofs. – ROOD SCREEN. This must
have been a fine example of the Dunster–Devon type when the
mullions and tracery still existed. Now there is only the dado,
and the ribbed coving with leaf decoration, and an exceptionally richly carved cornice. – PARCLOSE SCREENS. That

to the s chapel has three-light sections and a dado with the simplest linenfold panelling, that to the N chapel is identical in tracery, but the linenfold is a little more finely laid. Over the door the names of the donors. – TYMPANUM of plain plaster on a strong beam above the rood screen, a rare survival.

28b — PULPIT. Something unique in the county, a wooden pulpit with undamaged figures of saints. Small angels hold on to the crocketed gables above the saints. The figures have draperies falling in angular folds and probably belong to c. 1500. Their faces are all of one type, and there is nothing of the consummate skill or power of characterization of contemporary German wood-carving. – BENCHES. A large and interesting selection of benches, probably of c. 1530–40. The date 1560 and the signature of ‘*Simon Werman*’ is above a quite different seat against the back wall. This has finely pleated linenfold panelling. The benches are much like others of the district, such as Kingston 1522 and Crowcombe 1534. Apart from the Instruments of the Passion, big leaves, plants, tracery, Renaissance vases and profiles, there is here a complete little procession of men. A priest in cope, a man with a shrine, a man with a book, a man with a taper, a man with a processional cross. All very rustic. – STAINED GLASS. In the chancel E and S windows unusually much of C15 glass, the Virgin, St John, St Michael, St Margaret, St George. – N aisle NW window by *Kempe* 1899, N aisle w window by *Kempe & Tower* 1913. – PLATE. Flagon 1731; two Chalices 1847.

(BARN, at Steart. The MHLG mentions this as of timber-framed construction, dating back perhaps to the C16.)

CHILLISWOOD FARM. Mostly of the second half of the C16, but drastically remodelled c. 1830–40. A plaque bears the date 1594. Excellent original roof.*

TRUNDLE RING CAMP *see* BICKNOLLER

9020 ## UPTON
4¼ m. ENE of Dulverton

ST JAMES. Only the w tower stands, heavily laden with ivy, and the lowest courses of nave and chancel. The tower is unbuttressed and with its low E arch can hardly be later than the first half of the C14. – PLATE. Chalice 1573.

* Information kindly supplied by Mr A. D. Hallam.

VEN HOUSE

6010

½ m. E of Milborne Port

Ven House was begun in 1698 and completed before 1731.[53b]
It represents a type familiar in the Home Counties and the
Midlands (*Francis Smith* of Warwick), but rare in Somerset:
a brick block with stone dressings, seven by five bays, two
storeys, with a third as an attic storey. The lower two floors are
tied together by giant pilasters marking the angles and the
angles of the three centre bays. Top balustrade; no pediment.
The doorway towards the entrance from the road has an open
scrolly pediment on attached columns (the porch is a later
alteration), that towards the garden a heavier segmental pediment. Inside a fine big two-storeyed Hall in the centre, with
heavy stone fireplaces to the l. and r., flanked and surmounted
by overmantels on broad Ionic pilasters carrying pediments.
At the back of the Hall a gallery on Ionic columns, curving
back elegantly in the centre. Finely turned balusters. The
plasterwork of the ceiling must be somewhat later. It surrounds a darkened painting of Time and Beauty. Originally a
large two-arm staircase went up behind the Hall. This was
replaced by living-rooms about 1835–6, that is at the time
when *Decimus Burton* added offices on the E side and a nice
conservatory with glass walls divided by columns on the W
side.

WADEFORD see CHARD

WALFORD HOUSE

2020

½ m. E of West Monkton

Late Georgian. Five bays and two and a half storeys, brick
plastered, three-bay pediments. The middle window on the
upper floor has a pediment. On the ground floor a colonnade
of Tuscan columns runs along the whole front. Entrance
under Tuscan porch on the W side. Large open-well staircase
below oval glazing.

WALTON

4030

HOLY TRINITY. Mostly by *John Norton*, 1866. Perp W tower
at the E end of the S aisle with pyramid spire. The interior
with much naturalistic foliage carving. – PLATE. Cover of
1737. – MONUMENT. Effigy of a Priest, *c.* 1300.

OLD PARSONAGE, w of the church. A remarkable house, largely of pre-Reformation date and worth investigating.* Two ranges parallel and one behind the other. The one further s has on the first floor two three-light windows with transom and the same tracery as e.g. the refectory at Cleeve Abbey. At the back small two-light window. Others with different (slightly later) tracery in the block further N. The bay-window facing N is said not to be original, although it was in existence when Buckler drew the parsonage in 1830.

SHARPHAM PARK FARM, 1 m. N. An eminently interesting house historically and archaeologically – historically in that it was a residence of the abbots of Glastonbury, probably the house in which the last abbot, Richard Whiting, was arrested, and also in that it was the birthplace of Sir Edward Dyer, the poet, and of Henry Fielding, the novelist. The archaeological evidence is confused and not satisfying. Of the Glastonbury time the only survivors seem to be several heraldic plaques and the FRONT DOOR with its elaborate iron work, a type familiar in churches but rare in houses. Otherwise there are some mullioned windows under hood-moulds and an C18 doorway with heavy pilasters. The staircase dated 1726 is at the Victoria and Albert Museum in London. The remaining staircase is of the Jacobean type with symmetrical balusters.

₂₀₀₀ # WAMBROOK

ST MARY. E.E. chancel, renewed. Nave and low w tower Perp. Set-back buttresses, battlements, higher stair-turret. w doorway with quatrefoil frieze over. One blocked N window has Somerset tracery. – Some old BENCH ENDS, square-headed, with blank tracery and long finials. – PLATE. Elizabethan Chalice with its price, 35/–, engraved on it.

₀₀₄₀ # WASHFORD

ST PANCRAS CHAPEL. Now a house. Single-chamfered s doorway, lancet window on the N side of the chancel, and a curious squint in the w wall, perhaps connected with an ankerhole or anchorite's cell.

CLEEVE ABBEY, see p. 126.

BRITISH BROADCASTING CORPORATION. 1933, by *Wimperis, Simpson & Guthrie*. A heavy square building against the tall

* Recently alas painted a bright rose colour.

graceful lattice pylons. The same design was used at Brookman's Park, Herts.

WATCHET

0040

ST DECUMAN. On a hill outside the little town, but with its tower oddly close to the square brick chimney of a paper mill which seems just as incongruous in the fields as the church. The church is one of the largest in the district, and with the exception of the chancel all Perp. The chancel is of the C13. The E window has three stepped lancet lights and plate tracery of two trefoiled and one quatrefoiled circle above. Inside it is shafted. On the N side of the chancel a lancet window with a pointed trefoiled rere-arch inside. Also inside a Piscina with remains of shafting. Now the late medieval work. Big W tower of grey ashlar masonry. Set-back buttresses, higher NE stair-turret, battlements. Four-light W window and three-light bell-openings with a transom and Somerset tracery. On the S side a flat statue in a niche. The N aisle is embattled with quatrefoils in the crenellations and has an embattled rood-stair turret and three-light windows. For the S aisle – as in so many other churches in the same part of the county – a special effort was made. E window with a transom and the peculiar slightly mannered but very effective tracery of Dunster etc. On the S side one window of the same type and three with normal tracery flanking the S porch. The floor of the porch is made of old roof slates placed on end. It forms a handsome chess-board pattern (cf. Cornish churches such as Fowey). Inside the church the N and S arcades are of four bays. Then follows the rudimentary chancel arch, and then chapels of one bay. Piers of standard section (four hollows). On the N side most of the piers have the charming enrichment of niches for images. In one of them all four statuettes are preserved, in the pier by the pulpit St George and St Anthony. The sculptural quality is low. The moulding of the arch to the N chancel chapel is like that of the nave arcade. The S chapel has a wave instead of the hollow. Depressed pointed arches. Very good wagon-roofs on angel supports in nave, chancel, and S aisle. Decorated wall-plates and bosses.

FURNISHINGS. FONT. Octagonal, Perp, with angel-busts against the underside of the bowl. – ROOD SCREEN. Four-light divisions. The main arches divided into two two-light sub-arches. Top parts modern. – PULPIT. Jacobean or rather later, with tester. – COMMUNION RAIL. Jacobean, the balusters sturdy and vertically symmetrical. – WYNDHAM PEW. With excellent foliage carving and the date 1688. Perhaps by the workmen who did the staircase at Dunster. – TILES. C13, probably made at Cleeve Abbey, some on the chancel floor, others in a frame in the N aisle. – PLATE. Elizabethan Chalice remodelled; Chalice and two Patens 1634. – MONUMENTS. Mostly in the Wyndham Chapel. The monument to Sir John Wyndham † 1574 is the most ambitious and the most interesting, because it has, in spite of its date, no hints whatever yet of the Renaissance. Tomb-chest with three square panels (instead of the Perp quatrefoils) and frames of undetermined ornamental forms. Canopy on four piers with curiously crude and amorphous piers. Round arch, but with Gothic panelling inside. A large and striking demi-figure of an angel peers out from the tomb across the chancel. The effigies are of brass, $2\frac{1}{2}$ ft long. Attic storey with buttresses and shields. – Upright against the E wall of the chapel, John Wyndham † 1572 and his wife † 1596, 4 ft brass figures. – Brass in the chancel floor to Edmund Wyndham † 1616. – Henry and George Wyndham † 1613 and 1624, two large kneeling figures both facing E, in a usual Jacobean surround. – John Wyndham † 1645 and his wife † 1633. Large plate against the E wall, with two portrait busts in relief, made of brass – an unusual treatment. The monument is probably by *Nicholas Stone*. – Sir William Wyndham † 1683. A very good standing wall-monument with two putti holding a shield in front of the big bulgy sarcophagus. Curly open pediment and a vase and two urns on top. The monument could well be in Westminster Abbey. – George Wyndham † 1845. Neo-Gothic tomb-chest with quatrefoils and shields. No effigy.

THE TOWN. A small harbour. The esplanade runs along it, but the best is not made of the sea. At the W end of the harbour the MARKET HOUSE, probably Early Victorian, with windows, etc., with broad bands and segmental arches. From here Market Street runs W, and SWAIN STREET runs up S. At its end the nice three-bay Late Georgian or Early Victorian house of the Westminster Bank. On the upper floor the centre is a niche with a vase. Outside the old town somewhat elevated and looking down into Swain Street the BAPTIST CHAPEL of 1824, painted maroon and cream, and looking extremely English with its odd curved pediment and its arched upper windows.

KENTSFORD FARM. The original house of the Wyndhams. Elizabethan or Jacobean porch and in the wing at the back plaster ceiling with thin ribs.

KENTSFORD BRIDGE. Two-arch packhorse bridge.

DAW'S CASTLE. Prehistoric Camp on the cliff edge, along the Blue Anchor road. Most of the embankment has now been eroded away by the action of the ocean and only a very small section testifies to the existence of what must once have been a considerable bastion against the recurrent danger of raids by sea.

WAYFORD
4000

ST MICHAEL. All renewed externally, but inside rere-arches, simple and pointed-trefoiled, to several lancet windows. – PLATE. Chalice and Cover 1370.

WAYFORD MANOR. Below the church, with the main façade to the W, and behind, bordering on the churchyard, a court with at least one late medieval building, perhaps the priest's house. Wayford Manor was built c. 1602 (date on the library chimney-piece) for Giles Daubeney. E-plan with plain gables over the fronts of the projecting wings. The l. (N) wing by *Sir Ernest George, c.* 1900. The porch is on the ground floor, opened in a handsome group of three arches. They are prettily decorated and stand on Tuscan columns. The porch is, as Mr Oswald rightly observed, remarkably similar to that at Cranborne Manor in Dorset. Inside the porch shell-headed niches comparable with those at Montacute. Mullioned and mullioned and transomed windows, that of the Hall of six lights, as is also that of the Library overlooking the forecourt. In the Hall ribbed plaster ceiling of c. 1900. The Library ceiling, however, is original, as is that above it. They both have the thin ribs arranged in cross and lozenge patterns as they are familiar in Somerset and all over England. Good heavy fireplace in the Library. Coupled Corinthian columns to the l. and r., and in the overmantel a strap cartouche in a heavy frame with egg and tongue moulding. The fireplace and plasterwork are reminiscent of Montacute (A. Oswald).

WEARE
4050

ST GREGORY. W tower of the type of this neighbourhood, characterized by the two blank windows l. and r. of the bell-openings and identical in design with them, and by the pierced

parapet of quatrefoils in lozenges. Angle pinnacles and intermediate pinnacles. Much restored and N aisle added 1846. –
FONT. Square, Norman, fluted on the underside. – PULPIT.
1617, with the usual short blank arches. – COMMUNION
RAILS and STALLS, lavish and made in connexion with the
restoration of 1901. Designed, it is said, by a lady at Plymouth.
The communion rails are of alabaster and have two large
figures of kneeling angels. The poppy-heads of three stalls
are carved with prettily stylized tree and leaf motifs. – PLATE.
Chalice and Cover 1573. – BRASS. John Bedbere, a merchant,
c. 1500, the figure 18 in. long.

₄₀₄₀ WEDMORE

ST MARY MAGDALENE. A large church, at first sight entirely
Perp. But the s doorway is an extremely good piece of c. 1200,
so much in the style of Wells that one can presume Wells
workmen. Two orders of colonnettes with excellent *mouve-
menté* stiff-leaf capitals. Finely moulded arch. Of the same time
probably the crossing piers and arches. The piers are altered,
but the low arches with their two slight chamfers are good
evidence. The chancel also may belong to the early C13. It
looks at least from the exposed upper parts of tall slender
windows as if there have been rows of lancets on the s and N
sides. They must have made a fine show. Then follows the SE
chapel, with a two-light E window of c. 1300 (cusped lights
and a spheric triangle above; pointed cinquefoiled rere-arch).
The rest is Perp. Upper parts of the crossing tower with set-
back buttresses, two-light windows below the bell-stage, and a
bell-stage on which the two-light bell-openings are flanked by
two-light blank openings. Parapet with blank arcading. Higher
stair-turret. Fan-vault inside. The W front is quite monumental in scale. Four-light aisle windows and four-light nave
window. The aisles have rising arcaded parapets. The same
parapets continue along the s aisle and on the three-storeyed s
porch tower, a special and impressive feature of the s façade.
The front then continues in a very multiform way. There is a
two-bay chapel E of the porch, then a s transept, then the s
chancel chapel already referred to, and then the projecting
chancel. On the N side the treatment is simple, but there also
are a transept and a chancel chapel. The aisle arcades are of
five bays, with very fragile piers (of four-hollows section) and
four-centred arches. A clerestory was not provided. The

transept arches have the same section but treated more heavily,
i.e. probably built earlier. The chapel E of the porch has a good
panelled ceiling. The N chancel chapel ceiling is equally good.
– PULPIT. A good large Jacobean piece. Blank arches as usual,
filled by plants. In the upper frieze tablets surrounded by
foliage scrolls, strapwork, etc. – SOUTH DOOR. With medieval
(?) ironwork. The date 1677 is nailed on. – PAINTING. St
Christopher, above the pulpit. Robust painting of c. 1520,
painted over one of the same subject. The head of the Child
Christ is visible and seems to be mid-C15. – CHANDELIER.
Brass, given in 1779. – PLATE. Paten by *Edward Holaday*
1710; Chalice and Cover by *Bayley* 1711. – MONUMENTS.
George Hodges, † 1634. Brass figure of a soldier. – William
Boulting † 1755 and his wife † 1751. Standing wall-monu-
ment, with a draped urn in front of an obelisk.

VILLAGE CROSS. Plain shaft, and lantern head.
Opposite a pretty three-bay cottage in the Gothic Revival taste
of c. 1800.

WELLINGTON

1020

ST JOHN BAPTIST. The best part of the church is its red
sandstone tower of good ashlar. Tall, sturdy, and with the
stair-turret rising high and placed in the Totnes position –
i.e. the middle of the S side. Battlements, groups of three
pinnacles on each corner of the tower, corbelled-out intermediate pinnacles, and nine pinnacles on the stair-turret. W
door with niches l. and r., four-light W window, then on the
S side a two-light window with Somerset tracery, and then
on all sides the two-light bell-openings also with Somerset
tracery. Nave with clerestory, a rarity as far W as this. Embattled aisles and S chapel. All windows Perp, and most of
them renewed. Projecting chancel, rebuilt in 1848. Does the
window represent that of c. 1300? It is of three stepped lights
with three quatrefoils in circles. Inside a white and clean
impression, hardly any stained glass. Tower arch panelled,
chancel arch panelled. Arcades of four bays with slim piers of
standard four-hollows section. In the E window of the S aisle
a 'lily crucifix' carved into the central mullion below the
tracery. Ceiled wagon-roof. Two late C18 W galleries in the
aisles. Two-bay chancel chapels. The piers again standard. In
the chancel a largely reconstructed Piscina with cinquefoiled
arch. Shafts on two original heads. Opposite a reconstructed

cinquefoiled recess and in this EFFIGY of a Priest, early C14.

23 – REREDOS. An important piece of *c.* 1380, stone, with many small figures in tiers and a Crucifixion at the top. Preserved at the Taunton Castle Museum. – FONT COVER. A recent addition, designed by *W. H. Randall Blacking.* – PULPIT. Assembled from early C16 and later C17 parts, an odd combination. – PAINTINGS. Two Flemish (?) C17 paintings, signed. – PLATE. Set by *Jacob Marsh* 1763; Chalice 1823. –

35 MONUMENT. Sir John Popham, Chief Justice in the case against Sir Walter Raleigh, † 1607. Statelier than most Jacobean monuments in Somerset. Big base with kneeling figures of children. Tomb-chest with recumbent effigies, canopy of eight-poster type with the centre of the long sides raised in an arch – in the manner of a Venetian window. Big achievements and obelisks. All of poor workmanship, and newly repainted.

THE TOWN. The centre of the town is the former TOWN HALL, built in 1833. Three storeys, five bays, classical. It faces SOUTH STREET, where the BAPTIST CHAPEL, also of 1833, is worth a glance. The long side runs along the street, with tall arched windows. On the front a four-column Tuscan porch and nice Egyptian lettering. The architectural details are just on the point of going Victorian-Italianate. To the E from the Town Hall the HIGH STREET runs towards the church. Here are the best Georgian houses of Wellington, though none are of any high merit. Note No. 17, five bays, segment-headed windows, and No. 71 of *c.* 1830 with a Greek Doric doorway. Also several other nice doorways and porches, e.g. No. 4 (Greek Doric). Behind No. 18 the FRIENDS MEETING HOUSE of 1845, yellow brick, three bays wide with three-bay pediment. To the W of the Town Hall the High Street is continued in FORE STREET (No. 20 is an oddity, early C19, with triangle-headed windows and diagonal glazing bars), and this in MANTLE STREET. In Mantle Street the URBAN DISTRICT OFFICES, Late Georgian, brick, with a broad canted bay; then OLD COURT, on its own, with lower one-bay wings, also Late Georgian, though older behind. To Old Court belongs a stable range with early C19 Gothic windows. Finally the R.C. Church of ST JOHN FISHER, built in 1833 as almshouses. Gothic, red brick and stone dressings. Seven gables, the middle one bigger and with the entrance. To the l. transomed windows have been inserted. Also in Mantle Street the former church of HOLY TRINITY, built in 1828 by *Carver* in the form of a Greek cross. The building is awaiting demolition. Finally, again from the Town Hall, to the N, outside the town at TONEDALE a group of early C19 factory housing, called FIVE HOUSES, built round a square. The main front has a curious arrangement of segment-headed windows with three pointed and two semicircular ones in the centre.*

WELLISFORD MANOR
1 m. N of Thorne St Margaret

0022

Essentially a brick house of *c.* 1700. Five bays with the original wooden cross-window casements and the original cornice. Hipped roof. At the back two later C18 bows.

WEMBDON
1½ m. NW of Bridgwater

2030

(St GEORGE. Mainly 1868–9 by *J. M. Hay.* – PLATE. Dish of 1712; Chalice 1728 by *J. Wilkes*; also Paten and Flagon.)

WEST BAGBOROUGH

1030

St PANCRAS. Perp. W tower with diagonal buttresses, high stair-turret, and battlements. The rest over-restored. Moulded tower arch. Arcade of three bays with standard piers (four hollows), chancel arch with a wave-moulding instead of the standard hollow. Original wagon-roofs. – BENCHES. Of the type of the district, mostly close tracery motifs, but also Renaissance details (cf. Crowcombe). – SCREEN at the W end, memorial of 1922 designed by *Comper* and carved by a local class. By *Comper* also the ROOD, the FONT COVER, and the STAINED GLASS. – PLATE. Chalice and Cover 1641; Plates 1778 and 1780. – MONUMENT. Henry Shuldham † 1806, by *Pierce* of Exeter. Elegant, with an urn in the Adam style.

BAGBOROUGH HOUSE. Late Georgian, of five bays with a handsome Ionic colonnade of coupled columns along the S front.

TRISCOMBE HOUSE, 1¼ m. NW. Late Georgian, remodelled by *Sir Ernest Newton* in 1904. His porch and pretty bay-windows on the W side are unmistakable.

* Information obtained from the MHLG.

WEST BOWER *see* DURLEIGH

WEST BRADLEY

CHURCH. Perp and not of importance. w tower with pyramid roof behind the battlements. Inside the tower a pretty star-vault. Perp nave and chancel; *see* the windows and the chancel arch. – PLATE. Chalice and Cover 1572.

BRADLEY HOUSE, NE of the church. A remarkable sight and difficult to explain. The detail – framed sash-windows below string-courses rising into hood-moulds – seems early C18, but the plan is certainly not of that date. A square, three storeys high, and at the angles projecting in square bays set diagonally – that is an almost completely symmetrical tower-like elevation. Can this plan be an Elizabethan conceit? There are Elizabethan cellar windows preserved.

CHAPEL COTTAGE, Plot Street. Pretty Gothick cottage of *c.* 1800, with pointed windows and over the doorway a cusped crocketed panel with the lamb and flag.

COURT BARN. Said to be the smallest stone tythe-barn in the county, but very elegant in the stonework. Early C15, with remains of a dovecote. Heavy roof with collar-beams on arched braces. Only partly original timber work.

WEST BUCKLAND

ST MARY. In a prominent position. The church contains C13, C14, and early C16 work. The latter will be seen first. w tower, built *c.* 1509, in which year John Peryn of Wellington left money to its building. Centrally placed s stair-turret, in the Wellington (and Totnes) fashion. Diagonal buttresses. Pinnacles and corbelled-out intermediate pinnacles. Plain two-light bell-openings with Somerset tracery. The church itself is much renewed. Battlements and three-light windows. Interior with two-bay arcade of octagonal piers – C14. The N arcade apparently a little earlier than the s arcade; similar details in the s chapel. Perp details in the N chapel. The single-chamfered chancel arch seems to be the oldest surviving part, probably C13, but altered almost beyond recognition. – FONT. Square, of the Purbeck type with shallow blank arches. Two sides were originally uncarved and received leaf carvings in the C15. – STAINED GLASS. One N window has glass by *Morris & Co.*, early 1890s. – PLATE. Salver 1802; Chalice 1806.

WEST BUCKLAND FARM HOUSE. Two good plaster ceilings,
one with thin ribs, late C16 or a little later, the other with
broad patterned bands instead of ribs, say c. 1620.

WEST CAMEL

ALL SAINTS. Essentially early C14. S tower in transeptal position. Unbuttressed, with two-light Dec bell-openings, corbel
table, parapet, and later lead spire. On a beam in the spire the
date 1631. Nave W doorway and S doorway with depressed
double-chamfered arches without capitals. The nave S side
has an early C14 window. The same windows chancel N and S.
They have rere-arches. Chancel E window reticulated with
trefoiled pointed rere-arch. Inside, the arches into the tower
(S transept) and the N transept are double-chamfered, that on
the N side on moulded corbels. In the chancel completely
renewed C13 Piscina and Sedilia with trefoiled pointed arches.
Just W of the Sedilia a bracket with holes. It was used to attach
the lenten veil to. – FONT. Norman, circular, with intersected arches. – SCULPTURE. Fragment of a C9 Saxon cross-
shaft, with band-like intertwined snakes or dragons and much
close interlace. – STAINED GLASS. Old fragments in the window behind the pulpit. – MONUMENT. Tablet of 1786 with
urn, by *King* of Bath.
Nice houses W of the church, especially the RECTORY with its
stone barn and circular dovecote.

WEST CHINNOCK

ST MARY. One original C13 lancet in the chancel. The rest of
1889. W tower with saddleback roof. Interior imitation-C13.
Circular piers, corbels with naturalistic foliage. Contemporary
Pulpit, Font, etc. – STAINED GLASS 1890, etc., by *Ward &
Hughes*. – PLATE. Chalice and Cover 1570.
Nice terraces of cottages S of the church. Higher up to the
S HIGH CROSS, three-bay front, dated 1604.

WEST COKER

ST MARTIN. NW of the village centre. Mostly rebuilt 1863–4.
The low semicircular stair-turret of the W tower is medieval
and has original horn windows. Perp N chancel chapel. –
PULPIT. Jacobean. – BENCH ENDS. Dated 1633. With large

flowers. – PAINTING. Christ tended by angels; Italian, early C17. – PLATE. Chalice and Cover, early C17. – MONUMENTS. Two kneeling daughters of Sir John Portman; one of them † 1661. – Tablet by *Regnart*, 1791.

MANOR HOUSE. An exquisitely beautiful small manor house built after a fire in 1457 and apparently into the C16 (Courtenay family). Additions made for Sir John Portman who bought the house in 1591. Much altering and pulling about *c.* 1875, and some rebuilding (SE wing, by *M. Webb*) in 1910. Built of Ham Hill stone on a simple plan. The Hall is in the centre, entered from the W by a porch dated 1600. It has tall transomed straight-headed two-light windows to the E, separated by buttresses. The bay-window on the entrance side which now houses the staircase also has two lights, but a two-centred arch. The open roof is given arched braces supporting collar-beams. The quatrefoil frieze, however, which takes the place of wind-braces may well belong to *c.* 1840. Fine big fireplace with a frieze of elaborately cusped quatrefoils containing shields. To the S were Kitchen and Offices, to the N on the upper floor is the Withdrawing Room. In this is an early C17 overmantel with plaster decoration. Another fireplace which dates probably from *c.* 1510 is in the room to the W of this. More original roofs visible on the upper floor. The windows of *c.* 1600 are of course plainly mullioned and carry hood-moulds. The house lies close to one of the streets of the village.

The village extends along the Exeter highway and off it to the S. Near the E entrance MANOR FARM with a curious Barn, dated 1764 and incorporating four plain Gothic doorways and windows. They are oddly simple in their *c.* 1300-looking mouldings and may well be original work brought in from a church or monastery.

To the SE of the Manor House the ALMSHOUSES, dated 1718. Doorways and windows arched with the usual heavy square abaci and keystones. No. 33 in the same street is dated 1733 and has a segmental pediment over the doorway but still mullioned windows.

ROMAN VILLA on the site of an Early Iron Age Encampment.

WEST HATCH

ST ANDREW. 1861 by *Ferrey*. Thus Kelly. The *Little Guide* says 'entirely rebuilt in 1865'. But both are incorrect. There was clearly much re-using of old parts. The W tower with set-back buttresses and battlements. The buttresses have pinnacles above the battlements, and there are in addition higher pinnacles in the corners on the battlements as well. Would Ferrey have invented that? Stair-turret with spirelet. Original re-used wagon-roofs. – PULPIT. Made of parts of the original screen.

WEST LYDFORD

5030

ST PETER. 1846 by *Benjamin Ferrey*, an early work of this pupil of Pugin's, and a remarkably competent one, charmingly placed with a strip of graveyard lawn stretching on its S side immediately to the river Brue. To the E of the church a C17 BRIDGE with five arches and a parapet pierced by five smaller overflow arches, in case of a flood. The church is archaeologically correct Somerset Perp, no longer picturesquely Gothic and satisfied with that. This turn to antiquarian exactitude was one which did not occur in the work of any of the pioneers before 1840. W tower with set-back buttresses and battlements. Eight pinnacles. Embattled nave, embattled N aisle, lower chancel with a pinnacled parapet pierced by quatrefoils in lozenges. Perp windows. The N arcade inside is entirely Somerset standard and could well be original. – STAINED GLASS. E window by *Wailes*, 1852 (TK). – PLATE. Paten 1706; Flagon by *T. Tearle* 1723; Paten 1783.

WEST MONKTON

2020

ST AUGUSTINE. Very tall, four-storeyed W tower, grey and bare, as though in opposition to the fripperies of Taunton. That interpretation is not tenable however; for the tower arch, which is triple-chamfered and dies into the imposts, is clearly earlier than any of the fine displays in and around Taunton, at whatever date the tower was finally completed. It has set-back buttresses, two-light bell-openings with transom, and battlements. No pinnacles. On the S side an image-niche, then a two-light window, and then the bell-opening. The tower arch may well be as early as *c.* 1300, and in that case it would belong to a church preceding the present and of which two more pieces survive: the S aisle W window, of two lights with plate tracery, evidently re-set, and the chancel arch, which has a continuous double-chamfer. As for the rest, the S and N aisles are embattled, the N aisle with three-light, the S aisle with two-light windows. Nave with clerestory unembattled. Simple standard arcade (four hollows) of four bays. The small capitals on the S side have rosettes. The same enrichment of the arches into the chancel chapel, from the W and the chancel. Good wagon-roof of the C15 with pretty carving – SCREEN made up of C17 and early C18 parts. – STAINED GLASS. In the W window figures entirely in the C18 tradition, but signed '*Gray & Son* facit 1827'. – PLATE. Set of 1716. – MONUMENTS. Brass, demi-figure of a priest, probably Henry Abyndon, *c.* 1440. – Alexander Popham † 1767, large wall-monument with very chaste and classical spiral-fluted urn.

MONKTON HOUSE. The typical large villa of *c.* 1840, with Italianate tower. The arches on the top of the tower are a hall-mark of the date. But the house is Georgian and was only remodelled.

WESTON BAMPFYLDE
₆₀₂₀

HOLY CROSS. The W tower is C13 in its broad lower stages with a W lancet and a small unmoulded pointed arch to the nave. The upper stages are octagonal and Perp. – FONT. Late Norman circular bowl with nutmeg top moulding and cable bottom moulding. – PULPIT. Jacobean. – PLATE. Chalice and Cover by *Lawrence Stratford* 1573; Paten 1635 (?).

MANOR HOUSE. E of the church, picturesque gabled C17 building, altered.

WESTON FARM
1 m. N of Wambrook
₂₀₀₀

On the porch the date 1672, at the back in a far from prominent position the date 1583 which fits the interesting features of the house better. They are the two plaster ceilings above each other in the back wing (drawing-room wing?) to the r. of the porch. The ground-floor room has heavily stuccoed decoration in panels between the moulded beams, the upper room has charming oak scrolls, an unusual motif in the county. The porch was originally three-storeyed and the whole front had dormers in addition to its two storeys. Mullioned windows.

WESTON ZOYLAND

St Mary. Lias and Ham Hill dressings. The tower is the tallest
in Zoyland (just over 100 ft), the s front a proper façade. The
tower is in four stages with set-back buttresses diagonally
connected across the angle of the tower. Plain doorway and
four-light w window. On the n and s sides this stage is
entirely bare. Towards the nave it has a tall panelled arch
opening into a fan-vault. Next stage two-light windows with
niches l. and r. Next stage the same again, but the windows
with Somerset tracery. Then the bell-openings. Three in a
row, each of two lights, with transom. Only the middle one is
a real opening; the others are blank. Somerset tracery. Battlements with quatrefoils, square pinnacles, and also intermediate pinnacles. The s façade has an embattled aisle, embattled clerestory, two-storeyed embattled porch (roof on
angel-busts), and embattled s chapel. The s window of this is
flanked by niches and has some unusual details in its tracery.
On one of the buttresses are the initials of Richard Bere, abbot
of Glastonbury (1493–1524). The chancel is lower, unembattled and a good deal earlier; for it has on the n and s sides
two-light Dec windows, with rere-arches on shafts inside. The
n side otherwise is similar to the s but plainer. n vestry with
big buttress and small lancet window. On entering the church
the nave roof is a sudden thrill. It is one of the finest of Somer-   20
set and typical of at least part of the county. The roof is of
moderate pitch, with big tie-beams on short arched braces
which rest on angel busts. On the tie-beams stand, seemingly
carried by big angels, the kingposts. To the l. and r. of the
kingposts all is close tracery in two tiers. The sub-principals
are decorated by a kind of pendant kingposts connected by
thin braces to the beams. Plenty of bosses. Nave arcades of
six bays; the piers of the standard four-hollows section. The
clerestory windows are of three lights and have four-centred
arches. The tower arch takes the whole height of the nave.
Fine roof in the s transept also, panelled, on angels, with many
bosses. Another angel supports the panelled w arch into the
chapel. At this junction it is clear (grey stone v. Ham Hill,
two-centred v. four-centred arch) that the nave arcade is
earlier than the s transept. – FONT. Perp, octagonal, of an
unusual shape, stem and bowl of about the same size, and as
decoration just a number of bold mouldings to divide stem and
bowl into layers. – ROOD SCREEN. 1933–9, but instructive;

for it has been given a loft and a rood. – BENCHES. Plain, square-headed, with large tracery motifs. Some poppy-heads. On one end the initials of Richard Bere. – STAINED GLASS. Original bits in the chancel s. Again on one fragment the same initials. – SOUTH DOOR. Original, traceried. – PLATE. Chalice 1573; Flagon 1612; Paten 1707. – MONUMENT. Effigy of a Priest, praying, c. 1300; N chapel.

Incorporated into a HOUSE by the church some three-light windows with pointed-arched lights, said to come from a monastic house.

WEST PENNARD

5030

ST NICHOLAS. Perp w tower with set-back buttresses. w door with niches l. and r. and a frieze above it decorated with three busts of angels. w window with niches l. and r. and a frieze above it again with three angel busts. Two-light upper windows with Somerset tracery, two-light bell-openings with Somerset tracery. Battlements and blank arcading, square pinnacles, lead spike. In the tower a star-vault. The tower arch with panelling between thin shafts. s aisle with parapet with blank arcading, N aisle with plain parapet, chancel with parapet with pierced quatrefoils, clerestory with the same. Arcade of four bays with four-hollows piers and four-centred arches, polygonal capitals to the shafts only. Ceiled wagon-roof on angels. Chancel roof panelled on angels. – ROOD SCREEN. With one-light sections with depressed ogee-arches and a little thin tracery; carved frieze. – DOORS. W as well as S door original, both traceried. – STAINED GLASS. An interesting collection of Early Victorian glass, the best probably of the 1840s, in the NW window of the chancel. Very Nazarene, and certainly not English. – In the aisles several windows (1842, 1851, 1865) by *Mèna* of Paris. – The NE chancel window by *Mayer* of Munich, 1890. – PLATE. Domestic Cup early C17; elaborately engraved Tankard 1605 (cf. Binegar); Paten 1711. – CROSS in the churchyard. With the Symbols of the Passion on the base.

WEST QUANTOXHEAD

1040

ST ETHELDREDA (St Audrey). 1856 by *J. Norton*. By the Lodge of St Audries facing a green or field and set against a wall of trees (Quantock State Forest). Doulting stone, pinkish buff. The roofing with stone slates. The front consists of the big

NW tower, with a higher stair-turret crowned by a spirelet, the W gable, and the S aisle W gable. All the details in the late C13 Geometrical style. The piers inside are monoliths of Babbacombe marble. The carved detail is due to *Farmer* and is naturalistic, à la Southwell Chapter House, also with head-corbels and angels supporting the roof principals. – COMMUNION RAIL, metal, by *Hardman*. – STAINED GLASS. E window by *O'Connor*, Crucifixion in large figures and strident colours. – Window with Christ, St Peter, and St John, by *Kempe* 1882. – PLATE. Chalice and Paten 1574; Tazza 1703; Service of domestic silver, inscribed 1775.

ST AUDRIES. Large Tudor mansion by *Norton*. Tall porch-tower. Hall to the r. of it with four large transomed four-light windows.

SCHOOL. No doubt also by *Norton* (cf. his school at Stogursey).

WHEATHILL

CHURCH. Nave with bell-cote and lower chancel. Apparently medieval, but too much restored to afford any evidence. – PLATE. Chalice and Cover of 1573; Paten 1674.

WHITE LACKINGTON

ST MARY. The two transepts are older than the rest. The windows and especially the large N and S windows are clearly of the early C14. They are of three lights with a large circle in the middle. In the circle in the N transept three trefoils, in the S transept three spheric triangles. The transept windows have all rere-arches, the N window has in addition shafts. In the N chapel also a Piscina with shelf and in the E wall a rich niche for a statue. The rest of the church is Perp. Nave arcades of three bays with standard piers (four hollows). Thin piers, wide arches, no clerestory. Perp windows. W tower, nothing special. Diagonal buttresses and battlements. Higher stair-turret. W door, and four-light W window. Three-light bell-openings with Somerset tracery. – STAINED GLASS. E window 1896 by *Kempe*. – PLATE. Tall Cup with Cover of 1616; plain Paten of 1712. – MONUMENTS. In the S transept on the floor two defaced effigies, a Civilian of *c.* 1350, and a Knight in armour of *c.* 1375. – Sir George Speke (?). Sir George mentions his tomb as ready prepared in his will of 1583. But the monument must be at least twenty-five years earlier. It is still

entirely in the flamboyant latest Perp style and has hardly
more than one frieze which shows a recognition of the Renaissance. Tomb-chest with shields in cusped lozenges. On it to
the l. and r. polygonal panelled shafts carrying big twisted
chimney-like finials. A third over the apex of the four-
centred arch. The inside of the arch is panelled and has three
heavy pendants. The sides behind the polygonal shafts are
pierced tracery panels. The back of the niche has a shield
with large lush foliage. – Two HELMS on two side finials. –
John Hanning † 1807, by *J. Richards* of Exeter. Wall-monument with small kneeling woman by an urn.

(MANOR HOUSE, next to the church. Gabled, probably C16
to C17, but the windows sashed.)

WHITESTAUNTON

2010

ST ANDREW. An all-Perp church. Plain w tower with higher
stair-turret and two-light bell-openings. Nave without aisles,
but roomy s chapel (Bluett Chapel) and small N chapel. The s
chapel has a doorway and an arch next to this which once no
doubt held the tomb of the founder of the chapel. The N
chapel is divided from the chancel by a stone SCREEN,
plain, with one-light divisions. – FONT. Circular, Norman,
with fluting at the foot of the bowl. – ROOD SCREEN. Original,
but of no special interest. – BENCH ENDS. A few, mid C16. –
TILES. Some old ones near the altar. – PLATE. Chalice 1658. –
MONUMENTS. Two tomb-chests in the s chapel, one of them
very re-tooled.

MANOR HOUSE. On the N side the existence of medieval parts
can be seen in the embattled porch and the attached big
chimney. Inside this evidence is borne out by the survival of
the fine C14 Hall roof, with collar-beams on arched braces and
cusped wind-braces of a very unusual design (two cusped
'lights' and ogee plate tracery). The Hall windows are
Elizabethan. A date 1577 remains indeed in the panelling of
the Dining Room. The windows are mullioned and still have
arched lights. Two asymmetrically placed gables on the N
front, more on the w side.

WHITESTANTON CAMP. Prehistoric Earthwork in Horse Pool
Copse, r. of the Chard–Yarcombe road. It is hard to locate.
Oval in shape, it measures 300 by 135 yards, and its banks rise
in places to a height of 12 ft.

ROMAN VILLA recorded at Whitestaunton.

WICK *see* STOGURSEY

WIGBOROUGH
2 m. SW of South Petherton

4010

MANOR HOUSE. 1585. Fine gabled mansion with mullioned and mullioned and transomed windows. The E side has the original façade. Four-storeyed porch. To its l. the Hall and leading from it in the place where one would expect the Hall bay-window a small separate room, panelled and with a plaster ceiling with a pattern of fine ribs. The date 1585 appears in the frieze. Further on, i.e. to the S, the projecting Parlour or Drawing Room, also with a good plaster ceiling. Above the fireplace a coarsely modelled plaster overmantel with two figures. To the N of the porch the former Kitchen with a big fireplace. On the first floor much panelling and above the Parlour another room with a plaster ceiling. (Two one-storeyed porches are, it is said, a bisected former lychgate of Norton-sub-Hamdon church.)

WILLETT'S TOWER *see* BROMPTON RALPH

WILLITON

0040

ST PETER. Mostly the work of *Giles*, who restored and enlarged the church in 1858. – PLATE. Elizabethan Chalice and Cover by *Ions*.

TOWNSEND HOUSE (Williton District Hospital). Built as the Workhouse. It must date from *c.* 1830–40. Centre block with four diagonally-set spurs, lower wings, and yet lower gatehouse range. Quite a dignified design.

(THE COMBE. Built *c.* 1774.)

BATTLE GORE. Earthworks in a field known by this picturesque name on the road to Watchet. The earthworks are difficult to detect, and are related to a mound or barrow at their centre. Local tradition connects them with a battle in the year A.D. 918, and it is not unlikely that they are in fact Saxon in origin. Or are they, like so many other structures of similarly indeterminate character, connected in some way with the Civil War? There are three barrows altogether in Battlegore field, and they are known collectively, for some obscure reason, as Grabburows – presumably a corruption of Grave Barrows.

WILTON
½ m. s of Taunton

St George. Although the church appears normal Perp from outside, it is evident that it goes back very much further. In the w wall of the n aisle are traces of Saxon long-and-short work, in the w wall of the s aisle of quoining which must also date from a time before the church had aisles. Yet the interior reveals that already in the c13 it was fully aisled. Five-bay arcades. Circular piers with four attached shafts, just as at St Mary Magdalene, Taunton. The c15 or early c16 added four-centred arches. The chancel was rebuilt in 1837 (by *Carver*), the w tower in 1853, the s porch in 1870. – PLATE. Chalice 1636.

Grove Lodge. Good c18 gate of wrought iron.

WINCANTON

St Peter and St Paul. Perp w tower, now at the w end of the n aisle. It was originally at the w end of the nave, which became an aisle when the church was rebuilt by *J. D. Sedding* in 1887–9. s porch with segmental pediment, probably by *Ireson* (*see* below), and probably of 1735, the year when Ireson built the s aisle of the church. Interior with aisles and outer s aisle. The arcade between the two s aisles may be genuinely Perp. It has standard piers (four hollows). – SCULPTURE. An interesting though damaged relief of a scene from the life of St Eligius (n porch) – STAINED GLASS. E window by *Clayton & Bell*, 1889. Bell was born near Wincanton. – PLATE. Chalice and Paten 1695; Dishes 1712 and 1729. – In the churchyard MONUMENT of 1772 to *Nathaniel Ireson*, an architect from Warwickshire who moved to Wincanton from Stourhead in 1726 and died in 1769. Standing statue on a pedestal. The EAST GATES of the churchyard are later c18 with elegantly shaped urns on the piers.

The church lies at the bottom of the town. Church Street runs up E from the churchyard gates to the Market Place. Wincanton had a big fire in 1747, and in the following decades many houses were rebuilt in handsome stone and with handsome classical or semi-classical façades. The best are in the Market Place and the High Street. The MARKET PLACE is of elongated, irregular shape, hardly more than a widening between Church Street and High Street. On the s side the

TOWN HALL, red brick, 1878 (by *Willcocks*), and rather an eyesore with its ugly turret. There are, however, it seems, some C18 pieces re-used, such as the Gibbs surrounds. Opposite Messrs Townsends (and other shops) with a central Venetian window and the GREYHOUND HOTEL, Early Georgian (1743?) with an archway with Doric pilasters and a canted bay-window above. Top parapet. Stepped keystones of the windows in groups of three. Pretty wrought-iron inn-sign bracket. Then the BEAR HOTEL also with a wrought-iron sign bracket. The archway is round-headed rusticated. The house is dated 1720. The chemist's shop opposite had originally two Venetian windows in the rusticated ground floor.

In the HIGH STREET many Georgian houses, with and without pediments. Door cases and surrounds of various patterns. Especially ornate the WHITE HORSE HOTEL, with heavy rustication, heavy pediments, and groups of keystones. Two storeys with quoins, the attic storey above with short tapering pilasters at the angles. The house is dated 1733. It is rustic, and not at all metropolitan or courtly. Higher up also brick houses. The last house of note is the DOLPHIN HOTEL with evenly rusticated quoins and Gibbs surrounds to the ground-floor windows. Wincanton was evidently a good place for coaching inns.

Of other streets and houses the following need mention: Off the High Street to the N on a hill in Grant's Lane IRESON HOUSE, built by *Nathaniel Ireson* for himself *c.* 1726, etc., and much altered *c.* 1851. But the doorway with pilasters decorated by intermittent vermiculated rustication, the angle pilasters of the centre of the façade, and also the Gibbs surrounds of some windows seem original.

Off the High Street to the S in Common Road BALSAM HOUSE, Jacobean, with, on the N side, two wings to the l. and r. of a narrow courtyard. Gables and mullioned windows. On the S side gabled porch. The gables carry obelisks.

Off the Market Place South Street continues in TOUT HILL. Here THE DOGS, a composition similar in its elements to Balsam House. Opposite TOUT HILL HOUSE, built before 1797. The stables have a Venetian window in the pediment. Also off the Market Place to the W, parallel with Church Street, MILL STREET. Here the CONGREGATIONAL CHAPEL and the BAPTIST CHAPEL, both Late Classical, the first built shortly after 1800, the second in 1832–3. At the foot of Mill Street Messrs Ureco, a mill in the Early Victorian *Rundbogenstil*. The florid cast-iron window grilles should be noted. In WEST HILL, RODBER HOUSE, five bays, brick, with parapet, and then DIAL HOUSE, dated 1690. Five bays, two storeys, quoins, and a canted bay-window above a Tuscan porch. Further out, i.e. off the Bratton road, STEDDON GRANGE with a long front with mullioned windows and a two-storeyed gabled porch; C17. Then HOLBROOK HOUSE, two-storeyed, Georgian with Victorian additions. A lodge by the road seems to be the work of *Eden Nesfield* (see *Architectural Review*, vol. 2, 1897).

(MOORHAYES FARM, 1½ m. NW of Wincanton. Gabled, late C16 manor house with a spiral staircase in a semicircular projection.)

9030
inset

WINSFORD

ST MARY MAGDALENE (formerly St Peter). The round-arched S doorway could be Norman, the chancel is C13 (*see* the doorway and lancet windows). The rest Perp. The chancel E window is a late Perp type specially popular at the time in this neighbourhood (cf. Porlock, Exford, Exton). It has a transom and an ogee arch to each light beneath it. Nave and aisles and W tower Perp too. The W tower quite big for the district in which it stands. Three stages, set-back buttresses, battlements, no pinnacles. Statue-niche on the S side. Higher stair-turret. Large W window of four lights C19. Aisle arcades of four bays with piers of standard section (four hollows), very primitively treated. Chancel arch of the same type. Above it two windows, a great rarity in this part of England. Nave and aisles under the same big roof externally (cf. Cannington, Norton-sub-Hamdon). The church was restored by *J. D. Sedding*, who died here in 1891 while carrying out the work. – FONT. Circular, Norman, with coarse blank arches, their shafts plaited. Saltire cross frieze above. – PULPIT. Jacobean, with the usual arches. – DOOR. In the S doorway, with heavy C13 ironwork. – STAINED GLASS. In the E window small figure of the Virgin; C14. – PLATE. Exeter-made Chalice, inscribed 1574; Paten by *I.M.* 1633.

PACKHORSE BRIDGE, ¼ m. from the centre, near the Vicarage. Of two arches, with a cobble track.

ROAD CASTLE. Prehistoric Earthwork on high ground above the Exe in Lyncombe Wood, on the Exford road. It has been severely damaged by agricultural operations, but in places the bank still rises 15 ft above the bottom of its ditch.

WINSHAM

3000

St Stephen. The plan is unusual and impressive, and the church is by no means small. Nave and chancel separated by a tower which, in the absence of transepts, cannot be called a crossing tower. It is a Norman plan (cf. e.g. Iffley), but the details are Perp. In the chancel lancets, and also Dec tracery. Rere-arches. Early c14 w window in the nave, with modest flowing tracery. The other nave windows, of three lights, are Perp. The tower is plain with higher stair-turret, and embattled. The 'crossing' arches have responds of the standard, four-hollow type. – FONT. Octagonal, Perp, with quatrefoil frieze. – ROOD SCREEN. Much renewed. The side sections are of four lights, with depressed arches and the middle mullion reaching right into the apex. – PAINTING. Large Crucifixion with the two thieves, the Virgin, and Mary Magdalene. Formerly the so-called Tympanum, i.e. the infilling of the arch above the screen. Rustic work perhaps of the mid c16. – PLATE. Cover 1570; Chalice *c.* 1573 and 1654; Paten 1708; Flagon 1759. – MONUMENT. Robert Henley † 1639, small wall-monument, with the then fashionable representation of the dead man in his shroud rising from his tomb. The figure is only half visible (cf. Rodney Stoke).

Leigh House, *see* p. 219.

WITHIEL FLOREY

9030

St Mary. Hidden between green hills, with only one farm close. The w tower partly c13. The rest Perp and much restored. – PLATE. Elizabethan Chalice and Cover.

WITHYCOMBE

0040

St Nicholas. The rare case in Somerset of a church without Perp enlargements. Pink-washed. The s porch tower c13, *see* the outer doorway and the small one-light bell-openings. Chancel of the late c13 to the early c14, *see* the s lancet, the s doorway with ogee rere-arch, the two-light Dec window, and the three-light reticulated e window. Nave of the same time, though with some Perp windows. – FONT. Circular,

Norman, with widely spaced vertical ribs on the bowl and a cable-moulding. – SCREEN. Of the local (Dunster–Minehead) type, with four-light sections, the arches divided into two sub-arches of two lights each. The mullions are a replacement. Ribbed coving, four carved friezes. – PLATE. Chalice and Cover of 1665; Flagon 1767. – MONUMENTS. In the s wall half hidden by the pews, under a low recess, Effigy of a Civilian, not well preserved, late C13. – Below a Perp window which must have replaced the former arch of the recess, Effigy of a Lady, c. 1300, flanked by two low broad castellated stone candlesticks. They are decorated by flatly carved naturalistic foliage and have also small heads. It is a unique arrangement and very attractive.

WITHYPOOL

St ANDREW. Low broad two-stage w tower. Largely rebuilt in 1901, but the tower arch towards the nave with its remarkable misinterpretation of Perp details looks C17 rather than C20. Nave and rebuilt chancel, straight-headed windows. Arcade of three bays, piers of four-hollows section. The capitals are reduced to one thin moulding. – FONT. Circular, Norman, the bowl with a fluted underside and a band of parallel chevrons. – PLATE. Chalice by *I.P.* 1572; Paten by *Elston*, inscribed 1726.

METHODIST CHURCH. Very pretty with Gothick ogee-headed doorway and windows. It looks decidedly c. 1800. The date 1881 on a tablet cannot apply.

STONE CIRCLE. Of Bronze Age date, s of the bridge over the River Barle. It is at a height of 1250 ft, and thirty-seven stones are still standing. The megaliths are small, only 1 or 2 ft tall, and are of local grey grit.

WIVELISCOMBE

St ANDREW. Red sandstone, rebuilt 1829 by *Richard Carver*, who was allowed to sign his name on the w gallery. In rebuilding the church some of the original window tracery was re-used. The N aisle E window, e.g. was the E window of the old church. The chancel of 1829 has been replaced by a polygonal one of 1872 by *Giles & Gane* (GR). The church has a w tower which with its set-back buttresses and battlements and even some Somerset tracery in the bell-openings keeps to the local character. It looks later than 1829, but no date is known. The N side of the church has symmetrical NW and NE porch bays with a kind of pediment gables. A similar gable at the E end of the nave. The E rose window of 1915 is in a French Late C13 style and singularly uncongenial and unattractive. The arcades inside are of five bays. They have piers of a design clearly modelled on the Somerset Perp standard, though characteristically altered. Depressed four-centred arches. – BOX PEWS of c. 1829. – ALTAR RAILS. With heavy balusters, said to be Flemish and C18. – PLATE. Chalice and Cover of 1573; Paten of 1713; Paten of 1759; Flagon of 1782. – MONUMENT. Humphrey Wyndham † 1622, and his wife † 1620. Two recumbent alabaster effigies of good quality, and fragments of the architectural surround. Ascribed by Mrs Esdaile to *Epiphanius Evesham*. – In the churchyard remains of a CROSS with a figure on the shaft nearly eroded out of existence. Pinnacled niche.

Immediately N of the church and in axis with the churchyard gates BOURNES, a house which, with its projecting wings, must be C17, though its porch belongs to the later C18. Inside a very rustic plaster ceiling of c. 1660 with a representation of 'Sine Baccho et Cerere friget Venus'.

To the SE of the church the GATEWAY to the former palace of John Drokensford, Bishop of Wells. It is depressed two-centred with a continuous double-chamfer.

Yet further S the new SECONDARY MODERN SCHOOL, 1953 by *R. O. Harris*. Light brick, with a higher centre emphasized by a hipped roof. The rest flat-roofed. The centre has some fanciful treatment of the brickwork. The two wings are of uneven length and design.

On the way from the school up into the town which lies NW of the church the METHODIST CHURCH of 1845 with lancet windows. Higher up, in the HIGH STREET, a good stretch of houses l. and r., before the former Town Hall is reached. On the r. the former Dispensary with a huge 1804 on the door, on the l. several houses of c. 1700 or a little later, see the even quoins of one and the depressed arch of the doorway of another (No. 6). Then at the turn towards the Town Hall one is faced by the NATIONAL PROVINCIAL BANK, a pretty composition of 1881 in the Norman Shaw style, all tile-hung, with dark woodwork, especially divers oriel windows. The former TOWN HALL of 1840, of grey brick with arched windows and pediment, is completely altered in its ground floor. To the NE of the little Market Square, down Golden Hill, the CONGREGATIONAL CHAPEL, built 1708, enlarged 1825. The doorway with its segmental arch is clearly of the first date, the windows of the second.

ABBOTSFIELD, ½ m. W. Designed by *Owen Jones* for Lacey Collard *c.* 1872. The house was meant to have a second floor instead of the present attics. Perhaps partly owing to that, this design by an architect of remarkably advanced ideas is a disappointment. It seems mixed in its elements and put together without much taste or character. Big tower with pyramid roof, mullioned and transomed windows, two-light windows with triangular heads, and a few more oddities. Richard Wagner stayed at Abbotsfield with Lacey Collard, and Adelina Patti sang from the terrace to an audience seated on the lawn.

OAKHAMPTON HOUSE, 2 m. N. Of nine bays and two storeys with an added third. Plastered walls. Quoins of even length. No decoration. The most likely date is Early Georgian. Kelly gives the date 1734.

KING'S CASTLE. Prehistoric camp on Castle Hill, N of the town. Originally the ramparts defended the whole crest of the hill, but now they have been eaten away by quarrying. Opposite this strong example of primitive fortification, on the other side of the valley, is a second smaller camp called MINNINGTON PARK CAMP. It is rigidly square in form and is 140 yards in diameter. Probably it served as an outpost to King's Castle.

3040

WOOLAVINGTON

ST MARY. The W tower poses a problem. It has heavy angle buttresses at the foot, and on examination inside they turn out to be wall fragments of a church no longer in existence. For inside the tower there are heavy triple-chamfered arches to the W, the E, and somewhat squeezed in the N and S. Only the E arch is now open. It forms the tower arch towards the present nave. The others presuppose the intention of building transepts and an extension to the W which can, from comparison with plenty of similar cases (e.g. Stoke St Gregory, Ditcheat), only have been a nave of which a structure on part of the site of the present nave was the chancel. And the arches with their continuous mouldings date this part of the church fairly reliably as *c.* 1300. However, there is a blocked N doorway which seems to be Norman and a (much restored) chancel chapel with coupled and triple lancets. Perp nave and chancel, Perp upper part of the tower, C17 pinnacles and C17 E window, C18 Vestry. – FONT. Octagonal, Perp, of a usual type. – PLATE. Taunton-made Chalice 1678; Paten 1727; Tankard 1730 by *John Elston Jun.*; Salver 1784.

COTTAGE. W of the church. Dated 1734, yet still with mullioned windows of five, four, and three lights, and their arrangement not even strictly symmetrical. Also the windows are not attached to string courses.

THE GRANGE, W of this house, has a thatched circular COCK-PIT 14 ft in diameter.

WOOTTON COURTNEY

9040 inset

ALL SAINTS. C13 the lower parts of the W tower, see its general shape and unmoulded arch towards the nave. The upper part with saddleback roof is of 1866. C13 also the chancel, although its three stepped E lancets are much over-restored. The rest C15 (N arcade and much-renewed N aisle W and N windows) and *c.* 1530. At that time the S side of the nave and E side of the aisle were provided with new windows by the atelier which did work at Dunster, Cleeve Abbey, Selworthy, Luccombe, etc. Handsome figures of angels and animals as hood-mould stops, inside and outside. C19 S porch. The details of the N arcade are standard: four-waves moulding, with small round capitals only to the shafts. Both piers have big canopied statue niches towards the nave. Ceiled wagon-roofs. The bosses in the aisle specially big (cf. Selworthy, Luccombe). Amongst the representations the Signs of the Evangelists, St George, etc. – FONT. Octagonal, Perp, with quatrefoil frieze. – PLATE. Chalice and Cover 1573; Flagon 1624; Paten presented in 1676.

WORMINSTER

1½ m. NNE of North Wootton

5040

VILLAGE CROSS. On steps. Polygonal shaft and capital. Probably C15.

OLD FARM HOUSE. L-shaped, with mullioned windows under hood-moulds.

WRAXALL
1 m. w of Ditcheat

HILL FARM HOUSE. The only remarkable thing about it is that it is dated 1671 and yet still possesses the gabled dormers and the whole apparatus of the Jacobean style. It should, however, be noted that the fenestration is symmetrical and the gables are also symmetrical.

WYKE CHAMPFLOWER

HOLY TRINITY. 1623–4, immediately attached to the Manor House, which has a Late Georgian s front. The church, in size no more than a chapel, has a fanciful W bell-turret, windows still in the Perp tradition (straight-headed with hood-moulds and cusped lights), and inside Jacobean BOX PEWS, a painted TYMPANUM between nave and chancel, a fine large stone PULPIT, also Jacobean (strapwork on pilasters and detached foliage, etc., on the frieze), and wooden PANELLING in the chancel. – PLATE. Chalice 1573; Paten 1623. – MONUMENT. Tablet to Henry Southworth † 1625, in the chancel, with two flanking columns and an open segmental pediment.

YARLINGTON

ST MARY. Perp s tower, not in the usual porch position. The rest of the church was mostly rebuilt (in a coarse Geometrical) by *J. A. Reeve* in 1878 (GR). – FONT. Perp, square with chamfered corners, decorated with quatrefoils and panel tracery. – PLATE. Chalice and Cover 1573.

YARLINGTON HOUSE. Built shortly after 1782. Nine by three bays, brick. Handsome E front of three broadly spaced bays. Doorway with Tuscan columns and metope frieze. Venetian windows l. and r., pediment over the centre of the façade.

YEOVIL

14 ST JOHN. A large church of very uniform design, Early Perp. Built of local Upper Lias limestone with Ham Hill dressings. Begun under Robert de Sambourne, Canon of Wells, and from 1362 till his death in 1382 rector of Yeovil. He left money in his will 'to the works of Yeovil church begun by me'. The only

element older than *c.* 1375 is the Crypt below the chancel. This seems *c.* 1300 or a little later, and the doorway from the chancel to the crypt agrees with such a date. Central octagonal pier and four quadripartite vaults with heavy single-chamfered ribs. The ribs rest against the outside walls on moulded corbels. As for the rest, the Early Perp date is noticeable in the comparative severity of the tower, the use of unpierced arcading for the parapets (N side unarcaded), and also the tracery. All windows are of five lights with panel tracery without any sub-panels. Between them are buttresses carrying pinnacles. The nave has outside four bays, then a transept on each side, with E rood-stair turrets, then two bays of chancel chapels and the chancel projecting a further bay. The total length is 146 ft, the width across the transepts is 80, the height of the tower 92½. The tower has strong set-back buttresses, not yet the thin later ones, a plain W doorway flanked by tri-angular shafts, a five-light window, a higher NW stair-turret, and a parapet with pierced arcading. This was probably the end of the building history. There is plenty of bare wall all up the tower. On the third and fourth stages two-light openings. The tower arch inside is moulded, not panelled. The S porch has an outer doorway with ogee gable and inside a panelled pointed tunnel-vault, all renewed.

The interior has tall arcades of five bays and no clerestory. The piers have the standard section (four hollows). The chancel is only slightly distinguished, and the chancel arcades are like those of the nave. Wall-shafts up the aisle walls and chapel walls between the windows. In the chancel N wall ogee-arched doorway with crocketed gable, again still decidedly C14-looking. – FONT. Large, octagonal, Perp, with quatrefoil frieze and a cresting above it. – LECTERN. Brass, *c.* 1450. Heavy, moulded base, on four lions. On the lectern itself engraved demi-figure of a priest, no doubt the donor. In-scribed Frater Martinus Forester. Heavy, bold finial. Prob-ably East Anglian. – STAINED GLASS. Much of *c.* 1850. The Prowse window in the N aisle by *Henry Holiday*, 1917–18. – PLATE. Flagon by *John Gibbons* 1704. – MONUMENTS. Brasses to Gyles and Isabell Penne † 1519; 2 ft figures. – Robert Phelips † 1855, demi-figure, frontal, life-size and very lifelike. By *Westmacott*. – Many minor wall-monuments, the most ambitious is one to the Hartson family, erected 1711, with two mourning cherubs, several cherubs' heads, and shields.

HOLY GHOST, R.C. 1894–9 by *Canon A. J. C. Scoles*. In front of the church head of a C15 CHURCHYARD CROSS with the Crucifixion.

HOLY TRINITY, South Street, 1843–6 by *Ferrey* (GR).

MUNICIPAL OFFICES, King George Street, 1926 by *Petter & Warren*. Neo-Georgian, of fifteen bays width, two-storeyed, with cupola. Opposite the POST OFFICE, 1932 by the Office of Works, also neo-Georgian and two-storeyed, with a daintier cupola. Finally, to complete the impression of an incipient Civic Centre, the BAPTIST CHURCH (1827, enlarged 1868, choir 1898) and the BAPTIST HALL of 1912 in South Street facing King George Street. They are also classical (the latter by *Vincent* of Southampton).

RAILWAY STATION, 1853 by *Tite*. Red brick with stone dressings. Long, low, flat, and of symmetrical composition. In the Tudor style, with gables over the wings. The tall chimney-stacks have alas been replaced.

Yeovil up to the C18 was quite a small town, with the church on an eminence in the middle. The shape was roughly triangular and outside that area lay C18 houses in their gardens. The perambulation starts at the corner of High Street and Princes Street. In HIGH STREET the MERMAID HOTEL, an entertaining Gothick version of the classical theme of the inn archway with a Venetian window above. The archway has coupled shafts and a trefoiled head, and the Venetian window has – is this unique? – ogee-headed sides and a pointed-trefoiled centre. At the widening where Silver Street starts, the five-bay pedimented house of Messrs Hill Sawtell Ltd, with its arcaded ground floor, looking as formal as if it had been the Town Hall. High Street is continued to the E in MIDDLE STREET with the GEORGE HOTEL, a timber-framed Tudor house of two storeys with two oversailing bays of different width. At r. angles from the meeting of High Street and Middle Street SILVER STREET leads down the hill, with the church and churchyard on the l., and a row of houses on the r. The HALF MOON INN has a nice wrought-iron inn-sign bracket. On the other side of the churchyard, i.e. w of the church, CHURCH HOUSE with a Georgian five-bay brick façade, and a former CHANTRY CHAPEL (Perp window) attached to St John's School (neo-Tudor of 1897). At the foot of Silver Street MARKET STREET turns E. Nice pair of houses: No. 21 Georgian and No. 23 Tudor or Jacobean. To the w of Silver Street COURT ASH with a five-bay stone house that has rock-faced string courses and surrounds. Probably Early Victorian.

Finally back along PRINCES STREET. Here are the best Georgian town houses. No. 23 shows (at the time of writing) how Ham Stone decays when left alone. The house itself is of seven bays. Nos 21, 19, 15 also have dignified Georgian façades.

More Georgian houses outside that narrow circuit. The most rewarding group is in HENDFORD. First the THREE CHOUGHS HOTEL, with a tablet bearing the date 1724, then more Georgian houses, especially the five-bay MANOR HOTEL and its recessed five-bay Stables and HENDFORD MANOR HOUSE (now S.C.C. Health Inspectors and Housing), of seven bays with a r. wing, a handsome porch, and a Venetian window. To the l. the former Stable Block (HENDFORD MANOR HALL), brick with on the upper floor a central Venetian window flanked by circular windows. Hipped roof. Other Georgian houses in KINGSTON, e.g. SWALLOW-CLIFFE, early C19 with Tuscan porch, and in HIGHER KINGSTON, e.g. the earliest part of the Hospital. – In the PRESTON ROAD the BRITISH LEGION and then the long range of 1837 of the SUMMERLANDS HOSPITAL.

WESTLAND AIRCRAFT COMPANY, Westland Road. New Drawing Office by *Farmer & Dark*, 1955, a plain, sound, two-storeyed curtain-walling job.

ROMAN VILLA. A fine villa of courtyard-type was excavated at Westland. It was occupied during the C3 and C4. Its domestic furniture, including mosaics, is now displayed in the local museum.★

YEOVILTON 5020

ST BARTHOLOMEW. Norman evidence the strip of decorative bits built into the S porch wall. The window rere-arches of chancel and nave date the masonry of these parts as late C13 or early C14. To the same period belong the odd windows of the porch with trefoiled rere-arches. One is a sexfoil the other two tiny lancets. C14 Piscina in the chancel with ogee arch. It rests on a bust corbel. Tower arch and chancel arch as well as outer arch of the porch are double-chamfered and die into the imposts. Plain Perp W tower with much uninterrupted wall (cf. Queen Camel nearby). Money for building the tower was left by Richard Swann, rector of Yeovilton, in

★ A very fine Bronze Age TORQUE of gold, made of three cunningly-twisted strands of the precious metal, was found on Handford Hill in 1905.

1486 (15 marks). Diagonal buttresses. Small two-light bell-openings with Somerset tracery, battlements and tiny pinnacles. Statue niche on the ground floor to the N. Statue bracket in the S wall of the nave inside. Wagon-roof with bosses (e.g. Christ, the Virgin, a two-headed eagle). – PLATE. Chalice and Cover by *Lawrence Stratford* of Dorchester 1573; Dish 1700.

Several good houses round the church.

GLOSSARY

ABACUS: flat slab on the top of a capital (q.v.).

ABUTMENT: solid masonry placed to resist the lateral pressure of a vault.

ACANTHUS: plant with thick fleshy and scalloped leaves used as part of the decoration of a Corinthian capital (q.v.) and in some types of leaf carving.

ACHIEVEMENT OF ARMS: in heraldry, a complete display of armorial bearings.

ACROTERION: foliage-carved block on the end or top of a classical pediment.

ADDORSED: two human figures, animals, or birds, etc., placed symmetrically so that they turn their backs to each other.

AEDICULE, AEDICULA: framing of a window or door by columns and a pediment (q.v.).

AFFRONTED: two human figures, animals, or birds, etc., placed symmetrically so that they face each other.

AMBULATORY: semicircular or polygonal aisle enclosing an apse (q.v.).

ANNULET: *see* Shaft-ring.

ANTEPENDIUM: covering of the front of an altar, usually by textiles or metalwork.

ANTIS, IN: *see* Portico.

APSE: vaulted semicircular or polygonal end of a chancel or a chapel.

ARABESQUE: light and fanciful surface decoration using combinations of flowing lines, ten-

drils, etc., interspersed with vases, animals, etc.

ARCADE: range of arches supported on piers or columns, free-standing; or, BLIND ARCADE, the same attached to a wall.

ARCH: round-headed; i.e. semicircular pointed, i.e. consisting of two curves, each drawn from one centre, and meeting in a point at the top; segmental, i.e. in the form of a segment; pointed; four-centred, *see* Fig. 1(*a*); Tudor, *see* Fig. 1(*b*); Ogee, *see* Fig. 1(*c*); Stilted, *see* Fig. 1(*d*).

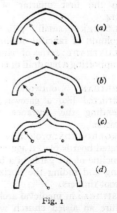

Fig. 1

ARCHITRAVE: lowest of the three main parts of the entablature (q.v.) of an order (q.v.) (*see* Fig. 11).

ARCHIVOLT: under-surface of an arch (also called Soffit).

ARRIS: sharp edge at the meeting of two surfaces.

ASHLAR: masonry of large blocks wrought to even faces and square edges.

ATRIUM: inner court of a Roman house, also open court in front of a church.

ATTACHED: *see* Engaged.

ATTIC: topmost storey of a house, if distance from floor to ceiling is less than in the others.

AUMBRY: recess or cupboard to hold sacred vessels for Mass and Communion.

Bailey: open space or court of a castle.

BALDACCHINO: canopy supported on columns.

BALLFLOWER: globular flower of three petals enclosing a small ball. A decoration used in the first quarter of the C14.

BALUSTER: small pillar or column of fanciful outline.

BALUSTRADE: series of balusters supporting a handrail or coping (q.v.).

BARBICAN: outwork, constructed like a gateway, defending the entrance to a castle.

BARGEBOARDS: projecting decorated boards placed against the incline of the gable of a building and hiding the horizontal roof timbers.

BASILICA: in medieval architecture an aisled church with a clerestory.

BASTION: projection at the angle of a fortification.

BATTER: wall with an inclined face.

BATTLEMENT: parapet with a series of indentations or embrasures with raised portions or merlons between (also called Crenellation).

BAYS: internal compartments of a building; each divided from the other not by solid walls but by divisions only marked in the side walls (columns, pilasters, etc.) or the ceiling (beams, etc.). Also external divisions of a building by fenestration.

BAY-WINDOW: angular or curved projection of a house front with ample fenestration. If curved, also called bow-window; if on an upper floor only, also called oriel or oriel window.

BEAKER FOLK: small bands of metal-using artisan-warriors from the Continent, heralding the onset of the Bronze Age.

BEAKHEAD: Norman ornamental motif consisting of a row of bird or beast heads with beaks pointing downwards and biting usually into a roll moulding.

BELFRY: turret on a roof to hang bells in.

BELGAE: powerful warrior bands from the Continent who established themselves in SE Britain shortly before the Roman Occupation. They came in two waves, *c.* 75 and 50 B.C., and gave rise to what is known as the Iron Age C culture.

BELL BARROW: type of Bronze Age barrow with a wide level shelf between edge of mound and ditch.

BELLCOTE: framework of stone on a roof to hang bells from.

BILLET: Norman ornamental motif made up of short raised rectangles placed at regular intervals.

BLOCK CAPITAL: Romanesque

capital cut from a cube by having the lower angles rounded off to the circular shaft below (also called Cushion Capital) (Fig. 2).

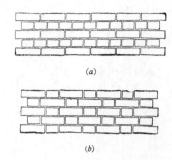

(a)

(b)

Fig. 3

Fig. 2

BOND, ENGLISH or FLEMISH: see Brickwork.

BOSS: knob or projection usually placed to cover the intersection of ribs in a vault.

BOW-WINDOW: see Bay-Window.

BOX PEW: pew with a high wooden enclosure.

BRACES: see Roof.

BRACKET: small supporting piece of stone, etc., to carry a projecting horizontal.

BRESSUMER: beam in a timber-framed building to support the, usually projecting, superstructure.

BRICKWORK: *Header:* brick laid so that the end only appears on the face of the wall. *Stretcher:* brick laid so that the side only appears on the face of the wall. *English Bond:* method of laying bricks so that alternate courses or layers on the face of the wall are composed of headers or stretchers only (Fig. 3a). *Flemish Bond:* method of laying bricks so that alternate headers and stretchers appear in each course on the face of the wall (Fig. 3b).

BROACH: see Spire.

BROKEN PEDIMENT: see Pediment.

BUTTRESS: mass of brickwork or masonry projecting from or built against a wall to give additional strength. *Angle Buttresses:* two meeting at an angle of 90° at the angle of a building (Fig. 4a). *Clasping Buttress:* one which encases the angle (Fig. 4d). *Diagonal Buttress:* one placed against the right angle formed by two walls, and more or less equiangular with both (Fig. 4b). *Flying Buttress:* arch or half arch transmitting the thrust of a vault or roof from the upper part of a wall to an outer support or buttress. *Setback Buttress:* angle buttress set slightly back from the angle (Fig. 4c).

CABLE MOULDING: moulding imitating a twisted cord.

CAIRN: any prehistoric mound of stones. Sometimes the stone core of a Chambered Tomb from which the earth has been eroded.

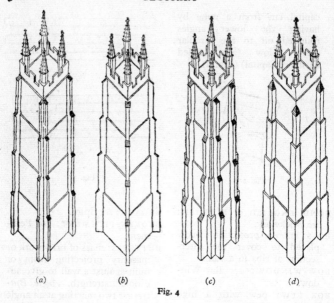

(a)   (b)   (c)   (d)

Fig. 4

CAMBER: slight rise or upward curve of an otherwise horizontal structure.

CAMP: Camps are generally either the simple rural encampments of the New Stone Age or the heavily fortified structures of the Early Iron Age. In Northern Britain they were being constructed during the whole of the Roman Occupation and beyond.

CAMPANILE: isolated bell tower.

CANOPY: projection or hood over an altar, pulpit, niche, statue, etc.

CAP: in a windmill the crowning feature.

CAPITAL: head or top part of a column (q.v.).

CARTOUCHE: tablet with an ornate frame, usually enclosing an inscription.

CARYATID: human figure used instead of a column.

CASTELLATED: decorated with battlements.

CEILURE: panelled and adorned part of a wagon-roof above the rood or the altar.

CELTS: The Celtic incursions into England occurred from c. 250 B.C. onward. The most important settlements were in Yorkshire and the SW. (N.B. *Celt*, pronounced with a soft *c*, is also a technical word for an axe of Old or New Stone Age origin.)

CENSER: vessel for the burning of incense.

CENTERING: wooden framework used in arch and vault construction and removed when the mortar has set.

CHALICE: cup used in the Communion service or at Mass. *Chalice with a lid:* also used in the Communion service or at Mass.

CHAMBERED TOMB: a burial mound of New Stone Age date, with a stone structure at the centre of an earthen mound. Wooden chambers were sometimes built in the Long Barrows of the New Stone Age.

CHAMFER: surface made by cutting across the square angle of a stone block, piece of wood, etc., at an angle of 45° to the other two surfaces.

CHANCEL: that part of the E end of a church in which the altar is placed, usually applied to the whole continuation of the nave E of the crossing.

CHANCEL ARCH: arch at the W end of the chancel.

CHANTRY CHAPEL: chapel attached to, or inside, a church, endowed for the saying of Masses for the soul of the founder or some other individual.

CHEVET: French term for the E end of a church (chancel, ambulatory, and radiating chapels).

CHEVRON: sculptured moulding forming a zigzag.

CHOIR: that part of the church where divine service is sung.

CIBORIUM: a baldacchino.

CINQUEFOIL: *see* Foil.

CIST: a small slab-lined receptacle to hold the bones or ashes of the dead in an inhumation burial.

CLAPPER BRIDGE: bridge made of large slabs of stone, some built up to make rough piers and other longer ones laid on top to make the roadway.

CLASSIC: here used to mean the moment of highest achievement of a style.

CLASSICAL: here used as the term for Greek and Roman architecture and any subsequent styles copying it.

CLERESTORY: upper storey of the nave walls of a church, pierced by windows.

COADE STONE: artificial (cast) stone made in the late C18 and the early C19 by Coade and Seely in London.

COB: walling material made of mixed clay and straw.

COFFERING: decorating a ceiling with sunk square or polygonal ornamental panels.

COLLAR-BEAM: *see* Roof.

COLONNADE: range of columns.

COLONNETTE: small column.

COLUMNA ROSTRATA: column decorated with carved prows of ships to celebrate a naval victory.

COMPOSITE: *see* Order.

CONSOLE: bracket (q.v.) with a compound curved outline.

COPING: capping or covering to a wall.

CORBEL: block of stone projecting from a wall, supporting some horizontal feature.

CORBEL TABLE: series of corbels, occurring just below the roof eaves externally or internally, often seen in Norman buildings.

CORINTHIAN: *see* Orders.

CORNICE: in classical architecture the top section of the entablature (q.v.). Also for a projecting decorative feature along the top of a wall, arch, etc.

COVE, COVING: concave under-surface in the nature of a hollow moulding but on a larger scale.

COVER PATEN: cover to a Communion cup, suitable for use as a paten or plate for the consecrated bread.

CRADLE ROOF: see Wagon-roof.

CRANNOG: prehistoric lake-dwelling on piles.

CRENELLATION: see Battlement.

CRESSWELLIAN CULTURE: term relating to the hunters who inhabited Cresswell Crags in Derbyshire during the Upper Palaeolithic. By extension, to similar cultures elsewhere in Britain.

CREST, CRESTING: ornamental finish along the top of a screen, etc.

CROCKET, CROCKETING: decorative features placed on the sloping sides of spires, pinnacles, gables, etc., in Gothic architecture, carved in various leaf shapes and placed at regular intervals.

Fig. 5

CROCKET CAPITAL: see Fig. 5.

CROMLECH: obsolete word, often used of a free-standing stone, but more properly applied to a Bronze Age stone circle.

CROSSING: space at the inter-section of nave, chancel, and transepts.

CRUCK: big curved beam supporting both walls and roof of a cottage.

CRYPT: underground room usually below the E end of a church.

CUPOLA: small polygonal or circular domed turret crowning a roof.

CURSUS: long strips enclosed between narrow banks at Stonehenge, in the Thames valley, and in Wessex. The best known is the one at Stonehenge. Their use is unknown, and they are of New Stone and Bronze Age date.

CURTAIN WALL: connecting wall between the towers of a castle.

CURVILINEAR: see Tracery.

CUSHION CAPITAL: see Block Capital.

CUSP: projecting point between the foils in a foiled Gothic arch.

DADO: decorative covering of the lower part of a wall.

DAGGER: tracery motif of the Dec style. It is a lancet shape rounded or pointed at the head, pointed at the foot, and cusped inside (see Fig. 6).

Fig. 6

DAIS: raised platform at one end of a room.

DEC ('DECORATED'): historical

division of English Gothic architecture covering the first half of the C14.

DEMI-COLUMNS: columns half sunk into a wall.

DIAPER WORK: surface decoration composed of square or lozenge shapes.

DISC BARROW: Bronze Age barrow in which the outer ditch and bank are more prominent than the inconspicuous mound.

DOG-TOOTH: typical E.E. ornament consisting of a series of four-cornered stars placed diagonally and raised pyramidally (Fig. 7).

Fig. 7

DOLMEN: obsolete word, signifying the stone chamber of a megalithic tomb after the outer structure of earth has been eroded away.

DOMICAL VAULT: see Vault.

DONJON: see Keep.

DORIC: see Order.

DORMER (WINDOW): window placed vertically in the sloping plane of a roof.

DRIPSTONE: see Hood-mould.

DRUM: circular or polygonal vertical wall of a dome or cupola.

E.E. ('EARLY ENGLISH'): historical division of English Gothic architecture roughly covering the C13.

EASTER SEPULCHRE: recess with tomb-chest usually in the wall of a chancel, the tomb-chest to receive an effigy of Christ for Easter celebrations.

EAVES: underpart of a sloping roof overhanging a wall.

EAVES CORNICE: cornice below the eaves of a roof.

ECHINUS: quarter round moulding carved with egg and dart pattern, used in classical architecture.

EMBATTLED: see Battlement.

EMBRASURE: small opening in the wall or parapet of a fortified building, usually splayed on the inside. See Loop.

ENCAUSTIC TILES: earthenware glazed and decorated tiles used for paving.

ENGAGED COLUMNS: columns attached to, or partly sunk into, a wall.

ENGLISH BOND: see Brickwork.

ENTABLATURE: in classical architecture the whole of the horizontal members above a column (that is architrave, frieze, and cornice) (see Fig. 11).

ENTASIS: very slight convex deviation from a straight line; used on Greek columns and sometimes on spires to prevent an optical illusion of concavity.

ENTRESOL: see Mezzanine.

EPITAPH: hanging wall monument.

ESCUTCHEON: shield for armorial bearings.

EXEDRA: the apsidal end of a room. See Apse.

EXTRADOS: outer vertical surface of an arch.

FAIENCE: decorated glazed earthenware.

FAN TRACERY: see Tracery.

FAN VAULT: see Vault.

FERETORY: place behind the High Altar, where the chief shrine of a church is kept.

FESTOON: carved garland of flowers and fruit suspended at both ends.

FILLET: narrow flat band running down a shaft or along a roll moulding.

FINIAL: top of a canopy, gable, pinnacle.

FLAGON: vessel for the wine used in the Communion service.

FLAMBOYANT: properly the latest phase of French Gothic architecture where the window tracery takes on wavy undulating lines.

FLÈCHE: slender wooden spire on the centre of a roof (also called Spirelet).

FLEMISH BOND: see Brickwork.

FLEURON: decorative carved flower or leaf.

FLUSH WORK: decorative use of flint in conjunction with dressed stone so as to form patterns: tracery, initials, etc.

FLUTING: vertical channelling in the shaft of a column.

FLYING BUTTRESS: see Buttress.

FOIL: lobe formed by the cusping (q.v.) of a circle or an arch. Trefoil, quatrefoil, cinquefoil, multifoil, express the number of leaf shapes to be seen.

FOLIATED: carved with leaf shapes.

FOSSE: ditch.

FOUR-CENTRED ARCH: see Arch.

FRATER: refectory or dining hall of a monastery.

FRESCO: wall painting on wet plaster.

FRIEZE: middle division of a classical entablature (q.v.) (see Fig. 11).

FRONTAL: covering for the front of an altar.

GADROONED: enriched with a series of convex ridges, the opposite of fluting.

GALILEE: chapel or vestibule at the w end of a church enclosing the porch. Also called Narthex (q.v.).

GALLERY: in church architecture upper storey above an aisle, opened in arches to the nave. Also called Tribune (q.v.) and often erroneously Triforium (q.v.).

GARGOYLE: water spout projecting from the parapet of a wall or tower; carved into a human or animal shape.

GAZEBO: lookout tower or raised summer house in a picturesque garden.

'GEOMETRICAL': see Tracery.

'GIBBS SURROUND': of a doorway or window. A surround with alternating larger and smaller blocks of stone, quoinwise, or intermittent large blocks, sometimes with a narrow raised band connecting them up the verticals and along the extrados of the arch (Fig. 8).

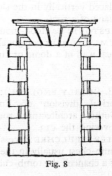

Fig. 8

GROIN: sharp edge at the meeting of two cells of a cross-vault.

GROINED VAULT: *see* Vault.

GROTESQUE: fanciful ornamental decoration: *see* also Arabesque.

Hagioscope: *see* Squint.

HALF-TIMBERING: *see* Timber Framing.

HALL CHURCH: church in which nave and aisles are of equal height or approximately so.

HALLSTATT CULTURE: the culture known as Iron Age A, brought from the Continent *c.* 500 B.C.

HAMMERBEAM: *see* Roof.

HANAP: large metal cup, generally made for domestic use, standing on an elaborate base and stem; with a very ornate cover frequently crowned with a little steeple.

HEADERS: *see* Brickwork.

HERRINGBONE WORK: brick, stone, or tile construction where the component blocks are laid diagonally instead of flat. Alternate courses lie in opposing directions to make a zigzag pattern up the face of the wall.

HEXASTYLE: having six detached columns.

HILL FORT: *see* also Camp, supra. The great hill-forts of the Iron Age were, for obvious reasons, usually sited on promontories, generally where the terrain afforded a natural barrier on one or more sides.

HIPPED ROOF: *see* Roof.

HOOD-MOULD: projecting moulding above an arch or a lintel to throw off water (also called Dripstone or Label).

Iconography: the science of the subject matter of works of the visual arts.

IMPOST: brackets in walls, usually formed of mouldings, on which the ends of an arch rest.

INDENT: shape chiselled out in a stone slab to receive a brass.

INGLENOOK: bench of seat built in beside a fireplace, sometimes covered by the chimney breast, occasionally lit by small windows on each side of the fire.

INTERCOLUMNIATION: the space between columns.

INTRADOS: underside of an arch.

IONIC: *see* Orders (Fig. 11).

Jamb: straight side of an archway, doorway, or window.

Keel MOULDING: moulding whose outline is in section like that of the keel of a ship.

KEEP: massive tower of a Norman castle.

KEYSTONE: middle stone in an arch.

KING-POST: *see* Roof (Fig. 13).

Label: *see* Hood-mould.

LABEL STOP: ornamental boss at the end of a hood-mould (q.v.).

LAKE DWELLINGS: villages of Late Iron Age date found in Yorkshire, East Anglia, Breconshire, and Somerset. Those of Glastonbury and Meare are by far the most extensive.

LANCET WINDOW: slender pointed-arched window.

LANTERN: in architecture, a small circular or polygonal turret with windows all round crowning a roof (*see* Cupola) or a dome.

LANTERN CROSS: churchyard cross with lantern-shaped top usually with sculptured representations on the sides of the top.

LA TÈNE CULTURE: the culture known as Iron Age B, brought from the Continent by Marnian overlords between 300 and 250 B.C.

LEAN-TO ROOF: roof with one slope only, built against a higher wall.

LESENE or PILASTER STRIP: pilaster without base and capital.

LIERNE: *see* Vault (Fig. 20).

LINENFOLD: Tudor panelling ornamented with a conventional representation of a piece of linen laid in vertical folds. The piece is repeated in each panel.

LINTEL: horizontal beam or stone bridging an opening.

LOGGIA: recessed colonnade (q.v.).

LONG AND SHORT WORK: Saxon quoins (q.v.) consisting of stones placed with the long sides alternately upright and horizontal.

LONG BARROWS: earthen structures characteristic of the New Stone Age, and not known subsequently.

LOUVRE: opening, often with lantern (q.v.) over, in the roof of a room to let the smoke from a central hearth escape.

LOZENGE: diamond shape.

LUNETTE: tympanum (q.v.) or curved opening in a vault.

LYCH GATE: wooden gate structure with a roof and open sides placed at the entrance to a churchyard to provide space for the reception of a coffin. The word *lych* is Saxon and means a corpse.

LYNCHETS: the eroded terracing of primitive field systems, usually in carefully devised strips: hence 'strip lynchets'.

MACHICOLATION: projecting gallery on brackets constructed on the outside of castle towers or walls. The gallery has holes in the floor to drop missiles through.

MAGLEMOSIAN CULTURE: term denoting the hunter-fishing culture of Baltic origin established along the eastern margin of Britain in Middle Stone Age times. By extension, to similar cultures.

MAJOLICA: ornamented glazed earthenware.

MANSARD: *see* Roof.

MEGALITHIC TOMBS: the chambered cairns of the New Stone Age, found with variations over SW England, Wales, Scotland, and particularly Ireland, with a small outlier in Kent. The inner tomb is constructed of large stone slabs, often disposed in accordance with an elaborate ground plan.

MENHIR: obsolete word, synonymous with Dolmen or

Cromlech, which are similarly vague and antique.

MERLON: *see* Battlement.

METOPE: in classical architecture of the Doric order (q.v.) the space in the frieze between the triglyphs (Fig. 11).

MEZZANINE: low storey placed between two higher ones.

MISERERE: *see* Misericord.

MISERICORD: bracket placed on the underside of a hinged choir stall seat which, when turned up, provided the occupant of the seat with a support during long periods of standing (also called Miserere).

MODILLION: small bracket of which large numbers (modillion frieze) are often placed below a cornice (q.v.) in classical architecture.

MOTTE: steep mound forming the main feature of C11 and C12 castles.

MOUCHETTE: tracery motif in curvilinear tracery, a curved dagger (q.v.) (Fig. 9).

Fig. 9

MULLION: vertical post or upright dividing a window into two or more 'lights'.

MUNTIN: vertical part in the framing of a door, screen, etc., stopped by the horizontal rails.

NAIL-HEAD: E.E. ornamental motif, consisting of small pyramids regularly repeated (Fig. 10).

Fig. 10

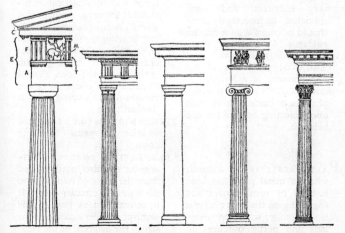

Fig. 11 – Orders of Columns (Greek Doric, Roman Doric, Tuscan Doric, Ionic, Corinthian) E, Entablature; C, Cornice; F, Frieze; A, Architrave; M, Metope; T, Triglyph

NARTHEX: enclosed vestibule or covered porch at the main entrance to a church (*see* Galilee).

NEWEL: central post in a circular or winding staircase; also the principal post when a flight of stairs meets a landing.

OBELISK: lofty pillar of square section tapering at the top and ending pyramidally.

OGEE: *see* Arch (Fig. 1c).

ORATORY: small private chapel in a house.

ORDER: (1) *of a doorway or window:* series of concentric steps receding towards the opening; (2) *in classical architecture:* column with base, shaft, capital, and entablature (q.v.) according to one of the following styles: Greek Doric, Roman Doric, Tuscan Doric, Ionic, Corinthian, Composite. The established details are very elaborate, and some specialist architectural work should be consulted for further guidance (*see* Fig. 11).

ORIEL: *see* Bay-Window.

OVERHANG: projection of the upper storey of a house.

OVERSAILING COURSES: series of stone or brick courses, each one projecting beyond the one below it.

PALIMPSEST: (1) *of a brass:* where a metal plate has been re-used by turning over and engraving on the back; (2) *of a wall painting:* where one overlaps and partly obscures an earlier one.

PALLADIAN: architecture following the ideas and principles of Andrea Palladio, 1518–80.

PALSTAVE: technical term for a Bronze Age celt with a pronounced stop-ridge to facilitate hafting.

PANTILE: tile of curved S-shaped section.

PARAPET: low wall placed to protect any spot where there is a sudden drop, for example on a bridge, quay, hillside, house-top, etc.

PARGETTING: plaster work with patterns and ornaments either in relief or engraved on it.

PARVISE: room over a church porch. Often used as a school-house or a store room.

PATEN: plate to hold the bread at Communion or Mass.

PATERA: small flat circular or oval ornament in classical architecture.

PEDIMENT: low-pitched gable (q.v.) used in classical, Renaissance, and neo-classical architecture above a portico and above doors, windows, etc. It may be straight-sided or curved segmentally. *Open Pediment:* one where the centre portion of the base is left open. *Broken Pediment:* one where the centre portion of the sloping sides is 'broken' out.

PENDANT: boss (q.v.) elongated so that it seems to hang down.

PENDENTIF: concave triangular spandrel used to lead from the angle of two walls to the base of a circular dome. It is constructed as part of the hemisphere over a diameter the size of the diagonal of the basic square (Fig. 12).

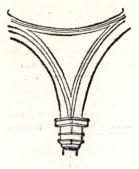

Fig. 12

PERP (PERPENDICULAR): historical division of English Gothic architecture roughly covering the period from 1350 to 1530.

PETERBOROUGH CULTURE: term denoting culture of Baltic origin that flourished during the New Stone Age.

PIANO NOBILE: principal storey of a house with the reception rooms; usually the first floor.

PIAZZA: square open space surrounded by buildings, in C17 and C18 England sometimes used to mean a long colonnade or loggia.

PIER: strong, solid support, frequently square in section or of composite section (compound pier).

PIETRA DURA: ornamental or scenic inlay by means of thin slabs of stone.

PILASTER: shallow pier attached to a wall.

PILLAR PISCINA: free-standing piscina on a pillar.

PINNACLE: ornamental form crowning a spire, tower, buttress, etc., usually of steep pyramidal, conical, or some similar shape.

PISCINA: basin for washing the Communion or Mass vessels, provided with a drain. Generally set in or against the wall to the S of an altar.

PLAISANCE: summer-house, pleasure house near a mansion.

PLATE TRACERY: see Tracery.

PLINTH: projecting base of a wall or column, generally chamfered (q.v.) or moulded at the top.

POPPYHEAD: ornament of leaf and flower type used to decorate the tops of bench- or stall-ends.

PORTCULLIS: gate constructed to rise and fall in vertical grooves; used in gateways of castles.

PORTE COCHÈRE: porch large enough to admit wheeled vehicles.

PORTICO: centre-piece of a house or a church with classical detached or attached columns and a pediment. A portico is called *prostyle* or *in antis* according to whether it projects from or recedes into a building. In a portico *in antis* the columns range with the side walls.

POSTERN: small gateway at the back of a building.

PREDELLA: in an altar-piece the horizontal strip below the main representation, often used for a number of subsidiary representations in a row.

PRESBYTERY: the part of the church lying E of the choir. It is the part where the altar is placed.

PRINCIPAL: see Roof (Fig. 13).

PRIORY: monastic house whose

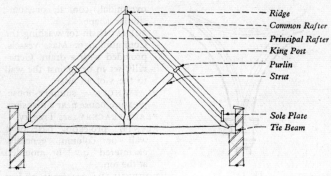

Ridge
Common Rafter
Principal Rafter
King Post
Purlin
Strut
Sole Plate
Tie Beam

Fig. 13

head is a prior or prioress, not an abbot or abbess.

PROSTYLE: with free-standing columns in a row.

PULPITUM: stone rood screen in a major church.

PURLIN: *see* Roof (Figs. 13, 14).

PUTTO: small naked boy.

QUADRANGLE: inner court-yard in a large building complex.

QUARRY: in stained-glass work, a small diamond or square-shaped piece of glass set diagonally.

QUATREFOIL: *see* Foil.

QUEEN-POSTS: *see* Roof (Fig. 14).

QUOINS: dressed stones at the angles of a building. Sometimes all the stones are of the same size; more often they are alternately large or small.

RADIATING CHAPELS: chapels projecting radially from an ambulatory or an apse.

RAFTER: *see* Roof.

RAMPART: stone wall, or wall of earth surrounding a castle, fortress, or fortified city.

RAMPART-WALK: path along the inner face of a rampart.

REBATE: continuous rectangular notch cut on an edge.

REBUS: pun, a play on words. The literal translation and illustration of a name for artistic and heraldic purposes (Belton=bell, tun).

REEDING: decoration with parallel convex mouldings touching one another.

REFECTORY: dining hall; *see* Frater.

RENDERING: plastering of an outer wall.

REPOUSSÉ: decoration of metal work by relief designs, formed by beating the metal from the back.

REREDOS: structure behind and above an altar.

RESPOND: half-pier bonded into a wall and carrying one end of an arch.

RETABLE: altar-piece, a picture or piece of carving, standing behind and attached to an altar.

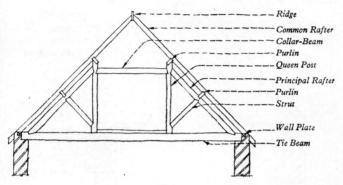

Fig. 14

RETICULATION: *see* **Tracery** (Fig. 19).

REVEAL: that part of a jamb (q.v.) which lies between the glass or door and the outer surface of the wall.

RIB VAULT: *see* Vault.

ROCOCO: latest phase of the Baroque style, current in most Continental countries between *c.* 1720 and *c.* 1760.

ROLL MOULDING: moulding of semicircular or more than semicircular section.

ROMANESQUE: that style in architecture which was current in the C11 and C12 and preceded the Gothic style (in England often called Norman). (Some scholars extend the use of the term Romanesque back to the C10 or C9.)

ROOD: cross or crucifix.

ROOD LOFT: singing gallery on the top of the rood screen, often supported by a coving.

ROOD SCREEN: *see* Screen.

ROOD STAIRS: stairs to give access to the rood loft.

ROOF: *Hipped:* roof with sloped instead of vertical ends. *Mansard:* roof with a double slope, the lower slope being larger and steeper than the upper. *Saddleback:* tower roof shaped like an ordinary gabled timber roof. The following members have special names: *Rafter:* roof-timber sloping up from the wall plate to the ridge. *Principal:* principal rafter, usually corresponding to the main bay divisions of the nave or chancel below. *Wall Plate:* timber laid longitudinally on the top of a wall. *Purlin:* longitudinal member laid parallel with wall plate and ridge beam some way up the slope of the roof. *Tie-beam:* beam connecting the two slopes of a roof across at its foot, usually at the height of the wall plate, to prevent the roof from spreading. *Collar-beam:* tie-beam applied higher up the slope of the roof. *Strut:* upright timber connecting the tie-beam with the rafter above it. *King-post:* upright timber connecting a

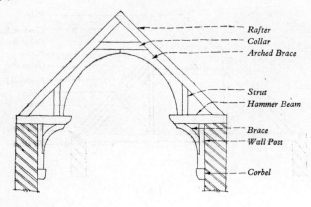

Rafter
Collar
Arched Brace

Strut
Hammer Beam

Brace
Wall Post

Corbel

Fig. 15

tie-beam and collar-beam with the ridgebeam. *Queen-posts:* two struts placed symmetrically on a tie-beam or collar-beam. *Braces:* inclined timbers inserted to strengthen others. Usually braces connect a collar-beam with the rafters below or a tie-beam with the wall below. Braces can be straight or curved (also called arched). *Hammerbeam:* beam projecting at right angles, usually from the top of a wall, to carry arched braces or struts and arched braces (*see* Figs. 13, 14, 15).

ROSE WINDOW (or WHEEL WINDOW): circular window with patterned tracery arranged to radiate from the centre.

ROTUNDA: building circular in plan.

RUBBLE: building stones, not square or hewn, nor laid in regular courses.

RUSTICATION: Quarry-faced if the surfaces of large blocks of ashlar stone are left rough like rock; smooth if the ashlar blocks are smooth and separated by V-joints; banded if the separation by V-joints applies only to the horizontals.

SADDLEBACK: *see* Roof.

SALTIRE CROSS: equal-limbed cross placed diagonally.

SANCTUARY: (1) area around the main altar of a church (*see* Presbytery); (2) sacred site consisting of wooden or stone uprights enclosed by a circular bank and ditch. Beginning in the New Stone Age, they were elaborated in the succeeding Bronze Age. The best known examples are Stonehenge and Avebury.

SARCOPHAGUS: elaborately carved coffin.

SCAGLIOLA: material composed of cement and colouring matter to imitate marble.

SCALLOPED CAPITAL: development of the block capital (q.v.) in which the single semicircular surface is elaborated into a series of truncated cones (Fig. 16).

Fig. 16

SCARP: artificial cutting away of the ground to form a steep slope.

SCREEN: *Parclose screen:* screen separating a chapel from the rest of a church. *Rood screen:* screen at the w end of a chancel. Above it on the rood-beam was the rood (q.v.).

SCREENS PASSAGE: passage between the entrances to kitchen, buttery, etc., and the screen behind which lies the hall of a medieval house.

SEDILIA: seats for the priests (usually three) on the s side of the chancel of a church.

SEGMENTAL ARCH: *see* Arch.

SET-OFF: *see* Weathering.

SEXPARTITE: *see* Vaulting.

SGRAFFITO: pattern incised into plaster so as to expose a dark surface underneath.

SHAFT-RING: ring round a circular pier or a shaft attached to a pier.

SILL: lower horizontal part of the frame of a window.

SLATEHANGING: the covering of walls by overlapping rows of slates, on a timber substructure.

SOFFIT: underside of an arch, lintel, etc.

SOLAR: upper drawing-room of a medieval house.

SOPRAPORTE: painting above the door of a room, usual in the C17 and C18.

SOUNDING BOARD: horizontal board or canopy over a pulpit. Also called Tester.

SPANDREL: triangular surface between one side of an arch, the horizontal drawn from its apex, and the vertical drawn from its springer, also the surface between two arches.

SPIRE: tall pyramidal or conical pointed erection often built on top of a tower, turret, etc., *Broach Spire:* spire which is generally octagonal in plan rising from the top or parapet of a square tower. A small inclined piece of masonry covers the vacant triangular space at each of the four angles of the square and is carried up to a point along the diagonal sides of the octagon. *Needle Spire:* thin spire rising from the centre of a tower roof, well inside the parapet.

SPIRELET: *see* Flèche.

SPLAY: chamfer, usually of the jamb of a window.

SPRINGING: level at which an arch rises from its supports.

SQUINCH: arch or system of concentric arches thrown across the angle between two walls to support a superstructure, for example a dome (Fig. 17).

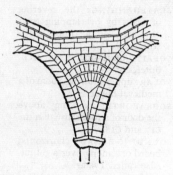

Fig. 17

SQUINT: hole cut in a wall or through a pier to allow a view of the main altar of a church from places whence it could not otherwise be seen (also called Hagioscope).

STALL: carved seat, one of a row, made of wood or stone.

STAUNCHION: upright iron or steel member.

STEEPLE: the tower or spire of a church.

STIFF-LEAF: E.E. type of foliage of many-lobed shapes (Fig. 18).

Fig. 18

STILTED: see Arch.

STONE CIRCLES: rings of standing stones without external earthworks. Probably of Middle and Late Bronze Age date.

STONE ROWS: single or double rows of standing stones, often associated with Stone Circles and of similar date.

STOUP: vessel for the reception of holy water, usually placed near a door.

STRAINER ARCH: arch inserted across a room to prevent the walls from leaning.

STRAPWORK: C16 decoration consisting of interlaced bands, and forms similar to fretwork or cut and bent leather.

STRETCHERS: see Brickwork.

STRING COURSE: projecting horizontal band or moulding set in the surface of a wall.

STRIP LYNCHETS: see Lynchets.

STRUT: see Roof.

STUCCO: plaster work.

STUDS: Upright timbers in timber-framed houses.

SWAG: festoon formed by a carved piece of cloth suspended from both ends.

TABERNACLE: richly ornamented niche (q.v.) or freestanding canopy. Usually contains the Holy Sacrament.

TARDENOISEAN CULTURE: Middle Stone Age culture named after a French type-site and extended to similar British cultures.

TAZZA: shallow bowl on a foot.

TERMINAL FIGURES (TERMS, TERMINI): upper part of a human figure growing out of a pier, pilaster, etc., which tapers towards the base.

TERRACOTTA: burnt clay, unglazed.

TESSELATED PAVEMENT: decorative floor or wall covering

made up of tesserae or small coloured cubes of stone, fitted into a bed of cement.

TESTER: *see* Sounding Board.

TETRASTYLE: having four detached columns.

THREE-DECKER PULPIT: pulpit with Clerk's Stall and Reading Desk placed below each other.

TIE-BEAM: *see* Roof (Figs. 13, 14).

TIERCERON: *see* Vault (Fig. 20).

TILEHANGING: *see* Slatehanging.

TIMBER-FRAMING: method of construction where walls are built of timber framework with the spaces filled in by plaster or brickwork. Sometimes the timber is covered over with plaster or boarding laid horizontally.

TOMB-CHEST: chest-shaped stone coffin, the most usual medieval form of funeral monument.

TOUCH: soft black marble quarried near Tournai.

TOURELLE: turret corbelled out from the wall.

TRACERY: intersecting ribwork in the upper part of a window, or used decoratively in blank arches, on vaults, etc. *Plate*

tracery: early form of tracery where decoratively shaped openings are cut through the solid stone infilling in a window head (Fig. 19a). *Bar tracery:* intersecting ribwork made up of slender shafts, continuing the lines of the mullions of windows up to a decorative mesh in the head of the window. *Geometrical tracery:* tracery consisting chiefly of circles or foiled circles. *Intersected tracery:* tracery in which each mullion of a window branches out into two curved bars in such a way that every one of them runs concentrically with the others against the arch of the whole window. The result is that every light of the window is a lancet and every two, three, four, etc., lights together form a pointed arch (Fig. 19b). *Reticulated tracery:* tracery consisting entirely of circles drawn at top and bottom into ogee shapes so that a net-like appearance results (Fig. 19c). *Panel tracery:* tracery forming upright straight-sided panels above lights of a window (Fig. 19, d & e).

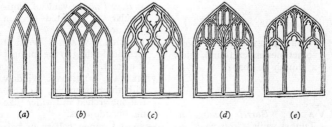

(a)   (b)   (c)   (d)   (e)

Fig. 19

TRANSEPT: transverse portion of a cross-shaped church.

TRANSOM: horizontal bar across the opening of a window.

TRANSVERSE ARCH: see Vaulting.

TRIBUNE: see Gallery.

TRICIPUT, SIGNUM TRICIPUT: sign of the Trinity expressed by three faces belonging to one head.

TRIFORIUM: arcaded wall passage or blank arcading facing the nave at the height of the aisle roof and below the clerestory (q.v.) windows. (See Gallery.)

TRIGLYPHS: blocks with vertical grooves separating the metopes (q.v.) in the Doric frieze (Fig. 11).

TROPHY: sculptured group of arms or armour, used as a memorial of victory.

TRUMEAU: stone mullion (q.v.) supporting the tympanum (q.v.) of a wide doorway.

TUMULUS: Term sometimes used of Cairns, but more usually of Chambered or Megalithic Tombs.

TURRET: very small tower, round or polygonal in plan.

TUSCAN: see Order.

TYMPANUM: space between the lintel of a doorway and the arch above it.

UNDERCROFT: vaulted room, sometimes underground, below a church or chapel.

VAULT: *Barrel vault*: see Tunnel vault. *Cross-vault*: see Groined vault. *Domical vault*: square or polygonal dome rising direct on a square or polygonal bay, the curved surfaces separated by groins (q.v.). *Fan vault*: vault where all ribs springing from one springer are of the same length, the same distance from the next, and the same curvature. *Groined vault* or *Cross-vault*: vault of two tunnel vaults of identical shape intersecting each other at right angles. *Lierne*: tertiary rib, that is, rib which does not spring either from one of the main springers or the central boss. *Quadripartite vault*: one wherein one bay of vaulting is divided into four parts. *Rib vault*: vault with diagonal ribs projecting along the groins. *Ridge-rib*: rib along the longitudinal or transverse ridge of a vault. *Sexpartite vault*: one wherein one bay of quadripartite vaulting is divided into two parts transversely so that each bay of vaulting has six parts. *Tierceron*: secondary rib, that is, rib which issues from one of the main springers or the central boss and leads to a place on a ridge-rib. *Transverse arch*: arch separating one bay of a vault from the next. *Tunnel vault* or *Barrel vault*: vault of semi-circular or pointed section (Fig. 20).

VAULTING SHAFT: vertical member leading to the springer of a vault.

VENETIAN WINDOW: window with three openings, the central one arched and wider than the outside ones.

VERANDA: open gallery or bal-

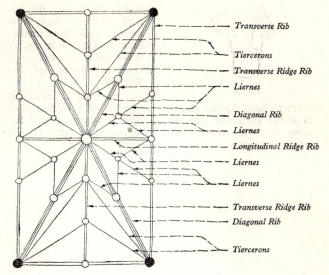

Transverse Rib

Tiercerons

Transverse Ridge Rib

Liernes

Diagonal Rib

Liernes

Longitudinal Ridge Rib

Liernes

Liernes

Transverse Ridge Rib

Diagonal Rib

Tiercerons

Fig. 20

cony with a roof on light, usually metal, supports.

VESICA: oval with pointed head and foot.

VESTIBULE: ante-room or entrance hall.

VILLA: according to Gwilt (1842) 'a country house for the residence of opulent persons'.

VITRIFIED: made similar to glass.

VOLUTE: spiral scroll, one of the component parts of an Ionic column (*see* Order).

VOUSSOIR: wedge-shaped stone used in arch construction.

WAGON-ROOF: roof in which by closely set rafters with arched braces the appearance of the inside of a canvas tilt over a wagon is achieved. Wagon-roofs can be panelled or plastered (ceiled) or left uncovered.

WAINSCOT: timber lining to walls.

WALL PLATE: *see* Roof.

WATERLEAF: leaf shape used in later C12 capitals. The waterleaf is a broad, unribbed, tapering leaf curving up towards the angle of the abacus and turned in at the top (Fig. 21).

WEATHERBOARDING: overlapping horizontal boards, covering a timber-framed wall.

WEATHERING: sloped horizontal surface on sills, buttresses, etc., to throw off water.

Fig. 21

WEEPERS: small figures placed in niches along the sides of some medieval tombs (also called Mourners).

WESSEX CULTURE: the fine, regal culture of high Bronze Age date in Southern England. Linked with Brittany, its floruit was *c.* 1750 B.C.

WHEEL WINDOW: *see* Rose Window.

WINDMILL HILL CULTURE: type-site of a culture of the New Stone Age, named from an important camp in Wiltshire.

INDEX OF PLATES

INDEX OF ARTISTS

INDEX OF PLACES

NOTES

NOTES